Regimes of Language

Publication of the Advanced Seminar Series
is made possible by generous support from
The Brown Foundation, Inc., of Houston, Texas.

**School of American Research
Advanced Seminar Series**

Douglas W. Schwartz
General Editor

Regimes of Language

Contributors

Richard Bauman
Folklore Institute, Indiana University

Charles Briggs
Department of Ethnic Studies, University of California–San Diego

Joseph Errington
Department of Anthropology, Yale University

Susan Gal
Department of Anthropology, University of Chicago

Jane H. Hill
Department of Anthropology, University of Arizona

Judith T. Irvine
Department of Anthropology, University of Michigan

Paul V. Kroskrity
Department of Anthropology, University of California–Los Angeles

Susan U. Philips
Department of Anthropology, University of Arizona

Bambi B. Schieffelin
Department of Anthropology, New York University

Michael Silverstein
Department of Anthropology, University of Chicago

Regimes of Language

Ideologies, Polities, and Identities

Edited by Paul V. Kroskrity

School of American Research Press

Santa Fe, New Mexico

School of American Research Press

Post Office Box 2188
Santa Fe, New Mexico 87504-2188

Director of Publications: Joan K. O'Donnell
Editor: Jo Ann Baldinger
Designer: Context, Inc.
Maps: Carol Cooperrider
Indexer: Bruce Tracy
Typographer: Cynthia Welch

Library of Congress Cataloging-in-Publication Data:
Regimes of language : ideologies, polities, and identities / edited by Paul V. Kroskrity.
p. cm. — (School of American Research advanced seminar series)
Includes bibliographical references and index.
ISBN 0-933452-61-6. — ISBN 0-933452-62-4 (pbk.)
1. Language and languages—Political aspects. 2. Language and culture.
3. Ideology. 4. Ethnic identity. I. Kroskrity, Paul V., 1949– . II. Series
P119.3.R44 1999
306.44'089—dc21   99-16251
                                                                      CIP

Cover: "Le Mois des vendages" ("The Month of the Grape Harvest") by René Magritte.
Oil on canvas, 1959. Photothèque René Magritte-Giraudon. Copyright © 1999
C. Herscovici, Brussels/Artists Rights Society (ARS), New York.

Contents

Table

Illustrations

Acknowledgments

The essays presented in this collection were first written for a School of American Research advanced seminar, titled "Language Ideologies," which met in April 1994.

For their generous support of the advanced seminar, I thank the School of American Research and the Wenner-Gren Foundation for Anthropological Research. For his hospitality and interest in this project, SAR President Douglas Schwartz has earned my warmest thanks. The participants, including myself, all benefited greatly from the organizational skills of SAR staff members Cecile Stein and Duane Anderson. They helped to make the SAR an ideal site for our deliberations. For help in all phases of the editorial process, I am grateful to Joan O'Donnell for her expertise, concern, and patience, and to the staff of SAR Press.

Regimes of Language

1

Regimenting Languages

Language Ideological Perspectives

Paul V. Kroskrity

[handwritten margin note:] Seem to have moved past English only legislation of the 1990s

Never before have the relations of language, politics, and identity seemed so relevant to so many. We live in a time when English-only legislation is zealously proposed in many of the United States; when many speakers of minority indigenous languages around the world struggle to retain their mother tongues in the face of all manner of state-supported linguistic discrimination; and when the mere mention of nonstandard varieties of languages such as "Ebonics" inspires animated debate on the subject of language and its educational virtues. Such current events are only more immediate reminders of long-term sociocultural trends, including centuries of nation-state formations. They serve to keep us aware of the status of language as a primary site of political process and of the discursive mediation of those very activities and events we recognize as political.

Partly in response to this escalating awareness, scholarship in linguistic anthropology has become increasingly cognizant of the sociocultural foundations of language and discourse and the need to complement the usual preoccupation with microanalysis (details of phonetic transcription, complexities of verb morphology, ethnographic detailing of specific speech events, sequencing of talk within a conversational "strip") with an understanding of how such patterns might be related to political-economic macroprocesses. Attempting to shed an outworn stereotype of their subfield as both arcane and irrelevant, many linguistic anthropologists today are concerned not with defending the autonomy of discrete levels of microanalysis but rather with demonstrating the relevance of their expertise in the linkage of microcultural worlds of language and discourse to macrosocial forces. For some of us, the time in which we live has prompted a recontextualized understanding of an important passage by Edward Sapir, patron saint of our subfield. In "The Status of Linguistics as a Science," Sapir (1949c:166) warned linguists against "failure to look beyond the pretty [formal] patterns of their subject matter" and exhorted them to produce more integrative research that would link language to the important issues of the day.

In the shadow of our interesting times and in the spirit of Sapir, ten linguistic anthropologists came to the School of American Research in Santa Fe in late April 1994 for an advanced seminar on "Language Ideologies." For one week we escaped the climates, the teaching responsibilities, and the committee work of our home institutions in their diverse locations in order to discuss papers we had prepared and circulated in advance. Although our original mission was a general exploration of the utility of the very heterodox concept of language ideologies, which has recently attracted a great deal of attention from anthropologists and other social scientists, our daily discussions and collaborative work produced some emergent unity and some unanticipated sense of direction. Our deliberations did not approach or impose a new synthetic orthodoxy on language ideological matters, but we were all struck by a current of political-economic emphasis. To be sure, this emphasis was hardly unexpected, given the acknowledged importance in much language ideological research of understanding the language beliefs and practices of social groups as strongly connected to group interests within society.

Even so, most of us were impressed by the magnification of political emphasis and by a collective analytical enlargement of scope that reflexively placed Western philosophies of language, European nationalist discourses, U.S. political discourse, and academic models of nationalism and identity into focus as language ideological acts. Before our group left Santa Fe, we had all intuitively recognized the appropriateness of "Regimes of Language" as a title for this volume. For many of us the phrase evokes an essential poetic tension between its major constituents. "Regimes" invokes the display of political domination in all its many forms, including what Gramsci (1971) distinguished as the coercive force of the state and the hegemonic influence of the state-endorsed culture of civil society.[1] Yet, as U.S. linguistic anthropologists, all of us had professional as well as cultural familiarity with many senses of "language" that, by contrast, emphasize its form (not its meaning), decontextualize its use, limit its role to providing labels for preexisting things, and otherwise represent language as an apolitical, even sometimes asocial, phenomenon. "Regimes of Language," as both image and title, thus promised to integrate two often segregated domains: politics (without language) and language (without politics).

We were aware that we were hardly alone in this quest. Not only were there well-established precedents in our own interdisciplinary field for studying linguistic inequality, forms of linguistic stratification, and the class-based reproduction of communicative codes (e.g., Bernstein 1975; Gumperz 1962; Hymes 1980; Labov 1972b), but the "linguistic turn" of poststructuralists like Bourdieu (1977, 1991) and Foucault (1972, 1980) had further influenced many social theorists and cultural critics with notions like "symbolic domination," models of "linguistic markets," and critiques of the power of regulating discourses within institutions. Surely such influential conceptual resources were invaluable in sensitizing scholars and researchers to the need to recognize critical linkages between linguistic practices and political-economic activity. Mindful of these and other informing works, we nevertheless felt that, as researchers who had a detailed knowledge of languages and texts as well as the sociocultural contexts of their speakers, we could provide an instructive perspective on politicized language and linguistic politics. "Language ideologies" provided an additional tool or level of analysis (Silverstein 1979) that permitted us to use the more traditional skills of linguistic anthropologists as a means of relating the models and practices shared by members of a speech community to their political-economic positions and interests.

The next sections of this chapter follow the triplet of the volume's subtitle—"Ideologies, Polities, and Identities"— to orient the reader to our main themes and identify our distinctive emphases. First, I will selectively introduce the notion of language ideologies, with special emphasis on the way this concept is elaborated here by these authors. I then turn more briefly to the interconnected domains of "polities" and "identities," discussing the authors' contributions to the understanding of the role of language ideologies and discursive practices in state formation, nationalism, and maintenance of ethnic groups, on the one hand, and in the creation of national, ethnic, and professional identities on the other.

LANGUAGE IDEOLOGIES

The concept that brought the seminar group together, under the generous auspices of the School of American Research and the Wenner-Gren Foundation for Anthropological Research, had already become increasingly visible in the pages of professional journals from a wide variety of fields (see Woolard and Schieffelin 1994 and Woolard 1998 for extended reviews). Indeed, since 1992, when the American Anthropological Association invited the first session on this topic, numerous symposia devoted to language ideology had occurred at meetings of the AAA, the International Pragmatics Association, and other national and international scholarly societies. Most of the papers originally presented at that first invited session were later published in a special issue of the journal *Pragmatics* (Kroskrity, Schieffelin, and Woolard 1992) and again, in further revised form, as the first anthropologically centered anthology on this topic, *Language Ideologies: Practice and Theory* (Schieffelin, Woolard, and Kroskrity 1998).

Many participants in the 1992 session reassembled for a 1993 AAA symposium, "Constructing Languages and Publics," which also examined the relationships between language, political economy, and language ideologies. This symposium too was later published as a special issue of *Pragmatics* (Gal and Woolard 1995), further indicating the emergence of language ideology as an enduring focus. Speakers in both these sessions who subsequently participated in the School of American Research advanced seminar did acknowledge the importance of language ideology as a conceptual means of resetting the scholarly agenda.

Members of the SAR seminar from which the present volume

emerged did not necessarily share a common vision of this concept or even a commitment to its development (e.g., Briggs 1992:401). But it is safe to say that all the participants were interested in further exploring "language ideologies" as an analytical resource that might be useful in our continuing efforts to produce a more integrative, sociopolitically engaged linguistic anthropology. Since the field has been insightfully reviewed so recently and comprehensively (Woolard 1998), my goal here is to offer a more selective introduction that allows the reader to appreciate how the authors in this volume have both taken from and given to this broad and still emerging theoretical movement.

One way to introduce the notion of language ideology and account for its relatively late arrival on the anthropological scene is to offer a language-ideological myth of origin. In such a myth, the concept of language ideology is the offspring of a union of two neglected forces: the linguistic "awareness" of speakers and the (nonreferential) functions of language. Both of these forces were prematurely marginalized by the dominant and disciplinarily institutionalized approaches to language, which denied the relevance—to linguistics, certainly—of a speaker's own linguistic analysis and valorized the referential functions of language to the exclusion of others. In effect, this surgical removal of language from context produced an amputated "language" that was the preferred object of the language sciences for most of the twentieth century.

Two of the many proposed definitions of language ideology emphatically restore the relevance of these contextual factors and provide an indication of the particular way the notion of language ideology is developed by the authors represented in this volume. Michael Silverstein (1979:193) defined linguistic ideologies as "sets of beliefs about language articulated by users as a rationalization or justification of perceived language structure and use." In a similar way, but with a more sociocultural emphasis, Judith Irvine (1989:255) defined language ideology as "the cultural system of ideas about social and linguistic relationships, together with their loading of moral and political interests." Both definitions place a focal emphasis on speakers' ideas about language and discourse and about how these articulate with various social phenomena. This emphasis on a form of "local" cultural knowledge may not seem particularly new to many cultural anthropologists (e.g., Geertz 1983). But for linguistic anthropologists it represents the opening of a book that had been closed by such ancestral figures as Boas (1911) in anthropology and Bloomfield (1944) in linguistics, who dismissed the importance of attending to indirect and inaccurate secondary rationalizations of members of a language community.

Boas was much more concerned with description of languages as categorization systems and with historical linguistics than with the understanding of culturally contexted speech. For him, native linguistic consciousness produced no useful explication but only "the misleading and disturbing factors of secondary explanations" (1911:69). A "direct" method that privileged the linguist's expertise bypassed the linguistic "false consciousness" of native speakers, who could not have accurate knowledge at the metalinguistic and historical comparative levels, knowledge only available to expert linguists. Instead, members typically explained linguistic forms by relating them often, in what Boas might have regarded as ad hoc explanations, to their own cultural worlds.

Boas's dismissal of such secondary rationalizations of linguistic structures made some sense, given his interest in more purely formal-categorical linguistic analysis. Nevertheless, it had the effect of suppressing research on the diverse cultures of language existing within the Native American speech communities that were among U.S. anthropology's first objects of study. Even later, when language usage— and not just linguistic structures—had become a routine object of analysis in research within such subfields as the ethnography of communication, correlational sociolinguistics (especially the quantitative paradigm), and discourse analysis, attention to members' beliefs and models regarding language was not consistently encouraged. Dell Hymes (1974:33) called for the inclusion of a community's local theory of speech, even if only as ethnography, and John Gumperz's (Gumperz and Blom 1972:431, Gumperz 1982) forays into interactional sociolinguistic and discourse analyses considered local theories of dialect differences and discourse practices. But William Labov quite explicitly diminished the importance of attending to speakers' linguistic ideologies. Interpreting his detailed study of a New York City English speaker, Steve K., as evidence "that a profound shift in social experience and ideology could not alter the socially determined pattern of linguistic variation" (Labov 1979:329), he found justification for his relative disregard of this presumably noninfluential level.[2] Even when local language ideologies were described—often in spectacular cultural detail, as in Gary Gossen's (1974) exploration of Chamula metalanguage— they were presented as cultural givens rather than understood as having any connection to political-economic factors.

Today, although students of language ideology recognize the limitations of members' explicitly verbalized models (Silverstein 1981, 1985), they do not view these knowledge systems as competing with expert or scientific models in the way that Boas and Bloomfield did. Rather, these local models are valued as constructs that emerge as part of the sociocultural experience of cultural actors. By definition "real" to members of the groups in question, they can provide resources for members to deliberately change their linguistic and discourse forms (Silverstein 1985; Rumsey 1990:357).

Like native consciousness, the nonreferential functions of language are a previously neglected aspect that language ideological work foundationally acknowledges. Semiotic models of communication were formulated by Jakobson (1957, 1960) and then in a functional idiom by Hymes (1964). Based on the theories of C. S. Peirce (1931–58), they recognized a variety of sign-focused "pragmatic" relations between language users, the sign vehicles of their languages, and the connections between these signs and the world. By contrast, most models—whether the ethnoscience models of cultural anthropologists or the formal models of Chomskian linguistics—reduced linguistic meaning to denotation, or "reference," and predication. One of the key advantages of such semiotic-functional models is the recognition that much of the meaning and hence communicative value that linguistic forms have for their speakers lies in the "indexical" connections between the linguistic signs and the contextual factors of their use—their connection to speakers, settings, topics, institutions, and other aspects of their sociocultural worlds.

As mentioned above, it is profitable to think of "language ideologies" as a cluster concept consisting of a number of converging dimensions. In the SAR advanced seminar's collective discussions of the individual contributions in their draft forms, four interconnected features of language ideologies were frequently acknowledged and confronted. Though the drafts have evolved into the chapters of the present volume, these features continue as prominent dimensions and provide a basis for recognizing the connection of these chapters to previous language ideological work and their contribution to this ongoing theoretical development.

First, *language ideologies represent the perception of language and discourse that is constructed in the interest of a specific social or cultural group.* A member's notions of what is "true," "morally good," or "aesthetically pleasing" about language and discourse are grounded in social experience and often demonstrably tied to his or her political-economic interests. These notions often underlie attempts to use language as the site at which to promote, protect, and legitimate those interests. Nationalist programs of language standardization, for example, may appeal to a modern metric of communicative efficiency, but such language development efforts are pervasively underlain by political-economic considerations since the imposition of a state-supported hegemonic standard will always benefit some social groups over others (see Woolard 1985, 1989; Errington 1998b, and this volume). What this proposition refutes is the myth of the sociopolitically disinterested language user or the possibility of unpositioned knowledge, even of one's own language.

Though interests are rendered more visible when they are embodied by overtly contending groups—as in the struggle for airtime on Zambian radio (Spitulnik 1998), the disputes of Warao shamans (Briggs 1998), or the confrontations of feminists with the traditional grammarian defenders of the generic "he" (Silverstein 1985), one can also extend this emphasis on grounded social experience to seemingly homogeneous cultural groups by recognizing that cultural conceptions "are partial, contestable, and interest-laden" (Woolard and Schieffelin 1994:58). Even shared cultural language practices, such as Arizona Tewa kiva speech (Kroskrity 1998), can represent the constructions of particular elites who obtain the required complicity (Bourdieu 1991:113) of other social groups and classes. Viewed in this manner, the distinction between neutral ideological analysis, involving the search for "shared bodies of commonsense notions about the nature of language in the world" (Rumsey 1990:346), and critical approaches that emphasize the political use of language as a particular group's

8

instrument of mystification and tool of symbolic domination may seem more gradient than dichotomous. But even though so-called neutral ideologies contribute to our understanding of members' models of language and discourse, an emphasis on the dimension of interest can stimulate a more penetrating sociocultural analysis by rethinking supposedly irreducible cultural explanations. In studies of the Pueblo Southwest, for example, a scholarly tradition of explaining such practices as indigenous purism by attributing linguistic conservatism as an essential feature of Pueblo culture had obscured the relevant association between purism and the discourse of kiva speech that is controlled or regimented by a ceremonial elite (Kroskrity 1998).

In this volume, the interested ideological construction of language is again a pervasive theme, and we see such interests in domains that are both purportedly nonideological and culturally proximate to those of the analysts. In Judith T. Irvine and Susan Gal's chapter, "Language Ideology and Linguistic Differentiation," the authors examine European linguistic confrontations with multilingual Senegalese and Macedonian speech communities. Irvine and Gal reveal the ideological bias of this linguistic scholarship and its effects on such practices as linguistic mapping, historical linguistic interpretation, and imputation of nationality. Their several case studies reveal different kinds of interests, ranging from a relatively unconscious colonial importation of European models of language (and of identity) to a more strategic representation of the subject non-Europeans as inferior Others, to outright politically motivated linguistic gerrymandering used as justification for redrawing national boundaries.

In separate chapters by Michael Silverstein and myself, this ideological focus on scholarship extends to the works of two social scientists. Silverstein's "Whorfianism and the Linguistic Imagination of Nationality" provides a language-ideological reading of the political scientist Benedict Anderson's influential *Imagined Communities* (Anderson 1991). Comparing that book with an important essay by the anthropological linguist Benjamin Lee Whorf, "The Relation of Habitual Thought and Behavior to Language" (Whorf 1956), Silverstein detects an ideological distortion in Anderson's argument that reveals his work to be as much an unwitting reproduction of European and (derivative) Euro-American linguistic nationalist ideologies as it is an analytical account of nationalist culture. My chapter, "Language Ideologies in the Expression and Representation of Arizona Tewa Ethnicity," focuses on the early scholarship of Edward P. Dozier, a Native American cultural anthropologist who conducted research in the late 1940s and early 1950s. I present Dozier's encounter with the multilingual Arizona Tewa community as a professionally endorsed misrecognition of their ethnic adaptation due to Dozier's own professional ideology—in this case, the relative inattention to linguistic beliefs and behaviors that had become normal practice for cultural anthropologists and the pervasive influence of an anthropological acculturation theory linked to assimilationist policies of the federal government. Both Silverstein and I found language ideological distortions (such as the properties of a homogeneous and hegemonic standard or the assumption of a one-to-one relationship between language and identity) embedded in the method and argument of these scholars' works.

Richard Bauman and Charles L. Briggs extend this ideological reading of scholarship to include two key language philosophers of the seventeenth and eighteenth centuries in their chapter, "Language Philosophy as Language Ideology: John Locke and Johann Gottfried Herder." They read the influential texts of these writers as ideological products that derive very specifically from their sociohistorically positioned perspectives. Though their works, very much still read, have had a resounding influence into the present, Locke and Herder focused on very different types of language in disparate national settings.

Writing in post-Baconian seventeenth-century England, Locke was concerned with creating an authoritative core language of rational and empirical science and with delegitimating all other forms of discursive (that is, textual and intertextual) authority. Through a close analysis of Locke's key relevant works, Bauman and Briggs demonstrate how this new "rational" language was based on conventionality of the linguistic sign, a cognitivist emphasis on linking these signs to ideas, and a privileging of denotation and propositional content. For Herder, writing in eighteenth-century Germany, language philosophy was centered around folk literature as an embodiment of emergent national language and identity, linking different poetic forms to the expression of distinctive national identities. Yet despite the very different languages they rationalized and romanticized, Locke and Herder, according to the emphasis on metadiscursive practices adopted by Bauman and Briggs, may actually be seen as both naturalizing their respective privileged positions and legitimating social inequality. Defining metadiscursive practices as "the capacity of discourses to represent and regulate other discourses," Bauman and Briggs follow Foucault (1970, 1972, 1980) in emphasizing the practices used in controlling the production and reception—in short, the regimentation—of socially dominant discourses.

Both Locke and Herder, despite their many differences, delegitimate "common people" (including women) as not controlling proper language—the cultivated, rational language of Locke, the language of intellectualized aesthetic appreciation of folk poetics of Herder. Illustrating an obvious class bias, Herder, for example, valorized a folk poetics that countered the tastes of a traditional aristocratic elite, then declared the peasant folk to be unable to fully understand their own productions, thus legitimating the interests of his own educated class. As Bauman and Briggs suggest, such metadiscursive strategies are relevant to the pervasive dismissal of "folk" linguistics within all academic disciplines until the reversal of this trend in the recent focus on language ideology. Their chapter allows us to observe the intellectual precursor to Boas's notion of (mere) secondary rationalizations of the vulgar or common folk.

Their chapter also proves instructive as a genealogical exploration of key points of European-derived language ideologies such as "language as reference" and "linguistic nationalism" and exemplifies, in "metadiscursive practices," a useful concept that directs analytical attention to projects of regulation of discourse that serve to promote the interests of the writers and their like.

Since Lockean and Herderian ideologies have had a profound impact, as language philosophies, on modern theories of linguistic nationalism and on the fetishization of language as a referential system, the Bauman and Briggs chapter can be read as informing all derivative work from these ancestral sources. Herder's use of folk verbal art as a nation-nucleating discourse is paralleled by Anderson's use of print capitalism and the consumption of nationalist realist novels as similar discursive touchstones of nationalist identity (discussed by Silverstein, this volume). Locke's emphasis on a rational language of science is still manifested in the modern period by the limited use of language in cultural research, such as Dozier's, which was influenced by both functionalist and acculturation theories. Herderian precedents such as declaring the innocence of the folk in terms of their discursive awareness are noted by Irvine and Gal as important preparations for later European scholarship in the middle of the nineteenth century. By that time, "it had become common in the scholarly world to see languages as crucially unaffected by human will or individual interest" (Irvine and Gal, this volume), as an order of form in their own ontic realm of "mind," whether biological or sociological. Later a homologous emphasis became foundational to American anthropology as Boas read the psychology of Native Americans directly from their ancestral language's word morphology.

Second, *language ideologies are profitably conceived as multiple because of the multiplicity of meaningful social divisions (class, gender, clan, elites, generations, and so on) within sociocultural groups that have the potential to produce divergent perspectives expressed as indices of group membership.* Language ideologies are thus grounded in social experience which is never uniformly distributed throughout polities of any scale. Thus, in Jane H. Hill's (1998) study of Mexicano linguistic ideology, when older Mexicano speakers in the Malinche Volcano area of Central Mexico say the Mexicano equivalent of "Today there is no respect," this nostalgic view is more likely to be voiced by men. Although both genders recognize the increased "respect" once signaled by a tradition of using Nahuatl honorific registers and other polite forms, "successful" men are more likely to express this sense of linguistic deprivation of earned deference. Mexicano women, on the other hand, are more likely to express ambivalence; having seen their own lot in life improve during this same period of declining verbal "respect," some women are less enthusiastic in supporting a symbolic return to practices of former times (Hill 1998:78–79).

Viewing language ideologies as "normally" (or unmarkedly) multiple within a population focuses attention on their potential conflict and contention in social space and on the elaborate formulations that the fact of such contestation can encourage (Gal 1992, 1993). This emphasis can also be maintained in the analysis of "dominant" ideologies (Kroskrity 1998) or those that have become successfully "naturalized" by the majority of the group (Bourdieu 1977:164).[3] As in Gramscian (1971) models of state-endorsed hegemonic cultures, there is always struggle and adjustment between states and their opponents, so that even "dominant" ideologies are dynamically responsive to ever-changing forms of opposition. By viewing multiplicity as the sociological baseline, we are challenged to understand the processes employed by specific groups to have their ideologies become taken-for-granted aspects and hegemonic forces of cultural life for a larger society.

A graphic example of the importance of multiplicity and contention in language ideological processes, one that has noticeably changed the grammar of English within my generation's lifetime, resulted from the feminist challenge to the once standard generic "he" (Silverstein 1985). Once upon a time, a sentence like the following would have been regarded as needlessly redundant: If a student wishes to be considered for financial assistance, he or she must complete an application. American feminist objections to the generic "he" sought to define it as untrue by virtue of referential exclusion and therefore emblematic of being unfair, viewing a previously accepted grammatical convention of the standard register as not just a neutrally arbitrary grammatical practice but as a discriminatory, gendered practice (Silverstein 1985). Relevant interest groups, in this case feminists, constructed a stance against a rule of grammar that speakers of standard English had been following for hundreds of years.

Many chapters in this volume examine not only multiplicity and contestation but also clashes or disjunctures in which divergent ideological perspectives on language and discourse are juxtaposed, resulting in conflict, confusion, and contradiction.[4] Contestation and disjuncture thus disclose critical differences in ideological perspectives that can more fully reveal their distinctive properties as well as their scope and force (Kroskrity 1998).

Bambi Schieffelin's chapter, "Introducing Kaluli Literacy: A Chronology of Influences," examines the disjuncture between indigenous language ideologies of a cultural group in Papua New Guinea and the "modernizing" and Christianizing ideologies embodied in a missionary-introduced literacy program. A small community in the Mt. Bosavi area of southwestern Papua New Guinea, the Kaluli did not experience significant foreign influence until the 1960s, when the arrival of missionaries opened the area to Christianization and modernization. Schieffelin's study looks at two decades of missionary engagement with local culture, demonstrating how Christianizing native literacy programs "challenged and changed Kaluli notions of language, truth, knowledge, and authority." These challenges were posed by missionary-introduced literacy practices and products pertaining to bible reading and interpretation and vernacular literacy instruction.

Among the literacy products examined are Kaluli primers written by missionaries, with the assistance of Kaluli speakers, to further their own objectives of Westernization. In her careful analysis of these works, Schieffelin effectively demonstrates how these primers "(re)presented and (re)constituted social identity." From the first, this promotion of "missionary literacy" within the oral tradition of the Kaluli introduced not only a new metalanguage of literacy for "books," "reading," and so on but also a fragmentation of language and a decentering of identity. In ways unfamiliar to Kaluli language ideology but seemingly naturalized both by Kaluli orthography and newly introduced literacy practices, the vernacular language was stripped of its cultural practices and severed from Kaluli discourses in church and school settings. The primers produced in the 1970s begin to oppose Kaluli local culture to the innovations of a Christian modernity. By referring to the Kaluli themselves as *ka:na:ka:* (a derogatory term for Pacific Island natives from Tok Pisin) and systematically depicting Kaluli practices as backward and inferior, these texts influenced the Kaluli to construct themselves from the pejorative perspective of outsiders.

A second and very important focus is on literacy events. Using audio recordings of literacy sessions in the 1980s, Schieffelin carefully explores the impact of these nontraditional practices as a critical site of the production of new models of textual authority. Books, as animated by Kaluli readers, "speak" the truth in a monologic voice of authority and, when talked about, are coded as agents that require appropriate ergative case marking. The goal of the literacy classroom—to produce a coordinated, unison vocal repetition of authoritative books—challenged traditional ideological preferences for locating "truth" in collective, multiparty, polyphonic discourse. Vernacular literacy classes taught by local pastors and based on Western models of classroom discourse and Christian sermons contributed, along with other missionizing activities, to the reshaping of local epistemology and aesthetics as part of a totalizing transformation of Kaluli culture. It is important to note that in this clash of ideologies, missionaries had a double advantage: they controlled the new technology of native language literacy and enjoyed the hegemonic support of the nation-state. Their ability to effect radical culture change through introducing Kaluli literacy thus linked modernity, Christianity, and the economic resources of the nation-state.

My "Language Ideologies in the Expression and Representation of Arizona Tewa Ethnic Identity" also concerns the disjuncture of imported and indigenous language ideologies. In this chapter I examine language ideologies of both a Pueblo Indian group and an anthropologist concerned with describing that group. In the first part of the chapter, I extend previous analyses (Kroskrity 1993, 1998) by emphasizing how a ceremonial elite among the Arizona Tewas used a dominant language ideology as a resource in the "erasure" (Irvine and Gal, this volume) of clan and class difference in order to create an "ethnic" identity as Arizona Tewa Villagers. In addition to noting this role in creating an ethnic identity, I also observe how specific ideological preferences like indigenous purism and strict compartmentalization promote the creation of repertoires of language and identity that encourage the maintenance of multiple, distinct languages and their associated identities.

The second part of my chapter examines Edward Dozier's confusion and resulting misrecognition of the Arizona Tewa pattern of multiethnic and multilingual adaptation to the Hopi majority on both First Mesa and the Hopi Reservation more generally. Dozier, one of the earliest "native" anthropologists, was a Santa Clara Tewa who enjoyed many real and imagined benefits in studying a group so similar to his own. But even Dozier's linguistic preadaptation for this research and his skill as an ethnographer could not save him from uncritically attending to "professional" anthropological linguistic ideologies that desensitized him to multilingualism and language use and insisted on an "acculturation" theory perspective in which assimilation was an implicitly assumed ideal. Dozier's professional ideology limited his interpretive choices: the Arizona Tewas had to be either "Hopi" or

"Tewa," although they gave ample evidence, in language ideology and linguistic practice, of being both.

As in Schieffelin's Kaluli study, the hegemonic force of nation-states is mediated through professions designed either to teach or to study other cultural groups. Missionaries and anthropologists certainly have contrasting immediate objectives—conversion and documentation, respectively—but they are often influenced by state support, thereby becoming agents, in a sense, of their respective nationalist regimes. As an examination of disparate ideologies of local cultural production and expert professional interpretation, the Tewa analysis resonates with Irvine and Gal's (this volume) treatment of the confusion experienced by European linguists who could not properly interpret local discourses of diversity or make sense of pervasive multilingualism and code switching in Macedonia and, seeing only disorder rather than a different kind of cultural order, chose to "orientalize" the region.

In Joseph Errington's chapter, "Indonesian('s) Authority," we find complementary if not contradictory language ideologies underlying the development of standard Indonesian. Errington examines the "conflicted efforts of the New Order to domesticate exogenous modernity and modernize domestic traditions." Though often viewed as a success story in terms of "the national language problem," standardized Indonesian does not readily conform to a number of facile claims by scholars and policymakers who share an instrumentalist ideology of language development in nationalism. Gellner (1983), for example, sees development of a national standard language as a key element in making the transformation to nationalism. Typically, according to Gellner, a state-level polity will emerge from a religiously based society anchored in local communities controlled by literate elites who derive their authority from knowledge of a sacred script. He correlates emergent nationalism with such contrastive attributes as secular- (versus sacred) and state-sponsored language standardization and mass literacy. Here standardized Indonesian is portrayed as an "ethnically uninflected, culturally neutral language" that is both universally available to its citizens and itself subject to development by the state. But Errington provides several key examples suggesting that the "instrumentalist" ideals of creating a linguistically homogeneous tool for economic development are clearly not resulting in a culturally neutral national language. Though the New Order attempts to efface the derivativeness of national high culture and national language by erasure of its ethnic and class sources, the language itself provides a key example of an apparent contradiction.

Errington employs Weber's distinction between bureaucratic and charismatic authority to help locate the "asymmetrical complementarity" of opposing influences on language development: the standardism of the state and the exemplarism of traditional elites. He examines recent lexical change and finds productive use of both archaic or archaicized terms traceable to Old Javanese and Sanskrit, as well as the incorporation of almost one thousand terms from English. This dual development of the lexicon can hardly be defended as "communicatively efficient" or as contributing to some neutral language widely available to all as an emblem of national identity. Rather, it represents a continuity with a supposedly abandoned linguistic past in which exemplary elites rule through a language over which they have specialized control. And since knowledge of the local prestige charismatic languages (Javanese and Sanskrit) and the prestige international language, English, is socially distributed, this standardizing project joins other nationalist projects in both creating and legitimating a state-endorsed social inequality (Alonso 1994). Errington's chapter thus succeeds in displaying the multiple, seemingly contradictory ideologies that provide disparate resources for the delicate balance of the ever-fragile Indonesian state.

In examining U.S. presidential political ideologies, Jane H. Hill also exploits the analytical value of recognizing ideological multiplicity. Her chapter, "Read My Article: Ideological Complexity and the Overdetermination of Promising in American Presidential Politics," asks the intriguing question of why American politicians are compelled to produce campaign promises despite the dangers of such public declarations. Informed with a comparative understanding of Samoan political oratory (Duranti 1993, 1994) and other English-language political discourse (e.g., Wilson 1990), Hill observes the critical relationship of promises to the "personalism" that is a pervasive feature of the American presidential system. Evaluative commentary on campaign promises by political journalists and by elite image makers provides an important site of explicit metapragmatic discourse. In such evaluation, Hill distinguishes two distinct language ideological discourses: the discourse of truth and the discourse of theater. The former is a more popular perspective grounded in expectations of "informed choice" and "full disclosure" and indexically linked to personalist readings of "moral character." The latter discourse is controlled by campaign specialists who worry about their candidate "performing" their "messages" in appropriately staged venues.

At the center of Hill's chapter is her analysis of George Bush's famous campaign promise issued in his 1988 speech accepting the Republican presidential nomination. Bush's "Read my lips: No new taxes" was a deliberately constructed and staged response designed both to talk "straight" and to index a masculine "street" vernacular in order to dramatically represent himself as a tough, determined, political leader, not a "wimp." When Bush later raised taxes in a 1990 legislative compromise with Congress, most analysts rejected the possible discourse-of-theater account that his statement was merely a dramatic "performance of a message" and instead insisted that his utterance counted as a promise that was subject to tests of truth and ultimately evidence of Mr. Bush's moral state. Bush was damaged by his campaign team's failure to see these two discourses of reception as potentially contradictory and their inability to recognize the greater scope and force of the discourse of truth. Hill concludes by viewing the demolition of George Bush by journalists and the general public as not only an example of the power of the discourse of truth as a source for the "moral character" of politicians but also "an important moment of reproduction of personalist ideology and the project of engendering masculinity that is central to it." By appealing to multiple ideologies of political discourse, Hill provides a valuable account of the strategic use of ideological resources in presidential campaigns and the importance of understanding language ideologies as deployed against relevant cultural backgrounds—here the "personalism" characteristic of local notions of personhood in American culture.

Third, *members may display varying degrees of awareness of local language ideologies.* While the Silverstein (1979) definition quoted above suggests that language ideologies may often be explicitly articulated by members, researchers also recognize ideologies of practice that must

18

be read from actual usage. Sociological theorists, such as Giddens (1984:7), who are concerned with human agency and the linkage of micro and macro allow for varying degrees of members' consciousness of their own rule-guided activities, ranging from discursive to practical consciousness. I have suggested (1998) a correlational relationship between high levels of discursive consciousness and active contestation of ideologies, such as those manifested in the disputes of competing Warao shamans (Briggs 1992) or feminist contestations of gendered speech practices in standard American English (Silverstein 1985) and, by contrast, the correlation of merely practical consciousness with relatively unchallenged, highly naturalized, and definitively dominant ideologies.

The types of sites in which language ideologies are produced and commented upon constitute another source of variations in awareness. Silverstein (1998:136) developed the notion of ideological sites "as institutional sites of social practice as both object and modality of ideological expression." Sites may be institutionalized, interactional rituals that are culturally familiar loci for the expression and/or explication of ideologies that indexically ground them in identities and relationships. In this volume Susan Philips clarifies the relationship between ideological sites and actual contexts for speech. She develops the notion of multisitedness in recognizing how language ideologies may be indexically tied, in complex and overlapping ways, to more than a single site, which may be a site of primary ideological production or a site of metapragmatic commentary. This distinction becomes especially important in the case of Tongan *lea kovi* 'bad language', discussed in Philips's chapter, "Constructing a Tongan Nation State through Language Ideology in the Courtroom."

Since "bad language" is a profaning topic, there are few opportunities for its explicit ideological elaboration in everyday contexts of use. The ideologically constructed site of use is "a hierarchically conceived familial dyad" in which members—here sister and brother—display "mutual respect" by strictly adhering to a variety of proscriptions on their discourse (including one on "bad language"). Though *lea kovi* is not explicitly discussed in this "site of use," it is indirectly modeled as a proscribed activity in culturally normative appropriate speech between male and female siblings. Ideological elaboration on this embarrassing usage as a topic does not occur in intrafamilial discourse but rather in the courts, where such notions must be clearly discussed as part of the legal process.

The legal setting thus becomes a site of "metapragmatic commentary" on *lea kovi,* which Philips carefully examines as an invocation and metaphorical extension of a culturally recognized *tapu* on "bad language" from the brother-sister relationship to other "potential" brothers and sisters—an extension that parallels the classificatory use of the kin terms for siblings for cousins. Magistrates also suggest that since individuals may not know whether all individuals present in a speech situation are or are not related in this manner, it is lawful to expect that one will behave as if such relatives are present. The young, unmarried women who are the victims of these crimes are framed and imaginatively interpreted as possible "sisters" to the defendant and to others who were present. This legal activity foregrounds a kinship-based aspect of social identity in which women are the foci of censorship. As the court officials exercise their authority, as representatives of the state, to constitute social realities as matters requiring the legal intervention of the nation-state, they also construct a distinctly Tongan gendered state.

But these magistrates also use local language ideologies like *lea kovi* and the kinship-based models they invoke as touchstones of traditional cultural authority. By invoking analogies between contemporary family and nation-state and between the precontact Tongan polity and the contemporary nation-state, these language ideologies use the moral authority of past and present Tongan culture to justify the political authority of the present-day state. As such, language ideologies play a significant role in the creation of both Tongan gender and national identities. By developing the concept of ideological sites, Philips also permits us to see ideological awareness as related to the number and nature of sites in which members deploy and explicate their language ideologies.

Awareness is also a product of the kind of linguistic or discursive phenomena that speakers, either generically or in a more culturally specific manner, can identify and distinguish (Silverstein 1981). Nouns, our words for things, display an unavoidable referentiality that makes them more available for folk awareness and possible folk theorizing than, say, a rule for marking "same subject" as part of verb morphology. The importance of attending to awareness as a dimension of ideology is both the reversal of a longstanding scholarly tradition of delegitimating common people's views of language—a tradition extending back at least as far as Locke and Herder and relevantly manifested in the modern period by Boas's dismissal of folk understandings of language as superfluous and "misleading" (Boas 1911:67-71)—and the recognition that when speakers rationalize their language they take a first step toward changing it (Silverstein 1979).

Finally, *members' language ideologies mediate between social structures and forms of talk.* The dynamic and synthetic role of ideologies is especially well captured in Silverstein's (1985:220) appeal to the necessity of including this often neglected and delegitimated level of language analysis: "The total linguistic fact, the datum for a science of language, is irreducibly dialectic in nature. It is an unstable mutual interaction of meaningful sign forms contextualized to situations of interested human use and mediated by the fact of cultural ideology." Language users' ideologies bridge their sociocultural experience and their linguistic and discursive resources by constituting those linguistic and discursive forms as indexically tied to features of their sociocultural experience. These users, in constructing language ideologies, are selective both in the features of linguistic and social systems that they do distinguish and in the linkages between systems that they construct.

Michael Silverstein, in his chapter here, reads Whorf as a pioneering figure in language ideological research. While embracing the Boasian program in his stance of relativity, Whorf refused to dismiss folk linguistic notions as irrelevant in the manner dictated by a Boasian preference for a direct method. Silverstein carefully details Whorf's argument, which was one of the first to include community members' folk linguistic extrapolations from their vocabulary, grammar, discourse, and general "fashions of speaking" as a contributing part of this dialectic process. The result is a relativity of consciousness across linguistic boundaries for such taken-for-granted though culturally constructed notions as "time" and "space." Silverstein details many structural analogies between Whorf's account of the production of Standard Average European "time" and Anderson's historical account of the emergence of a distinctive nationalist "we." He concludes by using the Whorfian model as a basis for critiquing Benedict Anderson's less penetrating treatment. Whorf, Silverstein argues, demonstrated a concern for examining the fit between cultural and linguistic tropes of reality suggested by actual usage and any codable reality that might be behind such a projection. Whorf demonstrated how "habitual thought" emerged from the dialectic of linguistic and discursive practices, on the one hand, and phenomenal cultural experience on the other. But Anderson, in contrast to Whorf, "seems to mistake the dialectically-produced trope...for the reality, rather than seeing...[their] dialectical workings...[as] the facts to be characterized and explained."

The mediating role of language ideologies is further explored and extended in Irvine and Gal's chapter, "Language Ideology and Linguistic Differentiation." The authors turn to semiotic theories of communication as an inspiration in order to develop three especially useful analytical tools for detecting productive processes that occur in interpretive understanding of linguistic variability over populations, places, and times. Irvine and Gal regard these language ideological processes as universal and "deeply involved in both the shaping of linguistic differentiation and the creating of linguistic description."

The three productive semiotically based features underlying much language ideological reasoning are iconization, fractal recursivity, and erasure. Irvine and Gal illustrate these processes in each of three sections devoted to detailed examinations of specific historical situations in Africa and Europe. Iconization, for example, emerges as a highly productive feature of folk linguistic ideologies as well as those imported by European linguists attempting to interpret the exotic languages of Africa and the Balkan frontier. Here iconization is a feature of the representation of languages and aspects of them as pictorial guides to the nature of groups. It becomes a useful tool for understanding how Western European linguists misinterpreted the South African Khoisan clicks as degraded animal sounds rather than phonological units and viewed the linguistic and ethnic diversity of the Balkans as a pathological sociolinguistic chaos that could only be opposed to Western Europe's transparent alignment of ethnic nation, standardized national language, and state. Irvine and Gal also see iconization as a typical feature of folk linguistic models in their account of how click sounds enter the Nguni languages through their "respect" or "avoidance" registers from neighboring Khoisan languages. By first viewing the clicks as sounds produced by foreign and subordinate others, Nguni language speakers can "recursively" incorporate such iconic linkages for use as a linguistic marker of a Nguni language register, or speech level, designed to show respect and deference under various culturally prescribed situations.

Erasure of differentiation is a selective disattention to often unruly forms of variation that do not fit the models of speakers and/or linguists. In their study of nineteenth-century European linguistic treatment of Senegalese languages, Irvine and Gal document the erasure of multilingualism and linguistic variation required to produce linguistic maps analogous to those of Europe. Erasure permits us to measure the difference between comprehensive analytical models, which attempt to understand a broad spectrum of linguistic differentiation and variation, and a more dominating or even hegemonic model in which analytical distinctions are glossed over in favor of attending to more selective yet locally acknowledged views. Erasure, like iconization and recursivity, is a sensitizing concept, loosely inspired by semiotic models of communication, for tracking and ultimately locating the perspectivally based processes of linguistic and discursive differentiation that inevitably represent the products of ideological influence on positioned social actors. All three processes provide useful means of describing and comparing the productive features of language ideologies employed by both nation-states and the social groups within them.

POLITIES AND IDENTITIES

Language, especially shared language, has long served as the key to naturalizing the boundaries of social groups. The huge volume of scholarship on nationalism and ethnicity typically includes language as a criterial attribute. Though much has changed since Herder and other European language philosophers valorized and naturalized the primordial unity of language, nation, and state (Bauman and Briggs, this volume), there are still features of contemporary Western European ideologies, such as "homogenism" (Blommaert and Verschueren 1998), with more than a family resemblance to their eighteenth-century conceptual ancestors. Contemporary scholars of nationalism use tropes of "invention," "imagination," or "narration"

(Hobsbawm and Ranger 1983; Anderson 1991; Bhaba 1990) to understand that complex social formation known as the nation-state. They appeal to the role of language and discursive forms in such nation-making (Foster 1995) processes as the invention of national traditions, the production of news reports and popular fiction, and the creation of state-produced narratives that locate citizens in the flow of national time (as described in Anderson 1991 and Kelly 1997). Though overtly different from Herder's preference for poetry from the *Volk* as a nation-nucleating force, these contemporary tropes and their associated theories all presuppose the existence and efficacy of shared language forms as a basis for making the discursive genres which, in turn, make the nation. Such continuity in theorizing nationalism by scholars is remarkable in its own right, but the foundational emphasis on homogeneous language is more an uncritical reproduction of folk theories than a considered interpretation of socially distributed linguistic variation.

Even as languages typically display socially significant variation indexed to such population variables as class, age, gender, network, and regional differences, speakers—and scholars of speech—just as typically erase much of this complexity. Guided by simplifying language ideologies, speakers construct languages more often by reifying their linguistic homogeneity than by confronting their internal variation. Though members of speech communities as large as New York City (Labov 1972b) and as small as the Tolowa (Collins 1998b) do recognize variation, they often embrace shared norms in both their embodiment of linguistic practice and their reflections on actual usage.

The Kaluli, as described here by Schieffelin, display a similar pattern. Though some older Kaluli people can remember the introduction of the imported and derogatory expression *ka:na:ka* and other loanwords by the missionaries who controlled the native language orthography along with the concept of writing, the Kaluli as a group were unable to resist the naturalizing impact of incorporating such words into the written/printed form of their native language. What might have been carefully distinguished and possibly compartmentalized (cf. the Arizona Tewas) as a missionary-imposed register with both foreign vocabulary and grammatically reduced forms was instead viewed as "the Kaluli language" by the Kaluli themselves. Of course, Kaluli acquiescence—and even enthusiasm—in accepting these new

Shobhana
leading to   what is eiappening
extend to South   to longuistic
Asiano   differences
here
REGIMENTING LANGUAGES

linguistic forms was greatly facilitated by the association of this new regime of language with the superior technologies and economic resources of a state-supported missionary vanguard. By appealing to the naturalizing unity of a "shared language," missionary control of literacy practices thus introduced the Kaluli to their new status, not as a self-defining ethnic group but rather as a racialized group within the nation-state, subordinated to the interests of national development.[6]

For the Arizona Tewas, these linkages between linguistic homogeneity and naturalization surface in a local language ideology that features indigenous purism and compartmentalization. Tewa language practices do not just assume or imagine a linguistic homogeneity; they attempt to impose it. Unlike the Kaluli, the Tewas retained control of how their language admitted new loanwords and could use it as a means of regulating the influence of culture contact. This is part of a discursive strategy, modeled on kiva speech, which maintains maximally distinctive languages by discouraging mixing and iconically connects each language to membership in its associated group. The Arizona Tewas have a well-developed "discourse of difference" that may actually imagine more linguistic differences than can be verified by observation (Kroskrity 1993). However, their "ceremonial ideology," centered on the kiva as a key site, constructs kiva speech as a shared linguistic resource, erasing clan and class distinctions in favor of an Arizona Tewa ethnic identity "diacritically" (Barth 1969) different from Hopi, Navajo, or Anglo identities. Though modern theories of ethnic group formation such as Barth's (1969) emphasize group self-ascription and the symbolic transformation of selectively distinctive cultural attributes into "badges of ethnicity," they tend to regard "ethnic languages" as a probable but not essential sources of these iconic badges.

Such modern theories attempt to account for "ethnic boundary maintenance" in situations of significant, even intensive, culture contact, and present ethnic groups as inherently oppositional even when culture change greatly reduces the number of persisting differences between group insiders and group outsiders. In such oppositional contexts, members are likely to erase internal linguistic differences in favor of producing a contrast of now homogenized languages that iconically fits the contrast of oppositional groups. Thus, for the Arizona Tewas, their project of ethnic boundary maintenance with the Hopis focuses attention more on the contrast of Tewa and Hopi rather than on their own internal linguistic differentiation. What is important about language ideological work is the appreciation of the role of members' ideological processes, such as erasure, in the production of homogeneous languages that can serve as emblems of group membership. Theorists of ethnic groups, like those of nation-states, tend to regard language homogeneity as a natural state rather than something that is constructively produced by language ideologies of the group and/or the analyst in relation to cultural practices. By doing so, they fail to investigate the role language ideologies and related linguistic practices play in helping to create the ethnic groups they are trying to analyze.

This reification of homogeneous language is also a common feature in the literature on language and nationalism. Gellner (1983), for example, represents standardized Indonesian—the product of state-sponsored language standardization and mass literacy—as an "ethnically uninflected," that is, culturally neutral, language that is equally available to all of Indonesia's citizens. But Gellner's portrayal, as interpreted by Errington (this volume), better fits the "instrumentalist" ideals (creating a linguistically homogeneous tool for economic development) than the linguistic facts. As noted above, many borrowings from English and a strong influence of classical languages like Old Javanese and Sanskrit suggest that standardized Indonesian is privileging the modern and traditional elites who control the various source languages.

Like Gellner, Benedict Anderson (1991) too naturalizes the process of linguistic standardization by assuming that such state-supported language policies produce a uniform linguistic product and a concomitant homogenizing influence on citizens through their consumption of newspapers and novels. Their shared, vicarious participation in these texts thus provides the basis for their sense of sharing of an "imagined community." Though Anderson clearly wants to reject Herderian thinking in his de-emphasis of primordial and iconic linkages of languages to national and racial essences, it seems more a permutation than a refutation of the nucleating role of a homogeneous language in fostering a nationalist consciousness (Gal 1989:355). To be sure, homogeneous language, for Anderson, is not a naturally given precondition for nationalism but a socially emergent effect of official-

consequences for how people experience enfranchisement

ized print capitalism. But, as Irvine and Gal state in their chapter here, "homogeneous language is as much imagined as is community." Further work on language and nationalism would certainly benefit from problematizing linguistic homogeneity as an issue of how language ideologies operate.

To analytically deconstruct the homogeneity of language is pervasive and problematic in the study of social formations like ethnic groups and polities like nation-states. But this project is also related to a second concern taken up in this volume: understanding the multiplex indexicalities of languages. There is a tense complementarity between scholarly approaches that emphasize the unifying effects of common language in the construction of national identity and those that emphasize the legitimation of social inequality created and imposed by either exemplary ethnic languages (e.g., Javanese) or standardized national ones. Representing the former is Anderson (1991:16) when he says:

> [The nation] is imagined as a community, because, regardless
> of the actual inequality and exploitation that may prevail in
> each, the nation is always conceived as a deep, horizontal com-
> radeship. Ultimately it is this fraternity that makes it possible,
> over the past two centuries, for so many people to die for such
> limited imaginings.

In this passage Anderson implicitly links the shared participation in print media publications, which produces an imagined community of nationalism, to a more egalitarian solidarity of citizens as comrades; here we can explain the development of powerful national loyalties among citizens who do not enjoy a high socioeconomic position. Other scholars, including cultural anthropologists like Alonso (1994) and Williams (1991), note that nationalist forms of community possess both horizontal and vertical dimensions and often acknowledge the complex alternations of egalitarianism and hierarchy that produce such apparent paradoxes as "a moral equality among all socially unequal persons" (Williams 1991:99).

But where Anderson iconically associates an overly homogenized standard with its uniformizing effects, Bourdieu (1977, 1984, 1991) views linguistic diversity as inextricably linked to the production and reproduction of social inequality. Linguistic varieties, like the standard and institutionally preferred linguistic practices, have value because they provide users with access to resources and are ultimately convertible into social and economic capital. Since control of state-legitimated linguistic forms—like a hegemonic standard language—is differentially distributed in stratified societies, even those who do not control the standard will often manifest compliance with its authority. For Bourdieu, this "symbolic domination" rests in members' iconic linkages between linguistic forms and social classes, with their associated power and resources. But whereas the symbolic domination of standard languages, as in the case of standard American English over New York City regional English in Labov's (1972b) research, rationalizes vertical, or hierarchical, relations, between speakers, it is doubtful whether processes like symbolic domination alone can provide a comprehensive account of how speakers find the horizontal camaraderie of citizenship in a nation-state. How then do we understand the dual role of standard languages as embodiments of both national identity and state-endorsed social inequality?

Language ideological research may provide some useful conceptual tools for better relating often simultaneous and pervasive processes of linguistic nationalism and the production of social inequality. Recognition of the multiple indexicality of many linguistic and discursive forms allows the analyst to see that, through ideological fractalization effects, the same linguistic signs or discourse practices can, be indexically linked by speakers to more than one group, at varying degrees of abstraction and inclusion, and at multiple sites of use and levels of awareness. As described here by Susan Philips, the practice of *lea kovi* is linked to the Tongan family in domestic sites while the rights and duties of metapragmatic commentary on its use or violation are reserved to Tongan magistrates as representatives of the state. These linkages tie such cultural speech practices to both the traditional family and the state and lend a multivocality to this culturally prescribed "avoidance" register. This multivocality is related to the different contexts in which language practices are produced and received. *Lea kovi*, as a multisited practice, also encourages Tongans to draw connections between local culture and the authority of the Tongan nation-state.

Presumably shared forms are also typically underlain by patterns of linguistic stratification. Kiva speech, for example, is constructed by a

Tewa ritual elite around a shared and unifying linguistic core; this creates an imaginably homogenous ethnic group by ceremonially erasing differences of class and clan (Kroskrity, this volume). Yet the very knowledge and practice of kiva speech is a major source of class stratification within the Tewa village, since only elites possess a full command of this register.

In Indonesia, the hegemonic standard was designed to erase ethnic or class linguistic bias and thus create a linguistic emblem of national identity. But like any standard, the presumably shared and artificial form, upon close inspection, reveals the differential influence of specific ethnic groups and elites (Errington, this volume) and validates a social hierarchy. Nevertheless, as Silverstein (this volume) observes of institutionally maintained state standards, "The standard that informs the language community's norm thus becomes the very emblem of the existence of that community." Susan Philips views states as very active in their nationalist appropriation of language ideologies. For her, the institutional maintenance of state-approved language and discourse—with institutions like government and education as sites—actively produces and reproduces an ideological consensus and converges with multiple nationalist discourses involving appeals to history, to tropes of kinship, and to oppositional others so as to legitimate both Tongan culture (including some of its social hierarchies) and, as its expression, the Tongan state. Her chapter reminds us that while language ideologies can be appropriated by the state, they are by no means the only discourses of self-legitimation for state regimes.

In nationalist discourses (Alonso 1994; Philips, this volume) the productive opposition to others does have important implications for students of language ideology. Other nations may not only speak other languages but may also use language in ways that are not compatible with language and identity relationships inscribed in state institutions and nationalist ideologies. Irvine and Gal's discussion of Western European linguists and their misrecognition of Macedonian practices of plurilingualism and code switching suggests the power that nationalist ideologies have on scholars of language. Silverstein (1996) has demonstrated how encounters with North American Indian communities, many displaying plurilingual adaptations or possessing linguistic repertoires that included "contact languages," led some early investigators to interpretations guided more by Eurocentric language ideologies than by observable linguistic practices. I suggest that the role of nationalist discourses on language and identity as a powerful, if indirect, source of influence is consistent with Edward Dozier's misrecognition of Arizona Tewa ethnolinguistic identity.

A scholar, as a citizen, can not avoid speciation into what Balibar (1991:93) termed *homo nationalis*—a member of a national community who enjoys or endures state support and regulation in daily routines from cradle to grave. The seductive naturalizations produced by language ideologies, especially those that regiment language and identity relationships, clearly require special attention from scholars who might otherwise reproduce assumptions and interpretations prefigured by nationalist ideologies rather than grounded in observable sociolinguistic patterns. Silverstein's (this volume) reading of Benedict Anderson is that the erasure of linguistic variation in Anderson's "imagination" of a homogenous standard represents just such a downloading of a nationalist ideology, and not its analysis.

Conceptual tools like fractal recursivity, iconization, and erasure (from Irvine and Gal, this volume) help to expose the often incompletely articulated models of community members and scholars and are particularly helpful in illuminating links between language and social experience. A focus on metadiscursive strategies (Bauman and Briggs, this volume), too, further reminds us of the role of "interests" in shaping texts normally perceived to be disinterested works about the true nature of language. Since language ideologies are both pervasive and pervasively naturalized, they are often difficult to see without the aid of these and other sensitizing concepts designed to denaturalize language and explore its connections to the political-economic worlds of speakers.

For scholars, the recognition of belonging perforce to the species *homo nationalis* alerts us to watch for the influence of nationalist projects on our own research, to take into account that, whether or not we admit it, we ourselves are profoundly influenced by our national identities. Though we may perhaps feel a reduced sense of heroic agency, there is no dramatic crisis of identity. In contrast, as presented by Schieffelin (this volume), the eventual incorporation of the Kaluli people into a nation-state was prepared by a sudden and dramatic "regimentation of identities based on cultural stereotyping." By importing a view of the Kaluli as just another subordinated racial group and naturalizing this view in the practices of an indigenous literacy program, missionaries and their local pastors played a key role in stratifying people during state formation in Papua New Guinea. Prescriptive gender identities were also entextualized in primers and other texts.

By introducing a new form of authority, the monological book, these same missionaries subverted local models of multiparty dialogical discourse as the key way of establishing authoritativeness. Imposed change of discourse norms by hegemonic forces are typically understood as attacks upon one's cultural identity (Basso 1979; Scollon and Scollon 1981). When hegemonic educational regimes require Cibecue Apache children to speak English exclusively and engage their teachers in mutual gaze, or when they force Kaluli students to answer in unison as part of highly regimented lessons, they attack those pupils' cultural identities and subordinate them to the nation-state.

For U.S. politicians, cultural identities are also at risk, as we see in Jane Hill's chapter; they too are constructed, in part, out of language ideologies. Regimes of personhood must be constituted on the basis of local cultural resources, including relevant language ideologies and personalism. The public reading of George Bush's attempt at impression management as a political promise was a victory for the discourse of truth which, coupled with personalism, required him to display exemplary intentional agency. Just as Mr. Bush's professional political identity would hinge on his and his advisors' decisions about appropriate professional comportment in language, so Edward Dozier's professional identity as a native cultural anthropologist would require some conformity to professionally accepted norms of conduct. Since anthropological research on Native Americans at midcentury was influenced by then-current U.S. nationalist projects of promoting urban migration and assimilation by terminating reservations, these were indirectly transmitted to Dozier as he acquired his professional identity. Ironically, then, Dozier's professional identity was at least partially responsible for his misrecognition of Arizona Tewa ethnic identity.

Before sending the reader on to examine the richness of the chapters that follow, it is appropriate to return briefly to a theme adumbrated at the beginning of this introduction, a theme that distinguishes this collection of essays from others on this and related topics. As linguistic anthropologists, the authors possess special qualifications in their appreciation of linguistic structure, sociolinguistic variation, ways of speaking, social structure, cultural practice, and political economy. They use these technologies of knowledge to address issues of concern not just to linguistic and cultural anthropologists but to a host of other fields as well, including sociology, political science, history, linguistics, literature, cultural studies, and folklore.

As a product of linguistic anthropology and as representative of a sample of research within this far from unified subfield of anthropology, the most distinctive attribute of the volume is an emphasis on reflexivity. This is not just the "reflexive" self-regulation (Giddens 1984:205) that social theorists ascribe when they see members' knowledge of social process as a critical part of the social system or of the metalinguistic and metapragmatic functions of "reflexive" language (e.g., Lucy 1993). By "reflexive" here I mean to tap into a slightly older tradition of use within cultural anthropology (e.g., Ruby 1982) to indicate a redirection of anthropological analysis to the anthropologist as well as to cultural Others. This type of reflexivity is perhaps especially welcome, even crucial, for those of us working on the role of language ideology in such processes as nationalism, ethnicity, and state formation. In these domains, as Alonso (1994:379) has aptly concluded about the danger of unintentionally importing commonsense knowledge, "Much of the misplaced concreteness that bedevils this scholarship results from an uncritical reproduction of common sense that poses intellectual as well as political problems."

Reflexivity takes several forms in this volume, including the analysis of European language philosophy (Bauman and Briggs), European historical linguistics (Irvine and Gal), U.S. academic ideologies of language from both anthropology and political science (Kroskrity, Silverstein), U.S. discourses of political commentary by journalists and elite image advisors (Hill), and the impact of Christian missionaries on natives in the Papua New Guinea highlands (Schieffelin). Chapters by Irvine and Gal and Kroskrity attempt to simultaneously consider members' local language ideologies along with those of the analysts who interpreted them. This focus on Western, Euro-American, and scholarly language ideologies is a necessary step in recognizing the unacknowledged role of language ideologies in all forms of language work.

Having suggested these connections, I leave it for readers to further explore the many links between language ideologies and the discourses of polity and identity that pervade this volume. Although many of the chapters treat both polities (states and ethnic groups) and identities (national, ethnic, and professional), they are offered in a sequence that begins with more macrolevel studies, typically emphasizing the nation-state (e.g., Irvine and Gal; Silverstein; Bauman and Briggs; Errington), and concludes with chapters centered more on microlevel analyses (e.g., Philips; Hill; Schieffelin; Kroskrity).

Notes

An earlier version of this introduction was written in 1997. I want to thank two anonymous reviewers appointed by the School of American Research for their helpful critiques on that original draft. I especially thank Susan Gal, Martha Hertzberg, Bambi Schieffelin, and Michael Silverstein for their detailed suggestions for revision over several draft versions. In addition I want to thank two of my UCLA colleagues, Karen Brodkin and Mariko Tamanoi, for their discussion of scholarship relevant to the work at hand. Of course, I alone am responsible for any shortcomings in the present treatment.

1. This Gramscian distinction between political society (the state) and civil society correlates with distinct mechanisms of control—coercive and hegemonic apparatuses respectively. According to some interpreters of Gramsci, the state— in both its narrow sense (as government) and its more general sense (as the source of state-endorsed culture)—employs these different mechanisms in an attempt to control citizens through both forceful domination of the state and consent-organizing "leadership" of its hegemonic culture (Buci-Glucksmann 1982:123).

2. It should be emphasized that Labov's argument about how speakers' ideological stances fail to dramatically alter their linguistic production rests on an analytical overreliance on phonological data (Errington 1988). It also is overly informed by the analyst's perspective rather than by members' judgments based on a wide range of linguistic phenomena, including lexical choice and grammar.

3. For a discussion of problems associated with the notion of dominant ideologies or cultural hegemony, see Gal (1989:348).

4. For more on the notion of disjuncture in ethnographic work, interested readers should consult Appadurai (1990).

5. Bambi Schieffelin (personal communication) objects to the characterization of the Kaluli as ethnic or racialized in "a country that is still based on tribal, village, and linguistic affiliations"; she sees the effect of the new shared language or "better, a shared discourse…[as] position[ing] the Kaluli in terms of being part of PNG as a Christian nation, and ultimately, something that was global, separate from the old, very local traditional, heathen scene." I would defend the analytic utility of a model (and associated imagery) of state-imposed hierarchies like race, for even if they are based on local categories of social differentiation, the imposed hierarchization that is often a product of nation-states (see for example Alonso 1994; Williams 1991) is race-like. My opting here for the imagery of "racialization," however in discord with local criteria, makes comparative sense.

2

Language Ideology and Linguistic Differentiation

Judith T. Irvine and Susan Gal

A language is simply a dialect that has an army and a navy—so goes a well-known saying in linguistics.[1] Although only semiserious, this dictum recognizes an important truth: The significance of linguistic differentiation is embedded in the politics of a region and its observers. Just as having an army presupposes some outside force, some real or putative opposition to be faced, so does identifying a language presuppose a boundary or opposition to other languages with which it contrasts in some larger sociolinguistic field. In this chapter we focus on the ideological aspects of that linguistic differentiation—the ideas with which participants and observers frame their understanding of linguistic varieties and map those understandings onto people, events, and activities that are significant to them. With Silverstein (1979), Kroskrity, Schieffelin, and Woolard (1992), Woolard and Schieffelin (1994), and others in the present volume, we call these conceptual schemes *ideologies* because they are suffused with the political and moral issues pervading the particular sociolinguistic field and are subject to the interests of their bearers' social position.

Linguistic ideologies are held not only by the immediate participants in a local sociolinguistic system. They are also held by other observers, such as the linguists and ethnographers who have mapped the boundaries of languages and peoples and provided descriptive accounts of them. Our attention here is therefore just as appropriately directed to those mappings and accounts as to their subject matter. There is no "view from nowhere," no gaze that is not positioned. Of course, it is always easier to detect positioning in the views of others, such as the linguists and ethnographers of an earlier era, than in one's own. Examining the activities of linguists a century or more ago reveals, via the wisdom of hindsight or at least via historical distance, the ideological dimensions of their work in drawing and interpreting linguistic boundaries. This historical inquiry also has a contemporary relevance, to the extent that early representations of sociolinguistic phenomena influenced later representations and even contributed to shaping the sociolinguistic scene itself.

Our discussion is less concerned with history per se, however, than with the dynamics of a sociolinguistic process. In exploring ideologies of linguistic differentiation, we are concerned not only with the ideologies' structure but also, and especially, with their consequences. First, we explore how participants' ideologies concerning boundaries and differences may contribute to language change. Second, we ask how the describer's ideology has consequences for scholarship, how it shapes his or her description of language(s). Third, we consider the consequences for politics, how linguistic ideologies are taken to authorize actions on the basis of linguistic relationship or difference.

To address these questions we have examined ethnographic and linguistic cases from several parts of the world, involving different kinds of linguistic differentiation. Since Africa and Europe are the sites of our own research, we have looked most particularly to these regions for examples of relevant ethnography, linguistics, and historical investigation. But whether in these parts of the world or elsewhere, in all the cases we have examined—those described in this paper and many others as well—we find some similarities in the ways ideologies "recognize" (or misrecognize) linguistic differences: how they locate, interpret, and rationalize sociolinguistic complexity, identifying linguistic varieties with "typical" persons and activities and accounting for the differentiations among them. We have identified three important semiotic processes by which this works: iconization, fractal recursivity, and erasure.

Before we offer more specific discussions of what these three processes are, let us note that all of them concern the way people conceive of links between linguistic forms and social phenomena. Those conceptions can best be explicated by a semiotic approach that distinguishes several kinds of sign relationships, including (as Peirce long ago suggested) the iconic, the indexical, and the symbolic.[2] It has become a commonplace in sociolinguistics that linguistic forms, including whole languages, can index social groups. As part of everyday behavior, the use of a linguistic form can become a pointer to (index of) the social identities and the typical activities of speakers. But speakers (and hearers) often notice, rationalize, and justify such linguistic indices, thereby creating linguistic ideologies that purport to explain the source and meaning of the linguistic differences. To put this another way, linguistic features are seen as reflecting and expressing broader cultural images of people and activities. Participants' ideologies about language locate linguistic phenomena as part of, and evidence for, what they believe to be systematic behavioral, aesthetic, affective, and moral contrasts among the social groups indexed. That is, people have, and act in relation to, ideologically constructed representations of linguistic differences. In these ideological constructions, indexical relationships become the ground on which other sign relationships are built.

The three semiotic processes we have identified are thus the means by which people construct ideological representations of linguistic differences. Examples will follow, but first let us describe the processes more particularly:

Iconization involves a transformation of the sign relationship between linguistic features (or varieties) and the social images with which they are linked. Linguistic features that index social groups or activities appear to be iconic representations of them, as if a linguistic feature somehow depicted or displayed a social group's inherent nature or essence. This process entails the attribution of cause and immediate necessity to a connection (between linguistic features and social groups) that may be only historical, contingent, or conventional. The iconicity of the ideological representation reinforces the implication of

37

necessity. By picking out qualities supposedly shared by the social image and the linguistic image, the ideological representation—itself a sign—binds them together in a linkage that appears to be inherent.[3]

Fractal recursivity involves the projection of an opposition, salient at some level of relationship, onto some other level. For example, intra-group oppositions might be projected outward onto intergroup relations, or vice versa. Thus the dichotomizing and partitioning process that was involved in some understood opposition (between groups or linguistic varieties, for example) recurs at other levels, creating either subcategories on each side of a contrast or supercategories that include both sides but oppose them to something else. Reminiscent of fractals in geometry and the structure of segmentary kinship systems—as well as other phenomena anthropologists have seen as involving segmentation or schismogenesis, such as nationalist ideologies and gender rituals[4]— the myriad oppositions that can create identity may be reproduced repeatedly, either within each side of a dichotomy or outside it. When such oppositions are reproduced within a single person, they do not concern contrasting *identities* so much as oppositions between *activities* or *roles* associated with prototypical social persons. In any case, the oppositions do not define fixed or stable social groups, and the mimesis they suggest cannot be more than partial. Rather, they provide actors with the discursive or cultural resources to claim and thus attempt to create shifting "communities," identities, selves, and roles, at different levels of contrast, within a cultural field.

Erasure is the process in which ideology, in simplifying the sociolinguistic field, renders some persons or activities (or sociolinguistic phenomena) invisible. Facts that are inconsistent with the ideological scheme either go unnoticed or get explained away. So, for example, a social group or a language may be imagined as homogeneous, its internal variation disregarded. Because a linguistic ideology is a totalizing vision, elements that do not fit its interpretive structure—that cannot be seen to fit—must be either ignored or transformed. Erasure in ideological representation does not, however, necessarily mean actual eradication of the awkward element, whose very existence may be unobserved or unattended to. It is probably only when the "problematic" element is seen as fitting some alternative, threatening picture that the semiotic process involved in erasure might translate into some kind of practical action to remove the threat, if circumstances permit.

By focusing on linguistic differences, we intend to draw attention to some semiotic properties of those processes of identity formation that depend on defining the self as against some imagined "Other." This is a familiar kind of process, one by now well known in the literature. Anthropologists, at least, are now well acquainted with the ways in which the Other, or simply the other side of a contrast, is often essentialized and imagined as homogeneous. The imagery involved in this essentializing process includes, we suggest, linguistic images—images in which the linguistic behaviors of others are simplified and seen as if deriving from those persons' essences rather than from historical accident. Such representations may serve to interpret linguistic differences that have arisen through drift or long-term separation. But they may also serve to influence or even generate linguistic differences in those cases where some sociological contrast (in presumed essential attributes of persons or activities) seems to require display.

In the hope that examples will illustrate and clarify these points, we have chosen three cases for discussion. One, from southern Africa, concerns the motivation of language change; the second, from West Africa, concerns linguistic description in grammars and dictionaries; and the third, from southeastern Europe, concerns political contestation.

THE MOTIVATION OF LINGUISTIC CHANGE: THE NGUNI LANGUAGES' ACQUISITION OF CLICKS

Our first case concerns the Nguni languages of southern Africa (especially Zulu and Xhosa) and their acquisition of click consonants. Clicks were not originally part of the consonant repertoire of the Nguni languages—the southernmost branch of the Bantu language family— but were acquired from the Khoi languages, indigenous to southern Africa at the time the Bantu languages arrived there. The question is why this change happened. It is common enough for otherwise unrelated languages in a geographical area, given sufficient time, to come to have certain resemblances to one another, or "areal characteristics." In this case it is possible to see something of how the resemblance came about. (We draw on work by Herbert 1990 and others, including Irvine 1992.)

Because they are conspicuous sounds that are unusual in the

phonological repertoires of the world's languages, clicks have drawn the attention of many visitors and newcomers to southern Africa over the centuries. Many early European observers compared them with animal noises: hens' clucking, ducks' quacking, owls' hooting, magpies' chattering, or "the noise of irritated turkey-cocks" (Kolben 1731:32). Others thought clicks were more like the sounds of inanimate objects, such as stones hitting one another. To these observers and the European readers of their reports, such iconic comparisons suggested (before our more enlightened days, at least) that the speakers of languages with clicks were in some way subhuman or degraded, to a degree corresponding to the proportion of clicks in their consonant repertoires. Commenting on clicks, the linguist F. Max Müller wrote (1855:lxxix):

> I cannot leave this subject without expressing at least a strong hope that, by the influence of the Missionaries, these brutal sounds will be in time abolished, at least among the Kaffirs [Zulu and Xhosa], though it may be impossible to eradicate them in the degraded Hottentot dialects [i.e., Khoi, which had more of them].

Clicks must also have sounded very foreign to Bantu-language speakers when they first arrived in southern Africa. The very concept of speaking a foreign language seems, unsurprisingly, to have been focused on the Khoisan languages, which were observably full of clicks. Thus the Xhosa term *úkukhumsha* [Zulu *ukuhúmusha*] 'speak a foreign language, interpret' borrows its stem from Khoi, as in Nama *khom* 'speak' (see Louw 1977:75, which also includes some other inferences, based on Nguni loans from Khoi, about early Nguni attitudes toward Khoisan-speakers).[5] Yet it was apparently for the very reason of their conspicuous foreignness that the clicks were first adopted into the Nguni languages, providing a means for Nguni-speakers themselves to express social difference and linguistic abnormality. The principal route by which clicks entered the Nguni languages seems to have been via an avoidance register, which required certain lexical items in everyday speech to be avoided or altered out of respect. By adopting clicks, Nguni-speakers could create lexical substitutions that were conspicuously different from their everyday equivalents.

The Nguni avoidance (or respect) register, called *hlonipha*, is

Becomes even more complex when dealing with issues of language access

reported for all the Nguni languages and is evidently of some antiquity among them. It also occurs in Southern Sotho, another Bantu language in the region and the only one outside the Nguni group to include a click consonant. In all these languages, however, *hlonipha* is tending to fall out of use today. It is still practiced among rural Xhosa women (see Finlayson 1978, 1982, 1984 for examples of recent usage), and perhaps also among some rural Zulu, but it seems to have become rare for Zulu in urban contexts. Published sources on Zulu *hlonipha,* while providing extensive lists of its vocabulary and some information on use, describe the practices of decades ago (see, for example, Bryant 1949; Doke 1961; Doke and Vilakazi 1958; Krige 1950), and Herbert (1990:308) reports that "many urban Zulu postgraduate students have described their reading of the *hlonipha* literature as 'like reading about a foreign culture'."

The norms of *hlonipha* behavior prescribe modesty and a display of respect in the presence or neighborhood of certain senior affines and, in precolonial times at least, of royalty. The norms apply to gesture and clothing as well as words: to *hlonipha* is to avoid eye contact, cover one's body, and restrain one's affectivity. Talk about bodily functions, for example, is to be avoided or, if not avoidable, to be mentioned only in conventional euphemisms. What the descriptions of *hlonipha* focus on most, however, is the importance of covering over or avoiding the linguistic expression of sound-sequences that would enunciate respected persons' names. Included in the prohibition are not just the names themselves but any word containing one of the name's core syllables.

The *hlonipha* words are thus lexical alternants that enable speakers to avoid uttering respected persons' names and any other word containing sounds similar to the name's root or stem. So, for example, if the name of a woman's husband's father happens to sound like *imvuɓu* 'hippopotamus', that woman must call hippos *incuɓu* instead. Where names are composed of meaningful expressions, as was traditionally the case, many ordinary words might be affected by the need to avoid name-sounds. As Bryant (1949:221) notes,

> Thus, if one of the [respected] persons were named *uMutí* (Mr. Tree), not only would this (the ordinary) word for 'a-tree' be disused, and the *Hlonipa* word, *umCakantshi,* substituted

for it, but, further, every other word containing within its root
the particle, *ti*, would be similarly avoided; thus, for *ukuTíba*
would be used *ukuPúnga*; for *umTákatí*, *umKúnkuli*; for
ukuTí, ukuNki, and so on.

The respectful substitute term could derive from a descriptive or
metaphorical construction, or it could derive from patterned phonological shifts altering a name-word's syllable-initial consonants.
Although there were several different patterns, the most common
kinds of phonological shifts were for stem-initial consonants to become
[+Coronal], especially the coronal affricates *tš* and *dž* (*j*), or to become
clicks.[6] Since—at least in the early phases of the process—the expressions from which names were constructed used ordinary Bantu roots,
which did not include clicks and most probably did not include coronal
affricates either (Herbert 1990:305; Finlayson 1982:49), a convenient
way to construct a *hlonipha* word would have been to substitute one of
these "foreign" sounds for the offending consonant. The result was a
click-laden respect vocabulary, perhaps consisting partly of idiosyncratic, ad hoc formulations but also including words that were widely
known as *hlonipha* alternants. The fact that the respect vocabulary
shows such a high percentage of click consonants, compared with the
everyday vocabulary, is one of the major pieces of evidence for supposing that it was the vehicle for these consonants' entry into Nguni
phonological repertoires.[7]

Table 2.1 gives some examples of *hlonipha* words in Zulu. The first
group of words illustrates consonant substitutions of various kinds,
especially substitutions of a click for a nonclick consonant. These words
are presumably name-avoidance forms; so, if a respected person's name
sounded like *aluka* 'graze, weave', the speaker must refer to grazing as
acuka instead. The *hlonipha* word *injušo* (for *indaɓa*, 'affair') is a lexical
substitution occasioned by avoidance of the name Ndaba, a Zulu royal
ancestor.

The second group of words in table 2.1 are forms referring to persons requiring respect because of their social positions. The creation of
hlonipha alternants may therefore have been occasioned as a respectful
way to refer to those positions, and not necessarily because of a need to
avoid particular names that might be based upon these stems. Bryant

TABLE 2.1

Zulu hlonipha (respect) vocabulary examples

	Ordinary	Hlonipha
(1)		
graze, weave	*aluka*	*acuka*
be dejected	*jaba*	*gxaba*
affair	*indaɓa*	*injušo*
hippopotamus	*imvuɓu*	*incuɓu*
lion	*imbuɓe*	*injuɓe*
house	*indlu*	*incumba*
our	*-ithu*	*-itšu*
thy	*-kho*	*-to*
(2)		
my father	*uɓaɓa*	*utšatša*
brother-in-law	*umlamu*	*umcamu*
chief	*inkosi*	*inqoɓo, inqotšana* (dim.)
(3)		
swing	*lenga*	*cenga*
annoy	*nenga*	*cenga*

Source: Doke & Vilakazi 1958

Note: c, q, x – clicks (gx = voiced click)

    ɓ= implosive bilabial stop

(1949:220) documents this process, which was not limited to words referring to persons: "For a Zulu woman to call a porcupine by its proper name, iNgungumbane, were but to provoke it to increased depredation in her fields; therefore it must be referred to 'politely' as 'the-little-woman', or umFazazana." The third group of words in table 2.1 illustrates the fact that the substitution of clicks for corresponding nonclick consonants sometimes created homonyms in the *hlonipha* vocabulary.

That the *hlonipha* vocabulary was the vehicle for the entry of clicks into the Nguni consonant inventories is argued in greater detail in

Herbert's (1990) paper. As he points out, however, some questions remain. Why would particular name-avoidance alternants be used, or even known, more widely than within the immediate circle of a respected person's dependents? And why are clicks now found in every-day words as well as in the respect vocabulary?

The first of these questions arises partly because the ethnographic literature tends to focus on a narrow portion of *hlonipha* behavior and so makes the practice appear more limited and idiosyncratic than it actually was. Drawing on participants' statements, observers emphasize the relationship between a married woman and her husband's father as the "explanation" of the *hlonipha* practice. That is, all *hlonipha* speech is supposedly based on the individual woman's respectful avoidance of a particular man's name. Were this the extent of the usage, of course, *hlonipha* alternants would be created idiosyncratically; each woman would have a different set (and men would use none); only a few vocabulary items would be affected for any particular speaker; and a respect alternant would disappear upon the daughter-in-law's death.

The focus on the daughter-in-law/father-in-law relationship seems, however, to be a folk rationalization—a piece of language ideology—that corresponds only in part to the distribution of actual usages. A wider distribution would be entailed even if *hlonipha* were practiced only by married women, since a married woman owes respect to all the senior members of her husband's lineage and household, and the respect terms deriving from these names would affect all women married into the same patrilineal, patrilocal community. But there is abundant documentation also of a much more widespread phenomenon involving male as well as female speakers, court as well as domestic contexts, and various kinds of respected beings. From Krige (1950:31) we learn, for example, that Zulu *hlonipha* terms were also used by men to avoid uttering the name of the mother-in-law, though the custom was "not so strict" for men as it was for women. Furthermore, "the whole tribe" must *hlonipha* the name of the king or chief, while those resident at the royal court must *hlonipha* the names of the king's father and grandfather as well (Krige 1950:31, 233). Bryant (1949:220) adds, "The men, or indeed the whole clan, may Hlonipa the name of a renowned chief or ancestor, as, for instance, the Zulus, a few generations ago, Hlonipa'd the words, iMpande (root) and iNdlela (path), calling them, respectively, iNgxabo and iNyatuko, owing to certain then great personages being named uMpande and uNdlela." Recall, also, Bryant's statement about the porcupine, to which he adds similar comments about cats, red ants, snakes, and lightning.

Among Xhosa, too, *hlonipha* repertoires were relatively large and widespread, as Finlayson's research indicates. A brief transcript of a conversation between two rural women (Finlayson 1984:139) shows that more than 25 percent of the words used are *hlonipha*. These women had some eight or nine affines in common, whose name-sounds were thus being avoided. But although the women's family members could point to particular persons who were being shown respect in this conversation,[8] it is not always obvious how the avoided words relate to their name-sounds. Indeed, some *hlonipha* words are or have become disconnected from specific name-avoidances, serving instead, as Finlayson (1984:140) notes, as a "core" respect vocabulary consisting "of words which are generally known and accepted as *hlonipha* words," used as a display of respect regardless of the particulars of individual names.[9]

In short, the daughter-in-law who avoids uttering her father-in-law's name-sounds is the cultural image, in Nguni language ideology, to which the respect register is linked. She provides the Nguni prototype for the respectful, modest behavior required of dependents and outsiders (nonmembers of a patrilineage, in her case). *Hlonipha* practice is not confined, however, to that particular in-law relationship. Instead, that relationship merely provides the model for what is actually a more widespread phenomenon, both socially, as regards the range of speakers and settings, and linguistically, as regards the range of words affected by the practice.

If clicks entered these languages via the respect vocabulary, how did they come to be found also in ordinary vocabulary? There are probably two routes by which click-including words could have entered the everyday lexicon. As Herbert (1990:308–9) notes, the adoption of clicks in *hlonipha* would have made them more familiar as sounds and therefore more likely to be retained in other lexical borrowings from the Khoi languages (i.e., words borrowed for quite other reasons, such as place names and terms for Khoi specialty activities and goods). The other source for click-bearing everyday words is the *hlonipha* vocabulary itself, because some *hlonipha* words may have gradually lost their "respectful" aura over time and passed over into everyday vocabulary. There, in turn, they would be subject to replacement by new avoidance forms.

This type of process, in which respect alternants behave like currency in inflationary conditions, is known to have occurred in other parts of the world (see Irvine 1992). The process seems to be hastened when speakers strive to mark their behavior as being extraordinarily respectful or conscientious. As Kunene (1958:162) remarks for Southern Sotho *hlonepha*, some speakers go so far as to replace almost all stems in daily vocabulary "due to an exaggerated loyalty to the custom, or to a competitive spirit, in order to outdo So-and-So, or to a desire to make assurance doubly sure…" In such circumstances, respect vocabulary, overused, eventually becomes commonplace and everyday and must be replaced by terms more conspicuously special.

Thus, by means of the conspicuous click consonants, seen as *icons* of "foreignness" in the early years of the process, the contrast between Nguni and Khoi consonant repertoires was mobilized to express social distance and deference within Nguni. To put this another way, a cultural framework for understanding linguistic difference at one level (the difference between Bantu and Khoi languages) was the basis for constructing difference at another level (a difference in registers within a particular Bantu language). This is an example of what we mean by recursivity. It is a process that led to phonological change in the Nguni languages, introducing click consonants into a special register that eventually began to leak, as respect registers will.

Notice that this idea of clicks as emblematically "foreign" and of their utterance as signaling deference ideologically emphasizes the sharpness of a boundary between Nguni and Khoi, and the domination of Nguni-speakers over Khoi-speakers. What the ideology ignores, that is, erases, is the historically attested complexity of Nguni-Khoi relations. Many Khoi were multilingual, living on the margins of Nguni society, moving in and out of it as their fortunes fell or rose. Some Khoi, moreover, served Nguni as traders and ritual specialists; some Nguni men took Khoi wives, and some Khoi men took Nguni wives; and some Nguni entered Khoi society as leaderless refugees, outcast from Nguni chiefdoms as a result of political disputes (Denoon 1992; Giliomee 1989; Harinck 1969; Prins and Lewis 1992). Another kind of erasure occurred when some European observers, writing about *hlonipha* after the power of precolonial kingdoms and chiefdoms had declined, described it as "women's speech"—ignoring its political dimension and its use by men.

This case is interesting for many reasons, among them the fact that its main outlines are precolonial and involve language ideologies other than the European or European-derived. However, it is hardly the only instance of the ideological mediation of language change. More familiar to a sociolinguistic audience is Labov's (1963) classic study of vowel change on Martha's Vineyard. Contrasts among ethnic groups of islanders (Yankees, Portuguese, and Indians) in the 1930s were replaced by a contrast between islanders and mainlanders in the 1960s. Islander phonology diverged ever more sharply from mainland forms after the development of the tourist industry made that contrast more socially significant than local, intra-island differences. Although Labov did not explore the content of the language ideology giving rise to these changes, the case seems to beg for just this kind of analysis and illustrates language change as an ideologically fueled process of increasing divergence. We can call the divergence ideologically mediated because it depended on local images of salient social categories that shifted over time.

LINGUISTIC DESCRIPTIONS OF SENEGALESE LANGUAGES

Our second case concerns the work of nineteenth-century European linguists and ethnographers who described the languages of Senegal, particularly Fula, Wolof, and Sereer. The question we explore is how representations of Senegalese languages and peoples were influenced by the ideologies of European observers interacting with Africans (who had ideologies of their own) in a complex sociolinguistic situation. The ways these languages were identified, delimited, and mapped, the ways their relationships were interpreted, and even the ways they were described in grammars and dictionaries were all heavily influenced by an ideology of racial and national essences. This essentializing move, when applied to Senegalese languages, involved the three semiotic processes we have discussed. Although our main concern is with nineteenth-century accounts, their representations of language have had some long-lasting effects, as we shall suggest.

Most linguists today agree that Fula, Wolof, and Sereer are three distinct but related languages forming a "Senegal group" within the Atlantic branch of the Niger-Congo language family. The languages in this group do not now constitute a dialect chain. Still, their geographical distributions overlap because of multilingualism and intermingling of speakers. Within the present-day country of Senegal, in the region north of the Gambia River (see fig. 2.1), Fula is most concentrated in the northeast and Sereer most concentrated in the south, but the three languages do not sort out into neatly discrete territories. Within this region, too, is a set of small linguistic islands—villages where still other languages are spoken. (These villages are located near the city of Thiès. In precolonial times they were enclaves within the territory of the kingdom of Kajoor and subject to its rule. See figure 2.1 for the region's precolonial kingdoms and some major cities.) These other languages, now known to linguists as the Cangin languages, form a group belonging to the Atlantic family, which is very diverse, but not to the "Senegal group," from which most linguists consider them quite different (see Wilson 1989). A century ago, however, Fula, Wolof, and Sereer were mapped as occupying separate territories; most linguists considered Fula unrelated genealogically to Wolof and Sereer; and Sereer itself was thought to include the varieties now termed Cangin.

Why have these representations of the Senegalese linguistic scene changed? Part of the answer lies, of course, in the greater accumulation of linguistic observations, the greater care in their recording, and the more stringent principles of genealogical classification that have characterized twentieth-century linguistics. Moreover, the territorial distributions of these languages have been affected by population movements during the colonial and postcolonial periods. But more is involved than the onward march of linguistic science and changing demographics. There have also been changes in what observers expected to see and how they interpreted what they saw.

At the beginning of the nineteenth century the languages of sub-Saharan Africa were scarcely known to outsiders. A comprehensive survey of the world's languages (Hervas y Panduro 1800–1805), published in 1805 and occupying six volumes, devoted only one page to African languages other than Arabic. During the next several decades, how-

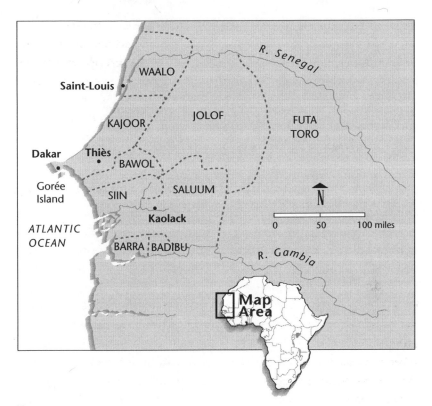

FIGURE 2.1

Geographical region of present-day Senegal and The Gambia, showing precolonial Senegalese states circa 1785 (boundaries approximate) and some modern cities.

ever, as European interests expanded into the interior of the continent, the task of mapping African languages was so enthusiastically pursued that by 1881 Robert Needham Cust was able to present to that year's Orientalist Congress a schedule of 438 languages and 153 dialectal subdivisions that filled in the entire map of Africa (Cust 1883).

At the most immediate level, the study of African languages involved control over communication with local populations, communication that would otherwise have to rely on African interpreters. Also important, however, were the ethnological, political, and cultural implications that were presumed to follow from the discovery of language boundaries and relationships. If languages were "the pedigree of nations," as Samuel Johnson had said, then identifying languages was the same thing as identifying "nations" and a logical first step in comparing, understanding, and ordering their relations to each other and to Europeans. As Lepsius (1863:24) wrote (in the introduction to his proposal for a universal orthography),

> From the relations of separate languages, or groups of languages, to one another, we may discover the original and more or less intimate affinity of the nations themselves ... [Thus] will the chaos of the nations in [Africa], Asia, America, and Polynesia, be gradually resolved into order, by the aid of linguistic science.[10]

Actually, for many post-Enlightenment scholars, languages coincided with nations in a cultural or spiritual sense but preceded any political realization of nationhood. As the expression of the spiritual (or even, some thought, biological) essences of particular human collectivities, languages were regarded as natural entities out there to be discovered—natural in the sense that they were consequences of a variable human nature, not the creations of any self-conscious human intervention. But if languages were prior to human political activity, they could then serve as its warrant, identifying populations and territories that could be suitably treated as political unities, whether self-governing nation-states (in the case of the European powers) or units for colonial administration.

By 1883, when Cust's survey of African languages was published, the European imperial powers were fully engaged in the "scramble for Africa" in which they divided the continent among their colonial empires. Concomitantly, Cust and others writing in the last decades of the century no longer normally referred to the speakers of African languages as "nations" but instead as "tribes" or "races," a change that reflects, among other things, Africans' loss of political autonomy—or at least their right to political autonomy in European eyes. Although some of those "tribes" are best understood as the population subject to a particular precolonial polity, to describe them in terms of language and customs made it possible to imply that indigenous political structures were epiphenomenal and dispensable.

Cust, a retired administrator from British India, likened his task to other imperial administrative projects (1883:6–7):

> With such a wealth of Materials pouring in upon me from every quarter, and a deepening conviction of the importance of the task, as well as the difficulty, I could only go on, and…lay down clear and distinct principles upon which this work should be constructed. Possessed of a trained capacity for order and method, a strong will and love for steady work, which is the characteristic of old Indians, I had to grapple with this entangled subject, just as twenty-five years ago I should have grappled with the affairs of a District in India which had got into disorder, or with the Accounts of a Treasury which had fallen into arrears.

Cust acknowledged that his task was difficult, but he never doubted the possibility that languages *could* be definitively identified and mapped, or that they corresponded to separate tribes inhabiting discrete territories. What was needed was to clear away the confusion of alternative and "unnecessary" names (pp. 10–11), to "avoid a lax phraseology," and to "place one foot firmly down upon Geographical facts, and the other upon such a statement of Linguistic facts as seem to my judgment sufficient" (p. 7). These principles being rigorously followed, any linguistic information that could not be made to fit the map was simply to be excluded because (Cust concluded) it did not exist: It was an error or fantasy. "Unless he [Cust's cartographer] can find a place in his Map for the tribe, the Language can find no place in my Schedule" (p. 8). Functional or superposed varieties, multilingualism, polysemous language labels, and contested boundaries were incompatible with this approach.

These assumptions were by no means limited to Cust or to British investigators, who, in any case, relied heavily on an international cadre of missionaries to conduct the basic fieldwork. By the late nineteenth century, European scholars of language, whatever their nationality, their particular opinions about grammatical forms and comparative methods, or their connection with specific colonial policies, generally concurred on many basic points. They had acquired a firm belief in linguistics' scientific basis, the naturalness and distinctness of its objects of study, and the relevance of linguistic classifications for models of evolutionary progress. Assuming, too, that ethnic groups were normally monolingual and that there was some primordial relationship between language and the particular "spirit" of a nation, they thought it obvious that the study of language could serve as a tool for identifying ethnic units, classifying relationships among peoples, and reconstructing their history. Ideas like these, then, informed the efforts of mid- to late-nineteenth-century scholars, administrators, military men, and missionaries who set about describing the languages of Senegal.[11]

The linguistic situation they encountered, insofar as we can reconstruct it today, involved a complex regional system in which linguistic repertoires were—as they still are—bound up with political and religious relationships. Fula had the strongest connection with Islamic orthodoxy because it was associated with the region's first converts to Islam in the eleventh century and with the strongest proponents of the late-eighteenth-century Muslim revival. Sereer, in contrast, was associated with resistance to Islam and with the preservation of pre-Islamic ritual practices. As a French missionary remarked (Lamoise 1873:vii), "The *marabouts* [Muslim clerics] have invented this false adage: whoever speaks Sereer cannot enter heaven." Wolof, meanwhile, was the dominant language in the coastal kingdoms where the French first established outposts, and it served as a language of politics and trade in other parts of the region as well.

Wolof's role in the political life of Senegal apparently dates back to the fifteenth-century heyday of the Jolof Empire, a state then dominating most of the region. In Jolof, whose very name is connected with the Wolof language, Wolof was the language of a political administration sufficiently centralized to keep the language fairly uniform geographically. (Arabic, not Wolof, was the official language of religion, however, although many of the Muslim clerics in the days of the Jolof Empire were probably of Fula-speaking origin.) This sociolinguistic pattern extended beyond the territories Jolof governed directly and persisted for centuries after the empire's breakup in the mid-sixteenth century. So even in the nineteenth century, in the kingdoms of Siin and Saluum (see fig. 2.1)—client states to Jolof's south which may never have been administered by it directly but were within its international sphere— Wolof lexicon was used for political offices and Wolof language for the conduct of high-level political relations, even though much of the population probably spoke Sereer as a language of the home.[12] In consequence many Sereer-speakers in the south were (and are) bilingual in

Wolof, while Wolof-speakers further north resist acquiring Sereer, which many of them associate with low-ranking, heathen peasants.

European observers in the mid- to late nineteenth century interpreted this regional situation in terms of a supposed history of race relations, migrations, and conquests. Assuming that a language ought to have a distinct territory and nation (or ethnic group or race) associated with it, scholars interpreted other kinds of language distributions as "mixtures," departures from some original linguistic and territorial purity. Assuming further that black Africans were essentially primitive and simple-minded people who knew no social organization more complex than the family group, these scholars explained African social hierarchy, multilingualism, and conversions to Islam in terms of conquering races from the north who supposedly brought Islam, the state, and some admixture of Caucasian blood and language to the region by force of arms and intellectual superiority. Fula-speakers, some of whom are lighter-skinned than their Wolof neighbors, were deemed "higher" in race and intelligence. Accorded an origin in Upper Egypt, they were thought to have brought their "superior" religion, hierarchical social organization, and language to bear upon the Wolof, who in turn (perhaps along with the Manding, a people to the southeast) influenced the "simple" Sereer.[13]

Informed by these notions, the language-mapping project was thus an effort not only to discover what languages were spoken where but also to disentangle the supposed history of conquests and represent legitimate territorial claims. In regions where the language of state or of an aristocracy differed from the domestic speech of the state's subjects, as was the case in some areas of Senegal, only one of these languages could be put on the map. In many such cases (Siin and Saluum, for example) it was the political language that was omitted from the map—removed just as the African state apparatus was to be.

Of particular interest with regard to language mapping are the military expeditions led in 1861 and 1864–65 by Colonel Pinet-Laprade, the French commander at Gorée Island, and General Faidherbe, military governor of the French colony at Saint-Louis. Part of the effort to extend French military domination to the east and south, these expeditions carried out research and cartography along with their military objectives. Expedition reports, published in the official journal

Annuaire du Sénégal, were accompanied by linguistic analyses, ethnographic notices, and a detailed map. The map (Faidherbe 1865), which shows towns and villages, lakes and rivers, and the frontiers between the French colony and the existing African states, also shows neatly drawn "lines of separation" between supposedly distinct Wolof and Sereer populations. Similar lines were drawn between each of these and the Manding, further south and east. The map does not extend as far as the main areas where Fula might be spoken in a village context, but it does show an area of "Peuls"—Fula-speakers—set off in a similar manner. These populations, identified by language, are thus accorded distinct territories in the map's representation of the supposed relationship between language, population, and territory.

To produce this representation, the cartographers had to ignore the multilingualism that characterized indigenous political life in the southern regions. But doing away with indigenous political institutions was the ultimate purpose anyway. Since the French colonizers' conception of regional history was that the Sereer had been enslaved and tyrannized by Wolof and/or Manding aristocrats and Muslim clerics, France would be justified in overthrowing these oppressors and substituting French rule. Until this was accomplished, and the French *mission civilisatrice* could get properly underway, wrote Pinet-Laprade (1865:147), the populations of "countries like Siin and Saluum…could not attempt any progress, because of the state of stupefaction *[abrutissement]* in which they were held under the regime of the Gelwaar [aristocratic lineages]." As for "Sereer" further north (i.e., Cangin), who, Pinet-Laprade suggested, were less thoroughly dominated by the Wolof state of Kajoor in which they formed an enclave, they were a simple, childlike people who would be easily led (by France) once the threat of Kajoor was removed:

> [The enclave populations] are, like all peoples in infancy, very little advanced along the way of social organization [*association*]: they are generally grouped by families, in the vicinity of their fields. This state of affairs will facilitate the action we are called upon to take on them, because we will not have to overturn established authorities, sever close ties, or combat blind fanaticism. (Pinet-Laprade 1865:155)

relationships
between U.S.
white U.S.
& African
American

→ model for U.S. →
other immigrants?

LANGUAGE IDEOLOGY AND LINGUISTIC DIFFERENTIATION

Notice that the mapping project involves our three semiotic processes. The language map depicted the relationship ideologically supposed to obtain between language, population, and territory (*iconization*), but it could only do so by tidying up the linguistic situation, removing multilingualism and variation from the picture (*erasure*). The multilingualism was supposed to have been introduced, along with religious and political complexity, through a history of conquest and conversion that paralleled the European conquest and the hierarchical relationships thought to obtain between Europeans and Africans—relationships of white to black, complex to simple, and dominant to subordinate. That is, relationships between Europeans and Africans were the implicit model for a history of relationships within Africa itself (*recursivity*).

This putative hierarchy of racial essences and conquests supposedly explained not only multilingualism but also the specific characteristics and relationships of the three African languages. Most linguists of the time, and indeed for generations afterward, refused to see Fula as genetically related to Wolof and Sereer at all, seeking its kin among Semitic languages instead. And Fula's linguistic characteristics, such as its syllable structure and its noun classification system, were taken by scholars such as Guiraudon (1894) and Tautain (1885), as well as Faidherbe (1882), as emblems of its speakers' "delicacy" and "intelligence" as compared to speakers of Wolof. The Wolof language, these scholars claimed, was "less supple, less handy" than Fula and signaled less intelligent minds.[14] Meanwhile, Sereer was considered the language of primitive simplicity.

To represent Sereer, with its complex morphology, as "simple" compared to Wolof—as Father Lamoise, the author of the first substantial grammar of Sereer (Lamoise 1873), claimed it was—seems to us something of an uphill battle. It required paying selective attention, regularizing grammatical structures, and interpreting complexities and variations as "interference." Accordingly, Lamoise suggested that if Sereer now deviated from its original purity and simplicity—the language God had placed among these simple people—the deviations were due to "errors and vices" (1873:329): either the errors of fetishism into which Sereers had fallen, or the vicious influence of Islam and its Wolof perpetrators. The missionary's task in describing Sereer was to retrieve as much of the pure language as possible and, Lamoise implied, to purge it of error. The task was difficult, for, as he commented darkly (in a section of his grammar discussing figures of speech), "everywhere, as one can see, the infernal serpent is to be found" (1873:284).

One way to retrieve Sereer's original purity was to select the variety that seemed to have the fewest traces of interference from Wolof or Islam. Lamoise selected the regional variety of Sereer spoken in Siin as the most "pure," yet it was still flawed and inadequate. Apparently rejecting or downplaying words and expressions he thought came from Wolof, he also seems to have avoided registers or texts that might incorporate a relatively large number of Wolof loans, such as aristocrats' political discourse relating to the state.[15] Since linguistic purity was, in his view, primarily a matter of returning to a divinely inspired condition, the purest Sereer of all was exemplified in the religious discourse he and his assistants could produce when translating Catholic prayers and religious writings. Actual prayers by Sereers themselves would not do, "since the rare aspirations that emerge from the mouths of the Sereers...are far too incomplete and inadequate" (1873:333).

Even while presenting Sereer as a language that contrasted with Wolof, however, Lamoise organized his description from a Wolof starting point, emphasizing Sereer's departures from a Wolof grammatical norm. His grammar of Sereer was modeled upon a grammar of Wolof recently published by his religious superior, the Bishop of Dakar (Kobès 1869). These descriptions of the two languages, though organized in parallel, highlight—perhaps even maximize—their differences by erasing variation and overlap. Just as Lamoise's description of Sereer and his text citations removed (among other things) most of the lexicon and discourse types associated with Wolof, so too the descriptions of Wolof tended to purge those registers connected with non-Islamic ritual (such as the language of non-Islamic portions of circumcision ceremonies) in which some vocabulary and expressions might be identified as "Sereer."

Each language, in short, was represented in an impoverished way to differentiate it from the other and to accord with an ideology about its essence. At the same time, regional varieties that seemed to overlap were ignored. An example would be the variety of Sereer spoken in Baol, which has been reported as a mix. Pinet-Laprade (1865:135) called it a language "derived from Sérère-Sine...and from Wolof"; a more recent linguist (de Tressan 1953) called it "Sinsin [i.e., the Siin variety of Sereer], penetrated lexically by Wolof." Unsurprisingly, this variety has never been studied in its own right.

The same notions of language purity that led nineteenth-century linguists to ignore "mixed" varieties, multilingualism, and expressions they could attribute to linguistic borrowing also discouraged research on African regional dialectology. Once a variety had been declared to belong to the "same" language as another, already-described variety, there was no reason to investigate it, unless its speakers stubbornly refused to speak anything else. So the languages today called Cangin— spoken by "Sereers" living northwest of Siin, in enclaves within the kingdom of Kajoor—were but little documented until the 1950s and 1960s. Since their speakers obligingly used Wolof in dealings with Europeans and other outsiders and had little contact with Sereer-speakers farther south, there was no pressing need for missionaries or administrators to worry about the fact that these ways of speaking failed to resemble the Sereer of Siin.

The real question is why these Cangin varieties were ever called Sereer at all. The difference was conspicuous enough to have been noticed early on by Faidherbe, whose 1865 report on Sereer includes some notes on one of the Cangin languages. But he and other European writers treated this diversity as dialect, rather than language, differentiation. A particularly important reason Faidherbe and others assigned the Cangin group to Sereer, despite linguistic differences, was that these people were called "Sereer" by their Wolof neighbors, who apply that label in a fairly sweeping way to non-Muslim peasant populations in the region regardless of linguistic niceties. Since French colonists had intensive contacts with Wolof well before penetrating any of the areas of "Sereer" occupation, Wolof identifications of other populations seem to have been accepted and imposed on language identifications even when the linguistic facts pointed in very different directions.[16]

Also supporting the "Sereer" label was the fact that the Cangin-speakers' social life fit relatively well with European notions of Sereer "primitive simplicity"—better, at least, than did the social arrangements of Siin. The Cangin-speakers' small egalitarian village communities, their resistance to Islam, their agricultural economy, and their relative lack of interest in military matters were characteristics thought to be typical of black Africans in general when uninfluenced by waves of conquest from outside, and of Sereers in particular. Since a language reflected the cultural or spiritual essence of a collectivity of speakers, the Cangin languages must be Sereer, for their speakers seemed to fit the ethnic label on other grounds. The reasoning was similar to that which rejected Fula's linguistic resemblance to Wolof or Sereer on grounds of supposed cultural and racial difference.

In sum, the Europeans who described these Senegalese languages in the nineteenth century saw their differentiation as reflecting differences in mentality, history, and social organization among their speakers. Working from an ideology that linked language with national and racial essences, European linguists represented the particular characteristics of Senegalese languages as emblematic of these supposed essential differences, which could be diagrammed in charts of genealogical relationship and located on a territorial map. Thus our first semiotic process, *iconization,* emerges in several aspects of these linguistic descriptions and analyses: in map drawing, in family trees and schedules of relationship, and in discourse describing the (emblematic) linguistic particulars, such as their "delicacy" or their "simplicity." The second process, *fractal recursivity,* is evidenced when, as we mentioned earlier, European representations of linguistic relationships within the Senegal group modeled these relationships upon contrasts supposed to obtain between Europeans and Africans. Recursivity is also involved when the differences among varieties of Sereer were ideologically interpreted as replicating the larger relationship between Sereer and Wolof; that is, less versus more thoroughly penetrated by Islam. Finally, those linguistic features and varieties that could not be made to fit an essentializing scheme were ignored or attributed to "outside" influence. They were assumed to be borrowings, forms that could be omitted from a grammar or dictionary. Those omissions are *erasures* whether they pertain only to representations, as when a linguistic description ignores some vocabulary or some registers, or whether they pertain also to some active policy of eradication, as when the French overthrew the "Wolofized" political administration of Siin and Saluum. As a result, descriptions of each language were impoverished, and, on a more practical level, the languages became indices primarily of ethnicity rather than rank, political status, or religious setting.

In sum, our discussion of this case has concerned the influence of language ideology on linguistic descriptions made during the period of initial colonization of Senegal. Nineteenth-century European ideologies of race relations, ethnic separateness, and African "simplicity" led to maps, schedules, grammars, and dictionaries that purged registers, ignored variation, and rewrote complex sociolinguistic relationships as ethnic relationships. Even though many linguists and anthropologists today no longer share our predecessors' essentializing assumptions—and so can see those assumptions as ideological more easily than our own—the influence of these earlier representations has been long-lasting. Not until the work of Greenberg in the 1950s and 1960s (if even then) were race-based arguments about Fula's linguistic relationships put to rest, and the Cangin languages were listed as "Sereer" until Pichl's study of them in the 1960s (Pichl 1966).[17] Meanwhile, many works by nonlinguists continue to assign Sereer ethnicity to Cangin-speakers without further discussion.

Indeed, the alignment of language with ethnicity—understood as subnationalism and reinforced by colonial policy—is a particularly important dimension of the representational process, though one that is hard to disentangle. Today it is difficult to reconstruct precisely what Africans a century and a half ago took labels such as "Wolof" and "Sereer" to mean—under exactly what conditions they applied such terms to linguistic phenomena, sociological phenomena, or connections they saw between these. Linguistically, for example, one cannot now be completely sure whether expressions that nineteenth-century linguists treated as borrowings were or were not considered so by Africans at the time. This is a hugely complicated matter. But despite uncertainties and complexities, what we would like to emphasize here is the role of ideological representations—European, African, or both—in "tidying up" a complex sociolinguistic situation through register stripping and boundary drawing. It is not just that language came to be taken as an index of ethnic group membership (thus delimiting an ethnic boundary), but also that the contents of a language—materials assigned to it, rather than to some other language from which it "borrowed" them—seem to have been rearranged to match.

LANGUAGE IDEOLOGIES IN POLITICAL
CONTESTATION: CONFLICTS OVER MACEDONIAN

For our final case we turn to southeastern Europe and consider attempts to identify and standardize speech varieties in Macedonia. Macedonia was never the colony of any European state. Nevertheless, as in the Senegalese colonial situation discussed above, nineteenth-century descriptions of the languages and peoples of Macedonia were crucially affected by the ways in which the linguistic ideologies of Western European observers interacted with the ideologies and communicative practices of speakers in Macedonia.[18] However, although we start with a discussion of this clash of ideologies, our further aim here is to focus on the political contestation surrounding contrasting scholarly claims. In Macedonia, linguistic relationships came to be used as authorization for political and military action that changed sociolinguistic practices, thereby bringing into existence patterns of language use that more closely matched the ideology of Western Europe. This ideology (often linked with Herder; see Bauman and Briggs, this volume) imagined inherent, natural links between a unitary mother tongue, a territory, and an ethnonational identity. It relied for its persuasiveness on the three semiotic processes we have proposed.

The Republic of Macedonia declared its independence from Yugoslavia in November 1991 and was accepted as a member of the United Nations in December 1993. The new country inherited over a century of acrimonious debate about its boundaries, its name, and its language, a debate that, in the rhetoric of nationhood, ultimately questions its right to exist. Each of Macedonia's current neighbors—Bulgaria, what remains of Yugoslavia (i.e., Serbia and Montenegro), Albania, and Greece—has made serious claims to parts of the same territory in the past century, always at least partly on linguistic grounds. Despite the official codification, recognition, and widespread use of the Macedonian literary language, Bulgarian and Greek scholars have continued to deny its existence and independent standing. By concentrating on the late-nineteenth- and early-twentieth-century antecedents to these conflicts, we aim to explore the semiotic processes through which they have worked. We consider first how popular Western European opinion viewed Macedonia at the turn of the century. Then we turn to the linguistic arguments and actions of the competing nationalisms within the region.

The political economy of nineteenth-century Europe is the crucial context for the clashes of ideology we examine below. Eastern and southeastern Europe had for four centuries been the site of violent competition in empire building among the Austria-based Habsburgs, the Russia-based Romanovs, and the Ottomans of Turkey. In the course of the nineteenth century, however, Turkey became increasingly weak, losing control of large parts of its European territories to nationalist movements in Greece, Serbia, Romania, and Bulgaria. During the same period, Serbian and Bulgarian Orthodox churches were successfully reestablished and gained considerable leverage in challenging the hegemony of the Greek Orthodox church within the Ottoman Empire. Finally, Greece, Bulgaria, Serbia, and Montenegro united to drive Turkey out of Europe in 1912, only to fight each other for control of the newly liberated territory of geographic Macedonia. The subsequent peace treaty divided geographic Macedonia between them, with borders that have since remained relatively stable though always contested (see fig. 2.2).[19]

Throughout this period, distant European powers, most especially Britain, France, Russia, and Germany, were intent on establishing or maintaining their presence and influence in the region to defend substantial economic interests as well as supply routes and military commitments to their colonial outposts in Asia. The strategic involvement of the Great Powers produced among Western Europeans a widespread popular interest in the region. Instigated by news of revolutions, wars, and exotic customs, this interest was further fueled, in the second half of the century, by a burgeoning literature of journalism, ethnography, philology, and travel.

Representations of Europe in popular and scholarly writing had been considerably altered during the eighteenth century. Scientific cartography had earlier established the boundaries of the continent, while in more philosophical approaches there remained the Renaissance trope of a civilized South endangered by the depredations of Northern barbarians. But by the start of the nineteenth century this axis of contrast had shifted significantly. The earlier North/South imagery had been transformed into a spatial opposition between a newly invented, backward, barbaric "East" and a civilized "West" (see Wolff 1994).

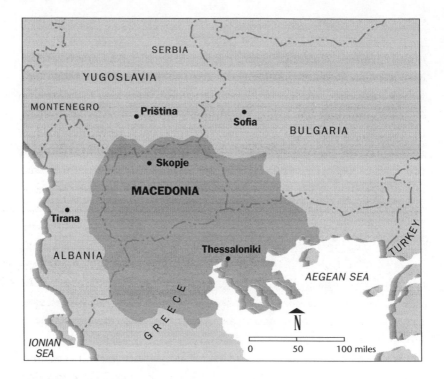

FIGURE 2.2

Republic of Macedonia (1995). Approximate extent of regions that have variously been considered geographic Macedonia.

Western European observers came to see the southeast of the continent through the lens of a dichotomizing orientalism that, as we shall argue, was also recursive.

In some respects the Balkan region was considered quintessentially European, indeed home of the heroic Christian defenders of the continent against the incursions of Asia and Islam during Ottoman campaigns of earlier centuries.[20] But this distinction between Europe and Asia, between East and West, could be deployed again and projected onto Europe itself, thereby producing a backward orient within Europe. Throughout the nineteenth century, the southeast of the continent was known as the "Near East" or *"l'Orient européen,"* or even part of the "Levant." Precisely because it was conquered for centuries by the

Ottomans, this region came to be seen as itself oriental, thus distinguished from enlightened Western civilization by its primitive lack of order: it was the least European part of Europe. It is telling that by the early twentieth century the term "Balkan," originally a euphemism for Turkey-in-Europe, had become a general pejorative meaning backward and, especially, subject to political disorder and disintegration. Finally, through this recursive logic, now applied to the southeastern region itself, Macedonia—one of the last provinces to be freed from Turkish rule (1913)—was seen as the Balkan of the Balkans. Accordingly, Macedonia was imagined in fiction as well as travel writing as a place of chaos and confusion, a veritable fruit salad—inspiring the French culinary term *macédoine*—of peoples, religions, and languages. It was alleged to lack the positive traits metropolitan Europe assigned itself. These traits included not only technological progress, economic development, and civilization, but most especially the prerequisite for all of these: the ideal political order of one nation, speaking one language, ruled by one state, within one bounded territory. (In fact, metropolitan Europe had by no means achieved this ideal itself.) [21]

This symbolic geography and its variants have received considerable scholarly attention recently (e.g., Bakić-Hayden and Hayden 1992; Brown 1995; Todorova 1994). What has not been noticed, however, is the role of linguistic ideologies in its formation. For example, Max Müller (1855:65) understood many of the characteristics of the "Slavonic" languages through their location "on the threshold between barbarism and civilization." More specifically, local Macedonian language practices and the metropolitan European linguistic ideology through which they were seen by travelers, scholars, and government officials were crucial to the construction of such images. Western European elites had come to think of language as the least socially malleable and therefore the most authentic indicator of a speaker's sociopolitical identity. As early as 1808 Fichte (1845–46:453) had declared, "Wherever a separate language can be found, there is also a separate nation which has the right to manage its affairs and rule itself." And a hundred years later, the noted linguist Antoine Meillet was calling language the principal factor determining national sentiment in Europe (cited in Wilkinson 1951:276).

In this context, Macedonia appeared doubly anomalous. First

there was its astonishing linguistic and ethnographic diversity.[22] At the turn of the century, the Englishman Brailsford likened the Macedonian marketplace to "Babel," where a traveler might hear as many as "six distinct languages and four allied dialects...one may distinguish in the Babel two Slav and two Albanian dialects, Vlach, Greek, Turkish, Hebrew-Spanish, and Romany" (Brailsford 1906:85). The Frenchman Lamouche (1899:1) equated this heterogeneity with disorder and an uncivilized past: "This region still presents itself to us with the variation and ethnographic confusion that reigned as the result of the barbarian invasions." Later British accounts called Macedonia "primitive," "barbaric," and "hybrid" (see Goff and Fawcett 1921).

Second, and perhaps more disturbing for Western observers, Macedonian linguistic diversity failed to correspond to social and ethnic boundaries in the ways that Western ideologies led them to expect. Describing a trip to Turkey-in-Europe, Lucy Garnett (1904:234–35) registered a widespread exasperation. In Macedonia, she noted,

> A Greek-speaking community may prove to be Wallachian, Albanian or even Bulgarian, and the inhabitants of a Slav-speaking village may claim to be of Greek origin...All these various ethnical elements are, in many country districts of Macedonia, as well as in the towns, so hopelessly fused and intermingled.

Garnett's comment was echoed in more scholarly—and more racialized—tones by a German geographer, Karl von Östreich (1905:270): "Instead of racially pure Turks and Albanians we find people who are racially mixed...and whose multilingualism misleads us about their real origins, so that they can be counted sometimes as Greeks, sometimes as Bulgarians, sometimes as Wallachians."

Other authors were "puzzled" at the "peculiar phenomenon" that members of "Bulgarian" families in Macedonia could be persuaded to become "Greek" or "Serbian" (Moore 1906:147). Brailsford (1906:102) reported with consternation that families often sent each son to a different school—Bulgarian, Greek, Rumanian, Serbian—whose language and nationality the child would then adopt. Western observers failed to perceive this practice as an attempt to extend social networks in uncertain times. Rather, the ethnic profusion and confusion predicated of the region as a whole, and implicitly contrasted with

"European" order, were seen to be reproduced within families. In the recurrence and persistence of such anecdotes we note again the workings of *fractal recursivity*. A somewhat later observer, writing about his journey "across the new Balkans" and the "Levant" (which for him began in Prague), demonstrated that this dichotomy of East and West was even projected onto individuals: "The Levantine type in the areas between the Balkans and the Mediterranean is, psychologically and socially, truly a 'wavering form,' a composite of Easterner and Westerner, multilingual...superficial, unreliable" (Ehrenpreis 1928:12).

The importance of this "composite" image for our purposes lies not only in its evidence of further recursivity but also in the way it shows that ethnolinguistic heterogeneity had consequences for the moral reputation of Macedonians. Ehrenpreis's comment explicitly links supposedly labile allegiances to linguistic practice. Multiple languages were assumed to indicate multiple loyalties and thus a temperamental flaw, a lack of trustworthiness. It was because linguistic practices and character were seen by Westerners as *iconically* linked that shifting language use could be used as evidence for equally shiftable, hence dubious and shallow, allegiances. Indeed, a French consul in Macedonia is reported to have declared that with a fund of a million francs for bribes, he could make all Macedonians French (cited in Brailsford 1906:103).

If recursivity and iconization are apparent in these turn-of-the-century accounts, the third semiotic process, *erasure,* is also evident. Because the relationship between linguistic practices and social categories in Macedonia diverged so fundamentally from the expectations of Western Europeans, the region appeared chaotic to them. These observers therefore missed—and their representations erased—the local logic by which the inhabitants of Macedonia understood categories of language and identity such as "Greek," "Turkish," "Bulgarian," and "Macedonian" during the long Ottoman period and before the rise of Balkan nationalisms.

One major constraint on local practices was the Ottoman *millet* system (often mistranslated as "nationality"), which categorized and administered populations according to religious affiliation irrespective of territorial location, ethnic provenance, or language. Moslems counted as "Turks," while Orthodox Christians, including people who spoke various forms of Slavic, Romance, Albanian, and Greek, were counted as "Greeks." During most of the nineteenth century, "Greeks" were officially ruled by the Greek Orthodox Church in European Turkey. But "Greek" and "Turk" were not merely imperial administrative categories; they affected local understandings as well. A Christian peasant in mid-nineteenth-century Macedonia would identify his "nationality" *(millet)* as Greek, regardless of the language he spoke. Similarly, Moslem peasants, even those speaking Albanian, identified themselves as Turkish well into the twentieth century (see, for example, Friedman 1975; Lunt 1984).

Yet Greek was not only a religious and administrative category but also a marker of stratification. As Stoianovich (1960:311) notes, "The Hellenization of the upper social strata of the non-Greek Balkan Orthodox peoples made possible the emergence of a single, relatively united, inter-Balkan merchant class which was of Greek, Vlach, Macedo-Slav and Bulgarian ethnic origin, but called itself and was known to others as 'Greek.'" When contrasted with "Greek," the designation "Bulgarian" was also, in part, a category of social stratification, particularly in the early part of the century. In Macedonia it could be equivalent to *raya*, that is, a rural, usually Christian, lower-class subject of Ottoman rule. It was not necessarily linked to the use of the Bulgarian literary language that was being developed actively during the nineteenth century. Moreover, a rural-urban contrast was also salient. Greek-speaking merchants and intellectuals, whatever their ethnic origins, tended to live in cities and towns; Slavic- and Albanian-speakers, whatever their religion, were more likely to be rural.

Clearly, multilingualism was widespread. "Greek" merchants of various backgrounds continued to speak diverse home languages, while using Greek for trade and intellectual activity. Ottoman Turkish was employed for administration and often for market activities by many speakers of other languages; *katharevousa* Greek and Church Slavonic were languages of liturgy and church administration in Greek Orthodox and (later) in Bulgarian and Serbian Orthodox churches, respectively. But these languages were not always strictly compartmentalized by function. Many a mid-nineteenth-century merchant wrote his accounts not in Greek, as might be expected, but in Bulgarian with Greek letters and Turkish numbers (Todorova 1990:439). The occurrence of codeswitching in mid-nineteenth-century folktales suggests that multilingualism was not limited to those persons directly involved in trade, administration, and religious institutions. Even many rural speakers or recent migrants to small cities could switch to Turkish and Greek or use other vernaculars—dialects of Slavic, Albanian, Rumanian, Greek, Romany—for everyday communication. Indeed, at least in urban areas, rates of multilingualism apparently increased as one moved down the socioeconomic ladder (Friedman 1995; see also Brailsford 1906:85–86).

These patterns of usage suggest that while there were regularities that systematically and predictably linked a range of linguistic practices to social uses and to categories of identity, there were no "total" categories in mid-nineteenth-century Macedonia that encompassed and subordinated all other categories while being also indissolubly linked to linguistic forms understood as single languages. In short, in the understanding of identity, the criteria of religion, region, occupation, social stratum, and language group had not been aligned, hierarchized, or regimented on the model of the Western, nationalist imagination.[23]

By the end of the nineteenth century, however, the reign of just such national ideas was well under way in the Balkan states that had gained independence from Ottoman rule. Hence, the multilingual situation we have described proved fertile ground for nationalist movements originating outside geographic Macedonia. Each "imagined" the territory and inhabitants of Macedonia as part of its own emerging "community." Well before the final expulsion of Ottoman rule from geographic Macedonia, neighboring elites were funding political agitation there and establishing schools run in each of their national literary languages. Local elites within geographic Macedonia were inciting action for independence. Relying on the very equation of nation, language, and territory that outside observers had earlier found lacking in Macedonia, advocates of Serbian, Bulgarian, and Greek expansion, as well as those calling for Macedonian autonomy, appealed to linguistic descriptions to prove the existence of *social* boundaries that would authorize their claims to popular loyalty.

At the same time, competing elites were also producing census figures, ethnographic and linguistic maps, and historical treatises written in national terms familiar to the West. They were all designed to convince Great Power audiences that one set of claims to Macedonian territory was more justified than others. These works appeared both before and after partition. They were written in Western languages and published in Paris, London, Vienna, Berlin, Zürich, and New York. As Wilkinson's (1951) compilation of ethnographic and linguistic maps of the period illustrates, this body of scholarship was often politically partisan, contradictory, and sometimes simply mendacious. We examine it here for what it reveals about the broader ideological assumptions concerning language and identity. By analyzing the arguments of Greek, Serbian, Bulgarian, and distinctively Macedonian positions, along with some of the policies they inspired, we can trace once again how the three semiotic processes work, this time in the fierce contestation among local linguistic nationalisms.[24]

To understand these controversies, it is helpful to start with aspects of Slavic dialectology about which there is general scholarly agreement. A dialect continuum in South Slavic runs from Serbian to Bulgarian through Macedonia (see fig. 2.2).[25] Dialects located in Macedonia share many lexical and phonological features with dialects in Serbia, but in morphology they bear a stronger resemblance to varieties in Bulgaria. For instance, West South Slavic dialects (Serbia) retain much of the complex declensional system of Common Slavic, but East South Slavic dialects, including those in what is now Bulgaria and the Republic of Macedonia, have lost inflections, replacing case marking with prepositions and syntactic features. Similarly, East South Slavic dialects share a postposed definite article as well as analytical rather than morphological forms of the infinitive and comparative (see Friedman 1975; Lunt 1984).[26]

In this context, we can see how the battles between Serbian, Bulgarian, and Greek claims to Macedonia provide examples of argument through *iconization*. "Deep" linguistic relationship was the key, identified by selecting some linguistic features and ignoring (or explaining away) others. Thus Bulgarian linguists emphasized the Macedonian dialects' relatively analytic morphology, which resembled literary Bulgarian, to argue for the languages' deep kinship; they explained phonological differences as superficial "new developments." Social relations of "closeness" and "distance" were projected iconically from presumed or claimed "closeness" of linguistic relations and were used to justify political unity. Indeed, the Bulgarian position simply asserts that Macedonian dialects are forms of Bulgarian, thereby erasing Macedonian altogether (see, for example, Brancoff 1905; Sís 1918).[27] Serbian linguists, on the other hand, picked only certain phonological features to emphasize, claiming they revealed the ancient kinship of dialects in Macedonia with those in Serbia (see, for example, Belić 1919; Cvijić 1907). Finally, Greek scholars argued that, because the Slavic forms spoken in Greek Macedonia were so heavily reliant on Greek lexicon, they were actually a dialect of Greek. A speculative history was iconically projected to explain this surprising hypothesis through historically "deep" social relations: it was argued that Greek-speakers in antiquity must have assimilated to later Slavic immigrants and, having gone through a period of bilingualism, retained the lexicon (though not the grammar) of their original language (see Andriotes 1957:15–16).

Iconization operated in other ways as well. Between the two World Wars, in the section of geographic Macedonia that had become part of Yugoslavia, Macedonian was treated as a dialect of Serbo-Croatian. In Macedonian-Serbian conversations a largely similar lexical stock assured that mutual intelligibility could be achieved, but at the price of a subjective impression "that the other was using an irritating kind of pidgin" (Lunt 1959:21). It was the Serbs who, on hearing the relatively simpler nominal morphology of Macedonian, took this as an icon of simple thought and so assumed Macedonians to be uncultivated country bumpkins. Through such iconization, the perception that Macedonian "had no grammar" apparently contributed to legitimating far-reaching political tactics. Serbs, who dominated the interwar Yugoslav government, "quickly became annoyed at the linguistic ineptitude of the mass of Macedonians and found [in this] a righteous justification for accusing them of stupidity and ingratitude and hence for treating the region almost as a colony" (Lunt 1959:22). Ironically, such characterizations of Macedonian as "simple" could only be sustained by focusing on the language's relatively few nominal inflections and ignoring, thus erasing, the complexities of its verbal system.

But processes of *erasure* in the arguments we are considering were often much more drastic than this. In linguistic maps of Macedonia from the turn of the century, evidence of the widespread multilingualism characteristic of the region disappeared altogether. The maps displayed neatly bounded regions, each in a different color to indicate the presence of speakers of a single, named language (see Wilkinson 1951). Maps drawn by Serbian and Bulgarian advocates each claimed all Slavic forms as dialects of their own standard languages. Furthermore, they showed virtually no one speaking Greek, despite the fact that some Slavic-speakers, especially in the south, continued to use it in commerce, writing, and intellectual life.

Greek maps, in contrast, showed great areas of Greek-speakers in Macedonia by counting only the use of "commercial language" rather than "mother tongue." Clearly driven by political motives, and vastly overstating the numbers, Greek arguments such as those of Nicolaïdes (1899) nevertheless allow us to see "mother tongue" itself as a deeply ideological construct that disallows claims of identity based on other linguistic considerations. After all, as we have seen, at least some urban, educated inhabitants of nineteenth-century Macedonia might well have agreed with Nicolaïdes's categorization of them as "Greek," despite the other languages they also spoke. Later Greek erasures were less benign, however. Between the World Wars, the existence of Slavic-speakers and Slavic forms was denied altogether in Greek Macedonia. Official policy prohibited their mention, census questions asked only whether individuals spoke Greek, village and family names were forcibly changed, and Slavic speakers were jailed. In the 1950s Slavic-speaking villagers were coerced to take "language oaths" promising never to speak Slavic again (see Karakasidou 1993).

In the debates among competing nationalisms, processes of *recursivity* were also evident, operating in tandem with erasures and iconization. As we have noted, within the logic of linguistic nationalism, the equation of a language with a delimited territory and population required the elision of multilingualism in maps and other representations. This elision ultimately led as well to the attempted elimination, through schooling and legal means, of repertoires in which different languages were used for different social functions. But the new conceptual opposition of "our own national language" versus "foreign language" that motivated such erasure was also recursively applied within the literary languages of the region as these were successively codified. The choices of language planners were often made at least in part to avoid or downplay similarities with competing languages nearby that were conceptualized as foreign because they "belonged" to other nations. For example, in the official codification of Macedonian in 1944, the preference for the Western dialects as the basis of the literary language was supported by historical precedent, since they were already evident in literary productions dating from the mid-nineteenth century. Another major motivation for this choice, however, was that it produced maximal differentiation from both Bulgarian and Serbo-Croatian standards (Friedman 1989:31).

Most significantly, heated debates about linguistic purity have involved the recursive application of this native/foreign distinction to the lexical stock of the region's languages. Ottoman rule had resulted in the heavy lexical influence of Greek and Turkish on all Balkan languages. As early as the 1840s Bulgarian language reformers engaged in what we have called "register-stripping": the attempt to purge Turkish elements from the literary Bulgarian then being created because such elements were now seen as "alien" despite their pervasiveness in colloquial speech. For familiar Turkish words the reformers provided unfamiliar Slavic glosses, often borrowed from Russian or revived from Church Slavonic (Pinto 1980:46). These latter languages were analyzed as historically related to Bulgarian and doubtless perceived to be, by iconic logic, less "foreign."

Equally interesting is the case of Macedonian, in which Turkish influence has included productive derivational morphology as well as the usual individual lexical items and calques of idiomatic phrases. What is significant is not the actual source of such elements but speakers' continuing perception of many of them as Turkisms. In Macedonian debates some planners in the 1940s argued for the replacement of Turkisms with Slavic forms in the literary language. Turkisms perceived as such suffered a stylistic lowering after the Ottoman's defeat, so that they came to connote archaism, local color, pejoration, or irony. Planners feared that their retention in the Macedonian literary language (especially after they had been purged from neighboring languages) would threaten to make all of Macedonian sound "lower" and less refined (Koneski, quoted in Friedman 1996). Thus, by an application of recursive logic, Turkisms (as both alien and low) were systematically stripped from the literary language. Simultaneously, registers perceived as native were newly "stretched" through neologisms or revival of dialect and archaic forms to cover broader functions (see Friedman 1989; Koneski 1980).

In sum, the complex Macedonian linguistic scene, and nationalist arguments within it, reveal all three semiotic processes we have discussed and show them to operate in a number of different ways. The continuing intensity of contestation over the representation of Macedonian speech forms is hardly surprising, given the consequences envisaged and authorized by the reigning language ideology and occasionally enacted under its auspices. It is an ideology in which claims of linguistic affiliation are crucial and exclusivist because they are also claims to territory and sovereignty.

IMPLICATIONS

The analysis we have presented here has implications relating to at least three intellectual arenas in social science research. The first is the study of historical fields of contact among peoples. European colonialism provides a major set of examples. In particular, part of our analysis contributes to the study of "colonial discourses," illuminating some of their semiotic properties. The second group of problems and issues we seek to address concerns ethnicity and its relation to communicative practices. The concept of "speech community," prominent in linguistic anthropology and sociolinguistics since the 1960s, is among the ideas we seek to reconceptualize. Finally, the third arena is that concerned with conceptions of language itself. Although these intellectual arenas have obvious overlaps, we now take them up in turn, adumbrating some of the implications our analysis has for each.

The semiotic processes we have identified, though not limited to any particular historical period, nevertheless always occur in history and operate in relation to contingent facts. The study of colonialism offers an important opportunity to study ideologies—linguistic and otherwise—because of colonialism's obvious consequentiality, the clash of interests at stake, and the evident differences in points of view. As scholars are increasingly recognizing, however, the colonial period is more than just an interesting topic for historical research. Ideas that were forged in that context have remained deeply embedded in our analytical frameworks.

A considerable body of recent research by historians and anthropologists has focused on the dichotomizing discourses of orientalism through which, in the nineteenth century and earlier, Europe created itself in opposition to a broadly defined "East" that often included not only Asia but also Africa. That "East" also found parallels elsewhere in the world, even within Europe itself, where a similar axis of opposition distinguished metropolitan centers of "higher" civilization from their "lower," especially their eastern, peripheries. As Mudimbe (1988), Olender (1992), Said (1978), and others have pointed out, scholars of language and ideas about linguistic differences played a significant part in the development of such categories of identity (see also Bauman and Briggs, this volume). Arguments about language were central in producing and buttressing European claims to difference from the rest of the world, as well as claims to the superiority of the metropolitan bourgeoisie over "backward" or "primitive" Others, whether they were residents of other continents, other provinces, or other social classes.

Language could be central to these arguments because by the mid-nineteenth century it had become common in the scholarly world to see language as crucially unaffected by human will or individual intent (see Formigari 1985; Taylor 1990b). For many scholars of the time, linguistic differences appeared to be the "natural" consequences of spiritual or even biological differences between collectivities of speakers, rather than the consequence of social action. August Schleicher (1869:20–21), for example, promoting a Darwinian model of linguistic evolution and differentiation, argued that "languages are organisms of nature; they have never been directed by the will of man...The science of language is consequently a natural science." In a more religious vein but with a similar implication, F. Max Müller (1861) proposed that a "science of language" should be theistic and historical, yet it should employ the methods of geology, botany, and anatomy, for the very reason that such a science—comparative philology—would deal with the works of God, not of man. Although later approaches differed sharply in many ways, the argument for a "science of language" that would be divorced from the everyday speech and social life of its speakers remained, Saussure's formulation being today the most familiar.[28]

Despite increasing awareness in recent years of these European ideologies of language and their historical contexts, anthropologists and linguists have not sufficiently explored their implications. Our disciplines' conceptual tools for understanding linguistic differences and relationships still derive from this massive scholarly attempt to create the differentiation of Europe from the rest of the world. We have sought to redirect this intellectual project. In this paper we have argued that linguistic differentiation crucially involves ideologically embedded and socially constructed processes. Moreover, the scholarly enterprise of describing linguistic differentiation is itself ideologically and socially engaged (see also Gal and Irvine 1995).

For instance, the Senegal case discussed above provides an opportunity to show how the study of language participated in colonial discourses. Such discourses reveal the complex interaction of ideologies, both the colonizers' and those of the colonized. Since then there have been many changes in the methods of linguistic analysis and the genres of linguistic description; nevertheless, those early discourses of language form the beginnings of a "culture of linguistics" of the region, a tradition to which scholars today fall heir. Contemporary understandings of language differentiation in Senegal thus have a complex history, with European and African language ideologies contributing to interpretations of local sociolinguistic phenomena.

In a parallel way, the case of Macedonia demonstrates the specific ways in which linguistic analyses have contributed to shaping "orientalist discourses." The perception of linguistic chaos in Macedonia emerged from an interaction of local and Western European language ideologies. And metropolitan Europe constructed its own self-image in opposition to just such representations of the sociolinguistic scene in the "East." As soon as Balkan elites appealed to Western powers in Western terms, moreover, linguistic scholarship became the ground on which political economic contests were fought. In such contests today, too, current linguistic scholarship in the region remains significant.

Recent scholarly reflections on colonialism and orientalism have focused on nineteenth-century Europe's discursive construction of boundaries and the projection of ideas and images across them. Thinking about boundaries and their construction has an older genealogy in anthropology, however. It is now many years since the publication of Fredrik Barth's *Ethnic Groups and Boundaries* (1969), a work that transformed anthropological thinking about ethnicity. Barth argued that ethnic groups represent a way people organize themselves within a larger social field—a way people identify themselves in contrast with others. Relationships *across* a boundary, Barth suggested, are thus more crucial to the existence and persistence of the boundary than are any group-internal attributes an anthropological observer might identify.

Barth's essay coincided with the appearance of sociolinguistic works (such as Gumperz and Hymes 1964, 1972; Hymes 1968; Weinreich, Labov, and Herzog 1968) that similarly emphasized the social organization of diversity and attacked the idea that any particular type of community, ethnic or otherwise, is the necessary outcome of homogeneous language. From those intellectual antecedents we derive our emphasis on functional relationships among linguistic varieties, relationships that lend systematicity to regional patterns of diversity. We also derive from the ethnography of speaking our concern with participants' ideas about the meanings attaching to the deployment of codes in a repertoire. Thus some of the themes we emphasize in this paper have been present in sociolinguistics and the ethnography of speaking from the beginnings of those fields' existence.

We believe, however, that the full potential of these sociolinguistic insights has yet to be felt. In sociolinguistics and the ethnography of communication, a concept of "speech community," though useful for understanding the organization of local repertoires, nevertheless neglected larger boundary relationships, cultural oppositions, borders, and conflict (see Gal 1987, 1989; Irvine 1987). Classic sociolinguistic research sought first of all to demonstrate that linguistic diversity did not necessarily produce or imply social disorder. This endeavor was not inconsistent with the sociological theories dominant at the time, theories that assumed consensus as the basis of social formations. So, while recognizing the importance and organization of social and linguistic diversity, this foundational research only rarely examined the ways in which identity is produced by ideas of opposition between culturally defined groups, and by practices that promote exclusion, divergence, and differentiation.[29] Later, an attempted switch in analytic unit from speech communities to social networks—though valuable in many ways, including its exploration of the nature of communicative ties—still did not give much attention to problematizing the boundaries of networks but instead treated them, in this respect, much like communities. The analytical focus centered on the social control and peer pressures that produce linguistic uniformity "within" them (Gal 1979; Milroy 1980).

In many branches of anthropology and other social sciences, meanwhile, the assumption persists that the communities anthropologists study will normally be linguistically homogeneous. Even so influential a student of ethnicity and nationalism as Benedict Anderson (1983:38) laments what he assumes to be the "fatality" of monolingualism: "Then [in the sixteenth century] as now, the bulk of mankind is monoglot." For Anderson it is this (supposedly) inevitable monolingualism that provides the fertile ground for linguistic nationalism, the indispensable context in which "capitalism and print created monoglot mass reading publics" (p. 43). He thereby ignores the variety of culturally and often politically significant linguistic differentiation—the registers, dialects, and languages—present in the linguistic repertoires of speakers before print capitalism and within contemporary states that are only legally or nominally "monolingual." Missing from Anderson's perspective, we suggest, is the insight that homogeneous language is as much imagined as is community. That is, Anderson naturalizes the process of linguistic standardization, as if linguistic homogeneity were a real-world precondition rather than a construction concurrent with, or consequent to, print capitalism (for discussion see Silverstein, this volume). An assumption of normative monolingualism tends to persist, as well, in schools of linguistics where dominant models of language are cognitively and not socially based. These models often include the supposition that dialects arise automatically out of communicative isolation and for no other reason.

We propose that what is needed is to shift attention to linguistic differentiation rather than community. But it is crucial to recognize that the differentiation is ideologically mediated, both by its participants and by its observers. It has now often been noted (by, among others, Cameron 1990; Ferguson 1994; and Irvine 1985) that linguistic differentiation is not a simple reflection of social differentiation or vice versa, because linguistic and social oppositions are not separate orders of phenomena. As Ferguson (1994:19) writes, "Language phenomena are themselves sociocultural phenomena and are in part constitutive of the very social groups recognized by the participants or identified by analysts." It is that mediating *recognition* and *identification*, together with ideological frameworks and pressures, whose relationship with processes of linguistic differentiation we seek to explore.[30]

A final implication of a shift of attention from linguistic communities to linguistic boundaries is to open the door to reflections on some fundamental questions about language itself. One set of such questions involves the mechanisms of linguistic change. In their study of language contact and language change, Thomason and Kaufman (1988) have shown that, contrary to what linguists have supposed for many decades, there are no strictly linguistic motivations of change that operate in lawlike fashion no matter what the social circumstances. Even such linguistic constraints as pattern pressure and markedness considerations are easily overridden by social factors. But Thomason and Kaufman's argument is primarily a negative one, showing that linguistic explanations alone are inadequate rather than supplying a substantial indication of what the social factors are or how they might operate. In this work we have tried to suggest how one might begin to supply that missing dimension. Our materials suggest that the direction and motivation of linguistic change can be illuminated if we attend to the ideologizing of a sociolinguistic field and the consequent reconfiguring of its varieties through processes of iconization, recursive projection, and erasure.

Another set of questions whose importance is signaled by our analysis concerns register phenomena. Our examples show various ways in which registers serve as sites for borrowing and for the negotiation of social relationships via recursive projections and/or claims about linguistic and social connectedness or distance. But we have also seen that an ideology of societal monolingualism and linguistic homogeneity renders functional varieties anomalous. That ideology, moreover, often imagines languages as corresponding with essentialized representations of social groups. Essentialized linguistic and social categories are made to seem isomorphic when ideologies omit inconvenient linguistic facts (such as "borrowed" lexicon, registers, or functionally specialized languages), or when they lead people to create linguistic facts (such as neologisms or new registers) to match the representation. We contend that scholarly analyses are improved when registers are systematically included in discussions of relationships among languages and dialects and in discussions of what competence in "a language" includes, rather than being omitted or inserted under those ideological pressures. To be sure, the concept of register is itself problematic and also subject to ideological pressures besides the ones we have discussed here (see Silverstein 1992).

Finally, we note that our analysis of semiotic processes in linguistic differentiation has implications for our understanding of sign relationships in language itself, such as the notion of the linguistic sign's quintessential arbitrariness. In our view, the notion of arbitrariness is more problematic than has generally been supposed. Saussure's assertion of the "arbitrariness of the sign" is often celebrated as the originary moment of modern linguistics. But publicly voiced claims about the inherent properties of particular languages, or of standards as opposed to dialects, have not abated in contemporary life. We suggest that a useful way to unpack this term and its dilemmas is to distinguish among the possible social positions from which the judgment of "arbitrariness" is made.

First, from the perspective of ordinary speakers, linguistic differences are understood through folk theories (ideologies) that often posit their inherent hierarchical, moral, aesthetic, or other properties within broader cultural systems that are themselves often contested and rarely univocal. The second perspective is that of contemporary linguistics. In constituting itself as an academic discipline, linguistics rejected precisely this culturally embedded speaker's perspective. It insisted instead on de-culturing linguistic phenomena and establishing the theoretical and thus disciplinary autonomy of language. Linguistics has its own set of relevances driven by changing theoretical considerations that differ from those of native speakers. Thus, from the perspective of many kinds of post-Saussurean linguistics, signs are indeed "arbitrary" because the cultural systems that make them iconic are stringently and systematically excluded from consideration, for the sake of science. This suggests a third, metatheoretical, perspective: As we recognize that ordinary speakers' theories about the nonarbitrariness of signs make a difference in the production, interpretation, and reporting of linguistic differentiation, we must add that the equally ideological theories of linguists do so as well.

The very real facts of linguistic variation constrain what linguists and native speakers can persuasively say and imagine about them.

Linguistic facts have a certain recalcitrance in the face of ideological construction. But, as we remarked at the outset, there is no "view from nowhere" in representing linguistic differences. Moreover, acts of speaking and acts of describing both depend on and contribute to the "work of representation." Those representations, in turn, influence the phenomena they purport to represent.

In sum, we have identified three semiotic processes at work in language ideologies as these apply to the question of linguistic boundaries and differentiation. The three are *iconization, fractal recursivity,* and *erasure.* We have argued that these processes operate worldwide; that they are not dependent on the historical contexts of European colonialism (although they do appear conspicuously there, they also appear elsewhere); and that they are deeply involved in both the shaping of linguistic differentiation and the creating of linguistic description.

Notes

1. The source for this saying, long a part of linguistics' oral tradition, is difficult to identify. Many linguists attribute it to Max Weinreich.

2. See, for example, the compendium of relevant statements by Peirce (1955) assembled by Justus Buchler under the title "Logic as semiotic: The theory of signs."

3. For further discussion and illustration in a contemporary ethnographic example, see Irvine (1989, 1990).

4. Well-known analyses of such processes from an earlier generation of anthropologists include Bateson (1936) and Evans-Pritchard (1940); more recent discussions include Abbott (1990), Gal (1991), Herzfeld (1987), and Wagner (1991), although the thrust of Wagner's argument about "fractals" is somewhat different from ours.

5. Notice, also, that entries in the Doke and Vilakazi (1958) Zulu dictionary seem to link click sounds, Khoisan languages, and chatter. Thus *nxapha*, a verb meaning 'to utter click sounds' (especially in annoyance or vexation), is exemplified in *Ulimi lwaɓaThwa luyanxaphanxapha*, 'The Bushman tongue is full of clicks'; the same verb also means 'misfire (of a gun)'. Another word, *qheɓeqheɓe*, refers to 'clicking (as of latch or catch)', 'liveliness', and a 'lively, talkative person, a gossiper'. These links are suggestive, although we do not consider dictionary entries of this kind to be actual evidence that speakers draw a conceptual link between a word's different senses.

6. We have identified these patterns mainly by examining the citations for *hlonipha* words given in Doke and Vilakazi's 1958 Zulu dictionary. Although there are some problems in the dictionary's treatment of these words (for instance, the seemingly haphazard collection of *hlonipha* lists from many regions, assembled for a pan-Zulu set of dictionary entries), the various phonological patterns observable in the dictionary are not contradicted by *hlonipha* data from other sources. See also Herbert (1990) for more discussion of *hlonipha* word formation.

7. See Herbert 1990 for discussion, and refutation, of some alternative views.

8. It is interesting that this conversation is a quarrel. Evidently, the speakers were showing respect not to one another but to third parties.

9. Herbert (1990:307) attributes the existence of this core vocabulary to urbanization and the decline of *hlonipha*. That it does not conform to the normative pattern of name-avoidance does not necessarily mean, however, that it is very recent or only urban. Finlayson (1984:140, 143) states, in fact, that she found the core vocabulary throughout the Xhosa-speaking area where *hlonipha* has been investigated. The change among some urban Xhosa is apparently not the emergence of a common *hlonipha* vocabulary but the loss of specific name-avoidances. The urban speakers display respect for tradition but do not orient their respect to the names of particular persons.

10. In the full text of this passage, Lepsius discussed the classification of African languages before continuing, "In like manner will the chaos of the nations in Asia..."

11. For a related discussion, see Irvine 1993.

12. For a historical discussion of Sereer-speakers' participation in a largely Wolof international system, see Klein (1968, especially pp. 7-8) and Diagne (1967). There is good documentation that kings and officials in Siin and Saluum dealt with nineteenth-century European visitors in Wolof, just as they did other outsiders; see, for example, the visit of the Kobès and other missionaries to the court of Saluum (Abiven n.d.).

13. Although most authors agreed on the main outlines of this picture, details varied. There was some disagreement between French administrators and missionaries—and among missionaries themselves—as to whether Islam, compared with animism, was a sign of higher civilization or of greater corruption. Another complication arose because of the sociological diversity of Fula-speakers. Some scholars claimed that it was only the pastoralist populations who came

close to a "pure" Fula racial type and that sedentary populations were the product of racial *métissage* (the supposed cause of social hierarchy in sedentary communities).

14. The role of supposed racial and cultural characteristics in analyses of Fula and, especially, in its placement in language families is relatively well known since Greenberg's critiques (see Greenberg 1963; note also Sapir 1913). For this reason we devote more of our discussion to Sereer, a less familiar case.

15. Space does not permit a detailed discussion supporting our characterization of Lamoise's work. We will just note that he does supply more examples of texts and discourse than is common in grammars of the period (or today), but some of them appear to have been composed by himself or his assistants, and none of them records aristocrats' political discourse. Other important evidence would come, for example, from his treatment of key pairs of words such as *Yalla/rôg* ('God'), each of which occurs in both Wolof and Sereer grammatical structures but in different situational contexts, which Lamoise and others seem to interpret as ethnic contexts.

16. Although Faidherbe accepted the identification of the Kajoor enclave populations (i.e., Cangin-speakers) as "Sereer," he did recognize its source (1865:175): "The populations *which the Wolof designate by the name of Sereers* speak two distinct languages: one called Kéguem and the other None...The populations who speak the None dialects do not understand Kéguem at all, and reciprocally" (emphasis added). So firmly was the label "Sereer" attached to these languages, however, that Faidherbe used it in all his later works, while other authors, including Cust and Lamoise, merely list "None" and other Cangin varieties along with other regional varieties of Sereer. (Note that Faidherbe's "Kéguem" was apparently a mistaken name for the same Siin variety of Sereer described by Lamoise [1873] and, more recently, Crétois [1972].)

17. Pichl's research was almost the first to be published on this language group since Faidherbe's brief notice in 1865. In a 1953 linguistic survey, however, de Tressan looked at these enclave languages and called them "faux-Sérère."

18. Many thanks to Victor Friedman for indispensable discussion and advice on Macedonian matters. There is considerably more agreement on the outlines of a geographic region called Macedonia than on the matter of which states have political rights to it. Historically, the following regions have been considered geographical Macedonia: the current Republic of Macedonia, the southwestern corner of Bulgaria, a northern province of Greece, and small parts of

eastern Albania. Figure 2.2 illustrates this distinction. For parallel discussions of this by several generations of scholars, see Wilkinson (1951); Friedman (1985); and Poulton (1995).

19. McNeill (1964) provides the classic account of interimperial competition. Some important milestones in the gradual dissolution of Ottoman rule in Europe—through a series of revolts, wars, and treaties—include Serbia's relative autonomy, secured in 1817; the independence of Greece, proclaimed after 1830; the establishment of Bulgarian schools in 1835 and the Bulgarian Church (exarchate) in 1870; and the final independence of Serbia and Romania, and the autonomy of Bulgaria, gained at the Treaty of Berlin in 1878. The Balkan Wars of 1912-13 reduced Turkish rule in Europe to its present boundary and produced the partition of Macedonia (for a useful summary, see Okey 1982).

20. The nationalist movements of nineteenth-century eastern Europe often claimed the distinction of having defended Europe, especially in literature targeted at Western audiences. Western views often recognized this claim, based on the earlier Christian/Moslem opposition, while also applying the contrast emphasizing civilization and barbarism (see Wolff 1994, chap. 1). For the Frenchman Lamouche, along with many other Westerners, the Greek struggle for independence was self-evidently a replay of "European civilization against Asiatic barbarism" (1899:134); Longfellow's poem about Skenderbeg, the early Albanian hero defending Christendom from the Turks, enjoyed considerable popularity in the late-nineteenth-century US; and as late as 1918 Lloyd George, as British prime minister, declared the Serbs to be "Guardians of the Gate" of Europe (Laffan 1918).

21. See, for example, Eugen Weber's (1976) discussion of the lack of cultural, linguistic, and political unity in the most centralized of European powers, France.

22. The views discussed here were very widespread despite the fact that, as Brown (1995) and Todorova (1994), among others, have noted, Western European observers varied widely in their class backgrounds, political commitments (e.g., socialist vs. conservative), national loyalties, and visions of what would be the best political solution for the Balkans.

23. For further complex examples and discussion see Brown's (1995) persuasive work on the 1903 Ilinden rising in Macedonia, showing how these cross-cutting categories were transformed and regimented into the familiar images of Western European national ideology.

24. For further discussion of different kinds of contestation among linguis-

tic ideologies, see Gal 1993.

25. The classic view of South Slavic dialectology adds a degree of regional organization to this picture. It maintains that in one part of this Balkan region, corresponding roughly to what is today the political border between Serbia and Bulgaria, a bundle of significant isoglosses permits Serbian and Bulgarian to emerge as linguistically distinct from one another. Farther south, however, isoglosses fan out. So while the dialectological transition from Serbian to Bulgarian in the north is relatively rapid, that from Serbian to Bulgarian through Macedonia (in the south) is very gradual. These claims about relative distinctness have recently been challenged, however (V. Friedman, personal communication 1998).

26. An early work describing these features is Lamouche (1899). Sandfeld's (1930) classic study on Balkan linguistics provides more detail. More recent and sophisticated descriptions include the cited works by Lunt and Friedman.

27. These arguments from the early years of the century continue unabated in attempts by Bulgarian linguists to deny the existence and historical depth of Macedonian. Macedonian linguists and historians, in turn, counter by producing evidence of early moves toward national autonomy in Macedonia, early literary production, and programmatic plans for a literary language; see Dimitrovski, Koneski, and Stamatoski (1978) and Lunt (1984) for summaries.

28. As Bauman and Briggs (this volume) show, important aspects have earlier roots in the work of Locke.

29. Noteworthy exceptions include Labov's (1963) research on Martha's Vineyard, Gumperz's (1958) study of linguistic organization in a North Indian village, and Fischer's (1958) discussion of social factors that influence phonological variation. A later example of a work focusing on linguistic aspects of culturally imagined opposition between groups is Basso's (1979) *Portraits of "the Whiteman"*.

30. Note our debt here to Silverstein's (1979) argument that language ideologies, in their dialectical relationship with the distribution of linguistic forms, introduce dynamics of change into sociolinguistic systems.

3

Whorfianism and the Linguistic Imagination of Nationality

Michael Silverstein

My discussion takes as its focus two important texts of linguistic ideology, one by Benjamin Lee Whorf, the other by Benedict R. O'Gorman Anderson. My aim is to show how Whorf's analysis of the semiotic mechanisms of language ideology can help us to understand what is problematic about Anderson's heavy reliance on language in modeling the cultural phenomenology of nationalism.

Whorf's name has shared the fate of those of many physicians who first propose a differential diagnosis, in that the condition or "disease" he diagnosed now bears his name, Whorfianism, with its neutralizing adjectival form, Whorfian.[1] These terms have generally been used as pejoratives in the linguistic literature because of a sad though understandable history of Whorf-stimulated psycholinguistic research in the behaviorist 1950s, followed immediately by the era of rabidly dogmatic anti-"relativism" orchestrated by and in the name of Noam Chomsky. These trends have taken Whorf to task for the earlier, misguided Whorfianism Whorf himself would have only seen as a further symptom of the disease.[2]

I shall attempt to sketch out in this essay the three lines of theoretical argument found in Whorf's oeuvre and will discuss the one central to the analysis of linguistic ideology. I will then turn to Benedict Anderson's brilliant little book, *Imagined Communities* (1991[1983]). It concerns the conditions under which nationalism has arisen as an ideological force and continues to exist and spread as a cultural form, exemplifying, however, classic Whorfian thinking. My point is this: that although Anderson's argument about the rise of nationalism recognizes the centrality of language as medium and even prototype of this cultural condition, it is itself a species of Whorfian construction from within that state or condition, a conceptual product of the linguistic conditions on which it rests.

THE THREE WHORFIAN THEMES
AND HOW THEY GREW

Let me begin with Whorf (1897–1941), whose centenary we celebrated in 1997. There has now been constructed about Whorf a multi-generational, intertextual edifice of projective misrepresentations that have followed the various "fashions of speaking" about language in several disciplines.

Whorf's Generally Boasian Intellectual Milieu

Whorf himself was a consociate of many of the now seniormost generation of anthropologically influenced linguists. He was in his most active professional phase during the 1930s, the last decade of his life, when he was part of the network of students and others that had, since 1931, formed around Edward Sapir at Yale. Coming into anthropological linguistics through his interest in Mayan hieroglyphs, Whorf demonstrated an analytic brilliance that still shines through in his detailed linguistic descriptions of Hopi, Aztec, Shawnee, and other Native American languages (see Whorf 1946a, 1946b, 1956c[1940]).[3] Indeed, Whorf shows himself to be perhaps the only Sapir associate who both theoretically mastered and was able consistently to put into practice the abstract conceptual machinery and methodological (analytical) dictates of commonly evolving descriptive linguistics in the American mode of the 1930s.

Having both an academic and a commercial professional identity, Whorf gave public voice to the enriching experience of a generation's collective enterprise of focused descriptive-linguistic work on Native American languages. He rearticulated various Boasian truisms from this experience and went beyond them: from his long-term ruminations on Einsteinian physical "relativity" (Hibbard 1991), he propounded inferences in an area we might term "relativistic epistemology," based on the contemporary scientific grammarian's understanding of language structure in relation to a cultural consideration of language use. It was, however, not Whorf's mentor, Sapir, who codified and ideologically framed the linguistics underlying this particular period of methodologically concerned Boasian relativism, but Leonard Bloomfield, in *Language* (1933), his comprehensive rewrite of Saussure's *Cours* (1916).[4] Whorf's work must be read in light of this.

Whorf, in other words, was committed to such Boas-derived anthropological linguistic issues as the structural diversity of specific languages, the problem of defining the grammatical (or "conceptual") categories of particular linguistic structures, (and comparing them in an appropriate typological framework); the question of doing deep linguistic history (comparative and historical linguistics) in North and Middle America to determine the "family" units of languages such as his own Uto-Aztecan specialty; and in articulating to a wider audience, both in the social sciences and beyond—especially outside of academia—the implications of the findings of these specialized studies for what Boas (1928) termed "modern life." But Whorf's vehicle for articulating these issues was a profound understanding of Bloomfieldian linguistic science, in which he was a superb practitioner at the same time that he was suspicious of, and indeed hostile to, the various obiter dicta of Bloomfield's outlook.[5]

The Bloomfieldian Irritant

Bloomfield was a born-again Vienna positivist (self-reconstructed in the image of Rudolph Carnap and Otto Neurath), a behaviorist (paying homage to his late friend Albert Paul Weiss and the tradition of German theorizing), and a fierce philosophical operationalist (hoping to do for linguistic science what Percy Bridgman and others were doing for physical science).

In the realm of philosophical positivism, Bloomfield (1936) declared that knowledge of matter (mass) in space-and-time plus knowledge of autonomous syntax are the foundations of everything knowable as "reality," including what reality lay behind received metaphysical speculation about human "mind," which linguistics was going to be able to reduce in the technical, logico-philosophical sense of scientific reduction according to the Viennese "*Aufbau.*"

In the realm of psychological behaviorism, Bloomfield declared that whatever structure underlies the stimulus-response episodes of human interaction constitutes the unstable psychobiological glue that holds individual organisms of this species together in societies and other, more ephemeral, social formations. To solve the problem of human mentality, we need only figure out (1) the principles of schedules of reinforcement versus extinction of effects of stimuli to which language forms appear to be the responses, and (2) how linguistic forms themselves can serve as stimuli to which an individual responds. In its recalcitrance to self-study, human mentality seemed to others to involve distinct a priori intentional, historical, dialectical, or sociocultural-order principles impossible to associate easily with an individual human biological organism. Such attempts, for Bloomfield confessions of primitive ignorance, he captioned with the pejorative term "mind."[6]

Finally, in the realm of scientific metatheory, Bloomfield, like all good operationalists, held that what he published in 1926 as "postulates" for linguistics as a science (1987a; see Silverstein 1978 for a commentary) were a set of unprovable but minimally essential and necessary heuristic "working methods"—indicating logically allowable operations of synchronic and diachronic linguistic analysis—from which emerged our scientific confidence in the existence of the empirical phenomena we deal with (things, and conditions relating such things). Thus all linguistic phenomena were to become abstract yet operationally locatable entities—operationalizable as equivalence-classes-under-distributional-rules—that one could never experience directly by sensorial means; operational postulates provide to the linguist the equivalent of laboratory meters for discovering unknowns. In this way the linguist could speak of (or 'model', as we now say) such "things" (linguistic units) in "structural" relations in specific analyses of the constitutive regularities inferred of grammar. The linguist understands in what sense such regularities are the norms that underlie particular stimulus-response phenomena in which linguistic noises or their equivalents play the role of stimulus or response.

Whorf had a profound and ready ability to utilize the Bloomfieldian conceptual and analytic vocabulary for articulating the nature of linguistic structure. (When Whorf writes "taxeme" or "tag-meme" or "morpheme" or "class meaning," he knows precisely what Bloomfield's famous 1933 text says and applies the terms accordingly.) Notwithstanding, his whole scientific and philosophical stance, indeed his whole framework of belief (in part derived from an unshakable New England spirituality; see Rollins 1972, 1980), lay elsewhere. His discovery of Boasianism in the network around Sapir allowed him to rearticulate misgivings about scientistic modernism (already long since articulated in polemics against Morganian evolutionary genetics, Einsteinian special relativity, and so on) that are specifically couched in terms of the lessons of linguistic science for a much broader, relativistic, and recognizably anthropological conception of humanity, and in particular of human *Geist* or 'mind-in-sociohistorical-"reality".' There are three component arguments, each with its own particular resonances with both Boasian and Bloomfieldian discourse.[7]

Linguistics as a Generalizing, Comparative Science

The first of Whorf's messages is a joyful celebration of linguistics as a human "science," something exceedingly important to Whorf, who came to the field from applied chemical engineering in the fire insurance business, and even more so to Leonard Bloomfield, who had a particularly bad case of science envy. In such articles as "Linguistics as an Exact Science," the second (of three) he wrote for the MIT alumni readers of *Technology Review*, Whorf (1956e) shows how mutual distributional patterning of formal units—the phonemes—in the phonological structure of English words is highly predictable. He thus demonstrates the power of the Bloomfieldian method that realized the Saussurean vision of language structure as rules for "syntagmatic" compositionality of equivalence-classes or "paradigms" of more elementary linguistic forms. Just like a chemical formula, a symbolic formula for English monosyllables—occurred, occurrent, occurring, and possible of occurrence under this grammatical system, note!—can be fashioned as a formally symbolizable generalization about this particular language's structure. Toward such generalizing descriptions, at all planes of linguistic structure, linguists' "laboratory" work with language consultants ("informants," in the idiom of Whorf's day) is directed, not only for a single language, but for all Language. In his concluding pep talk to outsiders to this field (who were insiders in the world of unquestioned "science"), he seems enthusiastically to endorse the Bloomfieldian translation of the Viennese positivist vision of the universe as susceptible of reduction to two kinds of forces:

> We all know now that the forces studied by physics, chemistry, and biology are powerful and important. People generally do not yet know that the forces studied by linguistics are powerful and important, that its principles control every sort of agreement and understanding among human beings, and that sooner or later it will have to sit as judge while the other sciences bring their results to its court to inquire into what they mean. When this time comes, there will be great and well-equipped laboratories of linguistics as there are of other exact sciences. (Whorf 1956e[1940]:232)

Whorf was articulating this ironically envious, tongue-in-cheek disciplinary boosterism at the end of a decade of the Great Depression to a scientific and technical audience for whom the invisibility of Whorf's linguistic "forces" contrasted with the obviousness of atomic and sub-atomic—"relativistically" conceptualized—forces. The impending Second World War and its Manhattan Project would ultimately make the latter even more salient to the general public as well as to physicists, chemists, and engineers.

In this first Whorfian thematic, the metaphoric and literal vocabulary of "relativity" would be Whorf's mode of introducing the argument common to all Boasian linguistics, practiced by Bloomfield as well as by Sapir and his students. We can summarize its major points as follows:

1. The grammatical categories of any particular language can be revealed only by analysis of distributional "patterning" or "configuration" of formal units one with another, as in Whorf's proposed formula revealing all possible syllable structures for an English monosyllable (see also Bloomfield 1933:130–37). This projects struc-

ture onto otherwise unanalyzed linguistic forms by assuming that linguistic form is to be modeled by an algebra of compositionality.

2. Such categories as we can define by linguistic-analytic methods differ from language to language as a function of the distributional structure of each language. This difference is structure-dependent but manifested in the way that apparent categorizations of the universe of experienceable or imaginable "reality" are projected differently into linguistic form in particular languages (see Boas 1911:24).

3. In terms of such conventional grammatical categories, a fundamental ontic intuition about the simplexes and complexes of the universe of denotation—a "meta-physics," in short—comes into being and is made available to some level of cognitive capacity of the users of a particular language. Languages, then, each seem to contain an implicit ontology as a function of structural factors of mapping from/projecting onto the universe of "reality," the uniqueness and nonlinguistic manifes-tation of which become critical issues.

4. It thus becomes possible to conceptualize gradiently equivalent constructive denotations of extensional "reality"—in effect, semiotically indistinguishable appli-cations of intentional linguistic representations to the universe of prelinguistic experience, save that they con-form to distinct structural starting points, as in two "lan-guages" differing in their fundamental grammatical cat-egories and modes of combining them (notwithstand-ing their use by speakers to achieve comparable deno-tational specificity).[8] This would allow us to "translate" from one structurally distinct language to another in a principled, theoretically grounded way rather than through mere Quinean shortcuts, guesses, and other leaps of "radical translation."

5. Development of linguistics as the field of comparative grammatical-categorial analysis is, therefore, a prerequisite to articulating the nature of the "relativity" of grammatical-ontological categories of different languages and their associated cultures. On this basis one can found a scientific, rational, and potentially universal framework for conceptual understanding among all humanity.

Conceptual "Relativity" Based on "Scientific" Grammatical Categories

"The relativity of all conceptual systems, ours included, and their dependence upon language stand revealed," Whorf tells his MIT peers in "Science and Linguistics" (1956d[1940]:214–15). He makes the Boasian (also Sapirian and Bloomfieldian) brief for the equality of all languages in their status as evidence "as to what the human mind can do" with experiential (or extensional) reality; for that "languages dissect nature in many different ways" at the intentional level is shown in their varying grammatical-categorial structures. He celebrates the existence in one language of directly coded categorial distinctions for certain areas of conceptualizable natural phenomena that are absent in another language. The type example is the coding of events seemingly composed of cyclic iterations, "naturally" occurring in an American Indian language, Hopi, that is at once different from the grammatical categorial structure coding these phenomena in "Standard Average European" languages like English, and at the same time is revealed to be closer to the very model of these phenomena made by the explicit formal-theoretic conceptual structure of alphanumeric "real" physical sciences, such as were familiar to his readership.[9]

In Whorf's less technical discussions, such as "Science and Linguistics" (1956d[1940]) and "Languages and Logic" (1956f[1941]), he used the linguist's method of presenting foreign language examples through the mechanism of glossing. This gives a feel for the strange categorial structure one would more seriously analyze by attempting a lexically focused piece-by-piece (morpheme-by-morpheme) calque of a foreign-language form into the language of the readership. In this way, Whorf attempted to reveal something of the grammatical-categorial structure of complex morphological constructions in polysynthetic and

incorporating languages of North America by keying the areas of denotational relevance of each piece of a complex word-form through a
familiar vernacular English word or phrase, rather than through precise grammatico-semantic terminology. Thus does the category of
'Plural' (as opposed to, say, 'Singular' and 'Dual' in a three-term paradigm of distinctions of 'Number') get glossed by Whorf as "many" or
"more-than-two" by this method of lexical calquing. Of course glossing
has no theoretical or methodological status in the scientific metalanguage of Boasian or any other structurally informed linguistics; it is a
shortcut we still use, attempting through translation of what Whorf
called mere "lexations" to bring two linguistic structures into view for
the naïve professional outsider.[10]

In more technical treatments intended for his linguistic peers,
Whorf makes quite clear that he is dealing with the complexities of
grammatical categories as projected from the Bloomfieldian formalization of the structure of grammars. In this view, apparent, durationally
experienced linguistic forms—what we call "surface segmentable
forms" in the contemporary idiom—are "lexical" expressions (Whorf's
"lexations"), from the smallest segmentable pieces of words up to the
maximal phrase-type, the sentence; they have associated with them certain regularities of denotational meaning. By contrast, from every such
lexical expression can be projected its grammatical organization, stated
in terms of a phonological plane of structure and a morphosyntactic or
more narrowly "grammatical" plane of structure. In order to project
grammatical structure(s) corresponding to (or immanent in, or
"underlying," as we now say) any specific lexical expression, the analyst,
like the native speaker, must know the grammatical structure of the
entire language (see points 1 and 2 above on the system-relativity of the
mappings between grammatical form and sense).

In turn, knowing such grammatical structures for particular languages in the empirical science of linguistics is a function of what we
know about grammatical patternment in general. The discovery of new
modes of such patternment in particular languages contributes to constant revision of our knowledge of patternment in general on a worldwide scale. Such general knowledge Whorf (1956h[1945]) calls "a
general science of grammar" (we now term it "universal grammar" or
"the study of linguistic universals"). He goes on to remark that

Only in such a sense can we speak of a category of "passive voice" which would embrace the forms called by that name in English, Latin, Aztec, and other tongues. Such categories or concepts we may call TAXONOMIC categories, as opposed to DESCRIPTIVE categories. Taxonomic categories may be of the first degree, e.g. passive voice, objective case; or of the second degree, e.g. voice, case. Perhaps those of the second degree are the more important and ultimately the more valuable as linguistic concepts, as generalizations of the largest systemic formations and outlines found in language when language is considered and described in terms of the whole human species. (Whorf 1956h[1945]:100–101)

Linguistics on a "universal" scale seeks in this manner to "calibrate" particular linguistic systems one with another through a framework of taxonomic categories.

Note how Whorf counterposes scientific linguistics, with all its theoretical, methodological, and formal-operational specificities, to the folk conceptualization of language, which he terms "Mr. Everyman's" view of his own language in relation to other people's languages, and which he mocks as naive and unscientific. (Did Whorf perhaps do this to appeal to *Technology Review* readers, linguistic Messrs. Everymen in the "other exact sciences," thus compelling their embarrassed agreement?) This folk view, Whorf says, considers linguistic structure as a "background" phenomenon and focuses on how well a particular language's lexical expressions correspond to the "reality" they denote. Messrs. Everymen compare two or more languages in this respect of referential and predicational "accuracy" or "precision" only in the shallowest and most unscientific terms, by in effect attempting interlinguistic glossing of one lexical expression by another, looking for matches and mismatches.

By contrast, the systematic, scientific study of grammatical-categorial structure reveals what is really transformed and what remains the same in going from one language to another, going from one implicit ontological reference-category framework to another. Linguistics is to provide the systematic and scientifically undertaken basis, the structure of Whorf's "taxonomic categories," to articulate a theory of ontological relativity (in Quine's [1968] felicitous phrase).

94

The Cultural "Mind" in the Language(d) State

There is, thus, a second substantive Whorfian theme that lurks in this discussion: how to account for the clear divergence between the folk views of Mr. Everyman, both on "Language" in general and on specific "languages" in particular, and the scientific views of the Linguist, both on Language in general and on specific categorial structures that linguists attribute to languages despite their lack of transparency to the native-speaker gaze.

The Everybodies that Whorf refers to range from the average MIT graduate to (by name) C. K. Ogden, H. G. Wells, and other well-intended amateur linguistic do-gooders of the 1930s.[11] Why, and how, does there emerge the folk focus on (mere) lexation and (mere) glossing in the face of the implicit richness of crosscutting categorial structuration in language? If, as linguistics purports, such structuration is the major "background" factor allowing the users of language—all of humanity, Whorf (1956d[1940]:212) claims—to use language

> in all our foreground activities of talking and reaching agreement, in all reasoning and arguing of cases, in all law, arbitration, conciliation, contracts, treaties, public opinion, weighing of scientific theories, formulation of scientific results…whether or not mathematics or other specialized symbolisms are made part of the procedure…

If such background phenomena underlie all this, how does the human mind remain unaware of them? How does the aware human intentionality come to the particular understanding it has of its own—and, through a glancing, surface-lexational gloss, of others'—linguistic usage?

Both Boas and Bloomfield had remarked on this limitation-in-principle of linguistic consciousness. Boas takes up the issue in his "Introduction" to the *Handbook of American Indian Languages*, particularly in discussing the "Unconscious Character of Linguistic Phenomena" (Boas 1911:67–73), meaning the categorial phenomena analyzed as part of grammatical descriptions and linguistic history, of which their users have no accurate, conscious, metalevel understanding. Discussing the "misleading and disturbing factors of secondary explanations" that emerge from native consciousness of such categorial phenomena, Boas provides numerous examples to demonstrate that the focus of native consciousness of language is on how lexical expressions, words and phrases, relate directly to the things and situations they appear to denote. He shows how, from the analyst's perspective, the native speaker's misrecognition of language relates to cultural practices both functionally and historically, playing a role also in the native's "secondary rationalistic attempt to explain a custom that otherwise would remain unexplained" (Boas 1911:69)—except, I would add, in anthropological theorizing.

Such secondary rationalizations by people of their own otherwise unconscious habitual customs constitute, for Boas, the principal cultural component of what are the very objects-of-study of most realms of ethnology other than linguistics. This fact privileges language among all such objects of anthropological study both for yielding a "true history" of human thought in the German neo-Kantian tradition (out of which came the disdainful Boas) and for yielding significant generalizations of humanitywide scope, increasingly a hopeless goal for anthropology, in Boas's view, as his career of negatively critical argumentation progressed.[12]

With the stance of the self-celebratory scientist, Bloomfield too takes up the issue of the relationship of native consciousness—generally limited to lexation and gloss—to those pervasive form-class differentiations in a Saussurean grammatical system that he terms formally demonstrable "categories" of the morphological system of grammar, the realm of word-structure. In Language (Bloomfield 1933:270–71) he observes:

> The categories of a language, especially those which affect morphology *(book : books, he : she)* are so pervasive that anyone who reflects upon his language at all, is sure to notice them. In the ordinary case, this person, knowing only his native language, or perhaps some others closely akin to it, may mistake his categories for universal forms of speech, or of "human thought," or of the universe itself. This is why a good deal of what passes for "logic" or "metaphysics" is merely an incompetent restating of the chief categories of the philosopher's language.... Our knowledge of the practical world may show that some linguistic categories agree

with classes of real things…for instance, that our non-linguistic world consists of objects, actions, qualities, manners, and relations, comparable with the substantives, verbs, adjectives, adverbs, and prepositions of our language. In this case it would still be true, however, that many other languages do not recognize these classes in their part-of-speech system. Moreover, we should still have to determine the English parts of speech not by their correspondence with different aspects of the practical world, but merely by their functions in English syntax.….Linguistic categories, then, cannot be defined in philosophical terms.

Bloomfield clearly understands that all the faults of grade-school grammars are but examples of the "metaphysical" tendencies of the Messrs. (and Mmes.) Everybody who see the universe denoted by their language as transparent from the perspective of, or through the lens constructed from within, one highly restricted part of the linguist's sense of the overall structure of the Everybodies' language. As Bloomfield points out, categories of morphological structure that get surface lexical expression so as to constitute words and their internal shapes are at issue in the Everybodies' consciousness. Bloomfield, like Boas, does not seek to explain this phenomenon but only warns against it as a scientific proposition (thus differentiating the "scientific" view of language from that of the Everybodies).[13]

WHERE DO SPECIFICALLY 'CULTURAL' CONCEPTS COME FROM?

Whorf takes up these themes of Boas and Bloomfield in his essay "The Relation of Habitual Thought and Behavior to Language" (1956g), which was originally printed in the 1941 Sapir memorial volume (Spier, Hallowell, and Newman 1941). The substance of the article concerns the "cultural" nature of concepts of 'space' and 'time', ontic categories the prelinguistic, precultural—indeed, absolute—nature of which Bloomfield himself espoused in his 1935 Presidential Address to the Linguistic Society of America (Bloomfield 1987c). Even if Bloomfield had to yield to the special-relativistic sense of 'spacetime' that was becoming the stock-in-trade of quantum physics—and recall that for Bloomfield, the investigable universe consisted of momentum (mass of a certain velocity-in-space) and syntax (categorial structure of language form)—Whorf is articulating here the "new kind of relativity" that epistemologically self-critical scientists would have to take account of, a relativity of "habitual thought" or default conceptualization that emerges from, but is distinct from, linguistic categorial structure.

In the year following Bloomfield's address, as shown in manuscripts published (1956a[1936]) in the collection edited by John B. Carroll, Whorf began to write about the Hopi language as a counterexample to such physicalist, positivist notions of what are presumed by Bloomfield and others to be the 'time' and 'space' universally organized by linguistic denotation. But the 1941 essay is Whorf's ultimate and most subtle development of his second theme, so subtle that it has long been merely assimilated to the equality-and-diversity argument of other writers and of Whorf himself, such as in publications like the *Technology Review* pieces (1956d, 1956e, 1956f) in which he addressed a linguistically and anthropologically uninformed readership in their idiom of "relativity."

Whorf begins by invoking this "linguistic relativity," which is embodied in an epigrammatic quotation from Sapir, the volume's honoree and Whorf's late mentor and patron. The quotation (in Sapir 1949c:162) merely articulates the standard Boasian view; perhaps it was the passage from the master closest to what Whorf was about to spell out, but it surely is on an inferior plane of conceptualization. For Whorf's essay actually goes on to schematize a truly pathbreaking explanation for why there might be culture-specific "metaphysical" concepts, the concepts of the purportedly absolute physical envelope of all our experience available to, for example, the Cartesian—or even Bloomfieldian—intuition.

Grammatical Analogy and Discursive Dialectics

The most sustained argument in Whorf's 1941 essay (1956[1941]) works through specific proposals about the complex, semiotic origin of 'space' and 'time' as "intellectual tools," that is, verbal captions and discursively manifested cognitive concepts that were supposed, by Bloomfield and those who inspired him, to be precultural and prelinguistic intuitions from "nature." In effect, Whorf proposes a seven-part explanation for how such cultural concepts emerge in the language(d) state of humanity. Its main points can be outlined as follows:

1. In the verbally captioned concepts of (meta)physical reality of a cultural group, we are dealing with a "relativity" of conscious, goal-directed language use as people attempt to communicate about normatively informed ("habitual") cultural practices of practical task orientation. This "relativity" emerges at the level of discursive practice (contrast the level of ontology implicit in grammatical categories), in which we can be consciously oriented to making a text-in-context determinately related to that context by representing (referring to and predicating about) it.

2. Such conscious language use in the denotational mode—the mode of describing and evaluating the universe of conceptually graspable "reality"—is biased for each linguistic group (e.g., a sociologically locatable language community) by what Whorf terms "fashions of speaking" about the phenomena of the universe. These fashions of speaking present degrees of phraseological givenness (conventionalization) and distinctness-to-domain ("literalness"); with them we encompass conceptualizable phenomena both familiar and unfamiliar in specific verbal ways, representing them in terms of assumed, or indexically presupposed, categorizations and dimensionalities. (Note that according to Boas and Bloomfield the internal grammatical-categorial structure of any fashion of speaking about a domain of conceptualizable reality will, in general, be transparent only to the analytic gaze of the linguist.)

3. The conscious native-speaker sense of the transparency of the universe to representation by one's own language, and perhaps to language in general, is a function of (a) language's fashions of speaking, through which the universe makes itself manifest to the speaker and which thus guide the conscious, common sense of the representability of the universe in language and its dependent representational systems.

4. Any fashion of speaking is a sociohistorical product that over the course of cultural process reaches a certain generativity (positive feedback toward emergent consistency in dealing with unfamiliar situations in new domains of representation). To the outsider, this looks like "metaphorical" transfer of fashions of speaking. Increasingly, a fashion of speaking that encompasses what at first might have been conceptualized as new domains of representation is understood as a straightforward, "literal" formulation of a fundamental aspect of the universe of experience.

5. At least in one central functional component, this generativity of a fashion of speaking is driven by apparent "analogy"—a technical linguistic concept (cf. Bloomfield 1933:275–77, 404–24; Silverstein 1978:245n26, 249n31)—within a grammatical system. Analogy results in the apparent (re)analysis of one surface (lexical) form in terms of the grammatical-categorial and related structural features of another form or class of forms in system-determinate ways. The existence of what we might term 'analogic forces' among surface lexical forms is dependent on how configurated structural categorizations are projectible from those surface lexical forms, with degrees of 'analogic force' (tendencies for imposition of reanalysis) depending on multiple such factors.

6. A growth point of a fashion of speaking involves essentially the working of analogic forces that make plausible for speakers of a language the projective misrecognition of the grammatical structure in the lexation targeted for analogic change, as we would describe such categorial structure with the usual machinery of grammar. This constitutes a predictive theory of analogy across fashions of speaking that inherently involves the structure of language in the technical linguistic sense, which is one of its points of origin.

7. The other, discursive and representational component of the generativity of a fashion of speaking is the practical, action-centered use of language in concrete situations of rational "thought," where linguistic expressions seem to their users to be indexically anchored to situations they are used to represent. To the speakers, language forms in actual use seem to be a metalanguage for the realia they describe. Critical to such beliefs in indexical anchoring is the ultimate authorization of the language-form-to-exemplar-of-reality, the "baptismal" (Kripke 1972) situation. Here, what we term a 'performative nomination' combined, perhaps, with a 'representative declarative', gives the fashion of speaking its originary denotational value in relation to an indexed aspect of reality. It does so upon validated use by someone socioculturally endowed with the authority so to do (a priestly incumbent, as it were, such as "scientist," "clergy," "judge," or "umpire").

It is through such a chain of connections—obvious to any thoughtful theoretician in the Boasian-Bloomfieldian milieu in which Whorf worked—that we can understand the argumentative movement in Whorf's discourse about cultural categories (see also Lucy 1992b:45–61). He starts from some linguistically simple fire insurance examples from the Hartford Insurance Company and moves, analogically, to the complex argument contrasting English and Hopi "space" and "time."

Starting from the simple analogies of fashions of speaking grammatically constructed as (adjectival) modifier plus (nominal) modified, Whorf demonstrates a semantic relation of denotational class inclusion between expressions constructed with the unmodified noun and expressions with the modified one. This productive and compositionally regular taxonomic relation of unmodified to modified compound head is the basis for a strong analogic force on any expression that seems to native-speaker cognition of language to be analyzable as modifier plus modified. Lo and behold, reconstructing the reasoning behind certain tragedies as analogy-based (based, that is, in language and not in "reality"), Whorf shows such analogic "error" to be consistent with the fire-insurance investigator's story of someone's carelessness that led to the origins of a blaze.

Thus the proper or "literal" class of denotata coded in the nominal head-word limestone- (itself a compound stem headed by the stem stone-), should bear a taxonomic relationship of class inclusion to the class of denotata of the modifier-plus-modified nominal construction, spun limestone-, with its modifying adjective being the passive participle of the transitive verb spin-. So 'spun limestone' ought, analogically, to denote a class of things that is basically a subclass of the class of things conceptualized as 'limestone', by virtue of 'having undergone spinning'. Here, grammatical analogy directs the cognition with respect to the denotatum of the expression spun limestone in instances of practical agency with respect to it, informed by this phrase as the "fashion of speaking" about the substance in industrial use, rather than by specific formulaic knowledge of its chemical composition—which turns out to be anything but 'stone'. And hence, to the commonsensical folk rationalist, the properties of the stuff, "spun limestone," which entail certain possibilities for "rational" action with respect to it, must subsume those fundamental to how one conceptualizes "limestone" and even "stone," the analogic foundational forms.

Seeking to contrast cultural concepts of "space" and "time," Whorf eventually looks to different cultures of mensuration, the institutional focus on practical acts of measurement that result in rational, denotational use of verbal expressions as "fashions of speaking" about a society's measurable phenomena. Such expressions of 'numerosity' or 'extent' or 'degree' are projectible as an area of grammatical construction we call Measure Phrases.[14] Whorf shows by example that using Measure Phrases in English implicates the grammatical fact of two great polar 'selective' (obligatorily distinguished) classes of nouns, the way these classes occur in Measure Phrases constituting for the grammarian their key differentiating diagnostic.[15] One such polar class, so-called Count Nouns (member: tree-), permits direct quantification with numerals, as in the three trees; the other polar class, so-called Mass Nouns (member: wood-), requires a special phrasal construction, as in the three blocks of wood.

Now Whorf, recall, is after the language- and culture-specific influences on the way explanatory concepts emerge in native theorizing to rationalize the applicability of denotational phrases to practical situations. He hypothesizes that there is a strong analogical pressure on speakers to understand the Measure Phrases for Mass Nouns in terms of the more basic but completely distinct structural (grammatical) arrangement of the same categories of lexical forms like the three statues of wood, the nine events of reference, the five matters of (some) delicacy, the seven consequences of truth, the two gentlemen of Verona, that is, noun phrases expressing material composition, manner, instrumentality, origin, provenance, and so on. In the latter type of phrase, each of the two constituent-heading nouns, for example, statue and wood, has its fullest, most autonomous semantic value, denotationally most transparent to the universe it describes from its canonical (or "literal") value of lexical categorization. One can even have appropriate plurals of either Count or Mass Nouns in the modifying phrase, as in the eight sculptures of finishing nails.

This structure of the noun phrase of material composition, with its pluralization of the Count noun that serves as its head, becomes what we call the "founding form" for the analogic folk interpretation of Measure Phrases involving Mass nouns. Note that the latter grammatically require a quasi-classifier Measure-Phrase noun to code semantic 'numerosity' of the denotata of the Mass noun ('singular' vs. 'plural' in English); this serves, moreover, as the grammatical head of the phrase for projecting agreement to verbs, and so on. In this way, Whorf reasons, the nouns in such phrases as (four) blocks of wood, (two) cups of sugar, (ten) board-feet of pine, seem plausibly to native speakers to be transparent lexical codings folk concepts of "dimensionalized, though essenceless, bounded configuration-s"—"block-s," "cup-s," "board-feet"— of "otherwise formless and nonbounded stuff, or essence"—"wood," "sugar," "pine." Whorf argues that linear, planar, and volumetric spatial measure terms like cubit, hectare, pint, and so forth, ultimately take on the folk-conceptual characteristics of the sequentially first nouns in Mass Measure Phrases, understood then to be bounded, recurrent as well as possibly concurrent, dimensionalized entities in an otherwise nonbounded realm of stuff (essence, the "[a]ether") called "space."

In the West, the invention of practical techniques of coordinating social intervals of experience and experienceable durations, "time"-

reckoning with clock mechanisms, has from the outset (ca. 1271 C.E.) depended upon linear or angular measures of distance traversed by a nonaccelerating indicator on a metricized background. Mediated over nearly six centuries by the evolution of increasingly authoritative mensurational practices centered on clock-mechanisms, the gradual "Standard Average European" (SAE) development of an elaborate, distinctively usable Measure Phrase terminology is an indicator of the emergence of a commonsensical, intuitively obvious and rational folk conceptualization of another nonbounded stuff, called "time," with its strongly presupposed linear dimensionalization.[16]

Whorf's point is that the cultural concepts of "space" and of "time" are just that: cultural concepts. For Whorf they emerged in the dialectic sociohistorical process between, on the one hand, language used (to its users) rationally and rationalizably as a way of representing the universe and of reasoning about it, and on the other hand, the universe of phenomena so represented. Someone's analogically driven use of an existing "fashion of speaking" about phenomena performatively baptizes some new situation as the parallel figuration ("metaphor") of something already encountered. In turn, this newly extended mode of representation is enriched with a whole new area of eventually "literal" denotational value from the analogical growth of the figuration in the new context. Whorf has, in a sense, given a constructive, dialectical account of Peircean 'abduction', that is, of empiricism in relation to theoretical concepts. His account gives the intersection of analogical process and grammatical-categorial structure the privileged generative capacity of the dialectic, though we must not forget the role of sociocultural practices, authoritatively centered, as absolutely necessary to the dialectic he hypothesized.

"Time," Tense, and Time

Such folk-theoretic concepts of "space" and "time" are particularly valuable for the Whorfian approach not merely as a reaction against Bloomfield and his Vienna Circle jingoism; they also allow Whorf to place the SAE metaphysics he sees therein in two fields of contrast. First, in this same paper (1956g[1941]), he contrasts a Hopi metaphysics of emergence to culmination in ordinal-like event series. He claims that this Hopi metaphysics does not distinguish "space" from "time" in the same way SAE metaphysics does. If SAE temporal practices dialectically emerge as congenial to the folk metaphysics of "time," Whorf sees a comparable fit in Hopi. Hopi cultural practices are carried on with respect to such emergent culminations (what we call, in SAE, events involving entities occurring at such-and-such time and place), and hence human agency involves the kinds of culturally understood "forces" with their applicable degrees of intensity that can be brought to bear on emergent culmination.

Second, Whorf rests his analysis of the culture-specific metaphysics of "space" and "time" on the contrasting analysis of the relevant grammatical coding categories in the two respective languages, against a backdrop of universal grammar. English is a language having Tense, Aspect, and a hybrid category of Perfection as regular grammatical categories of the predicating phrase; Hopi is a language having multiple layers of Aspect and a category of sender-receiver calibrated Epistemic Status. (Early on, Whorf calls the latter "tenses" and later rectifies this to "assertions"; see 1956b[1938]:113–15.) There is, for Whorf, a chasm between what universal grammar tells us about the way the grammatical machinery of Tense × Aspect × Perfection operates in English as an exemplary SAE language, and the native conceptualization of the transparency of this system to the folk concept of "time."

We can now see rather sharply, as few among Whorf's earlier addressees could, that he is talking the Boasian talk about contrasting ways that language structure is implemented in practical situations of denotation so as to give a compositional reading of the modalized referential-and-predicational values of particular grammatical categorial structures. These are, by our first Whorfian theme, different from language to language. And yet, in the Boasian or Bloomfieldian framework, he is able to compare two languages to show that each has sufficient formal machinery to encompass any practical demand of denotation, though their grammatical-categorial dimensions in particular empirical circumstances will, of course, differ.

Whorf's famous chart from "Science and Linguistics" (1956d [1940]:213) compares English and Hopi constructions used to communicate certain calibrated observations of an event or state of affairs. English uses its formal-categorial space of Tense × Aspect × Perfection, while Hopi uses its formal-categorial space of Aspect × Epistemic Status.

Both languages are "perfect"—or, equivalently, equally "imperfect"—grammatical engines for describing various practical situations, since they leave out certain differentiations as much as they include others. Where they differ is in how individual practical situations are, in effect, implicitly grouped or classified through the application of descriptive language to represent and reason about them. Whorf's chart shows this difference of grouping in contrasting English and Hopi.

Since English has Tense as an elementary and obligatory grammatical inflection within the predicating piece of a sentence (making at least one lexical verb in the sentence "finite"), we must consider, with Whorf, the difference, even disjunction, between the grammatical category of Tense and the "time" concept that speakers of English within the SAE metaphysics ascriptively see as its transparent realm of denotation. Tense is, by definition, an indexical-denotational taxonomic category. It indexes—points to—the occurrence of some reference-event and presents some denoted state of affairs as occurring in sequence with the reference-event ('prior-to' or 'subsequent-to' it) or nonsequentially, generally understood as 'simultaneous-with' the reference-event. Some tense systems distinguish only two specific paradigmatic values of Tense, a Past ('prior-to') versus non-Past (not 'prior-to'; by implicature, a Present-Future), as in English. Or they distinguish a Future ('subsequent-to') versus a non-Future (not 'subsequent-to'; by implicature, a Present-Past). Some languages, such as French, distinguish three such values, a Past, a Future, and the residual, unmarked "present" by markedness implicature. As William Bull (1960) has shown, systems become increasingly complicated by creating simultaneity/sequentiality relations between predicated states of affairs and second- and third-order reference events—themselves presupposed (indexed) to bear certain computable simultaneity/sequentiality relations with the default reference-event on which the whole system rests.

But if Tense involves only a relationship of simultaneity/sequentiality of events, one an indexed reference-event, the "here-and-now" of the presupposed communicational event in the primordial default case, how do people get the idea that Tense is "about 'time'?" Moreover, how do people get the idea that Tense is "about" (i.e., codes) what Whorf sees as "objectified" time, where "[c]oncepts of time lose contact with the subjective experience of 'becoming later' and are objectified as counted QUANTITIES, especially as lengths, made up of units as a length can be visibly marked off into inches" (1956g[1941]:140)? This is a very culturally local phenomenon, according to Whorf, in which the practical techniques of denoting experienceable durations of simultane-ities/sequentialities—by measure phrases in the linguistic realm, by clocks and such paraphernalia in the nonlinguistic realm—are brought to bear on the folk interpretation of the deictic grammatical category that points to this experience of simultaneity/sequentiality of dura-tions (event-intervals).

So the folk-practical and folk-conceptual realms of the infinitely divisible and mensurable timeline become the culture-specific back-drop for SAE folk interpretation of Tense, which, as an indexical deno-tational category, confirms the complexly produced intuition of "time" by seeming, to folk consciousness, to invoke it and point to it each time (!) we use an instance of a Tense category. It is an intuition that is his-torically locatable for Whorf in the emergence of clock and calendar techniques, as shown by the etymological rise of "time" words for the interval measures out of two different elements of earlier periods' cul-tural sense of simultaneity/sequentiality: (1) words and expressions that come from the linear, planar, and spherical geometries involved in iconic representations of motion-marked durations, for example, lengths of knotted ropes in water clocks or angular distances on circu-lar planes representing a cycle, such as (pars) minuta '1/60th part of a degree [of angular distance]'...>...Mod.F. minute; and (2) words and expressions that come from older notions of natural and social dura-tions within cycles, and their conventional subdivisions, for example, 'season', Greek ho:ra: taken into Latin as ho:ra...>...O.Fr./Mid.E (h)oure '1/12th of "natural" day [=light time]'.

Over centuries, terms that came from these two etymological sources became mutually calibrated in the practice of using Measure Phrases, for example the 'hour' (source 2) getting a fixed equiva-lence in 'minutes', 'seconds', etc. (source 1). Such a uniformity of grammaticosemantic usage of temporal terms in measure phraseol-ogy goes together with the emergent interpretation of them within the same "fashion of speaking." But this is the very emergent concep-tualization of a homogeneous envelope of-and-for eventhood, "time," in coding which these newly semanticized words emerge as pluralizable (Count category) head-nouns, as in <u>three</u> <u>minutes</u> (of "time").

From a strictly grammatical point of view, Tense is a configurational category unconcerned with any such direct and joint mensurability, continuity, and scalar or vectorial directionality of "time" as such, an etymological course established for the "time" words. This association is made plausible through the Whorfian disease of native speakers of SAE languages in the habitual world of SAE practices-as-representable. In the SAE "habitual thought" microcosm, as Whorf terms it, Tense transparently and locally codes "time" for its native speakers.

Homogeneous SAE space-time, in which we conceptualize ourselves to be "situated" in our habitual thought world, according to Whorf, though there is no specifically grammatical-categorial evidence for this in our systems of deictics. There is only the complex, analogically driven process whereby culturally specific concepts, and particularly culturally specific verbalizable concepts, emerge from the dialectic of grammatically anchored linguistic discourse and institutionally centered social practice, mediated by verbal and equivalent representational practices of both. By a kind of projective imagination, native speakers in such cultural universes "discover" that what is coded by expressions for these concepts are the essences of which "reality" is composed. This discovery is based on interpreting the indexical categories that anchor language to contexts of use with the aid of these discovered essences. For native speakers, then, indexical categories point to (presuppose) the very frameworks of essential properties of the universe that are revealed to habitual thought in fashions of speaking about the reality worked in/on by social practices. The unilingual cultural universe, though dialectic in its working, is ultimately quite closed in its efflorescence.

THE THEME NOT TAKEN

There is thus the third theme, darkly announced at the unhappy conclusion of Whorf's life, that perhaps all of the calibration of languages—and through language, of any form of cultural semiosis—is impossible because we just do not know how much of our own "calibration" of one grammatical categorial system with another through taxonomic categories of universal grammar rests on chimerical schemata of equivalently folk-theoretic emergents, as we have seen with "time" in SAE. That is to say, we are uncertain of the extent to which this Whorfian dialectic applies to grammarians' concepts about language structure as an object of practical focus, thus making them folk concepts rather than properly scientific ones. This dubiety into which Whorf leads us is the stance of what I term nihilistic relativism. It can be argued against not on general philosophical grounds, of course (viz. the folly of much postmodernist deconstructivism in launching the "Science Wars"), but only constructively, that is, empirically and pragmatically, by studying such phenomena. I will not have anything further to say about this third, deconstructive Whorfian theme in what follows.

OUR IMAGINATIONS, OUR SELVES

It should now be clear to those conversant with Anderson's *Imagined Communities* (1983, 1991) that an elaborate Whorfianism underlies its conceptualization of the cultural form in which "the magic of nationalism ... turn[s] chance into destiny" (1983:19; 1991:12). Within such a cultural order, nationality is a primordial aspect of one's very sense of selfhood. This primordiality appears to emerge out of an ontic realm beyond the contingent one of historical circumstances and happenings, such as one's birth or one's first job or any other life-event. To the subjectivity Anderson characterizes, nationality perdures above and beyond all these as a kind of essence of one's selfhood realized in and through such contingencies. Anderson's account locates the magic essence in what Whorf would term an unshakable metaphysical commitment that establishes the nationalist subjectivity.

And indeed, in the text, we do find two characteristic Whorfian themes. On the one hand linguistic and language-laden (or language-"relayed" [Barthes 1967:10]) representations, genres of text, contexts of interaction, and social-institutional structures form the central evidentiary material for Anderson's argument. On the other hand, the fields on which nationalism's imagination plays and the very figurations that dynamically comprise its game are crucially spatiotemporal at both literal and tropic planes: geopolitical areas and their maps, censuses, and other museologized/archivized exhibits; collective and aggregate events-in-time and their historiographies; people's synchronic—and synchronizable—memberships in groups, emblematically represented and performatively renewed; and so forth. By my count, twenty-one of Anderson's textual passages crucial to understanding his argument concern space-time and its structuring by and through nationalism as mediated by such language-laden semiotic forms; virtually all the rest straightforwardly address other, framing aspects of language and its textualized discursive forms. Here truly are exemplified the ingredients in social practices with which Whorf's most innovative discussions are fashioned about the ideological underpinnings of concepts of space and time.

In good Whorfian fashion, Anderson's *Reflections on the Origin and Spread of Nationalism,* as the book is subtitled, chronicles the emergence some two centuries ago of a cultural order of 'nationality' in the mediated image of its underlying linguistic order. The conditions of this emergence were essentially discursive in the Foucauldian sense; they comprised, centrally, (1) print-capitalist production, circulation, and consumption of (2) text-artifacts (newspapers, broadsides, pamphlets, novels, etc.) bearing (3) texts genred in realistically reportive voicings and composed in (4) standardized or emergently standardizing vernacular languages.[17] I will discuss each of these four intersecting preconditions of the nationalist "imagination" below.

Anderson goes on to describe the efflorescence of variant forms of nationalism as the cultural order these preconditions have licensed, and their global spread in distinct periods during the nineteenth and twentieth centuries. But notwithstanding the historical presentation, Anderson clearly believes that there is something common to the cultured phenomenology of the nationalist subject, itself in a way a condition perduring through global time and space: Everywhere it is a cultural order corresponding to an inclusive political entity that provides each social being with the essential property of national identity. And the cultural phenomenology of nationalism operates, Anderson theorizes, by projecting and constructing a homogeneous space-time of distinctive, differential membership. In this space-time every individual in a national population can be simultaneously located in relation to any other; and such bounded groupness as a habitable space-time—both synchronically and diachronically, as it were—is to be contrasted with that of any other such groups imagined to be included in other possible groupings of this overall cultural order (as one can note in the phrase, "the community of nations," for example, denoting that higher-order, overall space-time of space-times). Nationality is a taxonomy of differentiation of individuals as members of such groups, together with essentialized nondifferentiation of individuals within group boundaries.[18]

In practice a kind of classification that corresponds to having or seeking certain political rights, nationalism is thus a cultural phenomenon of very large, non-face-to-face social formations, in what we might term the superstructural order of collective consciousness. According to Anderson, it emerges from the way particular politicoeconomic modes of generating and circulating (particularly verbal) representations effect a "worldview." Nationalist worldview is experienced as a metaphysical sense of the primordiality of one's membership in the homogeneous groupness commonly associated with (or expressed by) a polity such as a nation-state. And there are nationalisms without nation-states in comparable "nationalist" cultural orders, for example so-called stateless nationalities, for whom an obvious telos is the achievement of autonomous nation-statehood. Within the contemporary United States, furthermore, comparable imaginations underlie concepts of ethnicity in particular. Increasingly, they also underlie how one imagines *any* demographically based dimension of identity as projecting one into a homogeneous, inhabitable attribute-space presupposed for collective political action, for denoting which the term "community" is in current use in the American English idiom.[19]

Anderson never makes clear if he is presenting a merely historical argument or a functional/evolutionary one. As a historical claim he would be contending that 'nationalism' emerged in the colonial Western Hemisphere periphery to the English and Spanish metropoles in the mid-to-late eighteenth century and that all further developments follow as mere events set into motion. The functional/evolutionary view would be that, where certain conditions are met, 'nationalism' emerges as a cultural form, a "worldview" of identity available to become linked to a political project. These conditions centrally involve the double mediation of print capitalism (or perhaps its electronic equivalents as well), aligned as both the axial institutionalization of discursive practice and a paradigmatic capitalism of production-circulation-consumption of commodities among "the reading classes" (Anderson 1983:73, 1991:75–76). Certainly, Anderson appeals to nationalisms "genuine" and "spurious," as Sapir (1949a) might call them. For he differentiates as phases of nationalism's historical course a kind of dialectical movement over time: first, implementing their rational, representationalist outlook and insight, the self-liberating bourgeois movements (good guys) that, second, seem to give way, particularly in the face of dynastic and imperial nation-statist forces (bad guys), to the cynical use of the now "modularized" paraphernalia of a kind of ersatz, merely ritual(ized) nationalism, so as to yield in turn, third, to local self-liberating possibilities of newly emergent, frequently postcolonial "creole" bourgeoisies (generally good guys). Such alternating-phase periodization in Anderson's story of the nineteenth and twentieth centuries sets up a dialectic internal to nationalist dynamics. But even this story seems to be presented as a "natural" or functionalist-evolutionary (Hegelian) dialectic of phases of the inevitable expression of "genuine" nationalism, the kind that is dependent on the functional relationships at the heart of Anderson's Whorfian analysis, to which I now turn.

THE DISCURSIVE REGIME OF NATIONALIST DEIXIS AND VOICING

Brought back to the realm of actual discourse and language, Anderson seems to be describing an imaginative sense underlying people's use of the verbal medium that "metaphysically"—in a term used by Whorf—presupposes the primordiality of "nationalist space-time." Distinct from the corporeally centered space-time of mere organismal physicality, this space-time has become a new contextual framing available for a definitive, or authoritative, indexical denotation using the personal deictic 'we'—in both "inclusive" and "exclusive" uses—and its equivalents in other languages. The nationalist 'we' concept differs from ones that preceded it; it emerges in particular places and spreads over the course of history.

This seems comparable to Whorf's SAE language users, for whose intuition, he inferred, Newtonian "space" and "time" externalize, systematize, and label concepts of "reality" that are pointed to by their related deictic (indexical denotational) categories, Locative-

Demonstratives for "space" and Tenses for "time." The Measure Phrases, or mensural expressions, of their language, by which SAE speakers denote extents of "space" and thence "time," play a mediating role in constituting this speaker-subjectivity of deixis. As was noted above, mensural expressions enter into analogical alignments as "fashions of speaking" about realities grounded in actual human actions-in-the-world calibrated to clock-ritual. Such mensural expressions orient speakers to a particular presupposed concept of "space" and of "time" in which these realms take on the properties of 'formless substances'—vast, homogeneous, all-enveloping. And, having indexical-denotational (deictic) categories aligned distinctively with "space" and "time," SAE speakers come to depend on the transparency of their pointing to the intuitively (and analogically) construed experiential context they understand to be confirmed also through the authoritative use of Measure Phrases.

Observe, then, how Whorf recovers this process that generates a set of cultural "physical" concepts (which he casts as "metaphysical") underlying deixis with categories of Tense and Locatives-Demonstratives. He seeks the denotational backing of these categories, the very shared conceptual warrants for speakers' regular use of them in acts of referring and predicating. He finds this backing in the ethnometapragmatics, the folk construal that projects transparency-to-context, of the structures implicit in Measure Phrases and other comparable expressions for talking about "space" and "time"; speakers assume this is the same "reality" determined by deictics. This characteristic speaker's assumption of universally available transparency of these verbal forms to pragmatic context of usage we might rephrase as an 'objective' framing of such mensural discourse. It is a stance presumed of both sender and receiver of such discourse with respect to the "reality" one is communicating about. It is, as Goffman (1979) would have it, an inclusive and objectivizing 'footing'; as Bakhtin (1981) might point out, it is an inclusively realist representational 'voicing' of factual states of affairs.

Seeing Whorf's argument in this way, as shown in the left column of figure 3.1, we can draw the parallel to Anderson's argument about the nationalist worldview, diagrammed in the right column. Here the deictic categories centrally involved shift from Locative-Demonstratives and Tense in Whorf's argument to categories of Person in Anderson's.

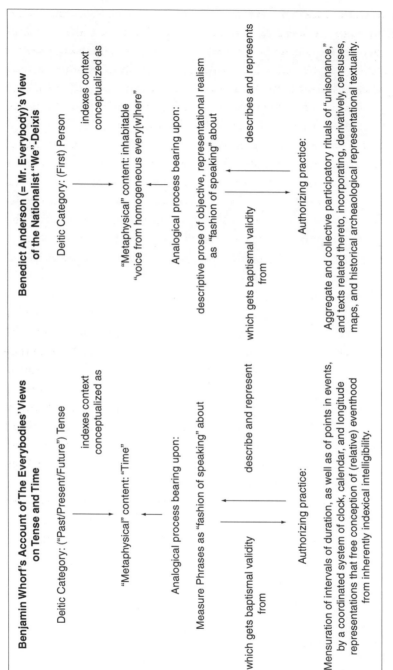

FIGURE 3.1

Schematic of B. L. Whorf's account of tense-deixis in Standard Average European, compared to B. R. Anderson's account of nationalist "we"-deixis.

In particular, Anderson's nationalist's indexical presupposition is mediated through the so-called First Person Plural, that is, the locus in the category-space of Person 5 Number that denotes the speaker or sender of a message as the defining member of a larger set of denoted individuals: speaker plus other(s). Anderson's point is that even where such first-person plural deixis is not explicit (though in much nationalist rhetoric, of course, it is), nationalism is an imaginative sense of Bakhtinian "we-voicing" that pragmatically frames whatever is narrated in its presupposition of unity of outlook. It is a denotational backing (framework of shared conceptual warrants) for first person plural deixis where this occurs, but it emerges in and from its own kind of discursive regime, according to Anderson. This "we"-ness constructs a normative consciousness that inclusively shares with others' consciousnesses a particular, homogeneous, nationalist space-time—a set of distinct, spatiotemporal, nationality-based presuppositions within a narrator's and a narratee's intersubjective normative consciousness.

Anderson thus recognizes the foundational evidentiary role of discourse in his survey of nationalisms. His discussion points us to the communicating "voice," that is to say, to the way that discourse indexically serves to position and group communicators, those communicated to, and the persons/things communicated about ("senders," "receivers," and "referents" in a communications-model taxonomy of basic inhabitable roles) in a common, essentially spatiotemporalized envelope of inhabitable mutual positionings. With Bakhtin (1981) and Williams (1983), he can recognize narrative realism as modern nationalism's most characteristic "chronotope" of voicing.[20]

So Anderson treats the opening passage of Jose Rizal's 1887 novel *Noli Me Tangere*, "today…regarded as the greatest achievement of modern Filipino literature" (1983:32, 1991:26), the first three paragraphs of which he quotes in English translation:

> Towards the end of October, Don Santiago de los Santos, popularly known as Capitan Tiago, was giving a dinner party. Although, contrary to his usual practice, he had announced it only that afternoon, it was already the subject of every conversation in Binondo…
>
> The dinner was being given at a house on Analoague Street. Since we do not recall the street number, we shall describe it in such

a way that it may still be recognized—that is, if earthquakes have not yet destroyed it. We do not believe that its owner will have had it torn down, since such work is usually left to God or to Nature, which, besides, holds many contracts with our Government.

"Extensive comment is surely unnecessary," Anderson observes (1983:32–33, 1991:27–28), for

> [i]t should suffice to note that right from the start the image (wholly new to Filipino writing) of a dinner-party being discussed by hundreds of unnamed people, who do not know each other, in quite different parts of Manila, in a particular month of a particular decade, immediately conjures up the imagined community. And in the phrase 'a house on Analoague Street' which 'we shall describe in such a way that it may still be recognized,' the would-be recognizers are we—Filipino—readers. The casual progression of this house from the 'interior' time of the novel to the 'exterior' time of the [Manila] reader's everyday life gives a hypnotic confirmation of the solidity of a single community, embracing characters, author and readers, moving onward through calendrical time. Notice too the tone. While Rizal has not the faintest idea of his readers' individual identities, he writes to them with an ironical intimacy, as though their relationships with each other are not in the smallest degree problematic.

The imagined community is the very envelope that "embrac[es] characters [as referents], author [as narrating sender] and readers [as narrated-to addressees]," all "moving onward through calendrical [i.e., SAE] time." This envelope, Anderson argues, has a particular and primordial (absolutely presupposable) character under a regime of nationalist imagination. It has the character of a homogeneous, bounded, continuous, and mensurable space-time in which the inhabitable frame of events of narrating (from which biographical author and readers step into the roles of sender-receivers) and the inhabited frame of events-as-narrated (where characters live as denoted referents) are not just indexically calibratable, but indeed are assumed and felt to be continuous one with another.[21]

There is thus a larger and inclusive framing of "we" out of which the

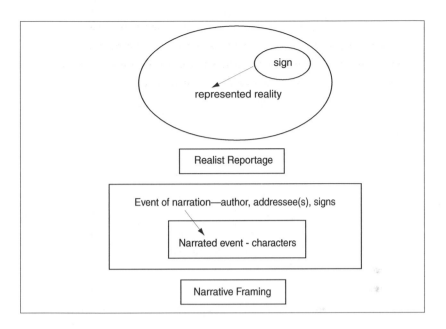

FIGURE 3.2

"Voicing" in realist reportage, schematically contrasted with the general role structure of narrative framing.

explicit narrative differentiation of "I/we," "you," and "he/she/it/they" (and even of the implicit voicing alignments that pragmatically correspond) is but a momentary configuration of communicative-role contingencies against a backdrop of uniformity. Contingencies like people's reportable events happen in history; they are temporal. People's membership in the presupposed space-time envelope is primordial and, in this contrastive sense, outside of any narratable time; indeed, such membership is sacred, a point emphasized in many nationalist rituals and other essentializing moves. Anderson's "we"-envelope of nationalism is thus a double de-diachronicization, an imagination that, manifesting itself in narration, synchronicizes membership in the community not only for potential consociates but even across vast orders of spatiotemporal change.

It is the kind of imagination whose "voicing" is caught in one of C. S. Peirce's most splendid images of an "indexical icon": someone using a stick in the sand of an island beach can scratch out an accurate map of that very island of which the sand and the beach are parts.[22] Differentiating representing microcosm and represented macrocosm in this Peircean image, let us note that the microcosm as constituted in and by the act of inscribing the map is a text produced in an act of communication that draws for its representational matrix on the same "stuff" as is being characterized in the macrocosm. At the same time, of course, the representing text constitutes the framing macrocosm within which the represented world of events-as-narrated exists as a microcosm of the imagination. The transduction of the strongly presupposed indexical relation of Peirce's image into the seemingly inverted, strongly entailed indexical relation that brings a narrated world into being through language is accomplished through the magic of "we"-voicing.

As figure 3.2 schematizes Anderson's analysis, the micro-/macro-relations are constituted between two frames of events. First, there is the frame of the event of narration, for example through the production, circulation, and consumption of a text-artifact like a book with a story communicated between author and reader(s). Second, there is the frame of the "real," that is, verisimilitudinous events-as-narrated, involving characters in various situations who are plausible inhabitants of the same space-time of circumstances as the individuals recruited as sender(s) and receiver(s) to the very event of narrative entextualization. But such is the utterable or even merely voiced "we" of report—even of 'reportively calibrated' (Silverstein 1993:49–50) fiction—in nationalist realism, according to Anderson, that the narrated-about characters, even the fictive characters, might as well be the folks next door, or even ourselves.

LOCATABILITIES AND LEGIBILITIES

If this sounds like Whorf's discoveries about our culture in SAE fashions of speaking, it should. Whorf wrote about what he terms a homogeneous yet mensurable "Newtonian space-time." Whatever its "truth" or pragmatic utility, it happens to be the cultural way SAE folks indexically experience their relationship to a dimensionalized physical universe about which, through acts of indexically grounded description, they can nevertheless reach a Cartesian metaphysical certitude.

Anderson's conceptualization of the nationalist chronotope adds a further, mystical dimension of homogeneous and even sometimes mensurable "we"-ness to the SAE Newtonianism. It more or less explicitly locates nationalism's historical emergence in the rise of a particular kind of bourgeois consciousness in a particularly structured Habermasian (1989) "public sphere" of discursive practice, where that type of communicative "rationality" that depends on reportive calibration under an objectivizing denotational realism becomes the standard-informing linguistic usage par excellence.

Bringing self-consciousness of identities together with indexical empiricism, Anderson's rationality of reportage is seen to be an expository style of an agentive empirical intentionality. It is, in short, the speaker's imagination (metaphysical presupposition) of inhabiting objectivity from anywhere within the confines of the group who share the chronotope. It is discursively like the much-vaunted expository stance of empirical science and other democratically "revealed" truths.[23] Normally, matters of relational identity are central to problematized footing and voicing in normal day-to-day social interaction—who one is and with whom one is communicating with respect to various contextualizing frameworks of social organization that determine centers of power, lines of discursive authorization, and so on. These are erased as factors or at least relegated to subsidiary status in the nationalist worldview of the underpinnings of communicative practice.

In effect, the practical discursive activity "literally" realizable in this nationalist stance (or footing or voice) is always already presupposed and presupposable as the shared orientational norm of agentive consciousness. Even "fiction" is encompassed in this chronotope, since figurative discourse can be experienced as a development out of the other, "expository" types by presupposing that the chronotopic parameters of the latter are the basis of tropically transformed denotational effect (thus, moving from "literal" to "metaphorical" locations within the chronotope). It is therefore possible to voice fiction with respect to the same presuppositions as one does scientific reportage. It is certainly possible to read and interpret fiction in this fashion, in an unproblematically scientistic approach that concentrates on indexically calibrating the denotation, without ever breaking out of the presupposed "unisonance" of pragmatic framing.

Indeed, Anderson characterizes the experiencing consciousness internal to nationalism, the "habitual thought-world," as it were, of the cultural phenomenology of nationalism, in compellingly vivid linguistic terms (1983:74; 1991:76–77):

> The pre-bourgeois ruling classes generated their cohesions in some sense outside language, or at least outside print language.... But the bourgeoisie? Here was a class which, figuratively speaking, came into being as a class only in so many replications. Factory-owner in Lille was connected to factory-owner in Lyon only by reverberation. They had no necessary reason to know of one another's existence; they did not typically marry each other's daughters or inherit each other's property. But they did come to visualize in a general way the existence of thousands and thousands like themselves through print-language. For an illiterate bourgeoisie is scarcely imaginable. Thus in world-historical terms bourgeoisies were the first classes to achieve solidarities on an essentially imagined basis.

"[A]n essentially imagined basis," Anderson notes, "limited by vernacular legibilities." Thus nationalism became "a 'model' of the independent national state...available for pirating" by "the marginalized vernacular-based coalitions of the educated" (1981;78; 1991:81) everywhere, just as he hypothesizes was first the case in the Americas.

The achievement of "imagined" solidarities, then, depends on mutual, even fictively mutual, imagination through inscribed and legible representations in which both the similarities and the differences underlying "we"-ness could be made and ordered. The condition of Anderson's "nationalism" seems to be one of a cultural consciousness of self- and other-placement in a dimensionalized space of uniform and interchangeable membership in an (extensionally) aggregated, (intentionally) collective order—the order in which it is possible to imagine everyone's individuated self in relation to an ideal one "from nowhere in particular" within it. The bourgeoisie, for Anderson, first achieve this condition, and it is interesting to see the images in this passage in which they are emblematized. It is the "factory-owner in Lille" and the "factory-owner in Lyon" who can read about each other within the chronotope of realist reportage or imagine one another in fictive narrative realism, and it is that condition of mutuality through universally available literacy that seems to mediate their class interest. It is a mutuality of words rather than of things (e.g., inherited property) or intermediate people (e.g., exchangeable daughters). Note the connection drawn between the condition of being bourgeois in the regime of factory-based capitalism, and realist literacy—"[f]or an illiterate bourgeoisie is scarcely imaginable." It is a connection of necessary conditionality, literacy seeming to fuel the very institutional engine of rationalized production that defines the socioeconomic base of the class at the same time as it is the personally enabling channel of self-reflective class communication and hence class imagination.[24]

THE IMAGED (LANGUAGE) COMMUNITY

But of course we already know in linguistic terms what kind of condition Anderson's bourgeoisie exists in: It is the order of a standardized language community (to be distinguished from a speech community; see references in n17). When a linguistic community has its norm informed by standardization, it is no longer just a group of people who can communicate by presupposing a determinate denotational code (a 'grammar' in the usual sense). Under standardization, speakers' usage of the denotational code furthermore reflects a sociologically differentiated allegiance, or at least orientation, to a norm informed by standardization. Standardization, in turn, is the imagination and explicit, institutionalized maintenance of a "standard" register—a way of employing words and expressions for reference and predication based on institutionalized prescriptions and proscriptions of various sorts— such that purportedly the best speakers and writers in the population index their adherence to all of them.

Manifested and enforced through such writing- and reading-dependent institutions as government, schooling, and so on, standardization is a modern and inclusive societal project in the classic Praguean sense (see the references in n17). One's familiarity with and ability to navigate within these various institutions becomes indexically tied to one's language use. Even outside them, one "voices" one's very identity in terms of the registers—for example, degree of standardization—that one controls and can deploy. Every speaker has a repertoire of registers that become, when used, second-order indexes (Silverstein

1996b) of class and related social positionings in modern social formations of inequality.

In this way a language community acquires what we would term a hegemonic standard relative to which variation is experienced as a pyramidical or conical space of divergence: standard-register usage is at the top-and-center, and each coherent cluster of variance is experienced as mere "dialect" (Silverstein 1996c and references therein). The standard that informs the language community's norm thus becomes the very emblem of the existence of that community, with a characteristic social distribution of strength and mode of allegiance that can be studied with some precision.[25] Those with the greatest allegiance to this emblem of community-hood tend to imagine the existence of the perfect standard-using member of the language community as a democratically and universally available position of inhabitance of the language community to which everyone can, and even should, aspire.

Those people with the greatest allegiance to standard-as-emblem imagine, furthermore, all kinds of good results that come to the user's mind, to users' communicative networks, and to society and its institutions as a result of inculcating the use of the standard register. Especially interesting here is the imaginative linking of the use of standard to what we might call expository rationality, purportedly evidenced in the act of making logically coherent denotational text, and the critical and empirical condition of mind this is said to make manifest. Paradoxically, inculcation of use of rigidly standard register is frequently seen as the very liberating instrumentality of fostering such a condition of mind, a kind of indexically calibrated empirical orientation as an individual subjectivity to the universe of cognizable and reportable phenomena. (The debate in educational circles of modern Western postindustrial democracies—sometimes linked to the Goody and Watt kind of reasoning mentioned in n24—is ongoing, of course.)

This is, to be sure, the condition of a specific, modern cultural order of language in which we and Anderson live (see Silverstein 1996c) and relative to which, as Bloomfield long ago (1987b[1927]) pointed out, many speakers of languages in such cultural orders cannot even conceive of any other kinds of linguistic phenomena, for instance, unwritten "languages," "languages" without standards, and so on. For such subjectivities from within cultures of standard, the very concept of "language" rests upon finding the various institutional paraphernalia of standardization, for example, literacy in relation to standard register, grammars and dictionaries and thesauruses, authoritative judgments of "correctness" enforceable in certain institutional sites of power over discourse, and so forth. Within cultures of standard, forms of language that lack these in some significant degree are relegated to some classificatory category other than "language."[26]

Clearly, Anderson can conceive of other kinds of cultural orders of language, as for example what he takes to be the functional predecessors of national languages, liturgical and dynastic languages, "the deader the better" (1983:20, 1991:13), languages connected through their cosmic and ritual axiality-of-authority (through a liturgical imagination, or an imagination of divine right) to exemplary centers and thence to the absolute and essential cosmic "Truth" in the realms beyond empirical reality. One's very "voice" in such an order of linguistic usage is always dependent on one's position with respect to liturgical or royal authoritativeness. For Anderson the new order of nationalist languages replaces those earlier orders in essential functional respects, so that one's "voice" is a function of one's participation in the mutual "realist" imagination of identities across narrated/narrating spaces, mediated by the market form of text-artifactual commodification.

But Anderson's imagination of this functional replacement for how "voices" are authorized in discursive usage has erased the processes—institutional, sociosemiotic, ideological—by which discursive regimes come into being and by which they effloresce and take hold of the subjectivities of populaces. Of course, just as in liturgically centered and/or royally embodied regimes of authorization of discursive voicing, the emergent forms of nationalist language community (especially as centered on standardization through bourgeois institutions) rest on the same kinds of exercise of power and control that any political regimes do. Explicating Whorf's sociolinguistic and dialectical intuition about the processually emergent and "metaphysical" content to deixis itself makes clear how complex has been the struggle in multiple institutional sites so as to result in the nationalist licensing of the Andersonian "we" in any particular empirical case and the silencing of other possible deictics.

Linguistic practice (and symbolic practice more generally) under standardization is an essentially contested order of sociocultural reality. So it is a mistake for Anderson, reading from one particular resulting discursive linguistic form, objective realist reportage, with its particular deictic presuppositions, to project therefrom a whole, homogeneous cultural order of subjectivity. Since the linguistic practice at issue is centered, in effect, on the category of Person, the objective realist "voicing" at issue depends on mapping across two framings so that indexed (invoked) identities of role-relational sender-receiver-referent(s) (in the framework of narrating events) and identities of denoted characters (in the framework of narrated events) can be grouped together by reference to a kind of "standard" identity—perhaps a "standard average" identity with a view from nowhere in particular that is most specifically emblematized by the speaker of a standard register of a "language." All of the processes of political (in)stability of (certainly hegemonic) standardization and its detailed institutional consequences—where forms of diversity must be at least effectively valorized to discerning cultural consciousness, if not outright suppressed—disappear from Anderson's account of the revolution in the metaphysics of "we"-identity. In this way, Anderson reads the synchronic (or functional) denotational linguistic practice of the authorized and self-declaring deictic "we." Suppressing all the contestation and social history, he in effect takes its meaning to be the straightforwardly and uniformly presupposed order of imaginable homogeneity-of-identity in the discursive-equals-discoursed-about spatiotemporal envelope of "the nation" (that is, the linguistic community informed by hegemonic standard) in which its speakers feel they reside.

Commoditized language—language commoditized through print capitalism—seems to Anderson to be the condition of experiencing that simultaneity/sequentiality with others in the imagined community of empty, homogeneous space-time. There emerges a natural "voice" of selfhood in this commoditized order, he is saying, a voice that is the cultural consciousness of self/other such as that described in Raymond Williams's (1983) "Notes on English Prose 1780–1950" or Mikhail Bakhtin's (1981) essay "Discourse in the Novel." Anderson wants to extend the cultural consciousness of the nationalist imagination from Whorf's making plausible a cultural analogy from "substance" to "space" to "time" to yet another domain, that of our mode of inhabiting—or of imagining ourselves to inhabit—the social world of groupness with millions of others with whom we have never interacted. From a Whorfian point of view, "we"-ness is an inhabitable trope that structures our very consciousness of being individuals in a social order, but one that needs an elaborate deconstruction to reveal its sociocentric constructivity as a cultural concept.

INHABITING THE TROPE

Whorf, we should recall, contrasts two perspectives on the problem of how language (structure and discourse) mediates between thought and thing. One is the "habitual thought world" of, for example, Newtonian space-time. Whorf sees this as a complex, emergent, partly analogically driven conceptual orientation that is absolutely "real" to the people in whom it emerges. For what he terms SAE language speakers, this cultural consciousness projects a homogeneously enveloping and fixed framework, mathematically a metric space, populated by objects and happenings in determinately measurable loci. We reveal and affirm this thought-world to ourselves each time we use fashions of speaking about matter in "space" and "time."

Such a thought-world contrasts for Whorf with what grammatical-categorial analysis reveals to systematic investigation. For from this perspective, space-time is grammaticalized in terms of asymmetrically dimensionalized contrasts—'marked' and 'unmarked' values—that are, within rather elastic limits, relationally indexed and thence denoted by the use of formal categories of Locational-Directional and Temporal deixis. In each case, these categories communicate at least a binary, 'proximal' versus 'distal' distinction in a radial geometric organization of deixis about the ever-moving, ever-changing 'here-and-now' of the discursive event as it unfolds. Whorf's point is that SAE language speakers in effect culturally reconstruct the universe indexed by such deictics in terms of the scalarizations of "space" and "time" that are local cultural emergents. The cross-linguistically valid deictic universe, of which the SAE grammatical systems point to theoretically permissible variants, and the processes by which the SAE cultural concepts emerge, are opaque to the typical SAE language speaker.

Whorf theorizes that such processes of production of a local cultural thought-world constitute a complex dialectic. To character-ize the dialectic moments, he seeks to demonstrate the disjunction between (1) the denotational-structural condition of language as a ref-erential and predicational communicative mechanism in practical, institutional contexts of reasoning and general cognitive functioning, and (2) the workings of mind in those conditions that rationalize them by finding a "fit" or transparency between the trope of reality that con-text-specific linguistic usage suggests and licenses, and any systemati-cally codable reality that might lie behind it.[27]

In contrast, Anderson seems to mistake the dialectically produced trope of "we"-ness for the reality. He seems not to see that the dialecti-cal workings of political processes that construct the sharable space of realist reportage in standardized language are the facts to be character-ized and explained. He diagnoses nationalist consciousness as essen-tially isomorphic to and emerging from a print-capitalism–mediated regime of standardization in a linguistic community with market-ratio-nalized public-sphere communication. He wants to project the nation-alist cultural consciousness from that condition, as a now imaginable and so imagined envelope of now doubly Newtonian individuals indexed-and-denoted, via "voicing," in their role-inhabitances we call I (we), you, and he/she/it (they).

As Bakhtin and Williams pointed out, one of the great achieve-ments of what we may term "nationalist" literary imagination as a kind of collective self-representation is the so-called realist novel, such as Rizal's 1887 *Noli Me Tangere*. In such a work, the presupposed perspec-tival jumble of interests in the society realistically portrayed finds its narrative linguistic trope in the figurated "polyphony" of voicing that depends on using linguistic "heteroglossia" to tropic advantage.[28] The "realistic" novel is like Peirce's map of the island in the sand, a swatch of plausible reality that it both represents and gives voice to. Thus, the objective authorial voice that calls us to identify with it rather than with any of the characters becomes the voice of objective and commonplace societal observation and judgment, the voice from everywhere and nowhere, exemplified, for both Bakhtin and Williams, in Dickens. By contrast, this trope to which Anderson calls our attention seems for him not, in fact, to be a trope.

Yet how else to explain the "modularization" of nationalism

Anderson recognizes in the nineteenth-century dynastic nation-state
and the official nationalisms of colonial and postcolonial orders?
Ironically, Anderson (1983:122; 1991:133) warns against the "mistake
[of] treat[ing] languages in the way that certain nationalist ideologues
treat them—as *emblems* of nation-ness, like flags, costumes, folk-dances,
and the rest."[29] Yet his examples present essentially organized textuality
in explicitly ritual contexts and canon-making literary forms that we
now understand to be the very essence of how language and discursive
voicing are authorized and warranted from their Durkheimian ritual
center (in these polities, moreover, their ritual top-and-center). Here is
an example of Anderson's kind of evidence (Anderson 1983:132–33;
1991:144–45):

> [O]ne notes the primordialness of languages, even those known
> to be modern. No one can give the date for the birth of any lan-
> guage. Each looms up imperceptibly out of a horizonless past...
> Languages thus appear rooted beyond almost anything else in
> contemporary societies. At the same time, nothing connects us
> affectively to the dead more than language. If English-speakers
> hear the words 'Earth to earth, ashes to ashes, dust to dust'—cre-
> ated almost four and a half centuries ago—they get a ghostly inti-
> mation of the simultaneity across homogeneous, empty time. The
> weight of the words derives only in part from their solemn mean-
> ing; it comes also from an as-it-were ancestral 'Englishness.'
>
> Second, there is a special kind of contemporaneous commu-
> nity which language alone suggests—above all in the form of
> poetry and songs. Take national anthems, for example, sung on
> national holidays. No matter how banal the words and mediocre
> the tunes, there is in this singing an experience of simultaneity. At
> precisely such moments, people wholly unknown to each other
> utter the same verses to the same melody. The image: uniso-
> nance.[6] Singing the Marseillaise, Waltzing Matilda, and Indonesia
> Raya provide *[sic]* occasions for unisonality, for the echoed physi-
> cal realization of the imagined community. (So does listening to
> the recitation of ceremonial poetry, such as sections of *The Book of
> Common Prayer.*) How selfless this unisonance feels! If we are aware
> that others are singing these songs precisely when and as we are,

we have no idea who they may be, or even where, out of earshot, they are singing. Nothing connects us all but imagined sound.

[6] Contrast this *a capella* chorus with the language of everyday life, which is typically experienced decani/cantoris-fashion as dialogue and exchange.

Notice the weight that language in its textualized realization bears for Anderson's argument. Language is the very emblem of the overcoming of diachrony, itself looming up with no discrete boundaries out of a past of indefinitely ancient depth. We recognize this, interestingly, in the highly ritualized context of the text-sign of a funeral service in which the living and the dead are indexically connected through prosaic substances, ashes and dust, made mystical in the instance so as to summon up nationality ("Englishness") as much as spiritual continuity in the Anglican Church. Again, language is the very emblem of simultaneity of inhabitance of homogeneous nationalist space-time, the emblem of overcoming the inequalities of social differentiation, when it is realized in the discursive form of "unisonance"—making in essence one "voice"—on occasions of singing anthems or collectively reciting prayers—or, we might add, of pledges of allegiance to flags as nationalist emblems. Such ritual occasions of textuality, with all their capacity to generate participatory effervescence by dense emblematization, draw Anderson's attention to language as the very emblem of nationality. Yet his argument is really about the "we-voicing" of objective realist reportage through the market-form of print-capitalist circulation of text-artifacts.

Here we see precisely the dialectic found in a complex linguistic community such as the emergently standardized ones with which Anderson's argument is concerned. The political—and political economic!—punch of such ritualized use of language at the processual top-and-center of social formations is its ability to warrant or authorize for those in the imagined community of standardization the polar opposite of ritual text: "literal, casual, or free" use of language in the expository, everyday-vernacular mode, the mode of objective realist reportage, among others.[30] The regime of language on which such a dialectic depends is a frequently fragile sociopolitical order, seething

with contestation that emerges from actual plurilingualism, heteroglossia, and like indexes of at least potentially fundamental political economic conflict. Such a regime of language is, however, energized and
in a sense maintained by the ritually emblematized trope of "we"-ness.
It seems to have taken in Anderson, who buys the trope as a transparently imagined "reality."

Notes

This chapter, ultimately revised in 1998, has had a vigorous life in commu-
nication of one sort or another, from regular classroom use in teaching at the
University of Chicago to samizdat circulation of earlier versions on special
request. It began as a paper, "The Imagination of Nationalities," given on
January 16, 1992, to the Midwest Faculty Seminar on the theme of "Nationalisms
Old and New" at the gracious invitation of Elizabeth Chandler, now associate
director of the Graham School of General Studies at the University of Chicago.
The 1994 draft of this paper, discussed at the School of American Research semi-
nar in Santa Fe, was fortunate in having Joseph Errington as its respondent.
Additionally, I thank the following in particular for providing written feedback
on aspects of earlier drafts that has been very useful in doing this one: John R.
Bowen, Susan Gal, Michael Herzfeld, John D. Kelly, John A. Lucy, Stephen O.
Murray, Richard J. Parmentier, Adam Rose, Elizabeth R. Vann, James M. Wilce,
and two anonymous reviewers for SAR Press.

1. Observe that the metaphorical disease-denoting noun phrases, Whorf's
disease, Whorf's syndrome, etc., would alternate with such phrases as Whorfian
disease, Whorfian syndrome, etc. The possessive forms with clitic 's neutralize
the grammatical distinction between naming the bearer of the disease or the
diagnostician who, like an author of a work or the creator of a painting or sculp-
ture, names it.

2. See Silverstein (1979:193–203, 1987:21–22), Lucy (1985), Lucy and
Wertsch (1987), and especially Lucy (1992b) and references therein for details
of Whorf's theoretical work and reasons for its apparent opacity to later writers.
As more people are again approaching Whorf's actual writings, their shock at
what has been represented secondhand—or at further remove (e.g., Pinker
1994:59–67)—has been manifested in a continuing series of articles (see, for
example, Smith 1996). By contrast, uninformed, Whiggish treatments mas-
querading as adequate intellectual history still abound, for example, Koerner
(1992).

3. For those of Whorf's writings reprinted by John B. Carroll in his 1956 edited volume of selected writings, the 1956 date of republication is immediately followed in square brackets by the year of original publication or, in the case of manuscripts, the year to which it was attributed by Carroll.

4. See Silverstein (1978), a lengthy review article on Charles Hockett's selected writings, for an explication of Bloomfield in relation both to Saussure and to Bloomfield's self-professed followers; cf. also Hall (1987), especially the letter to J. Milton Cowan on page 29. See also Joseph (1989).

5. Compare the condition nowadays of a serious social or behavioral scientist of language, most likely trained in Chomskian formalism but of course rejecting Chomsky's speculative psychological and philosophical obiter dicta! *Plus ça change...*

6. Who can forget Bloomfield's image of such commitments—common to Boas, Sapir, and most of the latter's students (cf. Silverstein 1986)—as "shreds of medieval speculation still hanging to the propellers of science and sometimes fouling them" (Bloomfield 1987d:278)?

7. This particular intellectual engagement of Whorfian thought has not been at all clear to intervening generations. To be sure, the persisting failure to see Whorf's oeuvre in a precise context of intellectual and social history is a problem of the poor state of the historiography of linguistics. But even when Whorf's writings were—posthumously—made available for the second time through the limited 1949 publication of *Four Articles on Metalinguistics,* the intellectual climate in both official and disciplinary politics had changed enough to make Whorf's discursive purport more or less uninterpretable, even to the well-disposed George Trager, who was paying homage to his erstwhile Yale friend and scientific collaborator (Whorf and Trager 1937). For, rather than dealing with the realm of the "meta"-linguistic (in Trager's usage, a term for what lies beyond the phenomena for which ("micro-")linguistics as such and "paralinguistics" take responsibility), these reprinted articles address two of Whorf's themes from what he must have considered the informed center of late 1930s Bloomfieldianism.

Moreover, by the time that the academic and other reading publics encountered the fuller selected writings of Whorf in 1956(entitled *Language, Thought, and Reality* by the volume's editor, the educational psychologist John B. Carroll and, ironically, published by MIT Press), post- or neo-Bloomfieldianism in linguistics and behaviorism-based experimental psychology were disciplinarily ascendant. The behavioral science world was then awaiting the formation and impact of the "cognitivist" movement at least retrospectively seen to have been initiated by the 1957 publication of its foundation text, Chomsky's *Syntactic Structures*. The climate was so completely different from that in which Whorf had written, and in a real sense has remained so, that it is difficult for current students of language and of "mind" to see what his three thematic messages were.

8. Observe how this vision of 'extensionally equivalent' but 'intensionally nonequivalent' language structures has played a key role in the analytic philosophical tradition of Quine (e.g., 1960, 1968), Kripke (esp. 1972), and Putnam (e.g., 1975, 1987). Quine ironically sees the difficulty in the position on reference that Whorf articulates, while Putnam uses the failure of intensional/extensional transparency to suggest an essentially "cosmographical" (see Silverstein 1986:69–73) and sociocentrically based theory of reference.

9. Compare the packaging of, and the public's reaction to, news that a certain group of so-called primitive people have traditionally incorporated into their folk pharmacopoeia practical remedies containing "active ingredients" equivalent to those used in drug therapies based on "science," and you will get the rhetorical flavor of this line of missionary argumentation that Boas, Sapir, and Whorf all vigorously carried on with respect to the realm of the world's linguistic-cognitive riches.

10. Whorf's later critics (Lenneberg 1953:464–66; Weinreich 1966:166–67; and others) seriously misconstrue the nature of Whorf's use of glossing as a pedagogical heuristic for the linguistically uninitiated. They are intent on seeing him—with a certain hostility, it is clear—as truly ignorant of the distinction between glossing of and by lexations on the one hand and structurally sensitive, grammatically informed translation on the other.

11. Paraphrasing Sapir's (1949b:219) *bon mot* about denotational equivalence, Whorf was aiming to show that Ogden and the average commercial lexicographer share equally ignorant views of linguistic structure and function.

12. Boas eventually despaired even of giving a "true history" for the unwritten American languages, where he saw only areally stimulated borrowing as the central process of language history, demonstrating his ignorance of comparative-historical method and his tendency not to see the forest for the trees; see Boas (1940a, 1940b).

13. In several of his papers, Whorf lays out typologies of what he will come to call grammatical categories. He captures Boas's concern with the degree of obligatoriness of coding certain distinctions by his contrast of category-types along the cline of 'selective' to 'modulus' categories (1956h[1945]:93–99). He captures Bloomfield's concern with categories of surface segmentability vs.

categories of overall grammatical structure by the distinction between 'overt' and 'covert' categories (1956h[1945]:88–93), for the latter of which he also used the suggestive term "cryptotype." It is this dramatic last formulation—in opposition to "phenotype," possibly echoing genetics—that perhaps encouraged delegitimating mirth among Whorf's critics. In fact, it was the discovery, in his terms, of what we now call "underlying representations" in language structure, as is obvious to anyone who understands both Bloomfieldian grammatical theory and contemporary transformations of it into formal syntax.

14. For a detailed comparative account of the grammar of 'numerosity' in relation to classes of nouns and systems of Classifiers, see Lucy (1992a:23–84). This account becomes the basis for a pioneering contrastive study in biasing effects of linguistic categorial systems on performing certain cognitive tasks.

15. In Whorf's terminology (cf. n13 above), the distributional behavior of noun stems in different Measure Phrase constructions constitutes the "reactance"—the overt, observable constructional evidence—of this relatively 'covert' (underlying) though 'selective' (obligatorily made) categorial difference among noun stems in English. A category for which there is only one observably differentiating context of occurrence is thus highly covert, and, we might say, only marginally grammaticized in the language concerned.

16. I cannot elaborate here on the emergence of the clock as a technology and an aspect of human life in Europe, or on the institutional ramifications of clock-focused practices relating to conceptualization of event simultaneity vs. sequentiality, temporal intervals (durational and conceptual), etc., that are at the heart of Whorf's understanding of our SAE culture of temporal mensuration and its concept of "time." Various historical works that focus on measures, clocks, and the temporal organization of society (Dohrn-van Rossum 1996; Kula 1986; Landes 1983; Le Goff 1980:1–97), though useful for certain details, do not really ask the questions about *mentalité* that Whorf did. Crosby (1997) does ask how "quantification" lies at the center of the conceptual and institutional transformation of European *mentalité*, but instead of answering the question, the author simply compiles a chronological catalog of poorly differentiated though broadly arithmetic practices.

17. Indeed, one of the principal means of standardization was precisely the fact that vernacular linguistic forms had newly achieved access to print-capitalist text artifacts that were intertextual with governmental and other forms of linguistic usage sited in, or associated with, command institutional loci. The political economy of text artifactuality—the establishment and control of institutional

creation, circulation, and consumption of printed text-artifacts—thus mediates the very process of linguistic standardization, through which is created a model of linguistic usage with authorizing force in a community of language users. On standardization see especially Garvin (1964, 1993); Garvin and Mathiot (1968); Havránek (1964); Heath (1980); Shaklee (1980); Silverstein (1996a, 1996c); and Stewart (1968:534).

18. These two perspectives on nationalism correspond to what Anthony Smith (1983:158ff.) would term the 'ethnocentric' and 'polycentric' nationalisms evidenced in ideological views. Ethnocentric constructions of nationalism are essentializing, locating and justifying power and value in the fact of an individual's group membership. Polycentric ones, seen as more politically "liberal," are diacritic and differentiating of multiple groups at that level of conceptualization, within the "family of nations."

19. Much of U.S. ethnic consciousness explicitly hearkens back to a preimmigration ethnogeography of actual nation-states or regions of empires, a place-from-which—an *Urheimat*—and an originary time-at-which—an *Urzeit*—a national-ethnicity imagines itself to have "come from." Hence the common American question, "Where do you/docs your family come from?" frequently intends to elicit national ethnicity in this sense. Of course, such *Urheimat-Urzeit* affiliations, and the group consciousness they warrant, shift over time and social circumstances.

20. This term, meaning 'space-time', is advisedly adapted by Bakhtin on the model of Einsteinian relativistic discussions. He uses it to mean what we would call the presupposed indexical bases and *origines* in an essentially spatiotemporal framework underlying characterization and plot in literary art (see Bakhtin 1981:84–85, 84n).

21. For the concept of indexical or pragmatic 'calibration' of denoted or otherwise signaled universes with the universe in which interaction takes place, see Silverstein 1993:48–53. Both Bakhtin's concept of 'voicing' and Goffman's concept of 'footing' (1979) are special, derived effects of the phenomenon.

22. The original draft of this paper stimulated, courtesy James Wilce, an interesting interchange on the "Language-Culture" electronic list (www.cs.uchicago.edu/discussions/l-c/html/archives). With help from William R. Kelley, Wilce got responses from Richard Parmentier, Anne Freadman, and Joseph Randsall, who located the Peircean construct in variants at three places: *CP* 8.122, 5.71, and a manuscript fragment (Robbins #637, pp.32–33). A Peircean 'icon' is a sign that represents its object by virtue of (generally preexisting)

"likeness"; a Peircean 'index' is a sign that represents its object by virtue of "real connection," i.e., spatiotemporal, causal, etc., continguity-in-frame. A sign that has both properties is an 'indexical icon' or 'iconic index', the choice of name loosely depending on which aspect is semiotically the more salient.

23. The late Ernest Gellner (1964, 1983, 1994) conceptualized the nation-state as a social formation at the mass level that centers on and makes manifest a modern, secular, and rational sensibility necessitated and mediated by the evolution of technology and its large-scale productive and consumption patterns. Gellner clearly saw the 'voice' of objective scientific discourse as necessary to this evolutionary stage of mass-order infrastructural project and, via that mediation, to the sociopolitical formation that harnesses and gives meaning to it, the nation-state. Smith (1983:155) quotes Gellner (1964:179) to the effect that "science is the mode of cognition of industrial society, and industry is the ecology of science." By seeing that scientific discourse—theoretically axiomatized and systematized canons of denotational textuality in the realist-reportive calibration—is central to what science is *qua* "cognition," a mode of knowing-that, we see the intimate connection to this conceptualization of nationalism of intellectuals and other bourgeois intelligentsia living under institutionalized regimes of scientific-expository linguistic usage. Here is a thread linking Anderson, Gellner, Karl Deutsch (1953), Anthony Smith (1983), Craig Calhoun (1993), and many others: All worry the same ultimately Whorfian issue not unrelated to the particular empirical-rational and at the same time political-economic "we"-ness of a Lockean intelligentsia that constitutes the *origo* of nationalist phenomenal "reality" (on which see Bauman and Briggs, this volume).

24. Note that in contemporary discussions, the nature of a putatively socio-culturally undifferentiated state-of-mind termed "literacy" has been at the center of debate about the gulf between the cognitive, social, and cultural conditions of "orality" and "literacy" since at least Goody and Watt (1963); see Goody (1968), Street (1984, 1993), and the concise overview in Besnier (1995:1–17). Among other things at issue is the causal or at least enabling relationships among these realms in which "literacy" is at once a mode of mental functioning, a medium—or, better, channel—for institutions of social production and reproduction, and an essential mediating instrument of collective consciousness through textualized representations. Anderson takes a position of transparent enablement, if not out-and-out causation, in the way "literacy" is linked to capitalism (see the authors cited in n23), perhaps via the market-form commodification of text-artifacts in print capitalism; for him, "literacy" transforms individual minds who are

the recipient entextualizers as intentional consumers of the circulated text-artifacts and therefore enables the nationalist political imagination.

25. Here I allude to the whole field of what we might term "variationist correlational sociolinguistics" that has developed out of Labov's (e.g., 1966, 1972a,
1972b) numerical operationalizations of the theoretical traditions of André
Martinet and Uriel Weinreich and applied with considerable success to language
communities in the condition of stratified and hegemonic standardization and
to some speech communities at the intersection of these. In all these studies, the
"evaluative" or "attitudinal" orientation of users to the variation in form of the
language being studied is essential to the project of determining the significance
of the variation, and itself shows interesting second-order patterns of covariation
of attitudinal and behavioral measures when viewed along demographic and
other dimensions. See Fasold (1984:147–79 and references there) for an
overview of "language attitude" research.

26. The contemporary presence of this cultural form can be observed in
the extraordinary public policy "debate" that took place in 1996–97 over so-
called Ebonics, that is, what linguists would term African-American Vernacular
(nonstandard) English (AAVE). The Oakland, California, school board had
resolved, in late 1996, to advocate recognizing it with realism and even perhaps
toleration in the classrooms where its speakers are students. Several interestingly
structured arguments prevailed among views opposing AAVE, all of which go
back to the culture of standard. On the one hand, antagonists claimed that
AAVE could not be a "language" because if it were, it would have a literature and
be subject to grammatical prescriptions/proscriptions, but as everyone knows it
is the "street talk" of the ignorant and unlettered, and consists just of "mistakes."
On the other hand, admission of AAVE to any sort of use in the classroom would
violate a clear pollution taboo in that only standard register can be inculcated in
the sacred precincts of school classrooms and only standard ought to be written
down and printed. So not only is AAVE not a "language," but to pretend that it is
would clearly be a danger—perhaps even a danger to the ideology!

27. In Whorf's view, moreover, the systematically codable reality is available
through the methods of the perfect, if not standard average, Boasian-
Bloomfieldian linguist, ironically, for whom comparative-typological modeling of
grammatical categories constitutes a key to the universe of conceptualizable and
communicable distinctions.

28. "Heteroglossia" translates a Russian term used by Bakhtin (1981) to
characterize the inherently variable condition of linguistic usage within a

language community, people of various demographic and biographical conditions showing characteristic differences of verbal behavior. "Polyphony," taken on analogy with the musical term, is the simultaneously in-play multiplicity of 'voices', i.e., inhabitable social perspectives on the unfolding of narratable happenings, that an author—a verbal composer, as it were—can use as an artistic device. Properly complex polyphony in a piece of narrative verbal art like a novel allows the writer, *qua* authorial speaker, to jump into the very world being described as just another person with a cluster of recognizable presuppositions of interested sociality. At the same time, polyphony manifested by a writer's deliberate mixing of heteroglossic variance from one or more groups or categories of people in one or more communities can be used as a trope of the contestation of perspectives that—at least for the somewhat idealist Bakhtin—characterizes modern society. For Bakhtin, who put forth his discursively centered "translinguistics" as an alternative to the Durkheimianism of Saussure and all structure-centered abstract linguistics, every language community, even those with fierce standardization, is characterized by heteroglossia as its most profound fact, language being "heteroglot" from top to bottom in his view.

29. Recall that an emblem is a text that serves as a conventional iconic index of that which it represents, *qua* index pointing to its existent object by virtue of a conventional system of naturalizing beliefs about consubstantial essences shared between the qualia of the text-sign and the object the text-sign represents as a (poetic) arrangement of those qualia. Thus, the American flag is said to be built out of the essences of red ('courage; valor'), white ('candor; ingenuousness'), and blue ('faithfulness; fidelity'), the (white) stars in (blue) heaven diagrammatically superimposed, "floating," above the (red and white) cultivated land. Similarly, Athena's owl becomes over time a transparent emblem of 'wisdom' in the Western world, and any owl-like features become emblematic decorative items for visual representations of personal qualities. Observe the dynamic intertextuality of emblematization, which also gives rise to fashions of speaking that rest on the existence of the emblematic text-signs.

30. I have developed the idea of this dialectic of text-ritually centered warranting or authorization of indexicality and ideologically warranted or authorized indexical value of discursive language (see particularly Silverstein 1996b, 1998; see also Silverstein 1979, 1993, 1996c). I use this dialectical model to understand many of the empirically discovered phenomena about language in sociocultural formations reported in recent literatures of linguistic anthropology and sociolinguistics, several contributed by my interlocutory partners in this vol-

ume. For example, Brenneis (1984) presents striking material on how men's gossip sessions constitute a kind of anti- or counter-ritual (with emblematic language use in a maximally nonnormative form, not dissimilar to African-American male 'signifying'; see Abrahams 1974) that performatively establishes and authorizes the prospective voicings of political factionalism in an otherwise "egalitarian" small-scale society (see also Besnier 1989; see Kroskrity, this volume, on this tension within the Hopi-Tewa community). The work of Jane and Kenneth Hill on "Mexicano" (Nahuatl) in the region of the Malinche volcano (Hill and Hill 1978, 1980; J. Hill 1998; see also Silverstein 1998:132–33) also pinpoints certain entextualizing occasions of usage—the very paragon of which is hyperstylized mutual greetings of *compadres*—as at least the imagined (though sometimes contested) authorizing center of a whole indexical stratification of Spanish and degrees of "pure" Nahuatl in the plurilingual community. Susan Gal (1998) has emphasized the contested aspect of ideologies that are performatively evidenced in ritual, such as state rituals like official funerals (Gal 1991). The volume on *Language Ideologies: Practice and Theory* (Schieffelin, Woolard, and Kroskrity 1998) might well be read as multiple and varied exemplifications of aspects of this larger dialectic.

With regard to standardized language communities in particular, such as those in Western Europe and many former European colonies, issues of the relationship between ritualized form of participation in regimes of standardization must distinguish—as Anderson does not—between the institutional contexts of emblematization of language to nationalist ends (where even in a unilingual community, ritual text becomes indeed flaglike) and those institutional contexts that more directly authorize the value of its expository prose form (whence enregisterment of genre and "style"). And note the fascinating ideological framing of San Francisco's antiplurilingual Proposition O in Woolard (1989); it becomes clear from Woolard's account that for many among the "rational" and not particularly "patriotic" left-liberal elites, the two issues—of participatory democratic patriotism (as in elections) and expository prose usage in English—came together. More generally, as is discerned by Bourdieu (1991:43–102; see also Silverstein 1996b, 1996c), the authorized standard register is endowed with the emblematically derived and ritually licensed indexes of belonging to privileged groups at the top-and-center of social formations that themselves license and control such membership. (Recall, conversely, Groucho Marx's quip about club membership!) As Labov's (1966, 1972b) and others' studies of highly developed regimes of stratified standardization have demonstrated, even the bourgeois consciousness of how one's use of standard register indexes one's top-and-center positionality is "false," as it were, a "misrecognition" that correlates with the phenomenon of Labovian "hypercorrection"—too much manifestation by speakers of an indexically good thing—in nonhighest and not-most-central groups in the conically shaped space of stratification about a standard of usage.

4

Language Philosophy as Language Ideology:
John Locke and Johann Gottfried Herder

Richard Bauman and Charles L. Briggs

What is philosophy?

To ask such a basic question about one of the most firmly established categories of Western discourse might seem banal, fruitless, or even perverse. But consider what issues would be raised if the question were asked from the perspective of a critical stance toward discourse. Now the focus shifts away from a concern with content, particularly with a construction of philosophy as comprising ideas that can be grasped by interpreting the referential content of philosophical texts. Such texts can rather be read subversively as powerful means of controlling the process of producing and receiving discourse.

Poststructuralists have detailed the role of philosophical texts in constructing ideologies of science, language, literature, society, gender, sexuality, the family, and so on. As students of language ideologies, our interest lies in how these texts construct and legitimate conceptions of language that both draw on and help shape other types of representations. In discussing the work of John Locke and Johann Gottfried Herder, we hope to identify ways that key texts seek to delegitimate particular practices of discourse production and reception while promoting others. Such practices, we suggest, are crucial tools for positioning discourses—along with their authors and readers—vis-à-vis textual and social hierarchies. In the transformations of European society that took place in the seventeenth and eighteenth centuries, these relationships of discourse to discourse and discourse to social life were of tremendous significance. In discussing Locke and Herder, therefore, we ask, "What is philosophy?" as a means of interrogating practices used in controlling the production and reception of socially dominant discourses.

Our readers might wonder what linguistic anthropologists can contribute to discussions of such widely debated figures; indeed we have asked this question of ourselves—and each other—repeatedly. This ground has, of late, been well trodden. Such writers as James Clifford (1988), Jacques Derrida (1967, 1974), Michel Foucault (1970, 1972, 1980), Julia Kristeva (1980, 1989), and Edward Said (1978) have stimulated critical revisionist histories of the emergence of Western thinking about language, literature, and culture, while Jürgen Habermas (1989) and Benedict Anderson (1991) have raised important questions regarding the role of discourse in the creation of civil society and the modern nation-state. We are, however, less concerned with rendering our own text authoritative by discovering something that has been left out by these critical rethinkings, some sort of Derridian gap, than with responding to a sense of frustration with our own efforts to grapple with fundamental questions regarding the relationship between discourse and authority. How can we best characterize the relationship between discourse production and reception on the one hand, and the means by which authority, legitimacy, and social inequality are generated and deployed on the other?

Although recent and important work in a wide range of fields has informed this question, it seems also to have widened the gap between the empiricist and often microanalytic approach taken by most linguistic anthropologists, linguists, and sociologists in defining "discourse" and identifying its constituents in a given discursive realm, and the more critical approach of practitioners whom we might loosely group under the rubric of cultural studies. This latter approach tends to address broad political and historical issues more squarely at the same time that it manifests a reluctance to provide close analyses of the operations that take place in the sites where "power," "institutional control," "logocentrism," "patriarchy," and the like are generated. We maintain that this hiatus between empirical discussions of linguistic forms and functions and critical analyses of race, class, gender, or nation is due, in part, to the way that academic discourses are embedded in extant processes of investing authority in particular methods of producing and receiving discourse.

As a host of writers have argued, one of the difficulties that haunts discussions of language emerges from ideologies that reduce discourse to systems of signs existing apart from history, social inequality, politics, and gender. This move acquired particular power through the universalizing rhetorics that predominated in the Enlightenment, as well as in much of the thinking that preceded and postdated it. Just as particular conceptions of "man," "nature," "mind," or "knowledge" were promoted to the status of essential characteristics of Homo sapiens always and everywhere, writers in the seventeenth and eighteenth centuries commonly focused their efforts on demonstrating that language was also possessed of universal properties and functions. The fruits of this universalization were clearly evident in the second half of the nineteenth century, by which time many scholars of language felt that they could focus on the empirical work of identifying phonological, grammatical, lexical, and semantic elements and relations and their historical constitution. Recent research has shown how these supposedly universal features emerged from socially, culturally, and historically circumscribed features of the languages spoken by, as well as the lived experience and political-economic interests of, their authors (see, for example, Silverstein 1985; Taylor 1990a, 1990b).

Such efforts at analyzing the linguistic ideologies that shape discussions of language can easily fall prey to the very ideological pitfalls that they seek to expose. As Woolard and Schieffelin (1994:57) suggest in their review of work in this area, language ideologies are generally framed as "ideas," "objectives," "beliefs," "notions," and the like, particularly insofar as they form "sets," "systems," and "shared bodies." A problem here is that studies that adopt such a focus may themselves be unduly shaped by the way the authors they study focus attention on abstract, generalized notions about language. It thus becomes more difficult to make a conceptual leap from the description of "systems" of "ideas" to questions of their social and political effects in social life. We suggest that Locke and Herder, founding fathers of Western ideologies of language, and their contemporary critics tend to divert attention from the way that discussions of language promote, resist, or run cover for particular practices of discourse production and reception.

We would like to suggest that these practices are evident in two important ways in discussions of language. They emerge, first, from the representational content of texts, as authors describe and analyze competing methods of writing and reading, speaking and listening, generally seeking to delegitimate competing strategies while arguing for the superior theoretical grounding and/or empirical usefulness of the ones they promote. Most of these discussions also attempt to draw on the power of what Silverstein (1993) refers to as implicit metapragmatics; here authors use the form and functions of features of their own texts as exemplars of preferred practices, thereby attempting to imbue both texts and practices with authority.

The practices that interest us more directly in this essay emerge from the capacity of discourse to both represent and regulate other discourses; in order to draw attention to this reflexive relationship, we use the term *metadiscursive practices* (see Bauman 1993; Briggs 1993). The power to represent and to constrain discourse clearly relates to more than referential content and stylistic characteristics alone, as important as they may be. Metadiscursive practices shape, both positively and negatively, processes of producing and receiving texts, affecting who is authorized to speak or write or to be listened to or read, and in what sorts of social and institutional spaces. As we have argued previously (Bauman and Briggs 1990), rights to recontextualize speech are of great importance as well. We are particularly concerned with how particular modes of producing and receiving texts are imbued with authority. By legitimating certain metadiscursive practices and suppressing others, Locke and Herder promoted ideologies of language that emphasized shared identity while at the same time generating means of creating hierarchical rankings of discourses and modes of producing and receiving them. These discursive hierarchies both reflected and helped create emergent forms of social hierarchy. We will argue that intertextuality—that is, explicit or implicit links between texts—is of critical importance in the efforts of these writers to authorize particular metadiscursive practices. Many of their assertions as to what sorts of texts and modes of creating and receiving them should be authoritative revolve around where intertextual links should be visible or invisible, how they should be generated, and what sorts of authority should accrue to them.

In centering our work on metadiscursive practices, we hope to provide ourselves with analytic resources for addressing the relationship between discursive processes and questions of authority and social inequality. By doing so, we hope to create a sort of unholy alliance between the empiricist and critical approaches to discourse analysis referred to above. In drawing attention to the interpenetration of discourses and to intertextuality, we draw on Bakhtin's (1981) social, political, and textual dialogism and Kristeva's (1980) characterization of intertextuality or "transposition." While an emphasis on *practices* certainly draws on the emphasis that has been accorded the term in the wake of Bourdieu's (1977) work, our usage here is most closely in accord with Foucault's (1972) concept of "discursive practice." We follow Foucault in drawing attention to discourse not simply as what was said or written but rather as practices that determine the limits of what can be expressed, the social relations of discourse production and reception, and the way discourse constitutes institutional configurations. Bakhtin, Kristeva, Bourdieu, and Foucault do not, however, offer a rich array of analytic tools for identifying how discourses intersect and exert control over discourse production and reception. We accordingly draw on Silverstein's (1976, 1993) work on metapragmatics and that of other linguistic anthropologists in attempting to analyze metadiscursive practices rigorously and at the same time to trace their social underpinnings and effects.

Our selection of Locke and Herder for this analysis is arbitrary in the sense that any major statement of linguistic ideology contains representations of practices of discourse production and reception. Our choice is also highly motivated, however, by the conviction that these authors contributed fundamentally to the establishment of two modes of connecting conceptions of language with metadiscursive practices that not only played a key role in the emergence of contemporary Western society but have hardly lost their force today. Locke attempted to delegitimate nearly all interactionally, socially, institutionally, politically, and historically based modes of producing and receiving texts. In his view, writing and reading, speaking and listening must emerge from connections between language and knowledge that are systematically stripped of all contextual and intertextual associations. By attacking textual authority, particularly as it is interactionally and intertextually produced, he rendered it less visible.

Herder, on the other hand, emerges as the Romantic champion of all that Locke sought to suppress: intertextuality, discursive authority, tradition, the social and cultural grounding of discourse, and the sensory celebration of poetics. By identifying the intertextual and social authority of discourse vis-à-vis its "authentic" connection with particular social formations (the patriarchal family, *das Volk*, "the German people," etc.), however, he rendered invisible the role of his own metadiscursive practices in constructing these social forms and subordinating them to the interests of the then emerging bourgeoisie and nation-state.

SCIENCE, RELIGION, AND THE MISSION OF LOCKE'S *ESSAY*

John Locke concludes his *Essay Concerning Human Understanding*, the work in which he presents his philosophy of language in its fullest terms, with a threefold division of the sciences: natural philosophy, practica, and the doctrine of signs (IV.xxi.1–4).[1] This classification argues for the need to place Locke's *Essay* in the context of the emergence in the seventeenth century of the "new science." The scientific movement created an epistemological shift; as it became more fully institutionalized over a century later, it had a profound effect on the structure of society (see Berman 1978). A transformation of language ideologies and metadiscursive practices was shaped by and helped construct and legitimate the intellectual, technological, and social revolutions associated with the emergence of modern science.

As Gruner (1977:114) notes, the mode of scientific inquiry that was formed during the seventeenth century is distinguished less by the kinds of objects it investigated than by its methods. Behind the differences that separate deductive from inductive approaches and rationalism from empiricism lie a host of shared assumptions. Perhaps the most basic of these is the role of abstraction and idealization in gaining knowledge of the natural world. As Hall (1963:235) suggests, the main object of the mechanical philosophy associated with such figures as Galileo, Boyle, and Newton is the principle of the simplicity of physical structure. In order to understand things scientifically, the experienced complexity and diversity of phenomena must be broken up conceptually into their basic components. Understanding nature thus entails discovering the fundamental elements that are the same everywhere and discerning their motions or relations.

The great conceptual breakthrough of Galileo, Newton, and others was to wed the concern with abstraction, idealization, and the uniformity of nature with mathematical reasoning. Mathematics, as Hall (1963:80) argues, provided science with a model for seeing nature as consistent and ideal, and allowed practitioners to generalize from one example to all similar instances with certainty. Abstraction, experimentation, and mathematical theorization enabled Newton and his followers to wage what Hall (1963:131) aptly refers to as "a joint attack on the complexity of things."

Hobbes, who applied Galileo's mechanical philosophy to politics, wrote that "[t]he Scripture was written to shew unto men the kingdome of God; and to prepare their mindes to become his obedient subjects; leaving the world, and the Philosophy thereof, to the disputation of men, for the exercising of their naturall Reason" (1968:145). As Gruner (1977) argues, both rationalists and empiricists made human beings—and particularly the human mind—the central point of reference. The mechanical philosophy of the seventeenth century rejected the search for the essential, intrinsic structure of nature in favor of the way it is experienced by humans through their senses. According to this philosophy, human beings possess no special insight into the ultimate nature of things, which is the purview of divine knowledge; on the other hand, humans could speak with authority regarding the way the world impinged upon their senses. Similarly, the study of Aristotelian final causes was rejected in favor of concern with efficient causes, again replacing a range of phenomena not fully accessible to humans with one that could be ascertained through experimentation.

Followers of the "new science" rejected the belief that humans could circumvent natural law through magic and alchemy and subscribed to the view that the world could truly be known only by human-made models that reduced the flux of experience to abstract principles and procedures. This conceptual step formed a necessary prerequisite to using science as a means of gaining power over nature. As we shall see, once the gaze of the new science was focused on it, language seemed particularly in need of reduction to fully accessible, elementary, and unified units and relations if it were to take its place alongside the scientific study of nature in the search for knowledge, utility, and domination.

The principal institutional agent of the new science was the Royal Society, formed in 1660, eleven years before Locke finished the first two drafts of his *Essay Concerning Human Understanding*. According to its 1662 royal charter, the Royal Society was intended "to be imployed for the promoting of the knowledge of natural things, and useful Arts by Experiments" (quoted in Sprat 1958:134; see also Purver 1967). Robert Boyle, Christopher Wren, and Robert Hooke joined the Royal Society a few years later, and Newton and Locke became members as well. After receiving assurance from the Dutch mathematician, scientist, and inventor Christiaan Huygens that Newton's mathematics was reliable, Locke incorporated Newton's scientific ideas into his own work and helped to create an image of Newton as a prominent philosopher (Hall 1963:297, 319). In his *Essay*, Locke (IV.vii.11) refers to Newton's *Principia* as a "never enough to be admired book." Aarsleff (1982:56) suggests that Locke knew and admired Boyle's work more than that of any other individual. The *Essay* was dedicated to Thomas Herbert, Earl of Pembroke, who was president of the Royal Society when the work appeared in 1690. In a lengthy "Epistle to the Reader," Locke (Epistle I:14) characterizes his role as that of "an under-labourer in clearing the ground a little, and removing some of the rubbish that lies in the way to knowledge," thus placing himself in relation to such "master-builders" in "the commonwealth of learning" as Boyle, Huygens, and Newton.

Locke had his task cut out for him. If we accept the origin myth that Locke provides for his own narrative, it was precisely the *failure* of discourse that prompted Locke to write the *Essay:* "I should tell thee, that five or six friends meeting at my chamber, and discoursing on a subject very remote from this, found themselves quickly at a stand, by the difficulties that rose on every side" (Epistle I:9). Locke thus seeks to legitimate his project by linking it to a master narrative of seventeenth-century England: the story of the individual male philosopher/scientist who finds himself surrounded by disorder and uncertainty. Virtually compelled by these circumstances to set out on a mission that seeks to provide a new conceptual foundation, he proposes a model for creating conceptual, scientific, and social order and exhorts his readers to promulgate it or at least to proclaim its legitimacy.

We would be rather naive in assuming, however, that Locke's purpose in writing the *Essay* emerged whole cloth in the course of this gathering of friends. In his Epistle (I:14), Locke explicitly ties his efforts to the widespread conviction that the abuses of language had degraded philosophy to such a degree that it impeded the advance of knowledge and "was thought unfit or incapable to be brought into well-bred company and polite conversation." Locke thus characterizes his *Essay*, a founding document of linguistic and semiotic inquiry, as an effort to make language and human understanding safe for science—and for society.

How could Locke establish confidence in phenomena that lacked the certainty, reliability, and subtlety of nature? Locke (Introduction I:28) reports that his efforts center on investigating the "original" of ideas in an effort "to show what *knowledge* the understanding hath by those ideas" and to explore the nature of faith or opinion. By attaining a firmer grasp on the powers of the mind, Locke hopes to prevail upon his readers "to sit down in a quiet ignorance of those things which, upon examination, are found to be beyond the reach of our capacities." We will return to this below, as it bears important implications with respect to the relationship between metadiscursive practices and linguistic hegemony.

Locke may have simply inherited the fundamental problem with which he struggled, but his proposed solution was brilliant and largely original. Bacon had argued in the *Novum Organum* (1863) that the fundamental failing of concepts and words is that they are less reliable than scientific observations and mathematical models as means of representing the nature of things. In his *History of the Royal Society,* Thomas Sprat (1958:62) went on to claim that Society members would free philosophy "not so much, by any solemnity of Laws, or ostentation of Ceremonies; as by solid Practice, and examples: not, by a glorious pomp of Words; but by the silent, effectual, and unanswerable

Arguments of real Productions"; the place of words in the presentation of scientific findings could be taken directly by "Inventions, Motions and Operations" (1958:327). If language was to be saved, and many doubted that it could be, it must be made to function like the more certain forms of knowledge. Turning this notion on its head, Locke argues that the value of language and thought as means of acquiring knowledge is derived precisely from their fundamental *difference* from the means by which we could come to know nature through observation. Language is, he claims, essentially reliable; reforming language thus involves developing a greater and more systematic appreciation of its particular nature rather than trying to make it look more like knowledge of the natural world.

Having indicated why we consider it productive to examine Locke's language ideology within the context of the emergent scientific epistemologies of the seventeenth century, we must recognize as well that religious factors played a significant role in shaping Locke's ideas on language and discursive practice. Ironically, it is a testimonial to the epistemological power of Locke's philosophy of science that we should have to do so, for his ideas were instrumental in relocating the boundary between the two domains at a considerable remove from the point at which he and his colleagues in the Royal Society would have located it. It is suggestive in this regard to learn that the subject of the discourse that engaged the five or six friends who met in Locke's chambers, according to one of the participants, was "the principle of morality and revealed religion" (James Tyrell, quoted in Woolhouse 1997:xi). This prompts Woolhouse to suggest, "Perhaps, then, the questions about which 'difficulties rose on every side' concerned the manner in which the principles of morality are discovered and known to be true, and the role and authority of religious revelation as a source and foundation of morality," hotly debated issues in the tumultuous public sphere of mid-seventeenth-century England. "Questions about the possible sources of moral knowledge specifically," Woolhouse (1997:xi) continues, "could certainly have exposed the need for a wider investigation into the extent to which knowledge of any kind is attainable by the human mind."

Religious knowledge was central to the program of the Royal Society. Thomas Sprat (quoted in Aarsleff 1994:254) declares in his

History that "the intellectual Disposition of this Age is bent upon a rational Religion," consistent with the notion that the goal of science was to illuminate God's hand in creation. Recognition of the place of religion in the scientific epistemology of Locke's day should make us aware in turn that the metadiscursive regimentation of science and of religion are mutually implicated in Locke's writings.

Toward a Doctrine of Signs

The significance of Locke's departure from established Western linguistic ideologies and practices cannot be overemphasized. As Aarsleff (1982) notes, Locke's *Essay* had a profound impact on thinking about language during the following three centuries. Before turning to Locke's treatment of metadiscursive practices, we will outline four facets of his conceptualization of language: (1) the notion that language forms part of a special domain that he termed the "semiotic"; (2) an approach to language that privileges abstraction and decontextualization; (3) the equation of linguistic order with atomistic, minimal units (signs) rather than larger discursive units; and (4) the proposition that signs were relatively arbitrary, conventional, shared, and context-free.

Locke concludes his *Essay* (IV.xxi.5) with the following sentence: "All which three, viz. *things*, as they are in themselves knowable; *actions* as they depend on us, in order to happiness; and the right use of *signs* in order to knowledge, being *toto coelo* different, they seemed to me to be the three great provinces of the intellectual world, wholly separate and distinct one from another." The third branch, which Locke terms "the doctrine of signs," is concerned with "the nature of signs, the mind makes use of for the understanding of things, or conveying its knowledge to others" (IV.xxi.4). Locke argues that words, as signs, stand not for "the reality of things" but for "ideas in the mind of the speaker." As such, the association of sound and idea is based not on a natural connection but on "a perfectly arbitrary imposition" that is created by "the free choice of the mind, pursuing its own ends" (III.ii.4–5, 12).

Locke argues that we can never know the internal constitution of things, which he refers to as "real essences"; the common view that words stand "for the reality of things" is accordingly mistaken. In building his theory of conventional and arbitrary associations between words and ideas, Locke makes a basic distinction between words that stand for simple ideas and general words. Simple ideas are products of sensation, "those impressions objects themselves make on our minds" (III.iv.11). Their meaning is accordingly determined by sense experience and cannot be defined through language. Their meaning must rather be characterized by specifying the sensations from which they are derived. While the mind is thus more passive in forming simple ideas, it does not simply reflect either things or sensations. A simple idea of an apple is abstracted from the sensations that emanate from a range of real, particular apples; in its formation, information is selected from the available range of sensory impressions.

Most words are, in contrast, general terms; unlike simple ideas, which are tied to classes of things, general terms are created by the mind by combining a number of simple ideas. Since the mind is free to combine simple ideas that are not associated in nature, it necessarily selects certain sensory characteristics and rejects others as a basis for creating a general term. "Mixed modes" thus refer directly to "ideas in the mind" rather than to things in the world, even though the process of construction is ultimately retraceable through reflection (III.v.1). This conception allows Locke to retain a commitment to the primacy of sense data while at the same time suggesting that sense data play a vastly different role in language than in knowledge of things in themselves.

Locke repeatedly discusses the central role of abstraction in the creation of general names. The abstract ideas that mediate between simple ideas and general names are derived by factoring out the particulars through which each simple idea differs and "retaining only those wherein they agree" (III.iii.9). Meaning and language itself emerge, in Peircean terms, from a suppression of indexicality—that is, ties to context—in favor of the creation of symbols. Locke (III.iii.6) points specifically to the crucial importance of abstraction from physical, social, and linguistic contexts: "Words become general by being made the signs of general ideas: and ideas become general, by separating from them the circumstances of time and place, and any other ideas that may determine them to this or that particular existence."

The equation of language with abstraction is rationalized in part by the need for economy. Noting that "the true end of speech...is to be the easiest and shortest way of communicating our notions" (III.vi.33),

Locke argues that the ability to encompass a number of particulars within a general class enables us to avoid wasting "our time and breath in tedious descriptions" (III.vi.30). A second consideration goes to the heart of Locke's concern with the nature of human understanding and the reason that language plays a central role in acquiring knowledge. Since things in themselves are only particulars, direct contemplation of things is incapable of yielding universal knowledge. Words, on the other hand, are signs of general classes created by the mind; since they are abstract, words provide means of creating the sorts of true and universal propositions to which Locke grants epistemological privilege. Once general terms have been combined in propositions, it is possible to derive conclusions that are universal, certain, and eternal. Truth and abstraction are one: "Truth, then seems to me…to signify nothing but the joining or separating of Signs" (IV.v.2). Locke repeatedly turns to mathematics as a model for discourse in view of its ability to use economical, basic terms with precisely defined values in generating universal, certain propositions (see, for example, Locke 1971:70, 91). He argues that the ability to derive general truths and abstract notions presupposes "the use of reason" (I.i.13); in arguing that the development of abstract ideas is progressive and not innate, Locke suggests that children, idiots, illiterates, day laborers, and savages are possessed of more limited capacities for abstract thinking than, we would presume, educated, adult Europeans.

Locke points to a crucial constraint on "the free choice of the mind" in creating signs. Sounds must be used identically by speaker and hearer in such a way as "to convey the precise notions of things." Maintaining a rigid one-to-one correspondence between sound and meaning is, accordingly, requisite for communication: "It is plain cheat and abuse, when I make [words] stand sometimes for one thing and sometimes for another" (III.x.5).

Here Locke has reconceptualized language in such a way as to counter the deep skepticism expressed by Bacon and by his fellow members of the Royal Society. Speech and thought are not only based in sense data; they also draw on means of abstracting from particulars that are just as systematic as those associated with experimental science. But Locke has really taken a much more fundamental step, not only making language safe for science but constructing an ideology of language modeled on the very properties of scientific knowledge that held the most cachet for its seventeenth-century proponents—and, we would argue, most twentieth-century proponents of a scientific outlook as well. According to Bacon and Sprat, language was damned as a means of acquiring knowledge by its intrinsic association with rhetoric, intertextuality, social interaction, and conflict, that is, with difference, politics, and historical particularity. Locke cut the conceptual links between language and society, politics, and history by arguing that the indexical grounding of speech in the social world is not its intrinsic character but is rather "plain cheat and abuse"—the way that misguided individuals get detoured from the true linguistic path. For Locke, language's essential nature remains untouched by these characteristics; it rather embodies the characteristics most highly prized by his fellows in the Royal Society, "a reliable, certain, but abstract relationship to particulars." Locke's perspective recasts efforts to create scientific practices that discard language entirely or invent artificial languages as unnecessary and misguided. Since language is intrinsically reliable, all that is needed to render it both a perfect mode of communication and a reliable means of generating universal propositions, knowledge, and truth is a program of reform that would clear away "the cheat and abuse" of words.

What is the source of language's contamination? In the *Essay on Human Understanding* as well as in *Of the Conduct of the Understanding* (1971) and *Some Thoughts Concerning Education* (1989), Locke attacks metadiscursive practices that promote referential ambiguity and variability, and he attempts substitute practices that are more in line with his characterization of language's conceptual foundation. Intertextuality lies at the core of unacceptable metadiscursive practices. Locke argues that discourse that is produced through explicitly intertextual links is deeply grounded indexically in particular texts, persons, and activities. Beyond being incapable of producing the abstract, general thinking that generates knowledge, such practices simply provide a cover for semantic indeterminacy, shifting definitions, weak arguments, and imperfections of knowledge (IV.xx.17). Practices that emphasize intertextuality lead squarely in the wrong direction for Locke, creating endless links between discourses that draw interlocutors further and further into language itself. The "intervention of words" (III.ix.21) should rather be strictly limited, leading us as quickly as possible out of language and into universal knowledge and reason.

Creating intertextual links, for Locke, is a passive process that deters individuals from following the path to truth and knowledge; the chain of signifiers accordingly must be broken and ideas derived from texts must be "divested of the false lights and deceitful ornaments of speech" (Locke 1971:93). Rather than making meaning immediately accessible, intertextuality embeds it in the discourses articulated by other people and in other times (III.ix.9–10). According to Locke, knowledge must be internalized by each individual through rational reflection at the same time that it is externalized by connecting it, through observation and sense perception, with reality. Otherwise, individuals will be discursively dependent on others "without being steady and settled in their own judgements" (Locke 1971:39). A person's reading "makes his understanding only the warehouse of other men's lumber" (1971:93). In a similarly individualistic and utilitarian metaphor, intertextuality is compared to "borrowed wealth" and "fairy money," which cannot be used as currency and "make no considerable addition to [one's] stock" (I.iii.24). Steven Shapin (1994) argues that members of the Royal Society took an emergent image of the independent gentleman—who did not need to lean on anyone for social, economic, or intellectual support—and used it in constructing a model of the natural philosopher; the growing cachet of science fashioned this figure into a dominant icon of the emergent modern social order. (See also Shapin and Schaffer 1985.)

Like Bacon, Locke attacked the notion that discursive authority should be vested in particular persons or texts. As is well known, Locke was a staunch opponent of the notion of innate ideas, which contradicted his conception of the arbitrary nature of signs and their ultimate derivation from sensation and reflection. His attack on innate ideas also stemmed, however, from his efforts to discredit extant metadiscursive practices. If we accept the proposition that some ideas are central, innate, and universal, Locke argues, these ideas will be used to create fixed intertextual bases for the production and interpretation of discourse. Such a practice would simply fill our heads with "other men's opinions"; the comprehension of truth and reason would thus be undertaken by another, and "what in them was science, is in us but opiniatrety" (i.e., opinionatedness; I.iv.24). No matter how true they might be, ideas gained in this fashion can contribute nothing to knowledge and reason. Locke strongly attacked textual authority itself; language must serve only as a neutral and transparent means of communicating ideas that exist in the mind of the speaker. Authoritative texts, he asserted, encourage belief at the expense of knowledge and comprehension. Whereas belief is dialogic, involving social and discursive relationships, knowledge is monologic, individual, rational, and universal. We will have more to say about this monologic internalization of the word later.

One rubric Locke uses to frame his attack on intertextuality is tradition. Locke conceived of tradition as intertextually constituted, a chain of testimonies with each successive link standing at a farther remove from the experiential base of true knowledge. "[A]ny testimony," he maintains,

> the further off it is from the original truth, the less force and proof it has. The being and existence of the thing itself, is what I call the original truth. A credible man vouching his knowledge of it, is a good proof: but if another equally credible, do witness it from his report, the testimony is weaker; and a third that attests from hearsay of an hearsay, is yet less considerable. So that *in traditional truths, each remove weakens the force of the proof:* and the more hands the tradition has successively passed through, the less strength and evidence does it receive from them. (IV.xvi.10)

Locke recognizes here the metadiscursive foundation of traditional authority in the course of denying its legitimacy. This is a resonant moment in the advent of modernity, as Locke advances "rational man" as the arbiter of "authentic truths," displacing "men [who] look on opinions to gain force by growing older" (IV.xvi.10).

According to Locke, it is especially difficult to extirpate intertextually based practices because they are closely associated with the way individuals acquire signs. Particularly in the case of signs that signify complex ideas, we first appropriate names through conversation without being sure that we grasp the ideas they signify. This process is of tremendous importance developmentally, in Locke's view, "in that children, being taught words, whilst they have but imperfect notions of things, apply them at random, and without much thinking, and seldom frame determined ideas to be signified by them" (III.xi.24). The metadiscursive practices that Locke attacks are, moreover, rooted in "custom," such that contextual and intertextual associations can be extirpated only with great difficulty. Here Locke constructs a dichotomy between discursive practices associated with rationality, involving logical relationships between decontextualized signs, and practices that order signs and shape their meaning indexically through contextual and intertextual links. Rather than leading "men" to a deeper grasp of the intrinsic nature of language, such practices deprive them of their common sense by filling their heads with "some independent ideas, of no alliance to one another, [that] are, by education, custom, and the constant din of their party, so coupled in their minds that they always appear there together" (II.xxxiii.18).

Although Locke asserts that his program of language reform through practices of linguistic self-help is generally applicable, he notes repeatedly that it is more applicable to some persons and in some discursive spheres than others. Arguing that language is used for "recording our own thoughts" and "for the communicating of our thoughts to others" (III.ix.1), Locke suggests that the communicative function is accomplished distinctly in civil and philosophical spheres. The *civil use* of words "may serve for the upholding common conversation and commerce, about the ordinary affairs and conveniences of civil life," but their *philosophical* use revolves around communicating "the precise notions of things" and general propositions regarding "certain and undoubted truths" that provide solid conceptual and discursive foundations (III.ix.3). Locke suggests that the requirements for semantic precision and referential constancy are more stringent in the philosophical domain, whereas "[v]ulgar notions suit vulgar discourses... Merchants and lovers, cooks and tailors, have words wherewithal to dispatch their ordinary affairs" (III.xi.10). He notes that "it would be well, too, if [the process of stabilizing and strictly delimiting significations] extended itself to common conversation and the ordinary affairs of life" (III.xi.10), but seems to doubt that individuals who must devote themselves to "ordinary affairs" are likely to benefit from his program of conceptual and linguistic reform. We will comment below on the importance of Locke's assertion that the language of some social groups is more susceptible to reform than that of others.

Locke's approach to remedying the abuse of words essentially boils down to two principles. First, we must reflect on the words we use to ensure clear and constant relationships between ideas and names. Individuals are to sit down and systematize the meaning of each word in their vocabulary through its correspondence with sense data. Each sign can then be placed in a constant and logical relationship vis-à-vis all other signs, and each act of speaking is to be guided by this internalized lexicon. Second, individuals who have undertaken this process of self-correction must be constantly on guard against the possibility that their interlocutors might not define signs in the same fashion.

The language ideology and metadiscursive practices that Locke proposes have profound implications for social inequality. In his treatment of understanding and language, Locke develops a strong cognitive and linguistic component to his doctrine of natural rights. All persons are born with "faculties and powers" that would enable them to cultivate their understanding and heighten their linguistic precision. Not everyone subjects himself or herself, however, to the "much time, pains, and skill, strict inquiry, and long examination" (III.vi.30) required for this process of linguistic reflection and reasoning. Locke makes it clear that social class, occupation, and gender create great gulfs in the ability of individuals to reason, the breadth of their understanding, and the degree of verbal competence they achieve. "The day labourer in a country village has commonly but a small pittance of knowledge because his ideas and notions have been confined to the narrow bounds of a poor conversation and employment" (Locke 1971:10); such "men of low and mean education" are similarly "no more capable of reasoning than almost a perfect natural" (1971:21). Philosophers and truth seekers, on the other hand, *must* develop their understanding, rationality, and verbal skills, and he deems such training necessary for the education of gentlemen. The relevance of gender as well as social class is clear here. Locke notes, for example, that women, like men whose business is confined to common life, can appropriately develop verbal skills entirely by rote; gentlemen and philosophers, on the other hand, should master grammatical rules and perfect the stylistic features of their speech (Locke 1989:224). Thus, as we ascend the social ladder in terms of both class and rank, consciousness of linguistic structure and language use becomes increasingly necessary. Locke's nascent sociolinguistics (of which more later) suggests that those who occupy the lower rungs are not able to gain access to the metadiscursive practices that promote conceptual and linguistic excellence.

The development of reasoning and linguistic precision is limited by the range of experiences gained through one's occupation and the amount of leisure time available. Differential competence in reasoning and using language properly becomes pronounced, according to Locke, through practice. He argues, "We are born with faculties and powers capable of almost anything...but it is only the exercise of those powers which give us ability and skill in anything, and leads us towards perfection" (Locke 1971:13). Locke observed long ago that social class is inscribed on the body as much as it is on the tongue when he suggested that it is training and practice that create differences in "carriage and language" between a middle-aged ploughman and a gentleman (1971:13). The ability "to reason well or speak handsomely" is limited by an individual's access to the metadiscursive practices that instill such competence—and thus quite clearly by class and gender.

In outlining his proposal for perfecting language by standardizing it, Locke suggests that the linguistically enlightened have the right and the duty to regulate the language use of their interlocutors. The self-disciplining process must accordingly be extended interpersonally: "In discourse with others, (if we find them mistake us,) we ought to tell what the complex idea is that we make such a name stand for" (III.xi.24). The inverse is true as well, such that the linguistically unreformed pose a conceptual if not social danger: "He that uses words without any clear and steady meaning" may "lead himself and others into errors," and thus "ought to be looked on as an enemy to truth and knowledge" (III.xi.5). Locke makes it clear that the rationalizing process accords individuals the right to discipline others; bonding together in a joint effort to make our words clear and ensure that we use them identically, we are "not to be unwilling to have them examined by others" (III.v.16). The linguistically enlightened can also play a special role in policing the language acquisition of children, "diligently to watch, and carefully to prevent the undue connexion of ideas in the minds of young people" (II.xxxiii.8). In the Epistle Dedicatory to *Some*

Thoughts Concerning Education, Locke argues that the most care should be devoted to the education of gentlemen: "For if those of that Rank are by their Education once set right, they will quickly bring all the rest into Order" (1989:80).

Having presented a new ideology of language, Locke seeks to legitimate a new set of metadiscursive practices by claiming that they can help perfect language by capitalizing on its real nature. For him, the discursive practices that are antithetical to rationality and science are embodied in the bête noire of rhetoric, particularly as it emerged in "the art of disputation." In Locke's view, rhetoric, especially as embodied in the discursive practices of the "schoole-men," brings into high relief what he regarded as the core of language: abstract and decontextualized signs with precise, nonoverlapping, stable meanings arranged in logical relations. At the same time, the dangers of rhetoric underlined for him the need to reform existing discursive practices. According to Locke, rhetoric fosters unexamined, imprecise uses of language ordered through intertextual and other types of indexical linkages. Since it confounds rather than clarifies meaning, "the admired Art of Disputing hath added much to the natural imperfection of languages" (III.x.6) and kept "even inquisitive men from true knowledge" (III.x.10).

Rhetoric becomes the foe of rationality and knowledge through its connection with passion, emotionality, and external authority. Locke's ideal discursive type—plain speech that conveys information with maximal economy through referentially stable signs—engages the rational capacity of the mind in an active process, one that enables it to create and evaluate clear arguments. Rhetoric and its devices (metaphor, figurative meaning, dialectic, syllogisms, and the like) rather render the mind passive and foster an emotional attachment to the words of others, thus engendering social as well as intellectual dependence. As Barrilli (1989:78–81) notes, Locke echoed the Baconian dichotomy that opposes the universality of logic to the particularity of rhetoric. Reason needs only the discursive common denominator, stable signs, to convey it, and it is accordingly free of the indexicality that links rhetoric to texts and/or discursive interactions. Discourse must be purified of interest—that is, free from the influence of individual agency, social location, and history. Rational discourse thus leads one to truth, which is characterized as universal, unimpeachable, and intrinsic knowledge, "the necessary and indubitable connexion of all the ideas or proofs one to another" (IV.xvii.2). Locke draws on cross-cultural comparisons to support his claim for the universality of plain speech and the marginality of rhetoric: men can reason quite adequately in Asia and America "who yet never heard of a syllogism" (IV.xvii.4).

Locke marginalizes rhetoric by aestheticizing it as verbal ornamentation and locating it in the realm of "wit and fancy" (III.x.34). Since it strives for entertainment and pleasantry, rhetoric can be tolerated "in discourses where we seek rather pleasure and delight than information and improvement" (III.x.34). Moreover, rhetoric is condemned as not only an art but a false one at that—"the art of rhetoric" really amounts to the "arts of fallacy." Locke urges that "in all discourses that pretend to inform or instruct, it is wholly to be avoided" (II:146). The discursive realm to which rhetoric is relegated must be tabooed not only for thwarting reason and knowledge but also for the seductive power of its beauty.

This forbidden terrain is occupied, for Locke, by two other superfluous and dangerous characters: women and poetry. By way of anticipating charges of "great boldness, if not brutality" for speaking against rhetoric, Locke (III.x.34) notes: "Eloquence, like the fair sex, has too prevailing beauties in it to suffer itself ever to be spoken against. And it is in vain to find fault with those arts of deceiving, wherein men find pleasure to be deceived." He creates a powerfully seductive analogy, aligning his dichotomy between knowledge, truth, universality, rationality, agency, and science, on the one hand, and passion, beauty, belief, passivity, particularity, error, deceit, and rhetoric on the other, with the relationship between men and women. Interestingly, Locke simultaneously denies women access as skilled practitioners into the feminine realm of rhetoric. Learning to speak and write in the "plain Natural way," that is by rote, will suffice for women and for those engaged in "the common Affairs of Life and ordinary commerce" (Locke 1989:224, 225). The way Locke connects gender and class in this assertion becomes more explicit as he goes on to suggest that all gentlemen should be taught grammar and rhetoric "since the want of Propriety, and Grammatical Exactness, is thought very misbecoming [to] one of that Rank, and usually draws on one guilty of such Faults, the censure of having had a Lower Breeding and worse Company, than suits with his quality" (1989:225). We will have more to say later about this contradiction in Locke's view of rhetoric.

Locke allowed even less space in his schema for poetics than for rhetoric. Poetry, for Locke, is simply referential redundancy. If the use of words is confined to the expression of clear and distinct ideas through stable significations, large tomes "would shrink into a very narrow compass; and many of the philosophers (to mention no other) as well as poets works, might be contained in a nutshell" (III.xi.26). In *Some Thoughts Concerning Education* (1989:230), Locke argues that poetry is socially useless, a waste of time that squanders estates rather than produces wealth and places one in "bad company and places." Poetry should thus be expunged from education, or at least from the teaching of gentlemen, and parents whose children possess a "Poetic Vein…should labour to have it stifled, and suppressed" (1989:230). Here Locke would seem to muster religious overtones in linking aesthetics with frivolity, desire, and sin.[2] Poetry, like rhetoric, embodies for Locke the excesses of language, the points at which language steps beyond "the true end of speech, which is to be the easiest and shortest way of communicating our notions" (III.vi.33), inverting the means-ends relationship with content in celebrating form for form's sake.

We hasten to note a fascinating exception to Locke's dismissal of rhetoric, one that emerges in *Some Thoughts Concerning Education*. There he is concerned with an aspect of "ill-breeding" that springs from failing to show "Respect, Esteem, and Good-will" for one's interlocutors (Locke 1989:203). According to Locke, the appearance of disrespect can spring from several factors. A "natural roughness" precludes consideration of the "inclinations, tempers, or conditions" of interlocutors (1989:201). Other sources of interpersonal friction include displaying contempt or censoriousness toward others or, on the other hand, flattery and excessive formality ("Ceremony"). Locke seems to have anticipated Bakhtin, Goffman, and reception theory by observing that only clowns and brutes fail to perceive "what pleases or displeases" their interlocutors or to "bend to a compliance and accommodate themselves to those they have to do with" (1989:201). The contradictory character of his call for dialogicality in conversation goes hand in hand with his assertions that such sensitivity will not only display good breeding but "bespeak the more favourable Attention and give great Advantage" (1989:205) and that more "Credit and Esteem" will be accrued by offering even an ill argument or ordinary observation "with some civil Preface of Deference and Respect to the Opinions of others" than by presenting a clever argument "with a rough, insolent, or noisy Management" (1989:203).

Locke specifically argues for the centrality of discursive interaction here. "*Good-Breeding*" is not essentially a matter of taking off hats and holding one's legs properly: "*Civility* being, in truth, nothing but a care to show any slighting, or contempt, of any one in Conversation" (1989:203). Locke astutely observes the range of channels that shape the conversational encounter—"Looks, Voice, Words, Motions, Gestures" (1989:200)—and anticipates both Benjamin Lee Whorf and sociolinguistics in arguing that such fashions of speaking are "as peculiar and different, in several Countries of the World, as their languages" (1989:204). Rather than giving children rules of linguistic etiquette, one should accordingly model the process of expressing love and respect "acceptably to every one, according to the Fashions they have been used to" (1989:204).

It seems clear that one of the primary motives for Locke's distrust of rhetoric and his general attack on the "cheat and abuse" of words was his clear conviction that such discursive practices are capable of generating conflict, even to the point of undermining the social order. The foregoing exception to his dismissal of rhetoric revolves around precisely this issue—conversation's potential for generating conflict must be defused. While the right to disagree with opinions and correct matters of fact must be preserved, objections must be raised "in the gentlest manner, and [with the] softest words [that] can be found" in order to preserve civility (1989:202).

As usual, "learned men" exemplify the dangers of unconstrained dispute and the disruptive potential of indexically grounded speech. Locke asserts that the learned men who "had the advantage to destroy the instruments and means of discourse, conversation, instruction, and society…did no more but perplex and confound the signification of words" (III.x.10). In areas that concern morality and ethics, for example, "Nothing can be so dangerous as *principles thus taken up without questioning or examination*" (IV.xii.4). Locke projected the abuse of words

directly onto the larger social stage, arguing that confused, indetermi-
nate, and shifting meanings, illogical relationships between ideas, and
particularly the metadiscursive practices associated with disputation
"establish the irreconcilable opposition between different sects of philosophy and religion" (II.xxxiii.18) and have "brought confusion, disorder, and uncertainty into the affairs of mankind; and if not
destroyed, yet in a great measure rendered useless, these two great
rules, religion and justice" (III.x.12). On the other hand, when language is reformed—restored to its true nature as shared, arbitrary, and
decontextualized signs, it provides a crucial social glue, "without which
laws could be but ill made, or vice and disorders repressed" (II.xxii.10).

This message is powerful: language is essentially ordered and rational. When discourse is shaped by metadiscursive practices grounded in
indexicality and intertextuality, however, language becomes a source of
irrationality, difference, and social disorder. Imposing metadiscursive
practices that center on rational self-disciplining is not only necessary
for scientific advancement; the fate of civil society hinges, at least in
part, on the development of new ways of speaking and practices for
imposing them:

> I leave it to be considered, whether it would not be well for
> mankind, whose concernment it is to know things as they are,
> and to do what they ought, and not to spend their lives in talk-
> ing about them, or tossing words to and from; whether it would
> not be well, I say, that the use of words were made plain and
> direct; and that language, which was given to us for the
> improvement of knowledge and the bond of society, should not
> be employed to darken truth and unsettle people's rights.
> (III.x.13)

Those individuals who have undertaken Locke's process of linguistic self-disciplining are accorded a crucial role in shaping how language
acquisition, discourse, and metadiscursive practices will be rationalized.

The fruits of discipline will, according to Locke, also provide a
basis for deciding what can be said, in that the process of rational
reflection will enlighten us as to the limits of human knowledge. These
epistemological limits mark another point at which metadiscursive vigi-

lance is necessary to forestall conflict. In the course of the *Essay*, Locke identifies many theologically founded bases of certainty and assent as beyond the reach of empirically grounded reason and knowledge. John Marshall (1994:351) suggests that the overall effect of these critiques, especially within the context of the theological debates and religious turmoil of the period during which Locke composed the *Essay*, "was to suggest that no theological doctrines beyond the existence of God were beyond legitimate debate and widely differing interpretations and assents." Locke was acutely aware of the susceptibility of theological debate to degenerate into social conflict, civil war, or state-sponsored persecution, and from this awareness sprang his vigorous advocacy of toleration. In his *Letter on Toleration* (1968), revered as a charter document by champions of freedom of expression, Locke frames the argument for toleration in terms of the necessary separation of church and state, but in the *Essay* it is couched in metadiscursive terms, keyed to the limits of certainty:

> Since therefore it is unavoidable to the greatest part of men, if not all, to have several *opinions*, without certain and indubitable proofs of their truths; and it carries too great an imputation of ignorance, lightness, or folly, for men to quit and renounce their former tenets, presently upon the offer of an argument, which they cannot immediately answer, and show the insufficiency of: it would, methinks, become all men to maintain *peace*, and the common offices of humanity, *and friendship, in the diversity of opinions*, since we cannot reasonably expect, that anyone should readily and obsequiously quit his own opinion, and embrace ours with a blind resignation to an authority, which the understanding of man acknowledges not. (IV.xvi.4)

Clearly, in Locke's view, if speech is "the great bond that holds society together" (III.xi.1), social order depends upon linguistic discipline to clear language of its imperfections as an instrument of pure reference and to purge discourse of the abuses to which interest, habit, and the practical exigencies of social life have made it susceptible. Those men who have submitted their own speech to the discipline Locke prescribes constitute a discursive elite, metadiscursive arbiters of epistemological and social order. Locke clearly counts himself among this linguistic elect and offers his *Essay* as a self-help manual for those who seek linguistic self-improvement. Not content simply to tell people what to do, Locke seeks to model the metadiscursive practices he advocates. He asserts that he has avoided intertextuality in the construction of his text, boasting that "I shall not need to shore...up [this Discourse] with props and buttresses, leaning on borrowed or begged foundations" (Epistle I:18). Locke believes that the practices he promotes will further social as well as intellectual order: "I shall imagine I have done some service to truth, peace, and learning if, by any enlargement on this subject, I can make men reflect on their own use of language" (III.v.16).

It seems worthwhile to stress that "language" here means English. Although gentlemen should learn Latin and scholars would be wise to study Greek, it is the ability to convey one's thoughts in English that really counts. Locke faults teachers who teach rhetoric and logic in Latin and Greek "but yet never taught [their pupils] how to express themselves handsomely with their Tongues or Pens in the Language they are always to use" (1989:242). In deriding those who exalt Latin and Greek but consider English to be "the Language of the illiterate Vulgar," Locke cautions that unnamed neighboring countries "hath not thought it beneath the Publick Care, to promote and reward the improvement of their own Language" through colleges and stipends (1989:244). National pride is thus mustered to the task of reforming the English language and asserting its discursive centrality.

Locke's discussion of the importance of English seems emblematic of the social implications of his take on discourse in general, just as it anticipates a vast range of efforts to regiment English. Once simplified and standardized, English can successfully serve as an essential social glue; through its rational and universal character it can help overcome rampant social disorder and impose civility. Nevertheless, only an elite minority of the population enjoys the leisure, education, and circumstances required to undergo the process of rational reflection, referential reduction, semantic rationalization, and stylistic polishing that is needed to become a linguistic model and a flawless communicator. Thus, that which joins ultimately separates; just as social class and gender restrict access to the practices that enable speakers to dominate this standardized code, an individual's speech closely indexes and legiti-mates her or his location in the social structure. Since speaking prop-erly is tied to understanding, rationality, agency, truth, and social order, linguistic competence à la Locke provides a powerful synecdoche of one's suitability and authority as a member of civil society.

The parallels between *An Essay Concerning Human Understanding* and the *Two Treatises on Government* (Locke 1960) are striking in this connection. Since they occupy different "provinces of the intellectual world" and are "wholly separate and distinct one from another" (IV.xxi.5), we would hardly want to suggest that Locke sees language and knowledge on the one hand and the moral and political determi-nation of human conduct on the other as identical. Nonetheless, both contribute in important ways to legitimating social inequality and a new social order. In these texts, Locke challenges established views that see property rights and language as intrinsically social in nature, arguing that both spring from the natural and universal endowment enjoyed by each individual. In each case, their fruitful cultivation is dependent upon an individual's use of reason; using language, labor, or property without exercising one's rationality creates conflict and social disorder.

In Locke's view, some individuals make much greater use of their natural reason. Everyone is naturally granted rationality, language, and the capacity to labor; all individuals thus possess a natural potential for rationally reflecting on their condition and use of signs.[3] Locke repeat-edly argues that people are only capable of utilizing capacities that they developed through sustained practice. Those who have expanded their rational capabilities can justifiably hold more property and alienate labor as well as provide models for the linguistic conduct of others. Since irrationality is associated with conflict and social disorder, those who differ, as MacPherson (1962:246) puts it, in "their ability or will-ingness to order their lives according to the bourgeois moral code" must accept their inferior position for the good of the society. Locke's writings on language thus seem to provide no less solid a foundation for naturalizing bourgeois society and social inequality than his politi-cal theory. In both cases, denying analytic status to difference and inequality paradoxically legitimated linguistic and political practices that created and sustained them.

LANGUAGE REFORM IN EIGHTEENTH-CENTURY GERMANY

If the language ideology of Locke is built on the foundation of an emergent scientific epistemology, that of Johann Gottfried Herder is founded on an equally emergent conception of national literatures. It would, though, be a misrepresentation of Herder and a disservice to our argument to suggest that Herder's ideology of language is solely or narrowly about language as a vehicle for literary expression. Literature, for Herder, was a frame of orientation for a conception of language that also encompasses history, culture, and politics and that views the place of language and literature as foundational to all of these dimensions of human existence.

It is not our intention to trace in detail the biographical factors, historical forces, and individual influences that contributed to the shaping of Herder's thought. Fortunately, that task has received the attention of a number of able scholars, including Aarsleff (1982:146–209), Bendix (1997:27–44), Blackall (1978),[4] and Clark (1969). We can, however, as we did for Locke, outline in broad terms some of the principal aspects of the intellectual context within which Herder's writings on language are to be understood.

In his wide-ranging study, *The Emergence of German as a Literary Language* (1978), Eric Blackall traces the intense preoccupation with the German language that characterized German intellectual life in the eighteenth century to the disastrous and lingering effects of the Thirty Years War, which engendered a widespread sense that Germany had lost its national pride and respect and a concomitant feeling that German culture was inferior to that of France. One manifestation of this cultural distress was a deep anxiety about the capacity of the German language as a vehicle for literature, philosophy, and other forms of intellectual expression (Blackall 1978:1–2). Importantly, however, as Blackall is at pains to establish, "the dissatisfaction was no passive despair; it was accompanied by a vigorous determination to improve the situation" (1978:1).

The intellectual stimulus for these efforts at reforming and reconstituting the German language came from such influential figures as Gottfried Wilhelm Leibniz, who tied his program for the promotion of the vernacular to the patriotic need for pride in one's fatherland, and

Christian Thomasius, for whom the cultivation of German was part of an Enlightenment vision that demanded liberation from past habits of thought and from the separation of the world of learning from everyday life perpetuated by a reliance on Latin for intellectual expression (Barnard 1965:8; Blackall 1978:2–18; Clark 1969:10). But the efforts at linguistic reform became more broadly based as well with the growth of "German Societies," nominally open to "all aficionados of the German language," but in practice made up largely of middle-class intellectuals—priests, teachers, professors, students—with links to the universities (van Dülmen 1992:45). While programs for language reform followed many lines, both practical and theoretical, we may identify two broad problems in particular that framed the efforts of German intellectuals to comprehend the nature of language and its role in the formation of German culture, namely, the origin and evolution of language and the relationship of language and literature to national identity.

Concerning the first of these, Ernest A. Menze and Karl Menges (1992:282–83) offer a useful and concise overview of the principal theological, anthropological, and epistemological issues and positions that shaped the debates. The central questions identified by Menze and Menges were three: Is language to be considered a divine gift or the result of an evolutionary process? Is language the decisive element that differentiates humans from animals? And, what is the relationship between language and consciousness? To these, we may add a fourth: Is language a precondition of society or an outcome of the human social condition?

Those who advanced a theologically founded theory argued that humans were endowed with language by divine inspiration but differed among themselves on the question of whether God's gift consisted of ready-made language or of the capacity to create language. The proponents of a rationalist theory, by contrast, viewed language as the product of the human capacity for reason and thus as representing a fundamental contrast between humans and animals. A third, "sensualist" position held that the emergence of language, like all human knowledge, is rooted in sensory perception and shaped by the evolutionary differentiation of the senses. All of these theoretical positions implicate conceptions of the nature of society by asking if language is prerequisite to society or a product of mankind's social nature. Indeed, the theological and the rational positions might easily be reformulated with "society" in place of "language." Further, theories of language origin are characteristically coupled with theories of its subsequent historical trajectory: progressive development, the maintenance of or degeneration from an original state of perfection, or an organic cycle of growth, maturity, decline, and death.

These problems of the origin and evolution of language were widely debated in the mid- to late-eighteenth century, deriving considerable stimulus from the contributions of Etienne Bonnot Condillac and Jean-Jacques Rousseau in France and the thinkers of the Scottish Enlightenment in Britain. The engagement of German scholars, like Johann Peter Süssmilch and Johann David Michaelis, with these issues took place within a broader intellectual arena that transcended political or linguistic boundaries and at the same time allowed for the valorization of particular languages as in some way superior to others (Aarsleff 1982:146–209). Indeed, one issue that raised the question of the relative capacities and merits of particular languages had to do with the second broad problem that gave focus to debates concerning language reform in eighteenth-century Germany, namely, the relationship between language and literary expression. At one level, the problem might be framed in general, universal terms, by asking, for example, what stage of linguistic development or what type of language is best suited to poetry or prose. For the most part, however, the particularities of specific languages figure prominently in consideration of language and literary expression.

As the debate was joined in eighteenth-century Germany, we find on the one hand proponents of Latin or French or even English as superior for literary purposes to German, and, on the other, champions of some variety of German—past or current, natural or constructed—as the only proper vehicle for an authentic German literature. This may state the terms of the debate in too oppositional a fashion, to be sure, for one of the most prominent figures in the arena, Johann Christoph Gottsched, advocated the German vernacular as a literary language while at the same time advancing French classical drama as a literary standard.

One prominent line of influence on German thought concerning national literatures came from the British philologists Thomas

Blackwell, Robert Lowth, Hugh Blair, and Robert Wood. Blackwell and Wood in their studies of Homer, Lowth in his classic work on ancient Hebrew poetics, and Blair in his defense of Ossian pioneered a historically, linguistically, and culturally relativist—that is to say, contextual—approach to literary expression. They insisted that the true literary qualities of the Homeric epics, the Old Testament, or the Ossianic epics could only be discovered and appreciated through a contextually grounded critical reading in which the particularities of time, place, and language were taken fully into account. In its strongest form, as in Lowth's *Lectures on the Sacred Poetry of the Hebrews* (1969), this demanded an interpretive effort that prefigures the ethnographic goal of "seeing through the native's eyes." Lowth is worth quoting in this regard:

> To all who apply themselves to the study of their poetry...difficulties and inconveniences must necessarily occur. Not only the antiquity of these writings forms a principal obstruction in many respects; but the manner of living, of speaking, of thinking, which prevailed in those times, will be found altogether different from our customs and habits. There is, therefore, great danger, lest, viewing them from an improper situation, and rashly estimating all things by our own standard, we form an erroneous judgment.
>
> Of this kind of mistake we are to be always aware, and these inconveniencies are to be counteracted by all possible diligence: nor is it enough to be acquainted with the language of this people, their manners, discipline, rites, and ceremonies; we must even investigate their inmost sentiments, the manner and connexion of their thoughts; in one word, we must see all things with their eyes, estimate all things by their opinions: we must endeavour as much as possible to read Hebrew as the Hebrews would have read it. (Lowth 1969(I):112–13)

The relativizing thrust of the critical method advanced by these British philologists, taken up by such influential German scholars as Michaelis and Christian Gottlob Heyne, fostered a conception of literature as a national phenomenon and of a standard of literary power and authenticity as achieved only through faithfulness to one's own national language and culture.

Language, Poetics, and Tradition in Herder

Johann Gottfried Herder's early essay, "On Diligence in the Study of Several Learned Languages," published in 1764, signaled his public entry into the intellectual arena we have sketched out in the foregoing pages and marked the beginning of a passionate lifelong engagement with language, literature, and the foundations of national culture. Although many students of Herder's voluminous writings fault him for a lack of intellectual consistency over the long course of his career, we share the judgment of those who find an overall coherence in his work. Accordingly, rather than offering a chronological examination of his writings on language, we will endeavor to delineate in general, synthetic terms the intellectual core of his ideology of language. We begin, though, with specific attention to his essay *On the Origins of Language* (1772), the work best known to students and historians of linguistics. The essay won the prize competition of the Berlin Academy for 1771, the topic of which was framed in the following terms: "Supposing that human beings were left to their natural faculties, are they in a position to invent language? And by which means will they achieve this invention on their own?" (Aarsleff 1982:194–95). Herder's victorious submission brought him into full intellectual prominence and established him as a significant participant in the language debates of the day.

The essay opens with a provocative assertion: "While still an animal, man already has language" (SW 5:5/Herder 1966:87).[5] As Herder develops upon this assertion, however, it soon becomes clear that this language that resides in our animal nature is but one species of language, not yet human language. The language that we have "in common with the animals," as sentient beings among other sentient beings, consists of "screams," "sounds," "moans," "wild inarticulate tones," responses to "violent sensations of [the] body" (SW 5:5–7/Herder 1966:87–88). This "language of feeling," to be sure, has communicative power, striking a resonant chord in other sentient beings of like feeling. But true human language, in Herder's view, rests on very specifically human capacities that clearly differentiate us from other animals. These capacities Herder terms *Besonnenheit*, reflection, one of the most fundamental concepts in all of his philosophy.

Besonnenheit is the "entire disposition of man's forces," a complex and unitary human capacity that encompasses "the total economy of his sensuous and cognitive, or his cognitive and volitional nature" (SW 5:28/Herder 1966:109–10; see also Barnard 1965:42–43). In the concept of *Besonnenheit*, Herder rejects the separation of faculties—reason, emotion, will, and so forth—on which Kantian philosophy is built. For Herder, "all such words as sensuousness and instinct, fantasy and reason are after all no more than determinations of one single power wherein opposites cancel each other out" (SW 5:31/Herder 1966:112); in the concept of *Besonnenheit* the Kantian antinomies vanish (Clark 1969:407).[6] In *Besonnenheit resides* "The distinctive character of mankind" (SW 5:29/Herder 1966:110) as well as the capacity for language: "Man, placed in a state of reflection which is peculiar to him, with this reflection for the first time given full freedom of action, did invent language" (SW 5:34/Herder 1966:115).

The process begins with the human animal immersed in a sea of sensations. By exercise of the power of reflection, one set of sensations is singled out, arrested; the sensory image thus selected becomes the focus of alert and conscious attention (SW 5:34–35/Herder 1966:115) and is recognized as a distinguishing characteristic of its source. It is worth noting here the *reflexivity* of the process. *Besonnenheit* is not merely reflection in the sense of focused consciousness but involves also consciousness of consciousness; in the exercise of *Besonnenheit* man must be "conscious of being attentive" (SW 5:35/Herder 1966:115).

In an extended argument that we need not recapitulate here, Herder concludes that sonic images are the ones most apt to be singled out in this reflective process. His central example is the bleating of a sheep: "The sound of bleating perceived by a human soul as the distinguishing mark of the sheep became, by virtue of this reflection, the name of the sheep, even if his tongue never tried to stammer it." The bleating is "a conceived sign through which the soul clearly remembered an idea—and what is that other than a word? And what is the entire human language other than a collection of such words?" (SW 5:36/Herder 1966:117). By this process, then, "human language is invented" (SW 5:35/Herder 1966:116).

It is important to emphasize that the language thus invented is not merely an abstract set of signs by which the reflective being apprehends the phenomenal world. In Herder's view, it "is in its very origin...a means of contact," a social instrument: "I cannot think the first human thought, I cannot align the first reflective argument without dialoguing in my soul or without striving to dialogue. The first human thought is hence in its very essence a preparation for the possibility of dialoguing with others! The first characteristic mark which I conceive is a characteristic word for me and a word of communication for others!" (SW 5:47/Herder 1966:128). *Besonnenheit* is thus doubly reflexive: a consciousness of one's own consciousness is inherently bound up with a striving for dialogue with others. Language, thought, and communication are all rooted in *Besonnenheit.*

Of course, the original human language that consists of onomatopoeic imitations of distinguishing sonic characteristics bears little apparent relation to language as we now know it. From its first emergence in this rudimentary form, language—and with it the human species—embarks upon a process of development that is intrinsic to its nature. The precise processes of change that Herder sets forth with regard to the formal structure of language are clearly untenable from the standpoint of current linguistic knowledge and need not concern us too closely. In Herder's understanding, for example, grammar is an emergent superaddition to language and "the more primordial a language is, the less grammar there must be in it, and the oldest language is no more than the aforementioned dictionary of nature" (SW 5:82–83/Herder 1966:159). Verbs develop prior to nouns because things are named initially for the actions by which they produce their distinguishing sounds (sheep is "bleater"); primitive languages are characterized by abundant synonymy because they have not yet developed general categories which require the capacity for abstraction; and so on (see, for example, SW 5:9–10/Herder 1966:91; SW 11:228–29/Herder 1833[1]:31).

The forces and mechanisms of development that Herder outlines, however, are important to our argument. He states these in a series of "natural laws" in the second part of the essay *On the Origin of Language,* focusing on linguistic development in the individual, in social interaction, and in the nation, or *Volk.*[7]

The first natural law is as follows: "Man is a freely thinking and active being whose powers work on in progressive continuity, for which reason he is a creature of language" (SW 5:93/Herder 1966:173). The motive force of this development derives again from the human power of reflection. The more reflective thought is exercised in the apprehension of the world, the more developed language becomes; it grows by experience. Better thinking makes for better speaking in the progressive realization of human potential.

By the same token, language develops continuously by virtue of our social nature: "Man is by destiny a creature of the herd, that is, of society; and the continuous development of his language is hence natural, essential, and necessary to him" (SW 5:112/Herder 1966:173). As explained in *On the Origin of Language*, the social development of language takes place first within the family as knowledge is shared between spouses and passed on to offspring, thus making for cumulative growth through the generations. But elsewhere Herder generalizes the process: "Language and speech are developed most intensely through conversations...Language originated through intercourse and not in solitude; through conversation every expression is sharpened and polished" (SW 30:223/English translation quoted from Ergang 1966:158). Thus, for Herder, as for Locke, the social use of language as an instrument of social interaction is not only part of the natural essence of language itself but also the inherent means of its progressive cultivation.

From the individual to small groups in conversational interaction, Herder's third natural law carries the process of development to social units of still broader scope, namely nations, *Völker:* "As it was impossible for the entire human race to remain one herd, so it could not remain restricted to one language. There ensued the development of diverse national languages" (SW 5:123–24/Herder 1966:173). Indeed, Herder's entire understanding of the social organization of language is founded on a recognition of linguistic diversification at every level of integration from the individual to the international. Because of individual differences of experience and learning, no two individuals speak exactly the same language. In like manner, every family, every group shapes language in its own distinctive way. In turn, these social forces, in interaction with environmental differences which—Herder believed—induce modifications of the organs of speech, give rise to dialects and eventually to national languages. Indeed, in Herder's conception, it is the possession of its own distinctive language that constitutes the touchstone of a people or *Volk*, the sine qua non of its national identity and spirit. And it is with this relationship of language to *Volk* that Herder is most centrally concerned.

In one of his earliest writings, Herder articulated this fundamental principle: "Every nation has its own storehouse of thought rendered into signs," he wrote. "[T]his is its national language: a store to which the centuries have added, and that has waxed and waned like the moon, that...has experienced revolutions and transformations...—the treasury of the thought of an entire people" (SW 2:13/English translation quoted from Morton 1989:135). The quotations from Herder's writings marshaled by Robert Ergang establish the radical centrality of language to national identity especially emphatically:

> "Has a nationality," a character in one of Herder's dramas asks, "anything more precious than the language of its fathers? In this language dwell its whole world of tradition, history, religion and principles of life, its whole heart and soul" [SW 17:58]. Language "is the bond of souls, the vehicle of education, the medium of our best pleasures, nay of all social pastimes" [SW 18:384]; "it expresses the most distinguishing traits of the character of each nationality, and is the mirror of its history, its deeds, joys and sorrows" [SW 11:225; 18:337]; "it is generally acknowledged to be the means for transmitting human ideas, inclinations and deeds; by means of it we bequeath the treasure of former times to later generations; through a common language all the members of a social group participate one in another to a greater or lesser degree" [SW 16:46]. (English translation quoted from Ergang 1966:149–150)

We will pursue the further implications of all of these dimensions of relationship between language and nation in the course of our discussion, but for the moment we would simply underscore the affirmative tone that colors Herder's observations: the complex anchoring of language in national character, history, and society is to be celebrated. What for Locke is an impediment to true knowledge is for Herder a quality to be treasured.

In order to comprehend more fully how it is that language comes to be "the treasury of the thought of an entire people," we must consider in some detail Herder's poetics as a central component of his ideology of language. Herder employs the term poetry (*Poesie*) in two related senses. In the first and primary sense, poetry designates a quality of language, intrinsic to its nature; in the second, the term takes on a textual component as well, comprehending all genres of verbal art, including proverbs, fables, *Märchen* (fairy tales), myths, legends, and various dramatic forms as well as forms of verse such as songs, odes, ballads, and epics.

For Herder, the foundation of poetry, its essence, is inherent in the origin of human language itself. Let us recall the nature of the first human language—"a dictionary of significant names, and expressions full of imagery and feeling" (SW 12:7/Herder 1833(2):7). "Imitation it was of sounding, acting, stirring nature! Taken from the interjections of all beings and animated by the interjections of human emotion! The natural language of all beings fashioned by reason into sounds, into images of action, passion, and living impact!" (SW 5:56/Herder 1966:135). But then, Herder goes on, "What else is poetry?" (SW 5:57/Herder 1966:136). That is, this first human language is "a collection of elements of poetry" (SW 5:56/Herder 1966:135).

The identification of feeling as essential to the poetic quality of this first human language stems clearly from the constitution of the language itself as built up of imitations of the natural language of feeling. In this conception, feeling and reference are inescapably joined. But the prominence of feeling in Herder's formulations makes it all the more necessary to emphasize that the original human language—and thus poetry as well—consists of an integration of feeling *and* form. The sensory impressions that flow in upon the first speaker have discernible form, and the first human utterances are shaped by that form as well as by feeling.

> From without, the forms of sense flow into the soul, which puts upon them the impress of its own feeling, and seeks to express them outwardly by gestures, tones, and other significant indications. The whole universe with its movements and forms is for the outward intuition of man...Thus what flows in on him from without, according as he feels it and impresses his own feeling upon it, forms the genius of his poetry in its original elements. (SW 12:6/Herder 1833[2]:6)

Thus, from the beginning, form plays a key role in Herder's

philosophy of language. We shall have more to say on this below.

Given the identity of language and poetry, at least in their origins, we must expect that poetry, like language, undergoes transformation over time. One significant developmental factor that affects the role of poetry is the functional differentiation of language, which, in Herder's speculative history of language, is bound up with the evolution of grammatical forms.

> For as the first vocabulary of the human soul was a living epic of sounding and acting nature, so the first grammar was almost nothing but a philosophical attempt to develop that epic into a more regularized history. Thus it works itself down with verbs and more verbs and keeps working in a chaos which is inexhaustible for poetry, which is very rich—when subjected to a little more order—for the fixing of history, and which becomes usable only much later for axioms and demonstrations. (SW 5:84/Herder 1966:161)

First poetry, then history, then formal philosophy, as verb forms (especially past tenses) and noun inflections are progressively systematized (SW 5:84–85/Herder 1966:161–62).

It is not only grammar, however, that evolves in relation to functional differentiation, but communicative style as well. As language develops still further, in Herder's view, the uses to which it is put continue to have a shaping effect on its formal organization. "Then, through poetry," he writes, "come into being syllabic meter, choice of expressive words and colors, order and impact of imagery; through history, come differentiation of tenses, precision of expression, then, through oratory, comes finally the perfect rounding of periodic speech" (SW 5:88/Herder 1966:165). Note that we have here arrived at a transition from the first to the second sense of poetry distinguished just above: features such as meter, order of imagery, or the rounding of periodic speech are features of *discourse*, formal devices that organize the discursive structure. From poetry as a quality of language, Herder's developmental schema has led us to the emergence of poetry as characterized by formal regimentation at the level of discourse. Ultimately, then, in the long course of language development, poetry recedes from being coterminous with language to being one among a range of functional varieties marked by special discursive regimentation. At the same time, poetry (like other functional varieties) is itself multifunctional. With it, the poet "instructs, reproves, consoles, directs, commands, contemplates the past, and discloses the future" (SW 12:22/Herder 1833(2):26).

Although the unfolding of this historical process, as Herder envisions it, does expand the communicative capacities of language, it also entails a potential loss. As the sphere of philosophy is extended and reason plays an ever increasing role in the shaping of language, it can impinge upon poetry, leading to increasing formalism, mechanical "counting of syllables and scanning of verses" (SW 5:189), and "delicate and overwrought refinement" (SW 11:230/Herder 1833(1):32). Again, it is not formal patterning to which Herder objects (as we shall see in more detail below) but the increasing insistence on formalistic regimentation. In this process, poetry can be distanced from natural feeling, with a concurrent diminution of its expressive capacity, its vitality, and its affecting power (SW 1:53–55/Herder 1992:106–7; Kamenetsky 1973:837). "What is it that works miracles in the assemblies of people," Herder asks, "that pierces hearts, and upsets souls? Is it intellectual speech and metaphysics? Is it similes and figures of speech? Is it art [artifice] and coldly convincing reason?" These can be effective, but they do not suffice (SW 5:16/Herder 1966:98). Poetry must strive to retain its ties to the language of nature: "[E]ven with us, where reason to be sure often displaces emotion, where the sounds of nature are dispossessed by the artificial language of society—do not with us to the highest thunders of rhetoric, the mightiest bolts of poetry, and the magic moments of action come close to this language of nature by imitating it?" (SW 5:16/Herder 1966:97–98). What Herder is expressing here is summed up by his distinction between *Naturpoesie* and *Kunstpoesie*, the poetry of nature versus the poetry of art, which is to say, of artifice (SW 32:73/Herder 1992:44; see also Kamenetsky 1973). Nature is not to be constrained, vexed, squeezed, molded, or rendered artificial, as Bacon would have it, but imitated, experienced as fully as possible. One must strive not to penetrate nature, but to be open and attuned to its sounding influence.

Nor is it only grammatical, stylistic, and functional differentiation that diminish the vitality and affecting power of poetry. A further critical development that may work to this end is the advent of writing. "The more distant a people is from artful cultivated thinking, language and letters," Herder observes, "the less will its songs be written for paper— dead literary verse." What is lost to the written word is the fullness of "animated representation" (SW 14:105/Herder 1968:178), the expressive power of performance. For Herder, the power of poetry resides maximally in the energy and immediacy (that is, unmediatedness, *Unmittelbarkeit*) of performance, both of which are diminished as poetry is dissociated from movement and music and rendered on the printed page (Fugate 1966:246). For Herder, the full power of poetry is a power of presence: "[T]he poems of ancient and savage peoples arise to a great extent from immediate presence, from immediate excitation of the senses, and of the imagination" (SW 5:185; see also SW 32:74 /1992:45). The more expression is informed by immediate sensory experience, the more true, genuine, and effective it will be. In foregrounding sensory experience and presence, Herder's view converges with the sensualist orientation of Locke. The critical difference, of course, lies in Herder's valorization of the emotional component of sensory experience, in marked contrast with Locke's insistence that sensory experience must be disciplined in the service of reason.

For Herder, the essence of poetry—as of language—lies in the union of feeling and form, born in immediate sensate experience. The external stimuli that flow in upon the senses and the imagination possess a natural form that is answered by the reflexive shaping capacities that render experience into human language and into poetry. From this formative moment, both language and poetry are set upon a course of further human development, but the essence and efficacy of poetry continue to reside in the union of living, present experience and expressive form:

> Upon the lyrical, upon the living yet at the same time dance-like rhythm of song, upon the living presence of images, upon the coherence yet at the same time upon the demanding urgency of the content, of perception, upon the symmetry of words, syllables, many times even of letters [i.e., of sounds], upon the cadence of the melody, and upon a hundred other things, which belong to the living world...upon these, and upon these

> alone depend the essence, the purpose, all of the wonder-work-
> ing power, which these songs have, to be the magic spell, the
> mainspring, the eternal heritage and joy in song of the people!
> …The longer a song should last, the stronger, the more sensual
> must these wakers of souls be, that they should spite the power
> of time and the changes of centuries. (SW 5:164)

This resonant inventory of elements that are constitutive of poetry, with its insistence on the present, living immediacy of inspiration and its balancing of experiential and linguistic form, establishes clearly Herder's conception of *Naturpoesie*.

Note, however, that it is not solely the immediacy of poetic expression that is at issue here, but its durability, its capacity to "spite the power of time" and to constitute "the eternal heritage…of the people." But how are the two principles to be reconciled? How can the ephemerality of the living inspirational moment "spite the power of time?"

Strength and genuineness of feeling clearly play a role: "The more true, the more recognizable and stronger the imprint of our sentiments proves to be, and the more genuine the poetry is, the stronger and truer her mark, effect, and duration will be" (SW 8:339). But feeling alone will not suffice, however strong it may be. The other necessary element, as we might expect, is form. Celebrating the great poets of all times, the Moseses and Homers, Herder proclaims, "You sang from inspiration! You planted what you sang in eternal metre, in which it was held fast; and thus it could be sung again for as long as men wanted to sing it" (SW 4:460/Herder 1969:85). Herder recognizes here the entextualizing force of formalization—variously "metre," "rhythm," "cadence," or "symmetry" in his terms—which makes poetic discourse memorable, repeatable, persistent. In like manner, formal patterning renders poetry pleasing and persuasive. In his extended appreciation of parallelism in *The Spirit of Hebrew Poetry*, Herder asks "Does not all rhythm, and the metrical harmony both of motion and sound, I might say, all that delights in forms of sounds, depend upon symmetry?" (SW 11:236/Herder 1833[1]:39), observing further that "It changes the figure and exhibits the thought in another light. It varies the precept, and explains it, or impresses it upon the heart" (SW 11:238/Herder 1833(1):41). Most importantly, Herder's observations on translation make clear that he saw form, content, and meaning as mutually constitutive and sustaining. The "meaning" or "internal feeling" of a poetic work depends on "the external,...the sensual, in form, sound, tone, melody" (SW 5:163).

Thus rendered meaningful, memorable, pleasing, and persuasive, the poetic texts created in the moment of inspiration are taken up by the people; they "share them with each other like reflected rays of the sun" (SW 8:340). The immediacy of poetic creation and performance thus gives rise to an *intertextually constituted tradition* as the people learn, remember, and pass on the texts: "The poet saw what he sang or he heard it alive...The circle around him was amazed, listened, learned, sang, and never forgot the proverbs about the gods; they were fashioned into the soul with nails of song" (SW 8:369). In this process of poetic continuity, form and tradition are mutually sustaining. Formal regimentation makes traditional continuity possible at the same time that particular formal structures—both linguistic structures and the artistic structures of poetry—become traditionalized through "acclimation of the ear," by repetition, imitation, and socialization (SW 5:165; SW 18:462): "He who has the sound of the Italian stanza or the Scottish 'Chevy Chase' song in his ear will, after ninety-nine stanzas and strophes be able to hear the hundredth. His ear desires the repeating cadence" (SW 18:462). Thus the poetic tradition is shaped by multiple dimensions of intertextual relationships. Poetic *texts* are passed on in a chain of transmission, while at the same time poetic *forms* become conventionalized and serve as orienting frameworks for the production and reception of new texts.

The poetic tradition was, for Herder, not simply a treasury of artistic diversions but rather the very foundation of culture itself. The central argument of his essay "On the Effects of Poetry on the Customs and Morals of Nations in Ancient and Modern Times" (1778) builds upon the conception of poetry that we have traced above:

> If poetry is what she should be, then according to her essence,
> she is influential. How could she not exert influence when she
> is the language of the senses and of first powerful impressions,
> the language of passion and of everything that passion created,
> of imagination, action, of memory, of joy or of pain, lived, seen,

> enjoyed, worked, received, and of the hope and fear to do so in
> the future—how could she not influence? Nature, perception,
> and man's entire soul flowed into the language and impressed
> itself into it, into this body, and therefore it affects everything
> which is nature including all like tuned and compassionate
> souls. (SW 8:338–39)

A people's poetry, then, becomes "the whole treasure of their life," giving voice to "teachings and history, law and morality, delight, joy and comfort" (SW 8:392). Like language, poetry stores up culture; it is "the archive of the folk" (SW 9:532).

The same process of socialization that imprints the formal patterns of poetic expression upon the minds of successive generations of hearers also imparts to them the culture of their nation:

> The ignorant child listens with curiosity to the tales, which flow
> into his mind like his mother's milk, like the choice wine of his
> father, and form its nutriment. They seem to him to explain
> what he has seen: to the youth they account for the way of life of
> his tribe, and stamp the renown of his ancestors: the man they
> introduce to the employment suited to his nation and climate,
> and thus they become inseparable from his whole life. (SW
> 13:304/Herder 1968:45)

The tradition, then, molds the worldview, the ways of life, the values, and the aspirations of a people, shaping the lives of children and adults alike. Its reflexive capacity allows a people to "portray themselves, and see themselves, as they are" (SW 9:532). Where Locke denigrates tradition as inimical to truth, Herder celebrates it as foundational to cultural identity.

There are, to be sure, certain fundamental enabling conditions that a poetic tradition must meet in order to be maximally efficacious and authentic. As we have established, true national poetry must be *Naturpoesie*, passionate, inspired, and natural. It must be consonant with the spirit of the people (*volksmässig* [SW 5:189; SW 9:529]), with time, and with place; it must be "created for these people and therefore …in the language, the morals, the way of thinking of the people and of no others in no other time" (SW 8:360). That is to say, once again, that

Herder's vision is popular and relativist in its principles, both culturally and linguistically, and firmly anchored in history. The true folk poet must articulate a *collective* spirit, a *collective* genius, must give expression to thoughts and feelings deeply shared by all. The folk poet may, it is true, be a named individual; Herder celebrates Moses, David, Homer, Ossian, and Shakespeare as great folk poets who articulate with special power the collective spirit of their people. Nevertheless, the demand of *Volksmässigkeit* foregrounds the shared, collective quality of the folk spirit, and for the most part Herder speaks of folk poetry as the collective and anonymous expression of a people. We will return to the further implications of this homogenizing tendency later in our discussion.

The necessary quality of *Volksmässigkeit*, which demands that authentic poetry be grounded in the historical moment and "no other time," might seem to be incompatible with the capacity of tradition to "spite the power of time." How can this apparent contradiction be reconciled? The answer lies in Herder's understanding of cultural continuity as shaped not only by the conserving power of tradition but also by a second human capacity that he terms "organic powers." "All education arises from imitation and exercise," he writes, "by means of which the model passes into the copy. What better word is there for this transmission than tradition?" He goes on, "[T]he imitator must have powers to receive and convert into his own nature what has been transmitted to him, just like the food he eats." Thus the traditional inheritance is creatively transformed: "Education, which performs the function of transmitting social traditions, can be said to be *genetic*, by virtue of the manner in which the transmission takes place, and *organic*, by virtue of the manner in which that which is being transmitted is assimilated and applied" (SW 13:347–48/Herder 1993:51). That is to say that a viable, productive, active tradition is a dynamic process insofar as the teachings of the elders are adapted anew by each successive generation. Tradition itself thus may be rendered *volksmässig*, consonant with the historical change that was so central to Herder's philosophy of history.

To identify poetic tradition as *the* constitutive cultural process is to vest great responsibility in the poet. In Herder's vision of culture, poets are the culture makers: "A poet is the creator of a nation around him, he shows them a world and has their souls in his hand to lead them there. That is how it should be" (SW 8:433). Moreover, the culture's continued viability rests on the poet's shoulders: "As long as there were bards, the cultural spirit of [a] people was invincible, their morals and customs could not be extinguished" (SW 8:392).

In identifying poets as "lawgivers" *(Gesetzgeber)*, Herder recognizes a centrally *political* dimension of the poet's role as culture maker. Thus Moses, for Herder the great poetic founder of the Hebrew nation (on Moses as poet, see, e.g., SW 11:309–10/Herder 1833[I]:108), is the "liberator and lawgiver" of the nation, and in ancient Greece, "The oldest lawgivers, judges of secrets and intimate worship, even, according to legend, the inventors of the most beautiful objects and customs made for morality of life, they were all poets" (SW 8:366). It follows that tradition, the process by which the poetic forms of a culture "are passed down from the earliest times, from the founders of the tribe" (SW 1:263/Herder 1992:179), is itself an essentially political process. The socialization of the child, the basic mechanism of tradition and cultural continuity, is, accordingly, the foundation of political culture. "Man is born under the very mild government of father and mother," Herder writes, "and since no authority transcends the parental authority, no wisdom the parental wisdom, no kindness the parental kindness, this government in miniature is the most perfect which can be found" (SW 9:313–14/Herder 1969:229). Here again, Herder makes explicit that it is poetic forms, manifested as "powerful sayings and proverbs…fables, genealogies, songs celebrating great deeds or virtues," and the like, by which this political authority is established: "all these are imprints of early paternal rule" (SW 9:313–14/Herder 1969:229–30).

Herder regarded the paternal and domestic government of the family, in which authority rests on the acquired wisdom of poetic tradition, as the most natural form of political order, the "most perfect which can be found" (SW 13:375/Herder 1969:317–18). Beyond the stage of family government, nature leaves off, and "it was left to man how to construct a polity" (SW 13:382/Herder 1969:322). The best of such polities, in Herder's view, were those in which the natural principles of family government were extended, allowing the people to choose the best and wisest of their number, the poet-legislators, to lead them. Herder admired especially the democracy and freedom of the

Greek republic: "All public affairs concerning the people were openly discussed and matters were decided on the spot according to the feeling of the meeting...The orator spoke to his own people, to a circle he knew...a multitude who were educated through poetry, songs, art, drama in the finest language in the world" (SW 9:325/Herder 1969:236–37). Consider what is being affirmed here: political community, founded in a sense of cultural cohesion, a shared set of understandings, mutual familiarity, and a sense of common purpose, in which political discussion is open and public, and action is based upon consensus, all resting on education through poetry, songs, art, drama, and language, that is, on a poetic tradition. Herder would never insist that any historical or cultural precedent should be erected as a standard for replication in another place or another period. Even the best of the republics he so admired "had aspects which we would not wish to bring back even for the sake of their orators and poets" (SW 9:377/Herder 1969:252). Still, the foundational principles that enabled these earlier polities to flower were, in his view, worthy of emulation in a form adapted to the particularities of German conditions, needs, and aspirations (SW 9:377/Herder 1969:252).

But Herder carries his naturalization of government from familial (and paternal) principles still further:

> It is nature which educates families: the most natural state is, therefore, *one* nation, an extended family with one national character...Nothing, therefore, is more manifestly contrary to the purpose of political government than the unnatural enlargement of states, the wild mixing of various races and nationalities under one sceptre...Such states are but patched-up contraptions, fragile machines, appropriately called state-*machines*, for they are wholly devoid of inner life, and their component parts are connected through mechanical contrivance instead of bonds of sentiment. (SW 13:384–85/Herder 1969:324)

Although this is at one level a condemnation of imperial conquest and domination, it is at the same time a clear affirmation of the need for organic purity as the only natural basis for a viable polity. The implication is unmistakable: a *Volk*, a nation, a culture, a polity must be homogeneous; diversity is unnatural and destructive of the bonds of sentiment that hold a people together. In this declaration, Herder has suppressed decisively the acknowledgment of diversity within the nation that we find in his essay *On the Origin of Language,* discussed above. Acceptable diversity, whether linguistic or cultural, begins at the national boundary. Here we encounter once again, this time in stronger terms, the homogenizing, standardizing thrust that we identified earlier as inherent in the principle of *Volksmässigkeit.*

Like all organisms, governments, no matter how perfectly they may be constructed, will ultimately decline, according to Herder's philosophy of history. "Each state has its period of growth, maturity, and decay" (SW 9:375/Herder 1969:250). Philosophical overrefinement and rational regimentation rob language of its expressive vitality; artifice, printing, and commodification rob poetry of its "living effect" (SW 8:411); the advent of despotic hereditary rule makes for a "warping of traditions" (SW 9:375/Herder 1969:251); and ultimately the nation sinks into the oblivion of history.

It is crucial to an understanding of Herder's philosophy of history and language to recognize that this trajectory of growth, maturity, and eventual decay, in his view, is neither uniform nor inexorable in its operation from one nation to the next. Perhaps most important, the course of development is susceptible to human intervention (SW 9:360/Herder 1969:360), and this is what motivates much of Herder's writings on poetry. In the larger interest of cultural revitalization and political reform, one of his principal instrumental goals was to reinvigorate German literature, weakened not only by an unbalanced reliance on reason at the expense of emotion but also by the misguided imitation of Greek and Latin literary models and—worse yet—by the adoption of French among the German intellectuals and nobility, who thereby distanced themselves from their own national tradition (SW 5:551/Herder 1969:209; SW 18:136/Herder 1993:142–43; cf. Wilson 1973:824). Herder's program for the revitalization of German literature consisted of two complementary elements, both centering on folk poetry, *Volksdichtung:* the study and celebration of the poetry of other peoples among whom it displayed its full expressive vigor, and the retrieval and revalorization of the remnants of vital poetic expression still to be found in those sectors of his own society least affected by the changes that had robbed cultivated poetry of its emotional power and efficacy.

The former enterprise led to Herder's celebration of the language and poetry of those he classified as primitive peoples, who included the ancient Hebrews and Greeks as well as Hurons, Brazilian Indians, Iroquois, Eskimos, and Tahitians. "What do you consider the most essential to poetic language?" asks Euthyphron, one of the interlocutors in the dialogue that constitutes the first volume of his *Spirit of Hebrew Poetry*. "No matter whether it belongs to the Hurons or Otaheitans. Is it not action, imagery, passion, musick, rhythm?"

"Undoubtedly," replies Alciphron.

"And the language that exhibits these in the highest perfection is the most peculiarly poetical," responds Euthyphron. "Now you are aware that the languages of people but partially cultivated may have this characteristic in a high degree," he continues, "and are in fact in the particular superior to many of the too refined modern languages. I need not remind you among what people Ossian, or at what period even the Grecian Homer sang" (SW 11:225/Herder 1833[1]:27). Euthyphron goes on to say of the Hebrews that "Their [poetic] productions are not loaded with delicate and overwrought refinement, but vigorous, entire, instinct with life and spirit...[T]he language seems to me, I confess, more poetical than any other language on earth" (SW 11:230/Herder 1833[1]:32–33).

Alciphron is not fully persuaded. When Euthyphron observes that "In this union of feeling from within and form from without...the Oriental languages [among which he includes Hebrew]...are the best models" (SW 11:231/Herder 1833[1]:34), Alciphron demurs. "Is it possible you are speaking of those barbarous and uncouth gutturals? And do you venture to compare them with the silvery tones of the Greek?" (SW 11:230/Herder 1833[1]:34).

"I make no comparison," Euthyphron replies. "Every language suffers by being thus compared with another. Nothing is more exclusively national and individual than the modes of gratifying the ear, and the characteristic habitudes of the organs of speech" (SW 11:231/Herder 1833[1]:34). This disclaimer is of the utmost importance, an expression of Herder's relativist vision, his respect for all languages and cultures in their own terms. In fundamental opposition to the universalist aesthetic of Kant, Herder insisted that the language and poetry of every people be assessed "with respect to time and place" (SW 14:98/Herder 1968:172); for each *Volk*, the authenticity and vitality of its poetry rested only on its faithfulness to "The genius of their nature, their country, their way of life, the period in which they lived, and the character of their progenitors" (SW 14:98–99/Herder 1968:172). Only by entering sympathetically into the spirit of a nation can one hope to achieve an understanding of its culture (SW 5:502/Herder 1969:181). This is in fact an extension and full generalization of hermeneutic and text-critical principles developed by eighteenth-century classical and biblical philologists such as Thomas Blackwell, Robert Lowth, and Robert Wood, all of whom influenced Herder.

In accordance with this insistence on rootedness in time and place as the touchstone of authentic poetic expression and interpretation, Herder did not valorize the poetry of other *Völker* in order to hold them up to his fellow Germans as models for imitation, for this would have undermined the very foundation of an authentic national literature (SW 1:140–41/Herder 1992:94): "if we mimic practices that are borrowed from foreign peoples and times, that are foreign to our inner sense, then we damn ourselves to Hades as we live and breathe" (SW 24:44/Herder 1993:102). Rather, he celebrated the poetic forms of other nations as demonstrations of how such authentic expression might be constituted (SW 1:444/Herder 1992:228]; this was the principal motivation for his influential collection of *Volkslieder*, published in 1778–79. For Germany, the corrective to a poetry of artifice must be sought in the German national tradition itself—in German folksongs, folktales, myths, and other poetic forms. "I am familiar with folksongs in more than one province," he proclaimed,

> provincial songs, peasant songs, which would certainly hold their own in liveliness and rhythm, in naive character and strength of language; but who is it who collects them? who concerns himself with them? with the songs of the people? in streets, and alleys, and fishmarkets? in the untutored roundelays of the country folk? with songs, which frequently do not scan, and are often poorly rhymed? who would collect them—who would print romances in handsome volumes? (SW 5:189)

Here, among the peasants and ordinary people of the towns, those "whom our ways have not yet fully deprived of their language and songs and customs, only to give them in return something misshapen or nothing at all" (SW 5:170), Herder found an authentic German folk voice, crude, perhaps, by the mechanical, formal standards of culti-vated critics, but full of the emotional energy and *Volksmässigkeit* he so valued as the essence of poetry (Schütze 1921:117). These songs are endangered by the privileging of foreign models and standards and the encroachments of a mediating literacy, but they must be saved: "I cry out to my German brothers! just now! The remnants of all living folk imagination are rolling precipitously toward a final plunge into the abyss of oblivion…the light of so-called culture is devouring everything about it like a cancer" (SW 25:11). A preoccupation with absence, a fear of imminent loss, suffuses Herder's writings on German folk poetry. The revitalization of German culture, the restoration of its vital balance, demands the recuperation of authentic folk culture to counter the "so-called culture" of a universalizing Enlightenment ratio-nalism (SW 9:530).

Herder's rallying cry to his German brothers stands as a critical moment in the symbolic construction of what we might call, drawing upon Susan Stewart's felicitous notion, the rhetoric and poetics of dis-tress that has attached to folklore since the term was first invented (Stewart 1991; see also Briggs 1993). Herder frames the poetry of the peasants, market traders, country people as multiply distressed: it is for-mally flawed and survives only in remnants, which are tumbling toward oblivion with no one to save them. The implication is that the people who still actively sing the songs cannot themselves hold them back from the abyss; others must intervene.

We encounter in this context a further dimension of Herder's usage of the term *Volk* (see Barnard 1965:73–75; Gaier 1990). In its most general sense, *Volk* designates a nation, a people, but it may also designate that portion of a more complex, stratified society that remains most firmly grounded in its inherited language and traditions and is still open to feeling, as distinct from those who have been dis-tanced from their roots and their feelings by overrational refinement or the adoption of foreign languages and alien ways. Herder is not always consistent in his usage, but in this more marked sense, the *Volk* is

"the largest," "most useful," "most venerable," and "most feeling" segment of a populace: peasants, artisans, burghers—essentially, the bourgeoisie *(das Volk der Bürger)* (SW 1:392, 6:104, 7:265, 32:60). The members
of the *Volk* are closer to nature than the intellectuals (SW 32:41).
Intellectuals may remain part of the *Volk (das Volk der Gelehrsamkeit)* as long
as they remain faithful to the *Volk* character, but the overrational, overrefined intellectual *(der Grübler)* is removed from the *Volk* (SW 7:265).
Likewise, as also in Justus Möser's conception of *Volk*, which influenced
Herder's own, the nobility *(der erste Stand)* are set apart (see, for example, SW 17:391; on Möser, see Sheldon 1970). Also excluded are the
rabble *(der Pöbel)*. Herder does not make entirely clear what he means
by this term—perhaps the dispossessed vagrants and urban poor whose
numbers were increasing in late eighteenth-century Germany
(Braunschwig 1974:106–16)—though his most explicit statement, "*Volk*
does not mean the rabble on the streets, who never sing and create
poetry, but shout and mutilate" (SW 25:323), does differentiate them
from the *Volk* in terms of poetic creation and performance.

Clearly, however, Herder's extended view of the *Volk* implicates
structures of inequality. When he speaks of a *Volk* in general, collective
terms as a nation or a people, the discursive and metadiscursive practices by which an authentic, vital cultural tradition is constituted
emanate from the social formation as a whole. From the more immediate perspective of his own society, though, the true folk spirit is
unevenly distributed. The autocratic and cosmopolitan nobility is
detached from folk culture—they speak French!—and the dispossessed
rabble, with their distorted, mutilated, and pathological discourse, are
incapable of participation in the authentic poetic discourse of the *Volk*.
The discursive practices that are fully authorized by Herder are those of
the bourgeoisie, the landed peasants, artisans, people of the marketplace. (It is interesting to note, parenthetically, that Herder celebrates
in the discourse of the marketplace precisely what Bacon and Locke
distrust. In addition to these members of *das Volk der Bürger*, Herder also
provides a place among the true *Volk* for certain intellectuals, those in
fully sympathy with the *Volksgeist*, among whom, by implication, he
would number himself and those who would join in his mission for the
rescue and nurture of German folksong.

But note the interventionist and recuperative role assumed by these members of *das Volk der Gelehrsamkeit*. It is the task of *intellectuals* to recover, collect, and preserve the folk poetry and to foster the use of the German language, to develop the educational and literary institutions that would sustain the authentic folk culture. It lies also with *das Volk der Gelehrsamkeit* to create the poetry that will renew the folk spirit of the German nation and carry it into the future. The simple folk alone cannot do it. They lack the ability to treat their own means of expression analytically, to recognize the reflexive capacity of language, or "to separate the *thought* from the *expression*." "[I]t would appear ridiculous," Herder suggests, "to see a peasant explicating words" (SW 1:387/Herder 1992:197). The unlearned "common man," at least, can be educated to scholarly pursuits; this requires that "I...speak *his language* and gradually accustom him *to mine*; I must not speak to him as if I were in the clouds, but stand on his level and slowly raise him to my sphere" (SW 1:390/Herder 1992:199). Women, however, differ in this regard. If a woman "is to develop herself into what *she is meant to be*, so that she may enhance her soul and be the delight of the male species, so that she may grow to attain the dignity of the burgher's estate, of motherhood, of a spouse, and of an educator," her "education must not reflect the *male* view or, still less, the *scholarly* view." Rather, it "must accommodate her mind," "her sphere," that is, "the *good common sense of life* ... the *common sense of the house and kitchen*" (SW 1:393–94/Herder 1992:201–2).

In recognizing *das Volk der Gelehrsamkeit,* Herder thus authorizes a metadiscursive regime of intellectual intervention in folk culture, founded on intellectual and gender inequality, the influence of which continues to be felt to this day. We will reserve further discussion of this metadiscursive regime for the conclusion of our paper.

Consistent with his self-assigned role, Herder repeatedly castigates his countrymen for selling out the culture of their fathers for a bloodless and overrefined cosmopolitanism. "Perhaps we could ask the flatterers of this century," he suggests, "what *is* this greater virtue that Europe is supposed to have acquired through enlightenment? Enlightenment! We know so much more nowadays, hear and read so much, that we have become tranquilized, patient, meek and inactive" (SW 5:555/Herder 1969:212; see also 1774:192). With bitter irony he observes:

> With us, thank God, national character is no more!…To be
> sure, we no longer have a fatherland or any kinship feelings;
> instead, we are all philanthropic citizens of the world. The
> princes speak French, and soon everybody will follow their
> example; and, then, behold, perfect bliss: the golden age, when
> all the world will speak one tongue, one universal language, is
> dawning again! There will be one flock and one shepherd!
> National cultures, where are you? (SW 5:550–51/Herder
> 1969:209)

Especially pernicious is the neglect of Germany's own national poets in favor of foreign models. Reproaching his countrymen "for the unwavering indifference with which they neglect and ignore the best poets of their own language in their schools and in the education of their young in general" (SW 18:136/Herder 1993:143), Herder warns of the linguistic and cultural consequences of such national indifference:

> Through what means is our taste, our style of writing, supposed
> to develop? Through what means is our language supposed to
> take on structure and rules? How else except through the best
> writers of our nation? Through what means are we supposed to
> acquire patriotism and love of country except through our
> country's language, except through the most excellent
> thoughts and feelings that are expressed in this language and
> lie like a treasure within it? (SW 18:136/Herder 1993:143)

It is in this spirit that Herder hopes that his writings on folk poetry will encourage his readers to recover what is left of the treasure of German folksong, so that Germany will be able to listen again "to the voice of its own poetry" (SW 8:392; see also 8:428).

In the political arena, Herder submits, this authentic national voice of the poets might offer a powerful corrective to the etiolated political discourse of the present, "corrupted through artifices, slavish expectations, fawning sneaky politics, and bewildering intentions" (SW 5:181). This critical inventory of political ills, in turn, points us toward the contemporary grounding of Herder's political ideology and reformist program. While we do not have the space here—nor is it our purpose—to describe fully, much less explicate, the broader contours of Herder's political theory in its historical context (see Barnard 1965, 1969), a brief account will help to clarify the grounding and implications of his emphasis on linguistic and poetic traditions as the foundations of an authentic political culture.

Late-eighteenth-century Germany existed as a unified entity in name only. Prussia, under Frederick the Great, dominated the political landscape, but in reality the empire consisted of more than three hundred essentially autonomous states, a significant common feature of which was the personal absolutism of their sovereign rulers. The concentration of absolute power in the hands of the ruling aristocracy diminished the status of the nonsovereign nobility, while the middle classes, lacking economic vigor and unified political consciousness, had no effective political presence.

Absolutism, to be sure, does not preclude political reform; in the aftermath of the Seven Years War, Frederick devoted great effort to reforming the machinery of government, and the commanding presence of Prussia in the political environment drew other rulers to emulate his example. Under conditions of absolute rule, however, reform can only be instituted from above, "enlightened" though it may be. One of Frederick's own administrators, in suggesting that Frederick's administrative accomplishment "could serve as a model and as an example to be striven after by the rest of the German states," observes as well that "everything was done by autocracy, there was no Estates constitution and no active state council to give unifying force; there were no institutions in which a community spirit, a comprehensive view and fixed administrative maxims could develop. Every activity awaited initiative from above, independence and self-confidence were lacking..." (quoted in Hubatsch 1975:233). The prevailing thrust of reform efforts centered on the progressive enlightenment of the rulers; the solutions put forward, founded on solid, rational, Enlightenment principles, recommended such reforms as the acceptance by the rulers of constitutional restraint and the rationalization of the administrative apparatus of government (Barnard 1965:19–22; Hubatsch 1975:148–68).

The ideology of the German *Aufklärung* (Enlightenment) accorded well with top-down programs of political reform. Henri Braunschwig, in his classic study of the Enlightenment in eighteenth-century Prussia, offers a trenchant characterization:

> In the case of the *Aufklärung*, culture…comes from above and
> moves downward, for the elite minds at the upper levels are
> often barely intelligible … The enlightened minority is con-
> scious of its merit; it has "raised itself" above the crowd, but in
> doing so it has parted company with the masses. Its ideal is to
> radiate above the masses and gradually to penetrate them, not
> to reflect them. It is not this minority which expresses the com-
> munity, but the community which painfully spells out a new
> alphabet of ideas which are alien to it. (Braunschwig 1974
> [1947]:90–91)

Herder, however, placed no faith in the corrective potential of
nobility-down political reform, especially if it amounted to little more
than hopeful tinkering with the administrative machinery and
remained dependent in the end on the personal will of an autocratic
sovereign. He believed deeply in the moral implications of the principles on which the reformers based their programs—that government
should be based on consent rather than coercion, that it should be
moved by law and reason rather than arbitrariness and the whim of
rulers, that the state should exist for the good of its members and not
the reverse—if not in the principles themselves. His conviction that
the natural foundations of government lay in the paternal authority
of the family, for example, led him to reject the principle of social
contract as a basis or justification for political organization. Likewise,
his radical historical and cultural relativism made him fundamentally
unsympathetic to universalistic notions of absolute individual rights
and like abstract ideals (Barnard 1965:141–42). Rather, Herder drew
inspiration from Rousseau's philosophy of the natural man, with its
celebration of sentiment and emotion, its valorization of education
on familial principles, its advocacy of popular sovereignty; from Justus
Möser's vision of political life as emergent out of custom, tradition
and local patriotism; and from champions of the intellectual, artistic,
and spiritual power of the German language, such as Christian
Thomasius, Friedrich Gottlieb Klopstock, and Johann Christian
Gottsched (Barnard 1965:18–29). As we have seen, he believed pas-
sionately that the true foundations of political community and political culture lay in the organic culture of a Volk, rooted in history,

sustained by tradition, and manifested in language and poetry.

For our purposes, it is especially important to emphasize that in Herder's view, this authentic political culture is discursively constituted. His sustained and passionate celebration of national languages and poetic traditions, his language ideology, vested authority in the metadiscursive practices that gave life to the language, poetry, and tradition of a people, to the living expression of their *Volksgeist*. In his vision, as we have attempted to establish, this spirit of a people resided in its most authentic form in that social formation he identified as a *Volk*—either a whole "uncultivated" society with a unified linguistic and cultural tradition or that segment of modern complex society that was least corrupted by modern overrefinement and that best sustained custom and tradition, that is, the peasants, artisans, and tradespeople of the farms, towns, and marketplaces. This was not simply a matter of according recognition and value to a suppressed voice in the social chorus. In authorizing the metadiscursive practices that were constitutive of folk-poetic tradition, Herder was in fact contributing powerfully to the *creation* of the Volk as a social formation and of folk poetry as the essence of folk culture.

CONCLUSION

We suggested in the introduction to this paper that our purpose in examining closely the philosophical writings on language of Locke and Herder is to elucidate the ways in which their respective ideologies of language establish a relationship between metadiscursive practices governing the production and reception of discourse and the establishment and operation of structures of authority, legitimacy, and social inequality. Our warrant for focusing on Locke and Herder is that they offer and are widely known for foundational articulations of contrasting linguistic ideologies that have had a deeply formative influence on subsequent thought and practice in regard to language. (Note that "foundational" here does not imply exclusive, fully original, or directly ancestral to all subsequent articulations of similar ideas.)

Hans Aarsleff, who has called Locke "the most influential philosopher of modern times" (1994:252), credits him with laying "the foundation of the modern study of language" (1982:24). Though we would not want to take such all-star rankings too seriously, Aarsleff's own eminence as an intellectual historian of linguistics gives weight to his assessment. Locke's theory of language, as developed in Book 3 of the *Essay Concerning Human Understanding*, stands as a cornerstone of "scientific" conceptions of language that rest upon the conventionality of the linguistic sign, the cognitivist linking of the linguistic sign to ideas, the privileging of the referential and propositional functions of language in the service of rational, philosophically rigorous thought and expression as against everyday "civil" discourse, and the suppression of indexicality (including prominently intertextuality) as inimical to pure reference (see, for example, Aarsleff 1982, 1984; Guyer 1994; Yolton 1970, 1993:115–20). These ideas occupy a wide space in modern linguistics; one index of their dominance is that the sociopolitical aspects of Locke's ideology of language do not figure in intellectual histories of linguistics, Aarsleff's included, although as we have endeavored to show, they are radically bound up with his overall language ideology.

For Herder, the reverse is true. Jakob Grimm, as early as 1851 (1984), used Herder as a foil against which to mark the break between older, unscientific conceptions of language and modern scientific linguistics. Even as sympathetic a reader as Sapir (1908) dismisses most of Herder's theory of language, valuing only the suggestiveness of his ideas concerning the nexus of form and feeling, ideas which have not figured prominently in subsequent linguistic theory. Rather, it is precisely for the sociopolitical aspects of his work on language that Herder is acknowledged: the populist celebration of ordinary people's language and poetry, the relativist insistence on the distinctiveness of national languages, their indexical grounding in time and place, their linkage to the worldview and ways of thinking and feeling of a people, and their essential role in maintaining national identity and cohesion (see, for example, Barnard 1969; Berlin 1976; Robins 1990). Herder is accorded a far more influential role in the development of disciplines outside linguistics, principally anthropology (in its Americanist guise) and folklore (see, for example, Broce 1981; Cocchiara 1981; Kamenetsky 1973; Murray 1985; Wilson 1973). Here it is the literary, philological, and expressive dimensions of his thought that are of principal significance: the idea that a people's culture is encoded in its traditional artistic texts and that these intertextually constituted traditions are the principal mechanisms of cultural continuity.

In playing up the contrasts between the Lockeian and Herderian views, our aim is not to posit two mutually incompatible intellectual traditions or to align Locke and Herder exclusively with separate disciplines. Indeed, the very enterprise of linguistic anthropology, the intellectual field with which we identify ourselves, is incompatible with such an oppositional vision, lying as it does at the intersection of linguistics, anthropology, and folklore, all of which have contributed to its intellectual foundations. Already in Wilhelm von Humboldt (1988) there are strong resonances both with Locke (for instance, on the semiotic linkage of the linguistic sign with ideas [pp. 56–59]) and with Herder (for instance, on language and poetry as the expression of the spirit of a people [pp. 42–46, 60]), and mixed strains may be found in varying degrees in much subsequent work. However, the core principles around which Locke's and Herder's respective language ideologies cohere contrast markedly in certain fundamental respects. Compare Locke's antipathy toward traditional authority with Herder's valorization of tradition; Locke's abstract and universalizing scientific rationalism with Herder's concrete, relativizing aesthetic particularism; Locke's suppression of indexicality and intertextuality with Herder's celebration of these associational principles as constitutive of culture; Locke's distrust of emotion with Herder's celebration of feeling and passion; Locke's primary focus on the word with Herder's emphasis on the text; Locke's rejection of the value of poetry and rhetoric with Herder's exaltation of poetic expression and its affecting power. Such fundamental epistemological and axiological differences cannot help but lead in different intellectual and ideological directions. Nevertheless it is important to take direct account of certain key areas of correspondence between the language ideologies of Locke and Herder and their implications for linguistic theory and practice. We focus especially on the structures of inequality that we have found to occupy a significant place in these ideologies.

For Locke, the referential precision and consistency that are essential to rational philosophical discourse are an inherent property of language. But the achievement of a fully realized language of reason demands reflexive effort on the part of its speakers, who must attend constantly and rigorously to the cultivation of a pure, plain language. In Locke's view, although every person is endowed from birth with the faculties and powers necessary to such reflexive awareness, the ability to exercise those capacities to the fullest is limited by social factors such as occupation, class, and gender. Manual laborers, those of "low breeding," and women do not have access to the experience, education, company, time, or opportunities for practice that the reflexive cultivation of thought and language demands; they are effectively barred from those metadiscursive practices that might allow them to perfect their faculties and thus their language. For such people, ordinary "civil" discourse will suffice, and under ordinary conditions, this will do no harm.

But Locke also saw in uncultivated language the potential for social disorder and disruption, as people fall victim to the imperfections to which language and linguistic practice are susceptible: the distortion of reference and meaning that results from lexicosemantic ambiguity, poetic frivolity, dependency on the authoritative words of others, the rhetoric of ornament, self- or partisan interest, and disputation, all of which may yield confusion, untruth, wastefulness, and even outright conflict. The remedy, in Locke's view, is to extend rational discourse into the arena of public affairs. The plain, direct, disinterested language of reason, which allows us to know things as they are, will inevitably have a unifying effect because truth is unitary and universal. Truly reasonable men will ultimately agree. Moreover, the language of this rational public discourse must be a purified, standardized, plain variety of the national language—for public affairs in England, English. Thus, in Locke's language ideology, the ideal metadiscursive order of the public sphere rests on a public discourse of one voice in one language, even as Locke recognizes that differences of opinion will inevitably exist and advocates toleration of this diversity.

[handwritten marginalia: dependent on exclusion (of women, lower classes) etc.]

Herder, as we have established, advocates a very different metadiscursive order, placing highest value on the inherent poetic quality of language and on poetic expression grounded in *Besonnenheit*, the unitary reflexive capacity that comprehends feeling, reason, will, all the human faculties. Again, all people are endowed with *Besonnenheit*—it is the quality above all others that makes us human. The means and forms of expression, however—be they languages, genres, or formal structures—are all variably shaped by differential experience, history, environmental factors, and cultural inheritance among the world's peoples. The most salient linguistic contrasts, in Herder's view, are those that differentiate national languages, which are at the same time the reservoirs for and the means of giving expression to the distinctive spirit of a people, its *Volksgeist*. The process is one of mutual reinforcement: the highest and most potent expression gives voice to the *Volksgeist*, and in so doing contributes as well to its progressive cultivation.

The chief means of this cultural realization are the poetic traditions that encode, preserve, and transmit the most powerful and distinctive meanings and values of a people. The best speakers, therefore, are poets, but all can participate in the cultivation of the folk spirit by learning and passing on the poetic traditions the poets have created and made memorable, affecting, and persuasive by giving them form. In the course of history, however, language and modes of expression are susceptible to potentially damaging influences—abstract and dispassionate philosophizing, artifice, the mediation of writing and print, which distance people from the sensuous experience of affecting performance, and cosmopolitanism—that rob the nation of its vitality. In Herder's own day, he felt, the vital traditions of the German people were fragmenting, sustained only in distressed remnants by the peasants, artisans, and market traders—*das Volk der Bürger*—who still sang the songs and told the tales that had been abandoned by the cosmopolitan nobility, the overrefined philosophers, and the rabble. Significantly, however, the very reflexive capacities of *Besonnenheit* that are so essential to human existence appear no longer to operate in this context as Herder depicts it. Those among whom the folk traditions are still to be found are unable to treat their own means of expression analytically, to reflect upon their language and poetry, or to stem their decline. The capacity for linguistic reflexivity is reserved to the intellectuals of *das Volk der Gelehrsamkeit,* who must intervene in the process if folk culture is to be revitalized. The male intellectuals, we might add, for Herder too felt that women are unsuited for the intellectual task.

Herder's language ideology, like Locke's, involved the extension of the metadiscursive practices he valued most highly into the public arena. The poetic traditions and their constituent expressive forms that give voice to the national spirit represent the authoritative basis for the cultural cohesion necessary to the establishment and maintenance of a viable polity. The desired goal of unification rests upon discursive unity, provided by the authority of tradition and a unified adherence to the national spirit. Here too, linguistic homogeneity is a necessary condition; in Herder's vision, a viable polity can only be founded on a national language resistant to the penetration of foreign tongues. Once again, a sphere of public discourse characterized by one voice in one language.

And so we arrive at convergent positions, whether we follow the path of Locke or of Herder. We conclude with two sets of implications to be drawn from these convergences, one scholarly, one more broadly political.

In the construction of their language ideologies, as we have seen, both Locke and Herder deny to common people and women the capacity for reflexive understanding of their own language and modes of linguistic expression; only the cultivated male intellectual can penetrate to the level of true linguistic understanding. The ideological legacy of this position has been deeply rooted in linguistic science. We hear it in Boas's insistence that "linguistic phenomena never rise into the consciousness of primitive man" (Boas 1966:59); it echoes through Bloomfield's stringent dismissal of secondary and tertiary responses to language (Bloomfield 1944); and we find it even in Hoenigswald's advocacy of the study of folk linguistics when he observes, "There is a habit, in itself honorable, indispensable, and deeply ingrained, of discounting informants' pronouncements on their language" (Hoenigswald 1966:17). One implication of this principled regimen of discounting is that the scholarly study of language has systematically organized itself around precisely those aspects of linguistic form and practice that are, or are assumed to be, most inaccessible to folk awareness or valid insight. People's pronouncements on their own language are either invalid or have to do with matters outside the proper province of linguistics as we conceive it. To be sure, there are larger epistemological problems at issue here that lie at a deeper level than we can tackle in this essay, including the principle that theory only stands as such if it is explicitly verbalized and framed in general, abstract terms; theory as manifested in practice is a contradiction in terms. Our point, though, is that modern Western ideologies of language, differ though they may in other fundamental aspects, repeatedly relegate folk linguistic knowledge to or beyond the margins of linguistic inquiry.[8]

We might add that much the same denial of the validity or even the existence of lay reflexivity has also guided conceptions of folklore, whether in the rationalist or the romantic mode. The Grimms (1987:2) made the argument early, in characterizing the *Märchen:* "Where they still exist, they live on in such a way that no one thinks about whether they are good or bad, poetic or (for intelligent people) vulgar." Kaarle Krohn (1971:26), the great codifier of the philological method in folklore, is more succinct: "The essence of folklore disappears with the development of contemplation." Stith Thompson (1946:451), the compiler of the authoritative reference works for the comparative study of the folktale, is more negative: "[T]he unlettered story-teller and his audience...may well insist upon their own distinctions which may seem quite arbitrary or illogical." Only the scholar is capable of valid analytical reflection—or perhaps any reflection at all—concerning folk discourse. And if the scholar can withhold validation, he or she can also confer it. One of the ideological underpinnings of the burgeoning movement toward staged public presentations of folklore in folklife festivals and allied forms of folklorized display is explicitly "the validation of...traditional cultures" (Santino 1988:122). The scholar is the ultimate arbiter of validity, legitimacy, and authenticity (see, for example, Staub 1988).

A further political implication of Locke's and Herder's language ideologies has to do with the nature and discursive organization of the public sphere. Locke has an established place in the Habermasian conception of the rational public sphere that has oriented much recent discussion (Habermas 1989), as in the broader historiography of modern democratic political ideology. As a number of critics have observed, the image of open participation in a public discourse that spans society has always coexisted with if not facilitated the exclusion of particular groups, issues, and forms of discourse (Calhoun 1992; Fraser 1993; Hansen 1993; Landes 1988; Negt and Kluge 1993). Our discussion of Locke suggests that tension between an ideally open public sphere and practices of exclusion and marginalization did not simply arise from some sort of gap between "theory" and "practice" or "ideology" and "action." By way of providing a theoretical basis of assertions of the social and political necessity of rational, disinterested, and dispassionate discourse, Locke theorized the exclusion of most of the population from this discursive realm and urged the institutionalization of metadiscursive practices that would naturalize and sustain the use of public discourse in preserving social inequality.

In contrast, Herder does not figure in considerations of the public sphere within the Habermasian frame of reference, notwithstanding his lifelong interest in the political public.[9] Certainly the conformation of the public sphere that Herder offers us is very different from that of Locke. It is a public sphere of poetic performance in which the vox populi gives voice to the authoritative traditions in which political community is grounded and political values are proclaimed. It offers a charter less for the political ideology of modern state democracy than for cultural nationalism in which language and folklore are key symbols of cultural identity and persistence; indeed, this romantic nationalism is taken as Herder's chief contribution to modern political ideology. But although Herder is justifiably celebrated as the populist champion of the common people, we have suggested that his populism is tempered by a politics of culture that demands intervention from above in the metadiscursive management of the public sphere. The structure of inequality that is masked in most historical appreciations of Herder, as in articulations of romantic nationalist ideologies influenced by his, is readily apparent in one of the last of his writings, published posthumously in 1803: "'Vox populi, vox dei' it once was said; and although this praise must not be extended beyond the limits of what the folk can articulate, it does at least point out that in those things that concern the folk their sense of truth demands respect" (SW 24:271–72). The limits of what the folk can articulate establish the interventionist baseline for those players in the arena of public affairs who are not so limited.

In addition to legitimating structures of inequality in the public sphere, the language ideologies of Locke and Herder converge in regard to the legitimacy of multiple voices and multiple languages in public discourse. Herder's vision of political community and national interest is clear in its principled insistence on linguistic and discursive standardization: social and political cohesion demand one language, one metadiscursive order, one voice. In the case of Locke, the situation is more complex. Locke's tolerationist principles allow a significant space for the protection of multiple voices, especially in domains with epistemological or practical limits to certain knowledge. In those domains where reasoned certainty is within the reach of human understanding, however, a similar ideology of one language and one metadiscursive order should prevail. The stronger and broader the claims for the reach of reasoned, certain knowledge, then, the stronger the press toward a monoglot and monologic standard as an ideal for the maintenance of social order. This ideology of a monoglot and monologic standard has provided a charter not only for homogenizing national policies of language standardization and the regulation of public discourse, but also for theoretical frameworks that normalize and often essentialize one society-one culture-one language conceptions of the relationships among language, culture, and society. We have argued here that the writings of both Locke and Herder, including the latter's relativist orientation, played key roles in validating this equation as both a philosophical charter and a political principle.

It is not our purpose here to offer an exposé of Locke's and Herder's ideological feet of clay any more than it is to worship at them. Our goal, rather, is to increase our reflexive understanding of the historical foundations of modern ideologies of language and metadiscursive practices more generally, toward providing a critical vantage point on our own work. Our examination of the philosophical writings of Locke and Herder in ideological terms might seem to represent a departure in certain key respects from the approach that characterizes most work on language ideology by linguistic anthropologists. For the most part, in such work, the cultural frame of reference selects for collectivist perspectives that emphasize "commonsense notions" (Rumsey 1990:346), "self-evident ideas and objectives a group holds" (Heath 1977:53), "cultural system[s] of ideas" (Irvine 1989:255), and the like. Locke and Herder, one might argue, are members of an intellectual elite whose highly cultivated philosophical formulations are anything but commonsense notions or self-evident ideas. We submit, however, that to exclude such classical European philosophy from the purview of linguistic anthropology is to acquiesce to the very language ideologies that Locke and Herder promulgated. To the extent that the notion of language ideology helps us to attain this critical recognition of the factors that underlie an ideology of separation between ourselves as modern Western intellectuals and those who are our objects of study, it is a valuable addition to our conceptual repertoire. Philosophy *is* language ideology insofar as its regimentation of the field of metadiscursive practice amounts as well to a regimentation of power relations and hierarchies of inequality.

Notes

1. We have used the Alexander Campbell Fraser edition of the *Essay* (Locke 1959[1690]). Citations follow the convention of Locke scholarship, with a succession of numerals designating internal divisions (book in upper-case Roman numerals, chapter in lower-case Roman numerals, section in Arabic numerals); references to Locke's "Epistle to the Reader" and "Introduction" cite the relevant portion of the work followed by volume and page number. This system facilitates the location of citations in any edition of the *Essay*. All italics are in the original.

2. Locke (1989:253) similarly notes that music ranks last on the list of educational priorities in view of the amount of time consumed in mastering an instrument, its unproductiveness, and the way it places an individual "in such odd Company."

3. Locke does note, however, that workers are so consumed by hard labor and a hand-to-mouth existence that they are largely incapable of reflecting on their condition. He thus lays more emphasis on socially and materially based limitations on the use of reason in the *Two Treatises* than he does in the characterization of rational examinations of signs in the *Essay*. As MacPherson (1962:245–46) notes, however, Locke suggests that since all persons are equally endowed with reason and that observed inequalities arise from the failure on the part of some to use their reason, social inequality can be deemed both natural and morally justifiable. See also Formigari (1988, 1993) on Locke's philosophy of language and its historical context.

4. See also Blackall's valuable survey of critical and bibliographical resources (1978:526 60).

5. References to Herder's works are keyed to the 1967 facsimile reprint of the standard Suphan edition (Herder 1967[1877–1913]), cited in the text as SW (for *Sämtliche Werke*). When we have drawn quotations from published translations, we cite those works as well. We have also drawn upon unpublished translations of the following: *Auszug aus einem Briefwechsel über Ossian und die Lieder alter Völker* (1773), translated by John Cash; *Über die Wirkung der Dichtkunst auf die Sitten der Völker in alten und neuen Zeiten* (1778), translated by Barbara Hummel; *Von Ähnlichkeit der mittlern englischen und deutschen Dichtkunst* (1777), translated by Clover Williams; and *Homer und Ossian* (1795), translated by Peter Bixby. We are

grateful to these colleagues for allowing us to use their work. The remaining translations are our own. All italics are in the original.

6. Herder was Kant's student at Königsberg but later became a strong critic of Kant's philosophy. On the relationship between Herder and Kant, see Clark (1969:41–46, 390–413).

7. The fourth natural law deals with the monogenesis of language and is not relevant to our discussion here.

8. Chomsky (1965:18–24) might appear exceptional here in granting importance to native speaker intuitions in the justification of grammars. Note, though, that he considers such "tacit" linguistic knowledge to be "obscured," "elusive," and "not…immediately available to the user of the language." In order for such intuitions to be activated and brought to consciousness, the linguist must intervene.

9. The political public is the subject of one of Herder's earliest published works, "Do we still have the Public and the Fatherland of yore?," first published in 1765 (SW 1:13–28/Herder 1992:53–64), as well as of the essay (SW 24:271–72) published posthumously in 1803.

5

Indonesian('s) Authority

Joseph Errington

In the afterglow of the Asian Pacific Economic Conference it had hosted the previous year, Indonesia celebrated its fiftieth anniversary in 1995 as a newly visible power on the international scene. Some saw the event as doubly vindicating for President Suharto, whose New Order regime had engineered this conspicuously successful project of national development (in Indonesian, *pembangunan nasional*). But the economic implosion of 1998, followed by Suharto's retirement, public unrest, and economic hardship, made some other aspects of the New Order's modus operandi—authoritarian intolerance of dissent, widespread patrimonialism, and entrenched corruption—too obvious for even Suharto's strongest supporters to ignore. The New Order's demise brought to the fore what critics had long seen as its "Javanist" cast: the colonial-era, ethnic-elite tradition that was reinvented to straddle the gap between "modern" and "traditional" modes of New Order authority and governmentality.[1]

My aim in this chapter is to examine the authority of the Indonesian language as "perhaps the most important single ingredient in the shaping of the modern [Indonesian] culture" (Liddle 1988:1) and in the New Order's version of the Indonesian national project. Indonesian is unusual in being a national language and instrument of state that lacks a primordial ethnic community of native speakers. Less nonnative than unnative, it was transparently bound up with the "palpable nexus of practice and institutional structure, extensive, unified and dominant" (Abrams 1988:58) that was the New Order state system. But Indonesian is also a way of talking, a symbol of Indonesian national identity that is "projected, purveyed, and variously believed" (Abrams 1988:58) in situated, everyday interaction. In this way, Indonesian helps to transform national ideology into nationalist doxa, "diffuse, full, complete, and 'natural'" (Barthes 1989:121), by bringing Indonesian-ness into the "order of [verbal] signs and [conversational] practices" that is conversational life (Comaroff and Comaroff 1991:23).

Thanks in large part to New Order initiatives, Indonesian has spread rapidly across Indonesian territory, giving rise in some places to bilingualism and scenes of language shift that are as diverse and complex as the ethnic communities the state is working to transform. (For a sketch of one such scene in Central Java, see Errington 1998a.) In this chapter, however, I consider just a few public uses of Indonesian as an ongoing "project for the assumption of 'modernity' within the modalities of an autonomous and autochthonous social-political tradition"(Anderson 1966:89). Anderson's prescient comment, which focused on the political elite of Jakarta, was published on the cusp of the bloody political shift that brought the New Order into ascendance. But his words are apposite here for a diagnostic sketch of some of the ambiguities of New Order political culture. In a similar vein, I work toward a sociolinguistic cum semiotic sketch of an ideology of linguistic differentiation (see Irvine and Gal, this volume) that developed under the New Order.

I suggest here that Indonesian's authority under the New Order had two broadly different grounds, presupposing and mediated by two broadly different features or genres of public discourse. Institutionally grounded in the nation-state, Indonesian is a standard language overtly set off from a plurality of subnational ethnic languages. I consider this distinctively unnative standardness through Indonesian's ideological links with the New Order program of national development. But I also suggest that the Indonesian language has derived authority from more covert, "exemplary" qualities of Indonesian discourse distinctive of speakers who tacitly embody or are perceived as possessing them. Such distinctiveness resonates historically with the language and political culture of the absolutist sphere of colonial Java's courtly elites, who were adopted as models by some of the highest figures in New Order circles.

MODERNIST STATE AND LANGUAGE

Indonesian has historical roots in dialects of Malay spoken natively on both coasts of the straits of Malacca (Sumatran and Malayan) and in nonnative varieties that served as lingua franca throughout the archipelago well before the Portuguese made their way to the spice islands—the Malukus of what is now Eastern Indonesia—in the sixteenth century. By some accounts, the pidginized Malay varieties often called 'market language' *(bahasa pasar)* were used as far north as the coasts of the (present) Philippines and southern Japan, as far west as the coasts of Madagascar, and throughout what is now the Indonesian archipelago. (For further information, see Collins 1998a.)

The Dutch placed severe restrictions on access to their own language for "natives" and so engendered longstanding controversy as to which variety of Malay would best serve their several purposes (trade, missionizing, military, and so on). The history of this debate reflects the changing nature of the Dutch presence: As the spice trade decreased in profitability, the Dutch exploitative focus shifted to inland agricultural and human resources on Java and Sumatra, lending new immediacy to issues of administrative communication. After the Dutch East Indies Company ceded power to the colonial government of the Netherlands East Indies, language issues became increasingly important in the context of efforts to increase knowledge of and extend control over local "native" affairs.

A standard Malay orthography was fixed at the turn of the twentieth century by van Ophuysen, whose work in the mainland Malay heartland led to the codification of a 'general, cultured Malay' *(algemeen beschaafd Maleis)*. This variety was in turn disseminated by a colonial office called the *Balai Pustaka*, established in 1908, to provide reading materials in "good" Malay (as well as major ethnic languages) for "a new class of potential readers, with different living and reading habits, with different expectations with regard to books, based on their school

experiences" (Teeuw 1973:112).[2] This literary publishing arm of the
state soon became a major force in "a long-term project to homogenize
and unify Malay" (Maier 1993:55).

Novels, poetry, and criticism produced by the Balai Pustaka were
exclusively in Dutch-propagated, standard school Malay, and markedly
Islamic or Chinese literature was neglected in favor of Western-
accented visions of modernity and humanism. This agency's literary
products were offered to a market created largely by the state's own
educational system—a community of Malay speaker/readers, most of
them employed, directly or indirectly, by the colonial system. If 'school
Malay' *(bahasa Melayu)* was artificial or "stiff," this was a correlate of its
"stability and uniformity" (Teeuw 1973:120). "Dominated by Balai
Pustaka," *bahasa Melayu* "provided a solid and trustworthy foundation
for the building of the present-day national language" (Teeuw
1973:124). Chronicling the rise of school Malay, Maier (1993:55) usefully deploys Bakhtin's observations on the centripetal effects of standardizing social authority in his discussion of the rising "awareness of
standardized language in a network of schools." "This particular kind
of Malay was strongly associated with Dutch Authority...[and] the
natives often referred to it with the term *Bahasa Belanda* (Dutch) rather
than *bahasa Melayu;* not all of them by any means felt compelled to use
it" (Maier 1993:57).

There is no date on which national Indonesian can be said to have
been born from this conspicuously colonial variety of Malay, but it does
have an identifiable baptismal event: the celebrated 'meeting of youth'
(Rapat pemuda) on October 28, 1928, in Batavia, then capital of the
Dutch East Indies. (A convenient source for general background is
Moeliono 1993.) At that meeting an ethnically diverse, Dutch-educated
native intelligentsia adopted a nationalistic program and simultaneously
renamed 'Malay' *(bahasa Melayu)* as 'Indonesian' *(bahasa Indonesia)*, the
language of their nation-to-be. Their famous 'oath of the youth' *(Sumpah
Pemuda)*, still repeated on its anniversary every year across the country,
conferred public, formal recognition on the project of a 'unified people'
(satu bangsa) speaking 'one language' *(satu bahasa)* in a 'single homeland' *(satu nusa)*.

So at the beginning of World War II, "Indonesian" was little more
than a new name for an artificial, state-supported dialect of administra-

tive Malay, hardly spoken natively in the former colonial empire. But by 1995 it had become the fully viable, universally acknowledged national language, native to relatively few but clearly ascendant over hundreds of ethnic languages spoken among more than two hundred million Indonesians. Notwithstanding difficulties in evaluating the results of censuses that include questions about knowledge and use of Indonesian (see Steinhauer 1994), such surveys provide grounds for broad consensus that Indonesia is well on its way to solving "the national language problem" and enhancing its status as "the envy of the multilingual world" (Lowenberg 1983:3). The slogan 'language indicates nationality' *(bahasa menunjukkan bangsa)*, which once expressed a nationalist hope, seems now to describe a national condition (Geertz 1973:315).

Much of the success of national language development has been due to the New Order. From its inception—after the fall of Sukarno in 1965 and the ensuing massacre of hundreds of thousands of putative members of the Indonesian Communist Party—the New Order oversaw a massive program of social and economic engineering in which Indonesian was a central object and instrument. Indonesian was thus a target for state efforts at language development designed to "reduce arbitrary social and linguistic heterogeneity through the fast growth of functional heterogeneity" (Neustepny 1974:37).

Because it has been both medium and symbol of development, Indonesian has also partaken of a broader ideology of state-fostered nationalism and social change aimed at 'achieved progress' *(kemajuan)* through 'development' *(pembangunan)*. It is worthwhile to briefly consider this unusual case of unnative Indonesian language development with an eye to Ernest Gellner's (1983) arguments about the codevelopment of nation-states and languages generally. His position corresponds well enough with the practice and ideology of New Order national development to help explicate what I call here Indonesian's "standardist" authority.

Gellner sees nationalism as broadly "delusional" in ways best explained (following Durkheim) with recourse to the organic division of labor which, he believes, it is the function of modern states to foster. Industrial and socioeconomic development, in Gellner's account, depend on radical breaks with prenational, premodern pasts and with the sacred script languages typical of agrarian states. As these are abandoned, together with the mystified symbolic realms in which they are anchored, small literate elites are succeeded by national citizenries for whom a homogeneous, standard national language is common property. Such languages come into ascendance with the rise of secular literacies. Echoing Hegel—"none, then some, then all can read" (1983:8)—Gellner argues that school-mediated, state-sponsored literacy is learned as citizens are "exo-socialized" into the crypto-religion of the state, which is nationalism.[3]

This view has salience here not because it has empirical value or predictive power but because it so usefully foregrounds a logic of symbiosis between standardized languages, economic development, and state institutions. In this latter respect, Gellner appeals to broadly Weberian notions of rationality that, he argues, are concomitant with the rise of modern state bureaucracies and market economies. Such rationality is bound up, in his account, with the distinctive capacities of modern national languages as referentially transparent vehicles of efficient communication. Alluding to Basil Bernstein's writings (e.g., 1971) on context-free "elaborated codes," Gellner claims standard national languages to be preconditional for thought and discourse that can be autonomous with respect to context and transparent with respect to topic. The distinctiveness of modern national languages resides in the fact "that all referential uses of [such] language[s] ultimately refer to one coherent world and can be reduced to a unitary idiom; and…it is legitimate to relate them to each other"(Gellner 1983:21).[4]

This argument places Gellner very clearly in the tradition of philosophers who have articulated what Charles Taylor (1985) has broadly called designative (as opposed to expressive) views of language and human nature. (See also Briggs and Bauman, this volume.) Centered as it is on language's noncontext-dependent, denotative capacities, Gellner's position likewise partakes of the core assumptions that Silverstein (1976) adduced as grounds for structural linguistic analysis on one hand and the ideology of "monoglot standard" languages (Silverstein 1996) on the other. Important here, though, is the strong resonance of Gellner's position with the New Order's own ideological justification of its program of national development, including national language development.

One of Suharto's first policy moves after assuming power was to decree that schools be built throughout Indonesia, with an eye to achieving what Gellner (1983:57) calls the progressive "imposition of a high culture on society, where previously low cultures had taken up the lives of the majority...of the [Indonesian] population." At the very inception of his regime Suharto thus recognized "the monopoly of legitimate education [to be] more important, more central than is the monopoly of legitimate violence" (Gellner 1983:34). Those schools became the primary institutional means for disseminating standard Indonesian language and nationalist sentiment to a new citizenry and have now helped to consolidate what Gellner (1983:57) calls a "school-mediated, academy-supervised idiom, codified for the requirements of reasonably precise bureaucratic and technological communication."

As medium and topic of development, Indonesian figured regularly in the means-ends rhetoric of New Order–sponsored conferences on language development, at which state functionaries repeatedly alluded to its institutional underpinnings. An example is the following: "The concept of national society *(masyarakyat bangsa*[5]*)* cannot be fully understood if one national language...does not exist. A country *(negara)* that has one general/common *(umum)* language known throughout society will be more advanced in development *(pembangunan),* and its political ideology *(ideologi politiknya)* will be safer and stabler" (Burhan 1989).[6] In such policy-oriented discourse, standard Indonesian discourse frames the Indonesian language as an object of institutional treatment, among many, within the state's purview.

The ideology that grounded Indonesian's development under the New Order can be seen to resonate remarkably well with Gellner's standardist conception of language, modernity, and rationality, thanks to the perceptive critique of Ariel Heryanto. Heryanto (1988) traces the emerging instrumentalist character of Indonesian development out of the shift in tropes of "development" that occurred between the pre-1965 era of Sukarno and the post-1965 New Order. Prior to 1965, development was figured in nationalist discourse with broadly organic metaphors through keywords derived, for instance, from the root *kembang* ('flower'). Its nominal form *perkembangan,* for instance, counts as a rubric for a "NATURAL PROCESS of change which is motivated primarily by some INTERNAL necessity, enforced primarily by its own INTERNAL energy, its pace and extent being PROPORTIONAL to its own nature" (Heryanto 1988:49–50, emphasis in the original). This version of "development," in all likelihood traceable to German Romanticist visions of language and nation, had its earliest and most eloquent expression in Takdir Alisjahbana's unabashedly modernist writings.[7] Under the New Order this gave way to mechanical, constructivist figurings of *pembangunan*—a nominal form of *bangun* ('to rise, become vertical')—as an agentive, instrumentalist vision of technical, expert, conscious construction. It is, as President Suharto (1971:4) put it, "like building a large building" *(ibarat orang mendirikan gedung besar)*. It "denotes CRAFTMANSHIP as well as ENGINEERING, with the chief emphasis on yielding MAXIMAL PRODUCT, in the most EFFICIENT pace and manner possible, by bringing EXTERNAL forces to bear upon the object, *bangunan.*" (Heryanto 1988:50-51, emphasis in the original).

Such is the instrumental rhetoric that legitimated the New Order's self-assumed role as a mediator of foreign influence, technocratic overseer of socioeconomic change, and socializer of Indonesians into a modern national citizenry. Indonesian, as the nation-state's standard language, counts as a developed, efficient, referential instrumentality, integrated at once into a translocal system of state institutions and the local lives of members of what Burhan (1989) called the national society.

EXEMPLARINESS AND PUBLIC LANGUAGE

Jürgen Habermas's seminal work on public discourse has provoked broad debate on the nature of public spheres and civil society in Western European nation-states. His stated goal was to explicate the nature and condition of the putative anonymity of print-mediated discourse which, being alienable from the person of any author or reader, represents "a kind of social intercourse that, far from presupposing the equality of status, disregard[s] status altogether"(Habermas 1989:36). Belonging to no one and so, ostensibly, to everyone, it takes on, in his account, a contextual uninflectedness rather like that claimed by Gellner for discourse in national languages more generally.

However persuasive and stimulating is Habermas's chronicle of the rise of civil society, it has far less purchase on New Order Indonesia than Gellner's economistic, state-centered account. (For further discussion, see Budiman 1990.) More useful here are his succinct comments on the medieval antecedents to bourgeois public spheres, what he calls the publicness of an absolutist public sphere. Such authority, he argues (Habermas 1989:7), was more "like a status attribute...displayed [by nobility] as [the] embodiment of some sort of 'higher' power." In this way prenational aristocrats engaged in representative publicity, performatively embodying distinctive, intrinsic attributes in courtly social contexts.

Habermas thematizes the "naturalness" of such public persons' attributes, citing Goethe's observation (in *Wilhelm Meister*) that nobles are set off by their right to *seem*, that is, to bear in their personal qualities—movements, voice, and "whole being"—a distinctive 'publicness' *(Öffentlichkeit)*. And where Goethe distinguished inalienable traits of nobles from alienable possessions of the bourgeoisie, so Nietzsche (cited by Habermas to the same end) nostalgically distinguished the (publicly representative) aristocrat by what he is from the commoner, who proves himself by what he can *do*. Bourdieu's (1984:23) comments on the modern "aristocracy of culture" in France center in broadly similar ways on the crucial misrecognition of differences between domestic and educational modes of acquisition of cultural capital.

Habermas's absolutist public sphere partakes of what Landes (1988:18-19), working in and against his gender-blind idiom, calls the "performative character" of "the official public sphere of the absolutist court." In this way, publicly representative verbal performance conflates the intrinsic conventionality of language with the intrinsic (im)mediacy of talk as conduct (doing) that indexes nature (a being). Distinctively authoritative speech, by this account, is imbued with perceivedly direct, indexical signs of inherent authority stemming from speakers' internal nature. Authoritative conduct in an absolutist public sphere will also be iconic, as Irvine and Gal suggest (this volume), insofar as it lends the *appearance* of "necessity to a connection...that may be only historical, contingent, or conventional."

These broad comparative observations resonate usefully with leitmotifs in premodern Southeast Asian statecraft and political culture.[8] They can be linked, for instance, to Anderson's broadly similar observations from his seminal article (1972) on the concept of power in Javanese culture. Anderson read traditional Javanese historiography and early Indonesian politics there in ways that suggest an interpretive notion of power as a quasi-concrete attribute of things and persons rather than (as Max Weber has it) as an aspect of social relationships. When authority is construed or presupposed as a tangible property inhering in persons, objects, and locales, it helps to define semisacred loci of singular rulers, whose persons define centers of territorial control and pinnacles of social hierarchies.

In this respect Anderson's argument anticipates Gellner's remarks on sacred script languages and the capacity of utterances to embody power. Archaic, exotic, and semiopaque languages—"Truth languages", as Anderson (1991:22) has more recently called them—are nonarbitrary "emanations of reality, not fabricated representations of it." Semantic opacity and syntactic idiomaticity do not just reduce the construability of exemplary discourse; they confer on it the significance of what Keeler (1987:139) has called "reserved reference," that is, "meaning held in readiness rather than released in intelligibility."

Persons possessed of exemplary authority and mastery of esoteric language manifest both through their capacity to affect the world in efficacious (and not just "meaningful") acts of speech. Then the describable and performable converge as the world is drawn into fit with the word, in John Searle's phrase (1983:171). (An example in Javanese literature is a king with the power to render someone insane by describing them as such, that is, by saying, "You [are] mad.") Textual specialists—paradigmatically, 'poet-scribes' *(pujangga)* of traditional royal courts and Islamic 'teachers' *(kyai)* steeped in a heavily Arabicized literature—were endowed with the privileged "ability to penetrate to and conserve old and secret knowledge" (Anderson 1972:47) in script languages.

What Anderson calls Truth languages make reality "apprehensible only through a single, privileged system of [orthographic] representation" (1991:22). Exemplary use of such languages similarly embodies and indexes ideologically grounded exclusivity—"the sacred character, separate and separating, of high culture" (Bourdieu 1984:34)—as a sign of distinctive knowledge and ability. Exemplary discourse in this way has social significance as perceivedly nonconventional, immediate evidence of a speaker's nature. Its indexical grounding resists report or reproduction in metalinguistic statements. Insofar as generic distinctiveness, semantic opacity, and syntactic idiomaticity are the so-called natural grounds for authoritative verbal conduct, they are grounds rather than objects of discourse. In this sense exemplary discourse is mute with respect to its distinctiveness and grounded indexically in the authority that it presupposes and entails.

READING INDONESIAN'S AUTHORITY

I proffer this ideal-typical contrast between "standardist" and "exemplarist" language, underwritten by Gellner's and Habermas's accounts of public discourse in modern nations, to motivate my two readings of Indonesian's authority. A few examples are presented here, not to catalog a range of variants but to illustrate the contextually shared, multiple guises those kinds of authority can be given. Two of these examples can be seen as symptomatic of the ongoing development of a covertly exemplary Indonesian genres. The first involves relatively stable, isolable lexical developments, the second a bit of public performance in a satiric play in which I perceive the self-conscious authority of a New Order figure. I juxtapose these examples to suggest that exemplarist and standardist modes of authority coarticulate in ways that are shaped by contextual factors, rhetorical goals, and speakers' personal qualities.

The third topic I broach here involves a noteworthy event in the history of Indonesian language development, one that tellingly articulated the broad institutional relation between the distinctiveness of standard and exemplary language. This was a government-sponsored conference predicated on Indonesian's authority as a standard language, one grounded not just institutionally by the nation-state but ideologically in its referential transparency as a means for describing Gellner's "one coherent world" in a "unitary idiom" (Gellner 1983:21). This event assimilated exemplary Javanese discourse to a unitary national world, fixing and exotericizing it in and through standard Indonesian. It showed Indonesian's authority as not just a language of state but an institutionally privileged means of metalinguistic objectification.

Lexical Change: Exemplary Javanese and Esoteric English

Over the past thirty years a vocabulary has developed in Indonesian that is generically distinctive thanks to its provenance in archaic Old Javanese and Sanskrit. (For further discussion of these issues, see Errington 1985.) Terms like *lokakarya* ('workshop') and *kridanirmala* ('epidemic control') are elegant archaic terms for very modern entities and programs that arose under the New Order; portentous phrases like *Parasamya Purnakarya Nugraha*, the name of an award given to provinces most successful in implementing development plans, are semantically opaque archaistic composites.

Ten years after the New Order's rise, Takdir Alisjahbana (1976:119), Indonesia's eternal modernist, ruefully observed "the tendency for using Sanskrit and old Javanese words…during the last decade as a result of the greater activities of the army in political, economic, and other aspects of social and cultural life…Many Indonesians still consider words from Sanskrit or Old Javanese finer and commanding of more respect than other words." He attacked such nativist and traditionalist influences as arising from "something mysterious in human feelings, which still leans to the magical and mystical" (1976:61–62).

Generalized from the particular borrowing he is considering and his own ideological orientation to culture and tradition, Alisjahbana can be read as diagnosing exemplary features of standard Indonesian discourse as "nativist influences" that impede national development. So, too, he appeals, along lines set out very clearly by Gellner, to ideals of discursive transparency, efficiency, and rationality. He recognizes, in effect, that these esoteric vocabularies work in the standard language against its standardist authority, allowing New Order officials and technocrats to figure themselves as initiates into an exemplary elite.

Public Indonesian discourse has also been heavily populated with borrowings from English, the quintessential language of international modernity. Many are new words that contribute to the communicative efficiency valued by technocrats and functionalist social theorists alike. They enable the sorts of precise, efficient reference to modern things in modern venues extolled by Alisjahbana and characterized by Gellner (1983:57) as "reasonably precise bureaucratic and technological communication." But by the same criteria, some of these exogenous borrowings appear communicatively gratuitous and seem instead to be distinguishers of covertly exemplary genres of discourse. Alisjahbana's remarks hardly extend, for instance, to English borrowings with discursive significances that outrun their referential usefulness. Does one really need a word like *mengakselerasikan* (causative transitive verb based on *akselerasi*) for 'accelerate' when *mempercepat,* from *cepat* ('fast'), exists? Why use *identik* rather than the Indonesian *sama dengan* (roughly 'same with')? The need for these and many others of the nearly one thousand English borrowings that turned up in Smithies' (1982:112) survey of Indonesian print media is, as he suggests, "highly questionable," and the tendency trend "shows every sign of increasing." Unnecessary from the point of view of referential completeness and communicative efficiency, such superfluous borrowings contribute to what Salim (1977:82) has called the Indo-Saxonization of the English language.

Alisjahbana's and Salim's remarks can be read as overstating and understating (respectively) a single basic point. Similarly, Smithies (1982:111) remarks that English borrowings "give the impression that users are steeped in alien concepts" and function as a "semiprivate language of the bureaucratic substratum" (1982:112). This may have deeper resonances with modes of discourse and power among an exemplary Javanese elite, which makes it worth noting how this new esoterica can enhance and reproduce old territorial disjunctions between educated city elites and peripheral peasants. (For further discussion of these relations in Central Java, see Errington 1989 and 1998a:35–50.) Even moderately educated younger villagers, literate in Indonesian, may recognize the new vocabulary as new-yet-old marks of social distinction of a "new" modern elite. Such is the tacit suggestion made in a cartoon (fig. 5.1) from the February 23, 1982, issue of the Indonesian news magazine *Tempo* (glossable as 'Time'), which the New Order later shut down for lack of self-censorship.

Almost all the new borrowings in this cartoon are recognizably cognate with English, as is the rubric under which it is printed: *Opini* ('opinion'). Only the caption—"Foreign terms enter the village"—needs translation. This wry comment on a government program called "Newspapers Enter the Village" calls into question the assumed need of a rural citizenry to follow national developments. Older villagers may be too far beyond the pale of the new national language to recognize the provenance of such exotic words, but their collective social diacritic significance, if not their respective referential senses, may not be lost on younger bilingual villagers. If a modernizing national ideology holds out

FIGURE 5.1

"Foreign Terms Enter the Village." *From* Tempo, *February 23, 1982.*

the prospect of a new language of public discourse, verbal esoterica may resonate with antecedent understandings of exemplary status.

Exemplary Indonesian in Performance

Lexicons are useful here as socially salient, metalinguistically isolable targets for development discourse (and editorial cartoons). Suitably codified, they can count as standard, public knowledge that is disseminated through Indonesian dictionaries (particularly those sponsored by the state). Less obvious and more ephemeral are nonlexical, less pragmatically salient distinguishers of authoritative discourse. I consider these here only briefly, with recourse to a skillful caricature by the Indonesian playwright Nano Riantiarno.

Riantiarno created a minor scandal in 1989 with his play *Suksesi,* a humorous, thinly veiled portrayal of social conditions in Jakarta whose plot centers on issues of succession. It concerns a king (Bukbang) who is growing old (like Suharto) and will soon be obliged (as, eventually, was Suharto) to relinquish power. The title character—whose

Indonesian-sounding name plays quite clearly on the English word 'succession'—may be the most sympathetic of the king's greedy children who are vying for the throne. In one scene (Riantiarno 1990:27) Suksesi sponsors a modern fashion show for wealthy wives of high state functionaries to raise funds for the impoverished masses. After the obsequious master of ceremonies lauds Suksesi's efforts to develop "a marriage between the present and the past," he invites her to address the gathering. The translation of her speech provided below approximates very imperfectly the tone of her words.[9]

> Ibu-ibu yang kami muliakan. Di dalam era pembangunan <u>daripada</u> kerajaan kita ini…di dalam era pembangunan <u>daripada</u> kerajaan kita ini, maka kita di samping harus melihat ke depan maka sudah sepantasnya <u>daripada</u> sekali-sekali kita menengok ke belakang untuk sudah melihat <u>daripada</u> sudah, sudah sejauh mana <u>daripada</u> perjalanan kita. Apa saja yang sudah kita lakukan, serta apa manfaat <u>daripada</u> yang sudah dipetik oleh <u>daripada</u> masyarakyat.

> Ladies whom we respect. In the era of development in this our kingdom…in this era of development in our kingdom we so we aside from looking forward so also it is most fitting <u>indeed</u> occasionally that we look behind in order to see <u>indeed</u> already, already how far <u>indeed</u> our journey has been. Whatever we have carried out as well as what benefit <u>indeed</u> has been grasped by <u>indeed</u> the people.

Unbeknownst to Suksesi, her father (Bk) is listening to her speech from his hiding place in the company of his faithful clown-servants Togog (T) and Bilung (Bl). He interrogates them about what he has just heard.

> Bk: Begitukah cara anakku berpidato kang Togog?
> T: Ya paduka.
> Bk: Dan kamu bilang dia menjadi makin fasih makin matang?
> Bl: Makdsudnya, kang Totog hanya mau memberitahu den ayu semakin fasih dan matang dalam mempergunakan kata kata "<u>daripada</u>."

> Bk: That's how my child makes speeches Togog?
> T: Yes Excellency.
> Bk: And you say she's getting more adept, more accomplished?
> Bl: He meant, Togog only wanted to say that Lady Roro Suksesi
> is increasingly adept and accomplished in utilizing the word
> "<u>indeed.</u>"

Togog (and Riantiarno) here allude to Suksesi's repetition of the communicatively superfluous word *daripada*, a common connective that can variously be translated into English as 'in relation to', 'whereas', or (as above) 'indeed'. This hypercorrect use of *daripada* contributes no more to the substance or clarity of Suksesi's speech than does "indeed" to its translation.

Riantiarno effectively lampoons elevated, tacitly exemplary public speech in which, as Bilung says, Suksesi keeps getting more adept. But it is interesting that Riantiarno deploys a strategy that speaks directly to the performative character of this talk's (putative) exemplariness. Suksesi's speech is self-authorizing or self-constituting in that it must accomplish a distinctiveness that it presupposes: the aura of natural-ness, which Habermas identified as characteristic of public conduct in an absolutist public sphere. Discourse that rests on or objectifies its own distinctiveness would be devoid of such natural authority. So it is that Riantiarno must ventriloquate his view by naming it from offstage, so to speak, in the metapragmatic talk of his characters, who circumscribe it in less exemplary, more sardonic performance.

This passage was probably among the least of the reasons the New Order government closed down *Suksesi* in very short order. But it suggests the ways in which covertly exemplary modalities of speech came to figure in New Order public Indonesian discourse. Empty of content (unlike new Indonesian lexicons), they mark distinctive authoritative speakership stylistically: Being peripheral for the reference-focused ideology that grounds standard Indonesian, they can confer a covert naturalness on such distinctively exemplary conduct. In this way they subserve the authority of what Barthes (1989:121) called encratic dis-course, "a diffused, widespread, one might say osmotic discourse which impregnates...the socio-symbolic field (above all, of course, in societies of mass communication.)"

Standard Javanese in Indonesia

Such developments have occasioned little sustained commentary in the Indonesian media, aside from occasional programmatic observations like Alisjahbana's. At the New Order's behest, however, the media focused on another dimension of state language development: the concerted effort to counter pernicious side effects of the success of Indonesian language development. It began with an effort to rehabilitate Javanese language and culture in 1991, when high-level Indonesian officials convened in Semarang, capital of Central Java, for a 'Javanese Language Congress' *(Kongres Bahasa Jawa)* that was opened by President Suharto (himself Javanese).

Six hundred Indonesian technocrats, politicians, and intellectuals (mostly Javanese) met to discuss (mostly in Indonesian) the current state of their nation's dominant ethnic language (Javanese) in the dynamic of national development. (See Errington 1998b for further discussion.) Suharto urged the attendees to discuss ways that Javanese philosophy, especially as contained in the Javanese orthography, could be used to develop and disseminate Javanese character. Claiming rather disingenuously to speak not as president of the Republic but as a Javanese, he pressed his hope for the Indonesian people to possess the "noble spirit" necessary for "proper relations" between people, people and the environment, as well as between people and God (*Editor* 1991).

Few Indonesian functionaries take seriously the notion that in the foreseeable future ordinary Javanese will be threatened by extinction through a massive language shift to Indonesian. Suharto's fond hope, and the institutional logic of the conference, presuppose instead that Javanese stands in need not of development (like Indonesian) but of preservation as an exemplary ethnic tradition. Suharto and others at the conference evinced particular concern for the widespread ignorance of 'Javanese orthography' (the *hánácáráká*), which was repeatedly identified as integral to the "noble Javanese tradition." This focus on prestigious, ostensibly moribund "high" Javanese is of a piece with the New Order's broader reinvention of Javanese tradition, well described by Pemberton (1994) and Florida (1987) as a lofty, monolithic, ineffable 'noble sublime' *(adhiluhung)*.

After suitable deliberation on and lamentation of this loss of heritage,[10] participants recommended that 'Javanese language'

(Indonesian: *bahasa*) and 'tradition' (Indonesian: *budaya*) be placed under the custodial aegis of the state—specifically, the Department of Education and Culture, which was authorized to establish (standardize) a version of Javanese to be taught in state schools. A formerly esoteric tradition thus came to be assimilated into a modern institutional framework and disseminated in newly exoteric form to the nation's Javanese/Indonesian constituency. The Javanese language enters schools in Central and East Java with the status of 'local content' *(muatan lokal)* in a translocal, state-established curriculum. In this way it has been effectively detached from its formerly exemplary loci: the courtly circles of Jogjakarta and Surakarta, erstwhile royal polities in south-central Java. Reframed as an exoteric subject of instruction, an ethnic language tradition is therefore on its way to homogeneity and uniformity across those parts of Indonesian national territory that happen to count as Javanese. In this way, restricted traditions of exemplary centers are being assimilated and subordinated to the institutions and ideology of the nation-state as objects in and for a standard public culture.

The second cartoon illustrated here (fig. 5.2) suggests something of the conflicted intent and effect of this congress, at least in the eyes of one shrewd Javanese Indonesian observer. It depicts what I presume to be an anonymous government official reciting the Javanese syllabary—represented in the cartoon along with its Roman alphabet equivalents—as he holds up a puppet from the 'shadow play' *(wayang kulit),* a traditional Javanese performance genre closely associated with courtly culture. To one side stands a young boy dressed in modern, not to say well-to-do clothes. At once audience and commentator, he says to his father, in idiomatic Indonesian, "Well, if you, Dad, of Javanese descent, don't understand it…all the more for me…" Interestingly, the boy identifies Javanese-ness with his father's 'ancestry' *(keturunan)* rather than as his social identity per se, as would have been true had he called him "a Javanese" *(orang Jawa).* Whether or not this youth affirms his own ethnic descent, the cartoon suggests, the associated tradition is as little known to his father as to himself, and hardly relevant to the lives of either.

Even if Suharto's language project fell short of imbuing Indonesian students with the ethos of their new-yet-old ethnic tradi-

FIGURE 5.2

"Well, if you, Dad, of Javanese descent, don't understand it…all the more for
me…" *From* Suara Pembaruan, *March 13, 1991.*

tion, it will not be considered a failure. To the degree it impressed
young Javanese Indonesians with the mere existence of an ineffable,
state-sponsored ethnic past, it licensed the state as custodian of and suc-
cessor to that tradition, which is now a reference point for territorial-
ized, subnational, ethnic identities. Newly exotericised, this counts as a
body of knowledge that could overtly and publicly enrich development
with Javanese content in a national frame. In this way too the New
Order sought to valorize as "nonnative" perceivedly uncongenial side
effects of the development program it sponsored.

As symbols of what Herder might have called "(sub)national character," exemplary forms of Javanese language and literacy helped the
New Order elite in its longstanding efforts to mediate the ambiguities
of ethnic and national identity in its own authoritative terms. By "reducing" this once esoteric, now standardized Javanese to the "unitary
idiom" (in Gellner's words) that is Indonesian, they elided the ambiguities of ethnic tradition in a modern national   present, and they did so
in authoritative discourse and contexts.

DISCURSIVE PUBLIC AUTHORITY

The hold of the "imaginary of development" (Escobar 1992) is strong enough, even in this postdevelopment era, to make possible persistent assumptions about sweeping modernizing transitions from the alpha of ethnic tradition to the omega of national modernity. I have worked against such broadly epochalist visions, so well articulated in Gellner's work, by foregrounding what I see rather as two faces or guises of Indonesian's authority under the New Order. I have contrasted standardist and exemplarist grounds of verbal distinction so as to make particulars of Indonesian usage speak to the doubled, perhaps conflicted legitimacy assumed by agents of the New Order regime.

To development's apologists and proponents, exemplarism may seem a dysfunctional residuum, part of an ethnic neotraditional syndrome that contributed to the New Order's demise. But even if Indonesian's authority partook of a peculiarly Javanese tradition, there is no reason to assume that authoritative discourse in other languages and nations does not partake of its own local, historically shaped modes of exemplary distinctiveness as well. Viewed within the history of Indonesia, in which the New Order counts as a chapter, Indonesian might be instead one specific, perhaps unusually clear instance of the asymmetric complementarity (rather than conflicted dichotomy) between standardist and exemplarist dimensions of authority. The asymmetry arises from standardism's overt grounding in dominant nationalisms and state systems, the paired ideological and institutional grounds against which exemplariness of whatever sort can be tacitly, performatively figured. In this way standardism's referentialist grounding, explicated very differently by Gellner and Silverstein, may leave a space for the kinds of performative variation or slippage that makes for exemplary personal conduct. But since it also gives standard languages the universe at large, it makes languages their legitimate (metalinguistic) objects. Symptomatic of Indonesian's political *cum* referential privilege was the Kongres Bahasa Jawa, the extended metalinguistic project, that discursively officialized and institutionally subordinated exemplary Javanese.

Kathryn Woolard has rightly pointed out how this complementarity can be broadened, insofar as standardism legitimizes forms and uses of a language (here, tokens of an Indonesian linguistic type), whereas exemplarist ideology informs the construal of conduct of particular speakers as covertly (un)worthy of respect and obedience.[11] If standardism, by its nature, is everywhere the same, the exemplary in authority's im-person-ations must be culturally and contextually variable. This asymmetry likewise informs standardism and exemplarism as a linguistically oriented version (as Richard Bauman suggested at the SAR advanced seminar) of Weber's ideal-typical distinction between bureaucratic and charismatic authority.

Like other abstract model-driven distinctions, including those of Gellner, Bourdieu, and Habermas, this distinction helps make the Indonesian case speak to broader comparative questions about the "imaginary of national (language) development" in postagrarian nation-states. Viewed cross-culturally, Indonesian's double development can be taken as an especially clear, linguistic symptom of the "combination of paradoxes [which] conspire[d] to make the tentacles of [New Order] state power appear to be discrete, disinterested, and diffuse" (Cohn and Dirks 1988:227). Studies of "language ideology" like this one can make verbal particulars diagnostic of contradictions and pathologies of power. As a student of Indonesia, however, I prefer to look to Indonesian as an enduring resource for shifting national identities in volatile, emergent sociopolitical contexts. I want to read not just against the developmentalist grain of the New Order, but with an eye to the broadly constitutive dimensions (see Ricoeur 1986) of Indonesian language ideology and its potential role in Indonesians' ongoing construal of and engagement with the social flux of everyday life. So I have sought to read Indonesian's authority in relation to local history and to situate broad comparative metrics with an eye to contextual and verbal particulars.

Students of language inside and outside the "developing world" are increasingly concerned with the production and political uses of standardized languages in postcolonial nation-states. My argument here is that sensitivity to language's uniquely articulated nature does not mean a distancing from power's broader conditions and effects. Rather, those particulars can inform locally nuanced readings of authority as it is mediated and legitimated through its verbal forms.

Notes

Material and issues in this paper have been taken over from Errington (1986, 1989, 1998a, 1998b). I gratefully acknowledge support from Yale University and the Center for Psychosocial Studies during the time I worked on all of these issues. However, none of the material provided or discussed in this paper derives directly from research in Indonesia. This paper is dedicated to the memory of *Tempo, Detik,* and *Editor* (*almarhum*), and to the hope for the ascendance of their true successors in post–New Order Indonesia.

1. See, for example, Anderson (1966); Florida (1987); Pemberton (1994); Robison (1983); Tsing (1993); Willner (1966). A representative journalistic treatment is in *The Economist's* (April 17, 1993) special survey on Indonesia, especially p. 18.

2. For a discussion of the politics and evolution of spelling reform, see Vikors (1992). For a more extensive overview of these issues, along with relevant sources, see Errington (1998a:51–64).

3. In this respect Professor Gellner is, by his own criteria, in the curiously conflicted position of being both demystifier/apostate and "high priest" of the secular religion of nationalism.

4. This same ideology underwrites Gellner's own authorial position and his story of a long, hard, developmentalist road that leads, finally, to the mode of thought presumably exemplified in his work.

5. That this phrase is difficult to translate suggests something of its breadth, if not its vagueness. *Bangsa* by itself suggests 'race' or 'group of people linked by common descent'; *masyarakat* invokes notions of 'people in society.' So one can refer either to *bangsa* or *masyarakat Indonesia,* meaning roughly 'the Indonesian people' and 'Indonesian society' respectively.

6. *Gagasan tentang masyarakat bangsa tidak akan dipahami dengan baik oleh masyarakat bila satu bahasa nasional ... tidak ada. Negara yang mempunyai satu bahasa umum yang dikenal oleh seluruh rakyatnya kan lebih maju dalam pembangunan, dan ideologi politiknya akan lebih aman dan stabil.*

7. For example: "A culture begins to bud, when there grows up within a society a conviction of the truth of a certain system of values...the ability of a culture to develop is not unlimited, for every culture contains within itself the dialectic of all growth. As the papaya seed, which sprouts in the fertile soil and joyfully thrusts up through it to greet the beneficent rays of the sun, must experience, the further it rises up out of the earth, an increasing remoteness from the soil, from which its roots suck up the sap, that makes it grow, so every culture

that gives expression to a definite system of values, must eventually experience the limits to the possibilities of its further development" (Alisjahbana 1961:3).

8. See, for instance, Geertz (1980) on exemplary centers and "theater states," and Tambiah (1976) on Thai kingship and the galactic polity of "Indic" Southeast Asia.

9. My thanks to Matthew Cohen for providing me with a copy and translation of this play. I have, however, taken liberties with the latter for my own purposes here.

10. As one congress attendee put it to me, "Everyone cried over the loss of high Javanese" *(Semua peserta menangisi kehilangan básá)*.

11. Woolard's comments were made on a previous draft of this paper, posted on the internet by the Language-Culture discussion group (to which my thanks for that opportunity). Space and time being what they are, I cannot do Woolard's thoughtful comments justice here. They can be read in their entirety at www.cs.uchicago.edu/l-c/archives/1995/Apr/msg00011.html.

A Note on Transcription

Standard Indonesian orthography is used. Consonant symbols have values close to their English equivalents, save that /ng/ represents a velar nasal. Vowels have roughly the following values: /i/ as in "she," /u/ as in "shoe," /e/ as in the first part of the diphthong in "shade," /o/ as in the first part of the diphthong in "shoal," /a/ as in "shot." Epenthetic glottal stops between vowels are not transcribed. Javanese words are transcribed with the same orthography, save that /dh/ represents a postalveolar dental stop, over and against dental /d/, and /á/ represents a low, back, semirounded vowel somewhat like that in "shore."

6

Constructing a Tongan Nation-State through Language Ideology in the Courtroom

Susan U. Philips

Recent work on language ideologies has given considerable attention to their role in the imagining of nation-states (see, for example,
Anderson 1991; Blommaert and Verschueren 1992; Spitulnik 1992; and
Irvine and Gal, Bauman and Briggs, and Errington, this volume). In
this paper I will consider some ways that language and language ideologies contribute to imagining Tonga as a nation-state. My goal is to
show how the harnessing or appropriation of language ideologies to
the end of imagining nation-states is both site-specific and multisited.
In particular I will show how the condemnation of crimes of bad language by Tongan court personnel on the grounds that brothers and sisters might have been present imposes a sister-brother relationship on
all Tongan citizens while they are together in public. The relevance of
their relationship is projected from the family onto the nation as a
whole. All Tongans are expected to treat one another in public as if
they were brothers and sisters. At the same time, this logic is but one
manifestation of nationalistic projections of family dyads onto the
nation as part of the imagining of a Tongan nation-state.

Tonga has many features of the ideal nation-state from a European point of view (Blommaert and Verschuren 1992). Tongans see themselves as a culturally and linguistically homogeneous group that shares a common history.[1] Tonga is a former colony of Great Britain, and its strongest international ties are with English-speaking countries. Although Tongan is the national language, English is a required second language for government employees, and many government documents are published in both languages. English is taught in the primary grades and high school and is the language of instruction in a small number of high schools. Since there is no significant conflict over these basic features of Tongan language policies, choice of a national language is not a focus of ideological work there as it is in places where the citizenry is self-consciously multiethnic and multilingual (see, for example, Errington, this volume; Spitulnik 1992). There is, however, a growing concern that particular highly valued styles of Tongan language use are being undermined and eroded by the attention given to English in schools. Relatedly, Tongan ideological work focuses on particular ways of using the Tongan language rather than on whole code choices, as we will see in the discussion to follow.

I argue here that Tongan nation-making ideology involving language, both in court and elsewhere, has four characteristics that are commonly attributed to nationalist discourses (see Alonso 1994): (1) Historical continuities between political regimes of the past and present are asserted as a way of legitimating present regimes. In postcolonial nations, this articulation of continuity regularly involves making connections between what are often referred to as "traditional" non-nation-state regimes of the past and "modern" nation-state regimes of the present (as in Errington, this volume). (2) The nation is represented through metaphors that draw analogies between nation and family, as in the terms motherland and fatherland. (3) The nation is represented as both internally homogeneous and externally different from other nations. This process regularly involves language ideologies that posit a common language for all members of the nation (as in Bauman and Briggs, Irvine and Gal, and Silverstein, this volume). (4) Nation-imagining ideology is multisited and site specific, so that the partial articulations of the three preceding processes take place in many contexts. Imagining of the nation-state is multisited even within the state.

Current awareness of the multisitedness of nation-making owes much to the work of Antonio Gramsci (1971) and Stuart Hall (1986). Gramsci argued that control of the state's governmental structures was sustained not only by force but also through cultural hegemony. He conceived of hegemony as an ideological process through which state institutions produced and reproduced ideological consensus within the citizenry. Hegemony emerges as a constant process in Gramsci's writings because he envisioned such ideological domination as never complete, as constantly giving rise to counterpositions that in turn had to be countered and appropriated by the group controlling governmental structures. A great deal of nation-making ideology, then, is produced by the state.

A crucial feature of Gramsci's writings is his conceptualization of the state in two distinct ways. He sees it, first, as consisting of the governing institutions of a nation. But he also sees it as encompassing the articulation of governing institutions with "civil" society, for example, with religious and educational institutions. In some contexts he writes of both state and civil ideological production as encompassed by the term "state." It is not my purpose here to fully develop Gramsci's concept of the state or other scholars' understanding of what Gramsci intended. But it is worth noting that his ideas about how state hegemony is achieved through ideological processes in a range of societal contexts have been influential in documenting ways that the state is imagined in a range of discourses outside of government itself (see Abrams 1988; Alonso 1994, 1995; Hall 1986; Joseph and Nugent 1994). Abrams (1988), for example, has argued that the idea of the state exists in many contexts within a society, in ways that convince citizens of its reality. Alonso (1994) suggests that in work developing this idea, civil society has been privileged. More attention has been given to the imagining of the state in areas of life that are outside of institutions typically associated with governing than within them.

For the purposes of this chapter, the importance of Gramsci's second concept of the state and its role in the constitution of nation-states is that it evokes an awareness of nation-state–making ideological practices as multisited. Discussing how some of Gramsci's key concepts can be used to analyze racism and postcolonial societies, Stuart Hall (1986:26) notes:

> Schooling, cultural organizations, family and sexual life, the pat-
> terns and modes of civil association, churches and religions, com-
> munal or organizational forms, ethnically specific institutions,
> and many other such sites play an absolutely vital role in giving,
> sustaining and reproducing different societies in a racially struc-
> tured form. In any Gramscian-inflected analysis, they would cease
> to be relegated to a superficial place in the analysis.

The term "site," which recently has been slipping into linguistic anthropological discussions of language ideologies (for example, Hill, this volume; Silverstein 1992), deserves some commentary at this juncture. It is worth considering the sources and appeal of "site," particularly since it overlaps in meaning with "context," a term already well developed in linguistic anthropology. "Site" is strongly associated with cultural studies and is used a good deal by Hall, a leading figure in the development of that field, as the material quoted above illustrates. It is not a concept that has been a focus of analytical treatment; in other words, it is not treated as a theoretical construct with specific uses or purposes. Rather it is a term that inflects cultural studies discourses in a way that invokes and evokes a particular theoretical orientation in much the same way that use of the term "construct" to talk about the construction of social realities is associated with ethnomethodology and conversation analysis.

"Site" is generally used to refer to a locus or focus of cultural studies analysis. Most notably, culture is written about as the general site of cultural studies analysis (for example, Hall 1981:21; Nelson, Treichler, and Grossberg 1992:5). The purpose of the focus on culture in cultural studies is to deconstruct it, revealing its ideological nature and the ways in which it is both a form and a source of power and authority, a regimentation by ideas. Part of the term's appeal lies in its metaphorical nature. "Site" is concrete, but it is applied to the ephemeral, to ideas, claiming a kind of materiality for them. This would be the converse of the metaphorical work done by the term "imagined," as in "imagined community," which renders what is thought of as very real as less real, more ephemeral, and more vulnerable.

But "site" is also used in cultural studies to refer to more concrete phenomena:

> There's always something decentered about the medium of cul-
> ture, about language, textuality, and signification, which always
> escapes and evades the attempt to link it, directly and immedi-
> ately, with other structures. And yet, at the same time, the
> shadow, the imprint, the trace, of those other formations, of the
> intertextuality of texts in their institutional positions, of texts as
> sources of power, of textuality as a site of representation and
> resistance, all of those questions can never be erased from cul-
> tural studies. (Hall 1992:284)

This is where the meaning of "site" most clearly overlaps with the meaning of "context" as it is used by linguistic anthropologists. "Context," however, has very salient methodological connotations. It refers to specific real interactions that are tape-recorded and video-taped, even though the interactions might otherwise be experienced as quite fleeting. In contrast, in cultural studies, even when the sites being discussed are material, as when geographers talk about places, the term continues to have the connotations of something ideologically constructed as part of a particular framework of ideas that has power over those who experience places as places or texts as texts. There is, then, in cultural studies, a tendency to avoid the idea we find in discussions of context of any strictly material reality. The appeal of "site" over "context" for linguistic anthropologists studying language ideologies probably stems from these ideological connotations.

Linguistic anthropologists are also developing ideas similar to the notion of "crucial sites" in cultural studies (see, for example, Hall 1986; Mills 1997). Like "site," "crucial sites" is not a term that receives analytical focus as a concept in cultural studies writing; rather, it conveys the sense that more important or powerful ideological work is being done in some forms of cultural activity than in others. The related idea emerging in linguistic anthropology is that some kinds of linguistic practices are more likely to be talked about than others in metapragmatic commentary about language and its use. Most notably, Silverstein (1981) has argued that some aspects of language structure are more subject than others to conscious awareness in a way that facilitates metacommentary. Specifically, words and other segmentable units can be commented on more readily than nonsegmental aspects of language structure.

The perceptual salience of words for humans is rooted in human cognition, but there are also cultural group–specific key sites that are brought up by members of a group when they are commenting on their own uses of language. Kroskrity's (1992) discussion of kiva speech as the key site referred to when Tewas call for linguistic purism, which by analogy is seen as desirable in other contexts as well, is the best-developed example of such a concept of site, but it can be seen in the work of others too. Irvine (1990) notes that the Wolof speech registers she describes are prototypically associated with praise singers' elevation of nobles, although Wolof of both these and other castes can activate the same kinds of register differences in their speech. And Hill (1992:270) points out that for Mexicano speakers, the most popular way to illustrate the respect conveyed by honorifics is with the example of greetings between ritual kin.

In the discussion of Tongan language ideology to follow, I will draw on these ideas in considering how, in Tongan courts, representatives of the state harness Tongan language ideology about the sister-brother relationship to the end of imagining a Tongan nation-state. I will argue that the court is a key site in Tonga for elaboration of language ideology about the sister-brother relationship, yet still part of a multisited language ideology that focuses on this relationship. I will focus on tape-recorded speech from Tongan magistrate's courts proceedings dealing with minor criminal cases of *lea kovi* ('bad language'). Typically in these cases, young unmarried women take men to court for speaking to them in public in an insulting or threatening way. Despite the diversity of circumstances in which bad language occurs, the magistrates and police prosecutors consistently interpret such language as a violation of Tongan moral order or *anga faka-Tonga* ('Tongan culture') because of the disrespect it shows to the sister-brother relationship. I argue that in this legal context the sister-brother relationship can be understood as a trope for a distinctly Tongan way in which citizens should conduct themselves in public with the opposite sex.

I first consider some of the broadest features of Tongan nation-making ideology, particularly those associated with the four features mentioned earlier as common elements in the ideological imagining of the nation: the continuity between past and present, the use of family imagery in talking about the nation, the characterization of the nation as internally homogeneous yet different from other nations, and the multisitedness of the ideological work that imagines nations. Attention then turns to how magistrates and police prosecutors in the courtroom invoke language ideology about the sister-brother relationship to explain why the crime of bad language is morally wrong. Finally, I will show how this ideological work by these representatives of the state exemplifies the four characteristics of nation-making.

IMAGINING THE TONGAN NATION-STATE

An independent constitutional monarchy in the South Pacific, Tonga comprises more than 150 islands and has a population of approximately 100,000, making it, along with Samoa, Tahiti, and Hawaii, one of the major Polynesian populations in size. Polynesianists see Tonga as having been one of the most centralized polities of the region before European contact. It has been characterized as one of the earliest and most radically Westernized societies of the Pacific and also as one of the most culturally conservative today. It is not difficult to resolve these apparently contradictory characterizations, however. Like many island groups in the area, Tonga began to experience frequent contact with Europeans in the late eighteenth century. Christian mis-sionization became profoundly effective and influential during the third decade of the nineteenth century. The island group's identity as a proto–nation-state began to emerge in the mid-nineteenth century. By that time Taufa'ahau, the man credited with unifying the island group, had already issued written codes of law and set up magistrate's courts that took power away from local chiefs and contributed to the further centralization of power (Latukefu 1974).

Tongan leaders early embraced the trappings of European nation-states as a strategy for keeping the colonial influence of Great Britain at arm's length without losing that country's protection from the preda-tory moves of other European nations. Thus, relatively early on, the island group created a national government that has continuity to the present. But that government appears to have been more shaped by local interpretive practices and less imposed upon by Western European interpretive practices than other political units of similar scale in the region during the past 150 years.

In Tonga today, nationalist discourses that link political regimes of the past and present are voluminous, multisited, and multifaceted. Contemporary Tongan political ideology connects the "modern" constitutional monarchy with a "traditional" polity ruled by a titled paramount chief through the embodiment of both polities in the living king, Tupou IV. The king also holds the same traditional title of Tu'i Kanokupolu that was bestowed on Tāufa'āhau, from whom he is directly descended. The present king's mother, Queen Sālote, who reigned from 1918 to 1965, is the twentieth-century Tongan most responsible for promulgation of these twin sources of authority for the contemporary state (Ellem 1981). Note that this overt double legitimation by both the traditional and modern is somewhat different from the links between traditional and modern described for Indonesia (Errington, this volume). In Indonesia, political rhetoric has it that the modern has supplanted the traditional, so that the latter can only be a covert source of authority in political discourse.

In addition to discourses linking the past to the present, there are also discourses that link the life of present-day commoners to the life of the present-day title-holding nobility. The nobles of today hold titles that carried prestige and power when they were bestowed on chiefs of the precontact period, and they benefit from the same kind of double legitimation as does the king. By implication, the entire social order of today is linked in this way to the social order of the past. I say "by implication" because there are no histories of commoners in Tongan public political spheres of the present in the way that there are histories of the nobility and the royal family, except insofar as commoners know their own family pasts to be tied to those of nobles and non-noble titled chiefs. The traditional polity, then, is imagined as if it could be equated with the present-day nation, in spite of considerable evidence that the islands that make up Tonga today were not unified under a single source of authority at the time of European contact.

As part of this ongoing nation-state project of double legitimation, characteristics of the nuclear family as it is experienced by present-day commoners are projected to the societywide level of both the nation of today and the imagined traditional polity of the past. Two dyadic nuclear family relationships in particular are the sites of ideological work relating family to nation-state: the father-child relationship and the sister-brother relationship. These dyads receive similar ideological treatment in some respects and are treated differently in others. Both relationships are represented as hierarchical. The child is subordinate to the father, and the brother is subordinate to the sister, although the latter relationship exhibits more complementarity than the former.

For both relationships, there are lists of behaviors that are *tapu* ('forbidden') to the subordinate position. In the father-child relationship, the child must not touch the father's head, eat his leftover food, use his cup, wear his clothes, or sleep in his bed. The *tapu* proscribing certain behaviors in the sister-brother relationship is more reciprocal, but there is a greater burden on the brother than on the sister to make sure proper conduct is adhered to. Traditionally, one is told today, this relationship was one of mutual respect and avoidance, with the brother portrayed as taking the active role of avoiding. Nowadays avoidance is not strictly enforced, and sisters and brothers are more often co-present in the same interactions. When they are together, they are expected to be emotionally restrained and decorous in their behavior. There should be no joking or hilarity, no expression of anger, and no reference to parts of the body. To this familiar and often repeated list, Tamar Gordon (1990:211) has added the following behaviors as not permitted in this relationship: private talking, exposure of private parts of the body such as genitals, chest, and thigh, dancing together, sitting together in a public place, and direct involvement in each other's clandestine courtships and marriages. Others who may be present along with the sisters and brothers are subject to the same constraints. People are expected to display the same respect for others' sister-brother relations that they display in their own such relations.

The sister-brother relationship is the cross-gender connection that is most ideologically elaborated among Tongans. Polynesianists writing about this relationship reflect a widespread view that women are more highly regarded and have far more power in family politics as sisters than as wives, particularly in Western Polynesia (Huntsman and Hooper 1975; Rogers 1977; Schoeffel 1978). Both Rogers, writing about Tonga, and Schoeffel, writing about Western Samoa, make it clear that the sister's higher status relative to the brother is a matter of her superior personal rank, which is to be distinguished from the legitimized political authority of the brother.[2]

There are key sites for the sister-brother relationship, that is,

scenes frequently and repeatedly mentioned by Tongans to instantiate
its nature not only when speaking to outsiders like myself, but also in
Tongans' reporting of life experiences to one another. Without a doubt
the most important of these is the sister's traditional right to ask for and
receive anything under the control of her brother, whether this be
food, material possessions, or money for her children's school tuition.
This right is controversial among Tongans themselves; there have been
written laws against it since the mid-nineteenth century, but the practice continues.

Interestingly, prototypical scenes demonstrating the sister's devotion to her brother are less salient. One that I am aware of is from a play
often performed by the students of Queen Sālote College, a girls' secondary school. In this play, girls are exhorted to produce traditional
forms of Tongan wealth in the form of bark cloth and mats for their
brothers. Sisters' devotion to their brothers was also made known to me
in more idiosyncratic forms. For instance, I taped the trial of a woman
who, while employed at the Bank of Tonga, had falsified a deposit
entrusted to her by a cousin by putting it into her brother's account so
that he could show he had collateral and thereby obtain a loan to build
a home.

The ability of sisters and brothers to give to one another is primarily associated with adults who have some control over their own
resources. The site most associated with relations between cross-gender
siblings at a younger age is that of young men's houses. Traditionally,
when boys moved into their teen years, out of respect for their sisters
they stopped sleeping in the main house with the rest of the family. A
smaller house would be built on the property where they could sleep
and socialize with other young men. Today this is an ideal that is not
necessarily practiced, although such houses are still built. In the village
where I lived with a Tongan family, I knew of two houses in which older
men lived alone and male youths regularly gathered in the evenings.
This seemed to be a modified version of the practice of separate houses
for young men. The purpose of Tongans in mentioning the separate
youth hut to me was to illustrate how the stricture on boys to avoid their
sisters intensified at adolescence, along with a greater freedom allowed
to boys than to girls.

Among commoners, the *tapu* complex associated with sisters and brothers is extended to other relationships. One extension of the respect given to the sister is the great respect given to the father's sister and the father's sister's daughter. Both of these relatives are prime candidates for the ritual role of *fahu*, the person who receives and controls distribution of women's material wealth at funerals and other occasions. Tongans say that in the past, the father's sister had to give permission in order for her brother's son to marry, and although this is no longer true, her support of her nephew's choice of a marriage partner can still be influential.

Of greater relevance here is the extension of the behaviors associated with the sister-brother relationship to cousins of the opposite sex to as many degrees of removal from the direct line of descent as can be traced. The term *tuofefine* ('sister') refers both to a male's siblings of the opposite sex and to his female cousins; the term *tuonga'ane* ('brother') refers both to a female's siblings of the opposite sex and to her male cousins. In relations between cross-gendered cousins, the demeanor called for is similar to that expected of true sisters and brothers, though a lesser degree of respect is involved. Here too sexual joking is inappropriate, and commoners are not supposed to court or marry their cousins. But whereas it is usually clear who one's true siblings are, Tongans aren't always sure of who their cousins are. For young men, concern to avoid sexual joking with cousins comes up as a conscious and articulated issue primarily and stereotypically around the practice of *kava* parties. When young men get together to socialize and drink *kava*, a narcotic drink derived from the root of the *kava* plant, they ask a young woman to join them as *tou'a*. The *tou'a* prepares and serves the drink, and the men competitively flirt and joke with her (Olson 1997). Men try to avoid *kava* parties in which the *tou'a* is a cousin, but if she is someone they don't know personally, they may unknowingly be with her inappropriately. This makes such gatherings in villages other than one's own more attractive, because there is less likelihood of encountering a female cousin there.

Young women likewise are concerned to avoid situations where they might unknowingly be co-present with a male cousin in activity involving inappropriate speech. I did not have a sense that there was a key site around which they ideologically elaborated this issue in the way that *kava* parties were for the young men. But I learned early in my research that the courtroom was one place young women knew it was dangerous for them to go, because the problems associated with their presence there were raised independently to me by young women who did not know each other. One such woman, a part-time interpreter in the Supreme Court, told me that she could not get full-time work because court personnel were concerned that a cousin could be present in the court unknown to her while she was hearing and interpreting bad language. My research assistants, who were young women, let me know that they and their father were uneasy about them coming to court with me for the same reason, although their desire to help me ultimately outweighed their reluctance. The likelihood that *tuofefine* and *tuonga'ane* would be co-present in a courtroom when cases involving bad language were heard was reduced by the court clerks' tendency to schedule such cases toward the end of the day, when fewer people were left in the courtroom.

The father-child and sister-brother relationships are projected into nation-state–making public discourses about the past and the present, and these discourses are experienced as having to do with all Tongans. Just as a father's duty is to love and take care of his children, it was the traditional chief's duty and is the king's and nobles' duty today to love and take care of the people under their rule. Just as it is the child's duty to treat the father respectfully, so too in the past it was the commoners' duty to show respect to titled chiefs and their family members, and it is their duty today to show respect to the nobles and the king. As with the family dyads, the duties of the subordinate party are elaborated and canonized to a greater degree than those of the dominant party.

This is the ideological context in which the term *lea faka'eiki* ('chiefly language') becomes relevant. In these speech levels, used when commoners are talking to or about a chief or the king, certain commoner lexical items are replaced with level-specific items to show respect. Construed within the framework of *tapu* developed for the family dyads, in which respect is conveyed primarily by refraining from what one would otherwise do, these lexical substitutions should be seen as avoidances of the common, as restrictions rather than elaborations.

Lea faka'eiki is described first and most often by Tongans as reserved for present-day nobles and the king and is understood to entail a symbolic identification between traditional chiefs and modern rulers, since its use predates European contact. However, terms associated with the kingly level are also used in church to refer to Jesus, God, and the Holy Spirit, and terms associated with the chiefly level are used in court to address the magistrate or judge, in church to address the congregation, and in public political meetings. (See Philips 1991 for a more detailed discussion of these aspects of *lea faka'eiki*.) Low frequency use of the most commonly occurring lexical items associated with the chiefly level are generally characteristic of speech in public activities in the village. When I asked why chiefly language was being used when no titled nobles were present, I was told on more than one occasion, "A noble might be present." Clearly, in metapragmatic discourse about *lea faka'eiki*, the higher speech levels are strongly associated with the present-day representatives of state authority, who in turn are linked to precontact representatives of authority.

The sister-brother relationship is also projected into public discourses about the modern nation-state and the traditional social order to which it is linked, in ways that specifically focus on the sister's ritually superior status. For example, Princess Pilolevu, the daughter of the present king, is a woman of great status. Her home on the main island is a regular tourist destination, she is eagerly sought to preside over a range of public events, and her doings are avidly followed in the press and commented on by Tongans. When she danced for her father at his seventieth birthday celebration, people rushed forward to kiss her feet. However, her superior ritual status relative to her brothers, one of whom will someday be king, was not a topic of ideological elaboration in my experience. Rather, the implications of the superior ritual status of the ruler's sister are developed in contemporary historical discourses about the traditional polity of the past. For example, referring to what he calls "the *moheofo* system," Mahina (1986) describes how the sister's superior ritual status was made use of in chiefly politics. In this system, which emerged in the seventeenth century, the then sacred ruler, the Tu'i Tonga, preserved the personal rank of his descendants as superior to that of the Tu'i Kanokupolu, the secular ruler, by marrying the secular ruler's eldest sister, the Moheofo. This strategy also gave him more control over the secular leader than he otherwise could have.

Several key points about Tongan nation-creating ideology should be highlighted here. First, Tongan discourses linking past and present political regimes have a certain shared logic, yet at the same time they are rich and diverse. Second, the metaphorical projections of ideas about the nuclear family onto the nation as a whole also have both coherence and diversity. Two key dyads within the family, the father-child dyad and the sister-brother dyad, are elaborated at both the family level and at the national level. Third, Tongan ideological links between past and present, and Tongan ideological projections of two family dyads to the nation as a whole, are displayed in a way that assumes internal homogeneity, that is, these ideological projects apply equally to all Tongans. Furthermore, Tongan national history and family metaphors are distinctive to Tonga. This means that these ideologies project a culturally homogeneous Tongan nation that is different from other nations. Fourth, as I have tried to show, Tongan nationalist ideology is multisited. It is concerned with both present and past and with both father-child and sister-brother relations. It is developed around both state and civil sites in ways that link these two ideological realms in imagining the nation.

I have been particularly concerned to demonstrate the multisitedness of sister-brother ideology. In discourses about this dyad, the key ideological site for adults is different than that for adolescents. The concerns surrounding true sisters and brothers are also somewhat different from those that focus on the extension of the sister-brother *tapu* to the father's sister, on the one hand, and to cross-gendered cousins on the other. There is also multisitedness in the projections of this dyad to the level of national polity, illustrated in the examples of the *moheofo* system of the past and the respect given to Princess Pilolevu in the present.

A fifth and final concern of this section has been to briefly display the ways that language ideologies are part of these nation-making discourses. Language ideologies per se are unevenly represented in nation-making discourses. At the level of rhetoric about the family dyads, the behaviors that are most notable in lists of what is *tapu* in the sister-brother relationship explicitly address what they and others must avoid in speech when they are co-present. Yet speech is not prominent in *tapu* lists for the father-child relationship. When these dyads are projected to the level of nation-state, however, the analogies to the father-child relationship—that is, the respect owed by people to their nobles and to their king are elaborated in *lea faka'eiki*. There is no equally salient elaboration of language constraints in national projections of the sister-brother relationship. If, however, we see the language ideologies involved in nation-making uses of family dyads as part of a broader semiotic system in which actions or nonverbal behaviors as well as speech are important, then ideological elaboration of both dyads and their projections to the national level seem more alike. Here such non-verbal behaviors as not entering the father's sleeping area or kissing the feet of Princess Pilolevu share symbolic significance with particular uses of language, all ways of displaying respect and subordination of the self to another

In the next section I will argue that when Tongan magistrates and police prosecutors interpret crimes of bad language as bringing harm to the sister-brother relationship, their language ideology is yet another manifestation of a broader Tongan nation-state imagining that metaphorically projects the sister-brother dyad into a national context, in this case a projection that focuses primarily on language use.

HOW CRIMES OF BAD LANGUAGE HARM
THE SISTER-BROTHER RELATIONSHIP

Tonga has a single unified legal system in which Tongan and British colonial ideas and practices are pervasively interlocked and integrated. The data I will be examining come from transcripts of tape recordings in two Tongan magistrate's courts during the period 1987 to 1990. These lower-level courts deal with minor criminal and civil cases. They are presided over by Tongan magistrates, and the procedures are conducted in the Tongan language. The criminal cases that do not involve vehicle code violations consist predominantly of public drunkenness, physical assault, theft, and bad-language cases.

By far the majority of those coming before the court as defendants and witnesses are male, as are all of the magistrates, police officers, police prosecutors, clerks, and lawyers. When women come before the court, their femaleness is explicitly noted in the way the magistrate and police prosecutor talk about the case. Thus female gender is marked both in the indexical relation between speech and speakers and in metastatements made about their presence and the events that warrant this presence in the court.

Lea kovi ('bad language') cases differ from other kinds of cases in that most of the victims and their witnesses are female, while the defendants are male. These are mainly cases in which young women take men to court for having directed bad language to them in a public context. In these cases, unlike the others, the femaleness of the women is explicitly mentioned, and the cross-gendered nature of the crime is noted by an explicit framing of bad language as a violation of the sister-brother relationship.

Bad language does not exist only as a concept for court cases. It was brought up to me and to other anthropologists working in Tonga as something to be negotiated with and by us. Most typically, it was mentioned—sometimes only playfully—as a kind of talk that we should not hear or learn the meaning of (Ernest Olson, Charles Stevens, Mike Evans, and Tamar Gordon, personal communications). *Lea kovi* is a very general term that appears in court talk about bad-language crimes. But the terms *kape* and the reduplicated form *kapekape*, which conveys more intensity, also are used to refer to bad language and have the more specific gloss of 'to swear'.

What distinguished talk about bad language in conversation from talk about it in court, in my experience, was that in court there was a systematic exposition of what it was and why it was bad. Such exposition seemed difficult if not impossible to come by in conversations or interviews without my referring to court proceedings in which bad language was at issue. Especially early on in my time in Tonga, I often had the feeling that to discuss bad language at all was in itself an identity-spoiling activity. It seemed to reflect badly on me, on the person I spoke to, and on our relationship, discrediting our reputations as respectable people. The magistrate's courts, then, are key sites for the ready explication and ideological elaboration of bad language by Tongans to Tongans.

Members of the legal profession and legal anthropologists are well aware that events defined as delicts of some kind undergo transformation through time as they are reconstituted in dispute management processes (Mather and Yngvesson 1981). In the court proceedings considered here, language ideology about bad language is double-sited, in that the metapragmatic talk about bad language systematically reconstitutes the past event in which it is supposed to have occurred. Many if not all language ideologies have both sites of language use or pragmatics that are the objects of language ideology, and sites of metapragmatic commentary on the items that constitute such objects.[3] These objects of metacommentary are actually being ideologically constituted or imagined *in* the metacommentary. The object may or may not be imagined as a real empirical context in which something was said in the past. Silverstein (1992) uses the term "site" to refer to language that is the object of metapragmatic discourse.

It is my sense that recent writing about language ideologies has devoted more attention to objects of language ideologies, or what I will refer to as the primary sites of language ideologies, than to sites in which metapragmatic commentary occur, which I will refer to as secondary sites. In part this may be due to the fact that it is often the researcher/author who is creating the secondary site in a published paper through her or his explication of a language ideology that is implicit in transcripts of tape recordings from primary sites. It may also partly be due to the fact that commentaries by people on their own language and their use of language often emerge when the researcher is interviewing a speaker of that language. Often it is not clear where commentary on language use will be heard in socially occurring speech outside of the anthropological interview.[4] Once sites that are objects of language ideologies and sites involving commentary on those objects are posited, the activities in which linguists discuss the pragmatic and the metapragmatic with consultants can be seen as tertiary sites in the study of language ideologies. If there are tertiary sites, the possibility arises that secondary sites in which language ideologies have been expressed in the ongoing life of speakers of a language can be imagined or created in the researcher's work with consultants, just as the primary sites can be imagined.

In this language of "sites," Tongan bad-language court cases are secondary metapragmatic sites where the primary object of language ideology is (re)constructed as a past, empirically real situation in which bad language harmed the sister-brother relationship. But as we will see, the metapragmatic representation of bad language is far from explicit, so I draw on tertiary sites of my own conversations with Tongans about what this metapragmatic work means in order to make sense of the cases.

Past interactions between people are reconstituted in bad-language court cases so that regardless of what they said to each other, how they conceptualized their relationship at the time, or where they were when the bad words were uttered, those past interactions are presented as having the following features: (1) The person identified as the defendant said certain specific bad words, with emphasis on the point that there was not just one word, phrase, or sentence, but multiple instances of such. Insults and threats predominate, but all of the bad words have in common that they can readily be understood as said in anger. (2) The past event being reconstituted is said to have occurred in a public place. While this idea is little elaborated in itself, it is necessary that there be a place identified because the statutes under which bad language is a crime are in a special section of the written law specifically concerned with order in public places. (3) Mention is made of actual or possible social identities of persons, notably ministers, church people, and sisters and brothers, who either were affected or could have been affected by these words. While *tuofefine* (sisters or female cousins of males) and *tuonga'ane* (brothers or male cousins of females) are always mentioned in some way, even if vaguely or abstractly, the other identities mentioned vary from case to case.

Through these three features, cases of quite diverse circumstances are rendered as instances of the same thing. The general idea is that the defendant is not relating to others in public in a way that is respectful, when clearly respect is called for because of the social identities of the people exposed to the behavior. However, although the identities of *tuofefine* and *tuonga'ane* may appear to be specific, the logic of the cases is such that these identities in fact encompass all citizens of Tonga.

In these bad-language cases there are three terms that Tongans hear as referring to the potential or actual presence of *tuofefine* and *tuonga'ane*: the words *tuofefine* and *tuonga'ane* themselves, the word *kāinga* ('relatives'), and the phrase *nofo feuluufi* or its reduplicated form *nofo feuluulufi* ('staying mutually respectful'). As one Tongan woman explained to me, *nofo feuluufi* refers to a situation in which a group of people are sitting together, don't know whether they are related, and specifically don't know whether the group includes *tuofefine* and *tuonga'ane*. In such a circumstance one must pay respect to all. Note that not knowing whether *tuofefine* and *tuonga'ane* are co-present, and therefore speaking respectfully, is analogous to the practice mentioned earlier of using chiefly language because a noble might be present. This makes it clear that, as noted above, cousins of the opposite sex and not just true brothers and sisters are included in the *tapu* on bad language in public since cousins, unlike true sisters and brothers, may not know one another.

I use examples from actual cases to illustrate these features of the language ideology of bad language and to show how diverse circumstances can be encompassed by a single interpretive framework. In the first example, the victim defines herself as being in a *tuofefine-tuonga'ane* relationship with the defendant. Of the cases to be considered here, this one is by far the most explicit about the relevance of this relationship to bad language. At the beginning of the proceeding the magistrate reads the charge against the defendant to him. (All names of persons and villages have been changed to preserve anonymity.)

1) MAGISTRATE: *Pita, faka'ilo koe 'i he 'aho hongofulu 'o 'Akosi, Kolovai. Na'a ke fakatupu maveuveu 'i ha anga kehe, 'i loto 'e he vaha'a 'o e ngaahi ngata'anga 'o e kolo ko Kolovai, feitu'u 'oku nofo'i 'e he kakai 'i ho'o 'oho ke tā 'ia Sela Havea, mo ke toe **kape, toe kapekape'i** ia 'i ho'o pehē kiate ia, "**Vale kai ta'e, toe si'i pea u hae ua koe,**" mo ngāue mo ho'o **ngaahi lea kehe 'e —ni'ihi** maveuveu ai 'a e loto 'o Sela. [3] Maumau ai e kupu 3N vahe 26 lao 'o Tonga 1967. 'Oku ke tali tonuhia pe 'oku ke tali halaia?*

Pita, you were charged on the tenth of August, at Kolovai. You caused a disturbance every which way, in the middle between the ends of two villages at Kolovai, a place where people stay, by rushing to hit Sela Havea, and you **repeatedly swore, repeatedly really swore** at her, by saying to her, "**Stupid eat shit, I might tear you apart,**" and doings and **other different bad words**, upsetting Sela. [3][5] Breaking section 3N chapter 26 Law of Tonga,1967. Do you plead innocent or do you plead guilty?

DEFENDANT: *Tonuhia 'eiki Sea.*
Innocent, Your Honor.

The highlighted terms refer to bad language and indicate its multiple or repeated nature. In this case, the defendant used insulting and threatening language toward the victim. The public place is described as an area between two villages. This case is unusual in that the defendant pleads innocent rather than guilty, requiring a trial. When the victim, who is the first witness, is called to the stand, the issue of the nature of her relationship with the defendant is immediately raised. The prosecutor begins by asking about her background and the circumstance in which the crime occurred. Immediately the victim claims that she and the defendant are *tuofefine* and *tuonga'ane*. The prosecutor starts to go on to other issues, but the magistrate shows interest in this topic, so the prosecutor asks for elaboration.

> 2) PROSECUTOR: *Kei nofo Kolovai, he taimi ko ia, 'oku ke 'ilo e tokotaha ko Pita Tupou, faka'iloa ko ē?*
> Still staying at Kolovai at that time, do you know anyone called Pita Tupou, that defendant?
>
> WITNESS: *'Io, ko hoku **tuonga'ane**.*
> Yes, he is my **tuonga'ane**
>
> PROSECUTOR: *'Aho 10 ko 'eni 'o Akosi 'o e ta'u ni, 1988.*
> On the 10th of August this year 1988.
>
> MAGISTRATE: *Ko ho **tuonga'ane?***
> Your **tuonga'ane?**
>
> WITNESS: *'Io.*
> Yes.
>
> PROSECUTOR: *Tamai taha, fa'ē taha?*
> Same father, same mother?
>
> WITNESS: *'Ikai, tautehina kui.*
> No, our grandparents are same sex siblings/cousins.
>
> PROSECUTOR: *'Io ko ho **kainga** pē. 'Aho 10 ko'eni 'o 'Akosi 'o e ta'u ni 1988 na'a ke mamata ai kiate ia 'i Kolovai?*
> Yes, he's only your **relative** [as opposed to brother]. On the 10th of August of this year 1988, did you see him at Kolovai?
>
> WITNESS: *Ko ia.*
> That's right.

After the witness gives her version of what happened, the magistrate addresses some questions directly to her, once again pursuing clarification of her relationship to the defendant:

> 3) MAGISTRATE: *Mahino ia, Sela, ko ho'o 'uhinga ki he lea ko'eni ko e **tuonga'ane**, ko e lea ia 'i he 'etau **'ulungāanga fakatonga**, 'e lava pē ke **tuonga'ane** neongo 'ene mama'o? Ka ko e hā hono 'uhinga 'oku ke pehē ai ko e **tuonga'ane**, ko e hā 'a e faka'iloa, ko e hā koā 'oku ke pehē ai ko e **tuonga'ane**?*
>
> You understand Sela your reason for that word **tuonga'ane**, it's a word used in our **Tongan culture**, and the use of **tuong'ane** whether near or far? But why do you say that he is your **tuonga'ane**, who is the accused, why do you say he's your **tuonga'ane**?
>
> WITNESS: *Lahi e tamai 'o e fa'ē 'a e faka'iloa, kae si'isi'i 'a e tamai 'o 'eku tamai.* [10]
>
> The accused's mother's father was my father's father's older brother. [10]

After some additional questioning, the magistrate condemns the defendant for his actions as he speaks to the victim.

> 4) MAGISTRATE: *'Io, tonu pē ho'o ui ia 'a'au ko ho **tuonga'ane**.* [4] *He ko homou **kāinga** he taha, he me'a maumau fakamanavahē ko e **'ulungāanga 'o Tonga** ho'o ngāue 'a'au.* [20]
>
> Yes, it's correct your calling him your brother. [4] Because you are **related**, the **Tongan culture** was terribly violated here [on account of] what you did. [20]

Note that in transcript excerpts (3) and (4), the magistrate specifically invokes Tongan culture as that which has been violated. This implies that Tongan culture has its own distinctive morality and that the magistrate, the victim, and the defendant are all part of the same moral community.

The defendant and the victim in this case were determined to be in a *tuofefine-tuonga'ne* relationship. In the next case, the prosecutor and the magistrate argue that the defendant and the victim *could have been* in such a relationship.

5) MAGISTRATE: *Na'a ke lea kovi'i 'i he hala pule'anga 'o e loto kolo 'o Vaini 'i ho'o* **toutou lea fakapalālangi** *'o pehē kia Mele Finau pea mo Fefita Taliai 'ā,* **"Bullshit, fuck you,"** *mo ha ngaahi* **lea kovi ni'ihi.**

You swore on the public road in the middle of Vaini by **repeatedly saying in English** to Mele Finau and Fefita Taliai, **"Bullshit, fuck you," and other bad words.**

The defendant used English swear words on the road in the middle of a village. The young women to whom he directed these words were Mormon missionaries, readily recognizable by their appearance as they go about their business. The police prosecutor makes moral work of their religious identities:

6) PROSECUTOR: *Ko e ongo fefine ko ē 'oku 'asi 'i he tohi fekau, Sea. Ko e ongo faifekau Māmonga. Na'e fai ki ai e kapekape fakapālangi ki ai 'a e tokotaha ni…Hange ko e me'a 'a e feitu'u na, Sea,* **'oku fai e nofo feuluufi.**

Those two women appear on the summons, Your Honor. They are two Mormon missionaries. This person swore in English there. As you say, Your Honor, *stay mutually respectful.*

Here the prosecutor makes reference to staying mutually respectful, which, as noted above, is advice given because of the possibility that people who are present are in a *tuofefine-tuonga'ane* relationship. The magistrate follows up on the prosecutor's remarks with greater condemnation, but a similar message:

7) MAGISTRATE: *Ko e 'ulungāanga palakū na'a ke fai. Na'a ō kinaua ko si'i ongo faifekau ke fakamafola. 'E fu'u kape mai.* **'Ikai ke 'ilo na'a ko homou kāinga.**

That was a disgusting thing you did. The two that were walking by were little missionaries spreading the gospel. You swore excessively. **No one knows if you were related.**

Here the magistrate raises the more specific possibility that the defendant and the victims could have been in a *tuonga'ane-tuofefine* relationship, without knowing they were related.

In the examples given so far, the prosecutor and magistrate focus on the actual or possible relationship between the defendants and the victims. In the next two cases, the focus is not on the relationship between defendant and victim but on others in the surrounding environs.

> 8) MAGISTRATE: *Na'a ke kaila 'o pehē*, **"Mata 'usi, mata lemu,"**
> **mo e ngaahi lea kovi kehe.**
> You shouted, saying, **"Asshole, rectum," and other bad words.**

In contrast to the first two cases, no victim is identified by name here. That is because the person being shouted at was a man rather than a woman, and he is the person who complained to the police. Within the Tongan logic of what makes bad language bad, he would not be considered a victim. Instead, it is people who have overheard the bad language that makes it the crime that it is:

> 9) PROSECUTOR: *Sea, ko e me'a 'oku tokanga ki ai 'a e talatalaaki,*
> *Sea, ko e* **nofo feuluulufi** *'a e fonua. 'Oku ke mea'i pē 'apē, Sea, ko e*
> *fa'ahinga lea kovi ko 'eni 'oku 'i ai 'a* **tuofefine** *mo e* **tuonga'ane,**
> *faifekau, 'oku 'i ai e kakai lotu.*
> Your Honor, what concerns the prosecutor is the relationship of
> **mutual respect in the country.** As you well know, Your Honor,
> this sort of bad language was in the presence of **sisters** and
> **brothers,** ministers, religious people were there.

Recall that it is not only *tuofefine* and *tuonga'ane* who must show respect to one another. Others in their presence must also show respect to them and their relationship. And note that this mutual respect is associated with the term *fonua*, which I have glossed as 'country', because it is used to refer to both land and the nation or country of Tonga. In this way a representative of the state lays claim to the idea that the necessity to be respectful applies to all of Tonga.

In the next extract, the magistrate's explanation to the defendant regarding why he has been charged with the crime of bad language is more explicit. It focuses exclusively on the *tuofefine-tuonga'ane* relationship and suggests just how strongly people feel about bad language.

> 10) MAGISTRATE: *Ko e 'uhinga ko e kaikaila 'oku ke fai ha kai efi-*
> *afi ha 'api 'oku feha'ofaki ai 'a e* **tuonga'ane** *mo e* **tuofefine.** *Hanga ai*
> *'e he tamaiki 'o tā koe.*

> The reason [you are being charged] is the shouting you did while an evening meal was going on in a nearby house where **brothers** and **sisters** were sitting around. Because of this the youth beat you up.

It is interesting that the people who are constituted in the court case as having overheard the shouted bad words don't have to have been in the public space themselves when the shouting took place, nor do they even have to be construed as having been visible.

In the final case to be discussed, the *tuofefine-tuong'ane* relationship has the least apparent real relevance to the circumstances of the bad language, yet that relationship is nevertheless made relevant. As in the first case, the man threatens the woman physically, but here there are sexual overtones to the threat perceived by Tongans I talked to about this material. The charge is presented by the magistrate:

> 11) MAGISTRATE: *Na'a ke **lea kovi** he feitu'u fakapule'anga 'a ia ko ho'o **lea kovi** 'i he hala pule'anga loto kolo 'o Hona 'i ho'o lea 'o pehē kia Amalia Vaiua ko ho'o lea kia Amalia, "**Mene, ule, ai pea u taa'i koe ke pihi ho mimi,**" mo ha ngaahi lea kovi kehe.*
> You **swore** in a public place with your **bad language** on the public road in the middle of Hona with your words said to Amalia Vaiua, your words to Amalia, **"Peel back [the foreskin], penis, I'll beat the piss out of you,"** and other bad words.

One Tongan consultant (an older man) interpreted these words as indicating the man was threatening to pee on the woman. A later reference by the magistrate to the defendant having shown parts of his body to the woman that she did not have is consistent with this. Although the nature of the relationship between the defendant and the victim is never mentioned in court, Tongans with whom I discussed this case suggested that the man would not have said what he did unless the two of them had been lovers. The prosecutor offered this evaluation:

> 12) PROSECUTOR: (a) *Pea 'ikai ke 'alu mu'a 'o **kapekape'i** ha motu'a tangata kae 'alu ia 'o **kapekape'i** e finemotu'a, e ki'i fefine ko'eni.*
>
> And he didn't go out and *swear* at a man, but he goes there and

swears at a woman, this young woman.

(b) *Sea ngaahi fu'u lea ko ena 'oku ha tohi.*

Your Honor, those excessive words are evident in writing.

(c) *Sea, ko e me'a 'oku tokanga ki ai e talatalaaki ai mu'a e founga 'oku sai.*

Your Honor, what concerns the prosecutor about it is a nice manner.

(d) *He 'oku 'i ai e kakai he kolo kae 'uma'ā 'a tu'a kau fine'eiki, kau faifekau, kakai lotu e kolo.*

Village people were there and also outside were respected women, ministers, religious people of the village.

(e) *Fai e fakapau'u holo he kolo.*

He is ill mannered all over the village.

(f) *Sea, 'oku fu'u kovi 'aupito 'aupito ha mai ai e ta'e akonaki'i.*

Your Honor, this lack of instruction is very very bad.

As in earlier cases, specific social categories calling for respect are listed here, but kinship relatedness is not referred to. It would not be appropriate to suggest that the two people involved could be related, if indeed they have been lovers. But see in the next excerpt how the magistrate manages to include (but not highlight, as in other cases) the *tuofefine-tuonga'ane* relationship, after berating the defendant at length:

13) MAGISTRATE: *Mo'oni e talatalaaki fanongo mai ki ai e kakai, kakai lotu, kakai maama, kakai poto ka kau faifekau, tangata 'i fonua, feuluulufi e nofo tangata mo fefine.*

The prosecutor is right that people heard about it, religious people, enlightened people, smart people, ministers, citizens, **mutually respectful-staying men and women.**

Here the magistrate suggests that there is offense not just if bad words are directed to or uttered in the presence of relatives, but even if women and men who treat one another respectfully hear about it. Although there is greater distance between the act and the offended parties in this case, an offense nevertheless was committed in its reaching them at all.

Taken together, these four cases reveal that bad language is bad not just if the defendant knows the victim is his *tuofefine*, but if she could

be. It is bad not just if the victim is or could be a *tuofefine* but also if people in a *tuofefine-tuonga'ane* relationship hear the bad words. And it is
bad not just if they hear the words but also if they hear about them. In
all these cases, then, the prosecutors and magistrates find a way to hold
up the respect associated with the *tuofefine-tuonga'ane* relationship as a
reason for bad language being morally wrong. Yet in their manner of
reprimanding the defendants, they acknowledge the different ways this
relationship is relevant in each of the cases.

DISCUSSION AND CONCLUSION

I have suggested that magistrates and police prosecutors are producing a nation-state–making discourse when they say that bad language is harmful because of the actual or possible involvement of
people in a *tuofefine-tuonga'ane* relationship. Here I consider how their
discourses have the four features identified at the beginning of this
chapter as common in the imagining of nation-states. First, when these
officers of the court invoke *tuofefine* and *tuonga'ane*, they are invoking a
relationship that establishes continuity between past and present political regimes. The distinctive features of the Tongan sister-brother relationship are viewed by Tongans as having existed prior to European
contact and as having been important in that earlier period not just in
family life but also in the politics of the paramount chiefs, as illustrated
by accounts of the *moheofo* system of marriage.

Second, reference to sisters and brothers in the bad-language
cases involves the projection of values and behaviors associated with an
important and ideologically elaborated family dyad to the national
level. By virtue of the commoner extension of constraints on sisters and
brothers to distant cousins, an individual will not always know whether
she or he is in a *tuofefine-tuonga'ane* relationship with other individuals
when large numbers of women and men convene in public gatherings.
So *all* Tongan citizens are subject to the constraints of the *tuofefine-
tuonga'ane* relationship when they are together in public, as the magistrates and police prosecutors would have it.

Third, magistrates and prosecutors present their concern about
protecting the *tuofefine-tuonga'ane* relationship as if that concern were
shared by all Tongans. They do this by explicitly linking the relationship to *anga fakatonga* ('the Tongan way'), thereby indicating that any-

one who is a Tongan will share their concern and conveying an assumption of national cultural sharedness and homogeneity with regard to the sacredness of the *tuofefine-tuonga'ane* relationship.

The sister-brother relationship and its associated language ideology also serve as national distinguishers, especially when Tongans are in dialogue with people from English-speaking nations, the nations that have posed the greatest threats to Tongan autonomy. Many Tongans know that the importance they attach to this relationship and the control that sisters have over brothers strike Westerners as distinctive. The potential of the Tongan sister-brother relationship to distinguish and differentiate Tonga from other nations may even help account for the continued ideological elaboration of this relationship.

Fourth, the officers of the court contribute to a broader nationalist discourse that is multisited, involving proper Tongan language use in relations conceived as dyadic between dominant and subordinate parties. At the same time, their moral evaluations in cases of bad language are site-specific in combining a focus not on true sisters and brothers, but on the more expanded category of cross-gendered cousin relations, with a focus on how angry speech violates the *tapu* against such speech in *tuofefine-tuonga'ane* relationships. The language ideology in the bad-language cases is also site-specific in the systematic way that it is double-sited. In the courtroom metapragmatic discourse about past talk, multiple reported bad words are attributed to the defendant as having been uttered in a public place where *tuofefine* and *tuoga'ane* were co-present, could have been co-present, or heard about it later. These cases are thus key sites for explicit representation of what counts as bad language that can offend the *tuofefine-tuonga'ane* relationship. Talk about bad language is far more explicit here than in other situations, even though the courtroom metapragmatic work cannot be fully understood without connecting it to other talk outside the courtroom about language use in the sister-brother relationship. In these ways, then, Tongan magistrates and prosecutors produce a discourse that is like other nation-imagining discourses, yet still specific to the legal concerns at hand.

This discussion makes clear that language ideologies can be both multisited and site-specific, and therefore partial rather than whole in their diverse manifestations. A single manifestation of a language ideology does not necessarily reflect the possible range of manifestations. In the imagining of nation-states, language ideologies not only can be but are multisited and site-specific. I have argued that language ideologies in nationalist discourses take on common properties of nationalist discourses in general. Language ideologies are appropriated from non-nationalist discourses such as those associated with the family and shaped to have qualities that will give them national relevance. Understanding this is key to understanding how the state can be "everywhere," because state harnessing of local language ideologies gives even their local expressions national relevance.

Notes

The research discussed here was funded by a grant from the National Science Foundation Linguistics Program. I would like to express my appreciation to the Government of Tonga for permission to carry out this research, and to the many Tongans who helped with data collection and analysis. I also want to thank the other contributors in this volume and Niko Besnier and Tamar Gordon, all of whom read an earlier draft of this paper, for their useful comments.

1. The small size of Tonga, the lack of potential for economic development, and the absence of a democratic form of government would all seem to undermine its status as an ideal nation from a European point of view. However, these features are not at issue in portraits of ideal and non-ideal nations as these are discussed by linguistic anthropologists.

2. Rogers (1977) points to the legally ratified forms of land inheritance from which women are largely excluded and to the patrilateral inheritance of titles as the most important evidence of men's legitimized political authority. I don't dispute this, but there is other evidence, including some from Rogers himself, that oldest sisters in particular have considerable institutionalized authority in even these domains, a point that Schoeffel (1978) makes for Samoa.

3. The distinction between the context of representation and the context represented, and the analysis of the relationship between the two, have been developed in a thoroughgoing way in the analysis of personal narratives (Chafe 1980; Hill and Zepeda 1993; Labov 1972c; Matsuki 1995). But not all of the many features of the way personal narratives link past to present apply to representations of the past that occur in other genres.

4. Briggs (1992) presents one of the clearer examples of socially occurring

articulation of language ideologies in his discussion of Warao gossip in which claims of shamanistic activity are discredited.

5. Numbers in brackets indicate the length of pauses in seconds.

7

Read My Article

Ideological Complexity and the Overdetermination of Promising in American Presidential Politics

Jane H. Hill

> His promises were, as he then was, mighty;
> But his performance, as he is now, nothing.
> —*William Shakespeare*, Henry VIII, *Act IV, Scene II*

> Presidents should never promise anything to anybody.
> I would like to see promises banned from presidential
> campaigns...Campaign promises are poison.
> —*One of Jimmy Carter's senior and most liberal advisors,*
> *quoted in Jeff Fishel*, Presidents and Promises

"Promising," as is clear from the epigraphs above, has long been both bane and necessity for political talk in the English-speaking world. The mystery of why politicians persist, often against their better judgment, in making promises, is a fitting object of inquiry for students of language ideology, understood as a "mediating link between social structures and forms of talk" (Woolard and Schieffelin 1994:55). This essay develops an insight into promising proposed by Alessandro Duranti. Building on Rosaldo's (1982) recognition that local cultural regimes of personhood pick out particular speech act types as exemplary performances of human agency, Duranti (1993) observed that promising seems to be essentially absent from political discourse in Samoa, where, he argues, the assignment of responsibility for speech is based on its results in the form of harmony or disharmony in human relationships, not on the intentions imputed to individual speakers. Promising, suggested Duranti, may instead be somewhat peculiar to regimes of personalism, which endow the speaker with intentions, motives, and knowledge and make the penetrating apprehension of these a central concern in the interpretation of talk.

Yet personalism, which is usually taken to organize the understandings of persons among dominant groups in Europe and the United States, has received little attention in the literature. Within cultural and linguistic anthropology, personalism has provided, in its embodiment in contemporary speech act theory, the "inspiration...and ...butt" (Rosaldo 1982) of antipersonalist critiques that denaturalize it by delineating alternative ideological regimes, as in Duranti's (1990, 1993, 1994) studies of Samoan political language. Students of English-language political discourse in disciplines such as communications and political science, among them Jamieson (see Jamieson 1988; Jamieson and Campbell 1992), Fishel (1985), and Wilson (1992), function almost entirely within personalism, which is invisible to them but forms the commonsense background of their critical and analytic work.

This essay aims to contribute to the study of personalism by focusing on a prominent site for overt metapragmatic discourse within this regime: the rich tradition of evaluative commentary around political promising. I analyze some journalistic discourse about the best-known political promise in recent American history, George Bush's "Read my lips: No new taxes." In his 1988 speech accepting the Republican presidential nomination, Vice President Bush told his audience that that was what he would say to a Congress greedy for new revenues. In 1990 Bush struck a compromise with the congressional leadership that included new taxes. This sequence of acts was represented by Bush's political enemies as a "promise" that had been "broken." By breaking the promise, they argued, Bush revealed that he lacked both "character" and "leadership," two moral qualities central to qualification for high office. That their representation prevailed is considered by many analysts to be the main reason for Bush's humiliating defeat in the 1992 presidential election, in which he received only 38 percent of the vote in a three-way contest against Bill Clinton and Ross Perot. Yet whether Bush's utterance was indeed a promise that the 1990 budget compromise broke is intensely contested; to this day, Bush supporters reject such an interpretation.

I argue here that this clash of interpretations was shaped by the interplay of two metapragmatic discourses that coexist among American English speakers in a Janus-faced relationship: a discourse of "truth" and a discourse of "theater." Philips (1998, and this volume) has pointed out that ideological discourse is variously developed at different sites, with ideological stances being prominent in some contexts, suppressed in others. This is the case here. The discourse of truth is, as we will see, highly elaborated in the journalistic evaluation of Bush's famous utterance. It is also, as far as I know, the dominant discourse of scholarly analysis of political language. The discourse of theater is most elaborated by campaign professionals in discussions of their craft. However, a few of its elements occur with some frequency in journalism.

The two discourses are often thought to be in opposition to one another. When scholars and journalists identify elements of the discourse of theater, for instance, they often claim that these are pathological, symptoms of a moral collapse in American politics. We will see several cases below where a discourse of truth is used to attack a claim made in the voice of the discourse of theater. I argue here, however, that interpreters of American political language always draw on both perspectives, even when only one discourse surfaces. That is, interpreters focused on truth must also evaluate performance, while interpreters evaluating performance require the textual dimension of the performance to make some kind of claim of referential grounding. Promising, in spite of its obvious dangers, continues to occur at a high frequency in American politics because both discourses recognize it as indexing an exemplary person, a hyperindividualized, hypermasculinized subject who is licensed thereby as qualified for high office.

While personalism or individualism dominated the discourse about George Bush and his promise, it is clear from some of the evidence examined here that journalists and other analysts do have knowledge of sociocentric and relational dimensions of personhood and of the contingent historical nature of political speech. But, especially as the attacks on Bush escalated, this knowledge was shaped almost entirely in the service of a personalist discourse that blamed Bush as an individual for his broken promise and attributed it to moral failings on his part. This intense discourse of blame can be seen as a key moment in the history of personalism as an interpretive process. By focusing on Bush as an individualized locus for moral scrutiny, these journalists played an important role in reproducing and producing the ideology of exemplary intentional agents.

THE DISCOURSE OF TRUTH

The discourse of truth prescribes that political talk should be a source of "information." Politicians should reveal in detail specific positions and goals, permitting voters to make an "informed choice" among candidates. Exemplary is an argument by McGeorge Bundy (1980): Politicians should practice "full disclosure," sharing with voters all the information that has shaped their positions. From this perspective, political talk falls squarely within the Gricean cooperative scenario (Sweetser 1987): Politicians are bound by Grice's (1975) maxim of quality to say only what they believe to be true and not to say what they believe to be false. This discourse privileges the referential function of language that analysts like Silverstein (1976, 1979) have argued is the dominant metapragmatic perspective for Euro-Americans.

Truth and reference need not be seen as localized within individuals, and indeed there are scholarly discourses in the English language that contemplate the distribution of knowledge across complex fields of collaboration that have deep histories (see, for example, Hutchins 1995). The vernacular discourse of truth, however, usually locates this quality in the utterances of an exemplary intentional individual who should be a source for "true" information. The degree to which interlocutors determine that some particular speaker is likely to speak truly depends on evaluation of an important moral quality, "character." Part of the evidence for character is a finding of referential consistency across the intertextual series (Hanks 1987) of statements that comprise a political career. Thus, the fact that George Bush went from favoring access to abortion to opposing it was held by both sides in the abortion debate to be a signal that Bush was unreliable, not that his position had changed as a result of careful reflection on the issue.

There should also be referential consistency between a person's series of utterances and his or her supposed deeds. For instance, a politician who makes the sacredness of the nuclear family a focus of policy should not be a known adulterer. This referential consistency is thought to index a consistent intentionality, the capacity to "keep one's word," that is central to character. Insofar as there is any distribution (Hill and Irvine 1993) of referential capacity away from individual politicians as exemplary loci of commitment to truth, it consists only of the understanding that politicians may require that experts provide them with information, which they must then balance and evaluate.

Most of the critique of American political language, from academics (see especially Jamieson 1988; Jamieson and Campbell 1992) and others, is conducted from this perspective. Failures of political talk are seen as failures of reference and truth, and thus of character. Considered from the perspective of the Gricean scenario, these failures are violations of the maxims of quality (speakers should say only what they know to be true, and not what they know to be false) or quantity (speakers should say as much as is needed, and no more). Apprehension of a violation of quality yields a search for motives like pride or greed that might make a politician speak "only to get elected" rather than to inform. Violations of the maxim of quantity are characterized as inadequately referential, inadequately susceptible to tests of truth, as mere imagery lacking the information necessary for a rational choice, and thereby intended to appeal to voter emotion, a baser quality than rationality. The media are often said to be at fault in such instances. Television especially is said to be driven by market forces and by the intrinsic nature of the medium to emphasize entertaining imagery over sober referential content, causing the degradation of referential language into "sound bites" that have become increasingly short (Jamieson and Campbell 1992).

A related critique places the fault with voters, who are thought to be irrational and emotional, lacking an appropriate orientation toward information. Fishel (1985), for instance, argues that recent presidential candidates have made many specific commitments and done their best to keep them. But if voters fail to understand the realities of governing, with its inevitable compromises, a sensible candidate will avoid making too many specific commitments as a necessary accommodation to voter irrationality.

THE DISCOURSE OF THEATER

Most popular political analysts and academic experts on political language deploy the discourse of truth almost exclusively. I will try to show that, although it is in most contexts far less developed than the discourse of truth, the discourse of theater is, in fact, ineluctably linked to it. The discourse of theater is most elaborated among political campaign specialists in what they represent as "insider" talk about the management of political careers. I owe much of my understanding of it to two recent popular books: Peggy Noonan's (1990) account of her years as a speechwriter for Ronald Reagan and George Bush, and a jointly authored campaign diary by Mary Matalin and James Carville (1994), campaign managers for George Bush and Bill Clinton, respectively, in the 1992 presidential race.

The central metapragmatic term of the discourse of theater is not "word" but "message." Message may appear to be a metasemantic item from the domain of reference, and thus appropriate to the discourse of truth, but it is not. Instead, message is a set of themes deployed through performance. Message includes talk and text, but it is dominated by the poetic function, with thematic material encapsulated in sound bites and slogans. The construction of message lies in the realm of art, with colors, lighting, music, costume, posture, and a variety of other signaling media at least as important as text itself.

Message is unerringly positive. Contrary to McGeorge Bundy's urging of "full disclosure," the inevitable negatives of any political program should never be mentioned. From the theatrical perspective, this is not a matter of misleading the voter. Rather, it is the recognition that message gains its power not by the density of information it delivers and the rational evaluation of this by the electorate but by "penetration" (Matalin and Carville 1994:80), meaning familiarity gained through constant repetition that sets up a complex performance-based resonance with critical groups of voters, a resonance that is at least as much aesthetic and affective as it is referential. To generate a favorable emotional tone in voters, message must play to their desires. Emotion is not, as within the discourse of truth, merely an enemy of rationality but a positive agentive quality of voters that can be exploited to turn swing groups in the desired direction.

The goal of politicians is to stay "on message," continually presenting their central themes in attractive packages. Opponents strive to throw them "off message" by attending to negatives. In the view of campaign experts, specific, referentially oriented denials of such negative attacks should never be made, because they shift the candidate off message. Instead, the best kind of reply is "spinning," the rhetorical reshaping of an attack away from its referential foundation so that it can be used to amplify message. We will see many examples of "spin" in the discourses of the Bush supporters quoted below.

An interesting example comes from the immediate aftermath of the 1994 congressional elections, in which the Republican Party gained control of both houses of Congress. Media interest in the new Speaker of the House of Representatives, Newt Gingrich of Georgia, was intense. This made it easy for his Democratic opponents to place a story that encapsulated important negatives: that Republicans were the tools of the rich and that Gingrich himself might be corrupt. Gingrich had signed a book deal with a publishing house run by Australian tycoon Rupert Murdoch and was to receive a multimillion-dollar advance. Gingrich spun brilliantly, seizing every opportunity to make statements like, "The Democrats are trying to distract the American people by talking about me. But it's not about me, it's about change." He cast himself as a "revolutionary," and the attack as an example of how his opponents, the forces of reaction, would "stop at nothing" to preserve the status quo. Gingrich's use of the term "revolutionary" simultaneously recaptured this word from the political left, invoked the 1776 American Revolution, and reinforced the message that Republicans, not Democrats, would bring about change—this word encapsulating, at the broadest level, the Republican message. Although Gingrich eventually was forced to give up the book advance, his successful spin, reported uncritically in the national press, gained him weeks of time during which he was able to devote his energies to rallying the House of Representatives for a major legislative push to the right.

As important as Gingrich's words was his pose of toughness, elaborated with a manic intensity that made credible his characterization of himself as a revolutionary. Gingrich was manifesting leadership, which is to the discourse of theater what character is to the discourse of truth. In contrast to the egocentric focus of "character," the internal quality that drives a politician's intentional relationship to truth as evidenced in referential continuity, "leadership" would appear to be intrinsically a more sociocentric notion. The claim to this quality is enacted by creating a tone of effervescence that is amplified through resonant interactions between a politician and his or her audiences. This resonance is not recognized within the discourse of theater as a fully relational and socialized dimension of the political process but rather is imagined as a sort of mirror in which a politician is reflected as a leader.

The theatrical perspective also opens the way to a more sociocentric apprehension of the campaign process. "Message" is not truth filtered by a politician from information presented by experts but an elaborate collaborative work of stagecraft, with directors, writers, lighting technicians, wardrobe experts, and crowd managers, in which politicians function as principal players whose public talk is as scripted as that of any Hamlet. However, "leadership," like "word" and "character," is seen as a quality of the individual politician and does not reside in this complex community, which stands in a merely prosthetic function. The discourse of theater, like its truth-oriented complement, thus is ultimately personalist in spite of its sociocentric potential.

The discourse of theater is normally little developed in journalistic text and talk, although examples do occasionally appear. Commentator Mark Shields, for example, speaking on the *MacNeill-Lehrer News Hour* a few days after the Oklahoma City bombing of April 19, 1995, praised President Bill Clinton's speeches in response to the incident, suggesting that they showed that Clinton understood that what was required of him as president was not just "words" but "music." The discourse of theater surfaces when journalists deplore the decline of oratory or attack politicians for focusing too much on information, for being dry and "wonkish." From the theatrical perspective, the production of sound bites and visual images is an art form cultivated by political campaigners, with television seen as an active medium of their performance instead of a constraint on the deployment of information. Although most analysis of the role of television in American politics strikes the pejorative note typical of the discourse of truth, the theatrical perspective does permit commentators to praise politicians for using television effectively—or condemn them for failure to understand the medium. The discourse of theater is not a product of the television era, however; such political figures as Daniel Webster (1782–1852) and William Jennings Bryan (1860–1925) were evaluated primarily from within its perspective.

Like the discourse of truth, the discourse of theater can yield a critique of the electorate. In the mid-1980s Gary Hart, a leading Democratic presidential contender, was rendered unelectable by difficulties of "character."[1] His supporters accused voters of being small-minded, unable to focus on the large picture of Hart's capacity for leadership, and criticized the press as being hungry for scandal, to the detriment of the national interest.

THE TWO PERSPECTIVES, PROMISING, AND THE CATEGORY OF THE PERSON

Promising is a speech act uniquely appropriate to personalism, the individualist ideology of intending agents, in that the syntax of promising actively constructs a singular locus. Silverstein (1979) points out that the commissives (speech acts such as promises that commit the speaker to a future course of action) are unique among the locutionary verbs in that they do not permit switch reference. The agent of the predicated act must be coreferential, or have overlapping reference, with the person who makes the promise. Even if there is overt change of reference, this presupposes that the promisor has appropriate power over the new agent (as when a parent says to a teacher, in Johnny's presence, "Johnny promises to hand in his homework on time").

My goal here is to show that personalist language ideology is more complex than we have heretofore recognized, being metapragmatically constructed in at least the two discourses of truth and theater. Promising is certainly an exemplary act from the point of view of the discourse of truth, because the use of the future tense in the formula for a promise focuses attention on referential continuity. Within the Gricean scenario, the hearer may infer that the propositional content, the designation of an act A, by the utterance of the promise means that a speaker has appropriate knowledge that A will come about, since speakers are bound by the maxim of quality to say only what they believe to be true and not to say what they believe to be not true. Such a future-tense utterance can then be regimented (Silverstein 1993) as indexing an intention to "keep one's word," a principal component of the character that is central to truth-discourse morality.

I have taken care to use gender-neutral language in the paragraphs above, but in fact the discourse of truth constructs a profoundly gendered subject. "Word," the continuity of reference from utterance to utterance and from utterance to deeds, which is important evidence of character, is prototypically an attribute of (heterosexual) masculine subjects. This is evidenced in a variety of routinized expressions—"He is a man of his word/She is a woman of her word"; "A man's word is his bond/A woman's word is her bond"—in which, while it is possible to say the second utterance in each pair, the evocation of the first is unavoidable: A woman so praised becomes an honorary male.

This gendering is perhaps the most significant moment of interconnection between the interpretive perspectives produced by the two discourses of truth and theater. Utterances are regimented as "word" in part by a performance of prototypical masculinity that can be read as "straight talk," characterized by ramrod posture, decisive gesture and gaze, a strong, low, slow-paced voice, and lexical material and sentence structure that model straightness by syllabic and syntactic simplicity, without any "fancy" or high-toned rhetorical frills that might be construed as feminine.[2] An understanding of American English language ideology that focuses exclusively on the privilege of reference cannot account for these obvious dimensions of political promising. Bush's "Read my lips: No new taxes" was straight talk par excellence. It was received with ecstatic applause by the nominating convention audience and seems to have become a permanent part of American political language.[3]

Recognition of the discourse of truth alone suggests that a bald, unelaborated statement predicating a future act should be adequate. Searle's (1969) analysis of promising helps us to understand why it is not and permits access to the sociocentric and performance-laden dimension of talk that is the special concern of the discourse of theater. Searle notes that promising requires a state of mutuality between speaker and hearer: the hearer's desire that the promised act be accomplished, the speaker's knowledge of that desire. By being tough and talking straight—qualities of language associated with leadership— Bush amplified his display of orientation toward audience desire and created intense resonances between himself and his audience that were manifested in exuberance and effervescence on both sides. Thus promising, because of its orientation toward desire, is exemplary within the theatrical perspective.[4]

Just as "word" and "character" are gendered, the performances of "leadership" are prototypically male. In both the Bush promise and the performance by Newt Gingrich discussed above, the speaker elaborated an image of a tough guy, a straight talker. Again we can easily identify linguistic evidence for the masculinity of "toughness:" in /ˈtʌf ˈgaɪ/ the unstressing of the second element suggests that masculinity is here presupposed; one could not say, "She's a /ˈtʌf ˈgæl/," only, "She's a /ˈtʌf ˈgæl/."[5]

Although promising is an exemplary act within the metapragmatic discourses of both truth and theater, it is also problematic in both systems. From the point of view of the discourse of truth, Searle (1969:65) makes the interesting point that wherever there is a sincerity condition, insincerity is possible. To recognize this possibility is analytically necessary, since a promise insincerely made is still a promise, for which the speaker can be called to account. Searle does not explain, however, why the presupposition of possible insincerity seems to be particularly available for "promise" as opposed to closely related commissive forms. Far from predicting this effect, he argues (Searle 1969:58) that people answer accusations with the expression "I promise" because this is "among the strongest illocutionary force indicating devices for commitment provided by the English language."

The noun form "promise," though, differs in its co-occurrence patterning from closely related metapragmatic designators in ways that suggest a special ambivalence. One can say of an unfulfilled commitment, "I guess it was just a promise." Less likely are, "I guess it was just a pledge/commitment/guarantee/vow/contract." The expression "empty promise" is highly lexicalized, but we are less likely to encounter "empty pledge/commitment/vow/guarantee/contract." The word "promise" can be used to imply its negative opposite, as in the following, lifted from my on-line *Oxford Dictionary of Quotations*: "I thought he was a young man of promise; but it appears he was a young man of promises," said by A. J. Balfour of Winston Churchill in 1899 (Churchill 1966[I]:449).

Finally, note the contrast between two stereotyped expressions: "Promises, promises" and "Lies, lies." MacLaury (1995) suggests that such reduplicated utterances express closeness or identity to a prototype. Thus, when I say, "I want a lipstick that's a red red, not an orangey red," I mean that the lipstick should be true red, as close as possible to the unique hue. When I say, "I want to invite people for a dinner dinner, not just a buffet," I mean that the event that I intend will be a sitdown affair with guests gathered around the table for several courses to be served by the hosts or their assistants, a "real dinner," close to some ideal prototype. Similarly, "Lies, lies" is an accusation that what has been said is absolutely untrue, fully a lie. But "Promises, promises" is an accusation that what has been uttered is either insincerely spoken or unlikely to be fulfilled.[6] Thus, there is evidence in ordinary English that "commitments" carry with them the possibility that the obligation they entail will not be fulfilled, and that this possibility is particularly available in the case of an utterance designated as a promise. To label a political utterance a promise thus entails a claim: this promise may be insincere; this candidate may lack character.

From the theatrical perspective, the great danger of promises lies precisely in the orientation to audience desire that makes them good vehicles for manifesting leadership. A retreat from a promised position may yield, in the "publics" picked out by the promise, a sense of betrayal that is intense in direct proportion to the effervescence evoked in the original moment of promising. The extremities of the response to Bush's retreat from his campaign promises on taxes exemplify this phenomenon. After 1990 the conservative Republicans for whom Bush's promise had been hand-crafted attacked him with extraordinary viciousness, accusing him of being a "liar" and a "back-stabber." The discourse of truth alone does not predict this intensity, which becomes intelligible only within the perspective on desire made available by attention to the theatrics of promising.

What is especially interesting is that the attacks on Bush from both perspectives were highly personalist, even given the seemingly intrinsic sociocentric dimensions of the theatrical perspective that I have pointed out above. The complexly socialized origins of the Bush promise, both within the dynamics of the Republican Party and within the campaign as an institutional structure, were thoroughly understood by his supporters and his enemies alike. Yet in the press coverage about his broken promise, Bush himself was the exclusive object of blame. Furthermore, while the material results of the 1990 budget compromise, the "new taxes" that Bush had negotiated, were known to all, almost no attention was paid to whether they were damaging or constructive. The discourse of attack instead focused entirely on Bush's alleged failures of character and leadership.

GEORGE BUSH'S PROMISE

My examples of discourse about Bush's 1988 campaign promise, the 1990 budget compromise, and its aftermath are drawn from a review of articles and editorials in three major newspapers, the *Washington Post (WP)*, the *New York Times (NYT)*, and the *Los Angeles Times (LAT)*. In the initial "firestorm" period, between May and November 1990, the volume of commentary was such that I decided to use only the *Washington Post*. In addition, I consulted books about the period by campaign workers, journalists, political scientists, and communications scholars. This method accesses a narrow range of representations in a complex and contested field, but they are undeniably influential; other media may take these "elite" newspapers as standards both for what is newsworthy and for what range of opinion about the news is appropriate (Jamieson and Campbell 1992:18–19). And although I did not undertake any surveys of ordinary people, the journalistic discourse I reviewed is quite consistent with talk about the Bush promise and compromise in which I participated in my role as a U.S. citizen. Readers should remain aware nevertheless that the texts I discuss here are those of authors with a distinct "inside-the-Beltway" bias. Finally, it is important to recognize that these materials do not reveal what those interviewed by reporters actually said. As anyone who has ever been "quoted" by a journalist can attest, such quotes often simplify or distort the original statement. Therefore I take the discourse to be that of the journalists themselves, and my ethnographic effort here is a discourse-centered analysis of one component of the written record around the promise, and not of "what really happened."[7]

Bush's Utterance in the Perspective of the Discourse of Theater

On August 18, 1988, Vice President George Bush ascended to the podium in the New Orleans Superdome to accept the Republican nomination for president of the United States. In the most memorable moment of his acceptance speech, Bush drew a series of contrasts between his own program and that of the Democratic nominee, Michael Dukakis. He built to a climax around a central theme of the Republican platform, fiscal conservatism and opposition to taxes:

> And I'm the one who won't raise taxes. My opponent now says
> he'll raise them as a last resort, or a third resort. When a politi-
> cian talks like that, you know that's one resort he'll be checking
> into. My opponent won't rule out raising taxes. But I will. The
> Congress will push me to raise taxes, and I'll say no, and they'll
> push, and I'll say no, and they'll push again, and I'll say to them,
> "Read my lips: No new taxes."

The last six words were a quintessential sound bite, a basic component of "message." Republican campaign consultants, testing some of
the most important lines from Bush's acceptance speech with focus
groups in the days after the speech, found that "Read my lips: No new
taxes" had an exceptionally high positive response. Based on this finding, Bush often repeated the line during his campaign (Bob
Woodward, WP October 4, 1992:A22). He continued to use "No new
taxes" as an applause line as late as his State of the Union address on
January 29, 1990. Bush's 1992 campaign manager, Mary Matalin
(Matalin and Carville 1994:51), thought the six words were "one of the
great political lines of the century."

Bush's text was amplified and regimented by multiple performance frames at the Republican convention. The visual setting was
spectacular, with floating confetti and balloons glittering in powerful
spotlights, the enormous, flag-draped arena, the banks of cameras,
Bush himself raised high above the huge crowd and backlit at the sanc-
tum sanctorum of the podium. The text exploits the quintessential
Western pattern number, three (Hymes 1981). Three times Bush
repeats that Congress will push, and three times he says that he'll say
"no." Each half of "Read my lips: No new taxes" is a triplet. Bush practiced the words repeatedly to achieve a highly rhythmic and measured
delivery (Bob Woodward, WP October 4, 1992:A23), such that the crucial six words, "Read my lips: No new taxes" emerged as a memorable
spondee.[8]

Peggy Noonan, principal author of the speech and a conservative
committed to the economic program entailed by the "No new taxes"
expression, has stated that her goal in writing it was to "lift" Bush, to
"vault him over the debris" (Noonan 1990:298) of Dukakis's double-
digit advantage in the polls. She liked "Read my lips: No new taxes"

because its combination of propositional specificity and syllabic condensation, its "definiteness," in her words, carried a sense of "leadership." When nervous aides tried to take "Read my lips: No new taxes" out of the drafts of the acceptance address, Noonan writes, "I kept putting it back in. Why? Because it's definite. It's not subject to misinterpretation. It means, I mean this" (Noonan 1990:307). Bob Woodward (*WP* October 4, 1992:A22) attributed similar language to Bush media consultant Roger Ailes, who was apparently explicit about the need for orientation to audience desire: "Ailes told Bush, 'Goddamit, you got to say something definite in these speeches. I mean people want something definite. Say something definite. If this is it, say it.'"

The "Read my lips" line was well known to have originally been written for the actor Clint Eastwood in his famous role of tough San Francisco cop Dirty Harry.[9] Associating Bush with Eastwood was thought to be a way to alleviate public concern that the vice president was a "wimp" (an image problem Bush encountered partly because of his patrician background and partly because he had been consistently deferential to President Ronald Reagan). Noonan arranged for a joke writer to prepare for Bush another line, "Make my twenty-four-hour time period," a parody of Eastwood's famous tag, "Make my day." This joke was intended to ward off criticism that the attempt to hypermasculinize the elegant Yale man Bush by linking him with the gritty Dirty Harry was reaching too far.

Noonan was concerned that the image of Bush conveyed by her speech be authentic, a sort of rhetorical exaltation of the actual person. She reports that she worked with Bush, encouraging him to help her express "how you see yourself" and make the speech "more personal and reflective" (Noonan 1990:302). In a particularly interesting passage, Noonan talks about how Bush finally "broke the 'I' barrier" by compiling a list of talking points entitled "Who I Am," which were eventually incorporated into the acceptance speech as the list of contrasts with Dukakis that culminated in the paragraph beginning, "And I'm the one who won't raise taxes." She was very concerned that Bush be fully a singular agentive locus in every detail of diction.[10]

At the same time, Noonan saw no difficulty in enlarging and exalting Bush's self-presentation with language borrowed from diverse sources, some of which might be thought to be in stark contradiction to what was believed to be true about Bush. For instance, although as a young man he had moved to Texas to found an oil business, Bush was notoriously a WASP patrician, the son of a wealthy Wall Street broker who had been a U.S. senator from Connecticut. Thus it is astonishing to learn that Noonan, upon reading a study of ethnic families by Michael Novak, thought "This is Bush; this is what he means" (Noonan 1990:310). In this intertextual construction of an exalted "I" for Bush, the lines from the Clint Eastwood films were pivotal, not least because Republican stereotypes of masculinity had placed Bush in a double bind. He was a certified World War II hero, an athlete and an outdoors-man, captain of the Yale baseball team, yachtsman, hunter, father of four. Yet many Republicans who were unswerving in their devotion to Ronald Reagan saw Bush as a weakling precisely because he had, as vice president, been entirely loyal to Reagan. Noonan, however, sensed in Bush "determination" (Noonan 1990:302), and thought, along with campaign manager Roger Ailes, that the Eastwood line hit exactly the note to convey this (Bob Woodward, *WP* October 4, 1992:A22).[11] Her use of street colloquial language to suggest determination is a clear instance of the way "word" and "leadership" are gendered, requiring an exaggerated, violent, working-class masculinization.[12]

The use of quoted speech—"...and I'll say to them, 'Read my lips: No new taxes'"—permitted an alignment of an intertextual series, an important component of message. The conservative wing of the Republican Party were "supply-siders" who held that taxes choked off growth in the productive sectors of the economy. Conservatives had never forgotten Bush's wisecrack, in the 1979 Republican primaries, that their supply-side theory was "voodoo economics," and they were deeply suspicious of his soundness on fiscal policy. So Bush, trying to find conservative support in anticipation of the 1988 campaign, agreed in early 1987 to sign a "no-tax" pledge letter, a million copies of which were distributed to party members (Germond and Witcover 1993:23). Bush thus succeeded in outflanking his major primary opponent, Kansas Senator Robert Dole, who had refused to sign. For an insider audience of conservatives, the acceptance speech text was thus a reminder of Bush's previous pledge. By using quoted speech and the future tense, Bush aligned his words with the future, with a moment when, as president, he would refuse to negotiate with the Congress, thus continuing to enforce the Republican consensus. And Bush uttered the words standing before the enormous audience in the Superdome, to immediate effect; they were being said in the present of the moment of utterance, and were amplified by a wave of applause.

The acceptance speech is one of a series of three important moments of ritual oratory in American presidential politics.[13] It is followed by the inaugural address and the four State of the Union speeches delivered to the Congress and the nation. The links to the inaugural address, delivered immediately after the new president takes the oath of office, may endow all of these orations and their contents with a sort of inherent "oathlike" quality. Furthermore, this series of speeches indexes the triumph of democracy. In the acceptance speech, the vast array of state and territorial delegations are labeled by signs and symbols, and the television cameras pan across them, picking up reactions to parts of the speech thought to be targeted at the various states and regions. The acceptance speech is also the crowning moment of the work of the party itself and the final element of a whole series of speeches by increasingly important party notables. The inaugural address takes place outdoors on the steps of the Capitol Building, with the great panorama of the federal city made visible to crowd and cameras. The chief justice of the Supreme Court administers the oath, aligning the new president with the highest powers of justice. The State of the Union speech is given in the chamber of the House of Representatives, with members of the Senate present as well, celebrating the legislative branch and the ideal of representative government. Thus the sequence of orations, taken as a total, (re)presents the American political system, evoking its past and projecting its future, and embodying it in the voice and presence of a single human being.

From the theatrical perspective, "Read my lips: No new taxes" was a triumph of the art of campaign stagecraft, a felicitous union of speech writing, the orchestration of the convention, the selection of precisely the right policy note, and Bush's skills as a performer. Kathleen Jamieson (1988:201) states that Franklin D. Roosevelt copied over speeches written by his amanuenses so that people would believe that he had composed them himself, but no public representations of the Bush speech ever suggested that Bush was its sole author or had delivered it extemporaneously. Speechwriter Peggy Noonan was a celebrity in her own right, and David Broder's report of the acceptance speech (*WP* August 19, 1988:A1–27) observed that the language of the speech "bore the earmarks" of Noonan's well-known style.[14] In her best-selling book—published in 1990, before the no-new-taxes promise was "broken"—Noonan wrote at some length about the highly socialized process of composition of the Bush speech. She credits Jack Kemp, a former Bush opponent, for suggesting that the speech "[h]it hard on taxes" (Noonan 1990:307) and says that in the final stages of preparation Bush's chief advisors went over every phrase.

Bush's staff never blamed him for breaking a promise in negotiating the 1990 budget compromise. An example of their tendency to distribute responsibility across the more sociocentric field permitted by the discourse of theater is found in Mary Matalin's argument that the budget compromise would never have happened had it not been for the untimely fatal illness of Bush's chief 1988 political operative, Lee Atwater, which left White House Chief of Staff John Sununu in sole control of day-to-day operations (Matalin and Carville 1994:51).[15] Bush's staff and supporters argued that it was unthinkable that the audience for the acceptance speech could have taken him literally, since it was widely known that experts agreed that it would be impossible to manage the federal budget without a tax increase. At the time of the budget compromise, some polls showed that two-thirds of the voters had not "believed" Bush's promise (*WP* June 27, 1990:A4). For these voters, "Read my lips: No new taxes" was not, in fact, a promise but a performance of the Republican message, an allusion to the different positions of the two parties on tax policy, a "slogan" (David Broder, *WP* May 13, 1990:C7). Bush's press secretary, Marlin Fitzwater, was quoted in the *Post* (June 27, 1990:A1) as saying, "He said the right thing then and he's saying the right thing now...Everything we said was true then and it's true now: No regrets, no backing off." When reporters asked whether he would agree that Bush had broken his pledge, Fitzwater is said to have replied, "No, are you crazy?"

Reportage of this exchange was shaped almost entirely within the perspective of the discourse of truth, a point of view from which Fitzwater's remarks seemed absurd. From the theatrical perspective, however, the notion of a continuity of truth is not really ridiculous. Within the discourse of theater, "truth," like "message," has a locally contextualized meaning. Fitzwater always took "the pledge" to refer to the Republican message of fiscal conservatism, established in an inter-textual series intended to penetrate the consciousness of the electorate, and not to any specific moment of definite reference. This perspective is very clearly articulated in Matalin's discussion of an event in the 1992 campaign. In September 1992, Bush, using a strategy developed by his staff of "apologizing" for the 1990 budget compromise (he never apologized directly for breaking a promise), ad-libbed in a standard speech by saying, "I found out the hard way, I went along with one Democratic tax increase, and I'm not going to do it again. Ever. *Ever.*" In response to press inquiries about the meaning of the remark, Fitzwater insisted that it "wasn't a pledge" (*LAT* September 11, 1992:A18); this statement was greeted with almost universal derision.

For Matalin, Bush's one-word departure from his standard text, one he had given "a thousand times," was a disaster:

> The second "Ever" was ad libbed.
>
> One extra word made the promise more definitive… Which required Marlin to go out and respond to the press, who were asking whether this was in fact a new pledge not to raise taxes…
>
> This is a classic case of political jargon conflicting with human jargon. To humans it meant what it looked like; he said he refused to raise taxes. To us, the "tax pledge" is a term of art, it doesn't mean what it means to normal people. It refers back to a specific fight during the 1988 New Hampshire primary over "taking the tax pledge." Marlin said the President did not "take the pledge," meaning, in political-speak, he refused to commit to not raising taxes. (Matalin and Carville 1994:330)

In defending Bush, the White House staff tried to represent the budget compromise as a testimonial to his positive qualities of leadership, such as courage. Some of their statements specifically addressed the emphasis in the discourse of truth on continuity of reference, arguing that courage (which can be a component of both character and leadership) should supercede this. In a press conference reported in full in the *Washington Post* (June 30, 1990:A8), Bush himself replied to the charge that he had broken his promise:

> I can understand people saying that…I think it's wrong. I'm pre-
> sented with new facts. I'm doing like Lincoln did, think anew.
> I've still got the principles that underlie my political philosophy
> and haven't changed my view about whether—you know—taxes.
> But we've got a major problem facing this country.[16]

Governor James R. Thompson of Illinois returned to the Lincoln comparison, stating that Bush, like Lincoln, "has the courage to change even deeply held beliefs."

As late as February 24, 1992, the White House continued to deny that any promise had been broken. All the major newspapers reported a statement on this point by Vice President Quayle on the television show *Larry King Live*. According to the *New York Times* (February 24, 1992:A15),

> Mr. Quayle said that Mr. Bush accepted the tax increase because
> the likelihood of war in the Persian Gulf then limited his ability
> to wage a domestic battle with Congress. [Quayle was referring
> to the final signing of the budget agreement in November 1990,
> after Iraqi forces had occupied Kuwait.] "He made a choice; the
> choice was a budget or no budget, and to get a budget, he had
> to give the Democrats in Congress a tax increase," Mr. Quayle
> said. "It was a compromise with Congress, and it was not going
> back on a campaign pledge."[17]

The discourse of theater is most easily identified in the language of Bush's supporters, but a few attacks on his leadership also used this discourse. For instance, it was recognized that many people were involved in arranging the budget compromise, with operatives like Sununu and Budget Director Richard Darman seen as especially blameworthy. (Darman, who had opposed the inclusion of the "No new taxes" lines in the acceptance speech, offered to resign after Bush confessed in March 1992 to having made a "mistake" in the 1990 budget deal.) This understanding opened the way not to an elaborated discourse of sociocentricity but to an accusation that Bush was a failed leader who was "not in charge" even in his own White House. Conservative columnists Rowland Evans and Robert D. Novak, for example, stated that calling Bush a liar (from the truth perspective) missed the point: The problem was not "presidential veracity" but whether "the kinder, gentler chief executive can gain control of the chaotic budget process" (*WP* July 2, 1990:A11). Evans and Novak used "kinder, gentler" to invoke Bush's campaign statements that, after eight years of "tough-guy" conservatism under Ronald Reagan, his presidency would bring about a "kinder, gentler America." By implying that Bush needed to make elaborate displays of being tough, firm, and in charge in order to reestablish his gendered capacity for leadership, Evans and Novak were raising the old schoolyard charge that Bush was really a wimp, not a tough guy at all.

Tom Bethell's *Los Angeles Times* opinion piece (November 11, 1991:M5) also tried subtly to associate Bush with more "feminine" qualities. Bethell suggested that Bush agreed to the budget agreement because he was vain and shallow, puffed up with unseemly pride in his reputation as a world leader: "Having traded away his most important promise to the electorate—his pledge not to raise taxes—the Democrats would surely admire his conciliatory nature. This would free him up to travel the world negotiating peace agreements, doling out foreign aid, and listening to bands play 'Hail to the Chief.'" Conservatives, Bethell concluded, might as well vote Democratic. "If we are to have our taxes raised…let it be done by someone who makes no bones about it. Let us be stabbed in the front rather than the back." Bethell's column exemplifies the dangers of performativity: Bethell is claiming the intense anger of a loyal supporter who has been deeply and viciously betrayed, "stabbed in the back."

Bush's Utterance in the Perspective of the Discourse of Truth

In spite of the obvious theatrical dimensions of the Bush speech, from the very beginning analysts chose to understand his famous words not as a skillful performance of the Republican message but as a strong commitment, susceptible to tests of truth. Thus David Broder (*WP* August 19, 1988:A27), reporting on Bush's acceptance speech the morning after it was delivered, wrote that Bush had made "an ironclad pledge to accept 'no new taxes' from Congress."

In early May of 1990, Bush agreed with congressional leaders that he would impose "no preconditions" on the upcoming negotiation of the federal budget. Opponents immediately accused him of breaking his "promise." On June 26, 1990, Bush agreed to the following statement, negotiated with congressional leaders who insisted that he take some responsibility for new taxes that seemed to them unavoidable:

> It is clear to me[18] that both the size of the deficit problem and the need for a package that can be enacted require all of the following: entitlement and mandatory program reform; tax revenue increases; growth incentives; discretionary spending reductions.[19] (Jamieson and Campbell 1992:100)

This statement set off the firestorm of attacks on Bush that continued through November 1990, when Bush signed a budget bill that included tax revenue increases on gasoline, tobacco, alcohol, and a variety of luxury goods, and an increase in the top income tax rate from 28 to 31 per cent. The attacks escalated throughout the 1992 presidential campaign. Led by conservatives in his own party, who made Bush's "broken promise" a centerpiece of their campaign against his reelection, the perception grew among voters that "Read my lips: No new taxes" had been a particularly firm and sacred commitment—an *omertá* (Mafia-ese for "death oath"), in the words of *Washington Post* commentator Jodie T. Allen (May 13, 1990:C7)—and that by compromising with the Congress Bush had broken it and thus had broken faith with the voters.

Many of the arts of stagecraft that are assigned positive value within the discourse of theater have a negative value within the discourse of truth. For instance, from within the discourse of theater, Peggy Noonan (1990) argues that the role of the speechwriter is to bring out the best in a candidate, to make voters see clearly qualities that were always there but that the candidate lacks the specialized skills to reveal. Kathleen Jamieson, a specialist in political communications, argues that, on the contrary, the use of speechwriters has caused a "divorce between speech and thought." Their skills, she states, make it "now possible to elect someone whose primary qualifications are a knack for creating news McNuggets, a willingness to speak the thoughts of others, a talent for doing so with sincerity and conviction, and a tolerance for feigning enthusiasm when delivering the same stock stump speech for the seventh time in a single day" (Jamieson 1988:237).

In theatrical perspective, every detail of Bush's inaugural address was intended to enhance his image as a leader and particularly to develop an imagery of ideal American masculinity, of toughness with the colloquial edge that Bush might share with someone "ethnic" or with a street cop like Dirty Harry, that would remove any lingering concern that Bush was a fancy-pants rich kid. However, the attacks on him as a breaker of a promise focused not on his toughness or leadership but on his sincerity and truthfulness, qualities of his character. The whole world knew that the speech was Peggy Noonan's work, but she was never blamed for making an insincere promise (although she was criticized for urging Bush to stick to his position [Hobart Rowen, *WP* July 19, 1990:A23]). When from time to time Bush was recognized as largely an animator of Noonan's entextualization of a conservative Republican message, he was blamed for "irresponsibility" (Bob Woodward, *WP* October 4, 1992:A22) in agreeing to utter the words. Most of the attacks completely neglected the socialized origins of Bush's speech and its place in the construction of the Republican "message" and treated him as if he had been author, animator, and principal of the famous words. Going straight to the referential jugular, Bush's attackers called him a liar.

Bush first hinted he might compromise on taxes when, on May 10, 1990, he told Democratic leaders that he was willing to enter into budget negotiations with "no preconditions." The Senate majority leader, Democrat George Mitchell, immediately announced this language. Speaker of the House Thomas Foley added that "everything was on the table," prompting one satirist to joke, "Who ya gonna call? Ethan Allen?" (Tony Kornheiser, *WP* May 11, 1990:D1). Sununu rushed over to the Capitol to reassure Republicans that Bush did not mean that he would permit new taxes. It was in reaction to the clashing signals from Bush and Sununu that the first use of the term "character" and other wording suggesting it, appeared in my materials. House minority leader Robert H. Michel of Illinois, a conservative Republican, expressed concern about the contradictory statements: "The decision has got to be made as to whether you go into one of these things in good faith, and being candid and open and honest with one another or I don't know that you have any prospects for success" (David Hoffman and John E. Yang, *WP* May 11, 1990:A24). In a *Post* editorial, Evans and Novak quoted "one GOP leader" as saying, "It is a test of character";

they concluded, "When the rank and file start talking about the character of their leader, the White House knows the message is serious" (*WP* May 21, 1990:A11).

James Kilpatrick, a conservative columnist, appealed to Bush in a dramatic evocation of "old-fashioned values," a mixed discourse that links the value of referential continuity explicitly to masculine heroism and the performances of leadership. Kilpatrick quoted the speech of Horatius from Macaulay's *Lays of Ancient Rome:* "And how can man die better than facing fearful odds, for the ashes of his fathers and the temples of his gods." "Mr. President!" appealed Kilpatrick:

> Stand like Horatius! Hold firm to your convictions!...Or be like Ulysses, who ordered sailors to bind him to the mainmast lest he succumb to the sirens' song. Or take your model from the boy who stood on the burning deck, whence all but he had fled. The old heroic ballads speak to us through the ages. This is a time for leadership. (*WP* June 4, 1990:A15)

"'Read my lips,'" Kilpatrick went on, "was a pledge of honor, and Bush is an honorable man." This tag, of course, could not fail to remind Bush's more literate enemies of Marc Antony's characterization of the traitor Brutus, murderer of Caesar, as "an honorable man."

Richard Cohen, a self-described liberal Republican who approved of the budget compromise, weighed in with a devastating opinion piece published under the head, "What does Bush Stand For?" Echoing conservative talk-show host Patrick Buchanan, Cohen asked, "Can Bush be trusted?", and concluded with a particularly damning figure: "[N]o question about it, when it comes to convictions, this man travels light" (*WP* May 11, 1990:A27).

On June 26, 1990, after a breakfast meeting between Bush and congressional leaders, a statement about the results of negotiations in the meeting (the "it is clear to me" statement quoted above) was posted stealthily in the White House press room (rather than being distributed in a press briefing, with opportunities for questions; Germond and Witcover 1993:32).No one was fooled, however. The conservative columnist George Will characterized the statement as "carefully crafted and crafty," distributed "like a scrap of wastepaper furtively discarded on a street corner by a litterer with just enough conscience to be uneasy about littering but not enough conscience not to litter" (*WP* June 29, 1990:A27). Will quoted the notorious June 27 headline in the *New York Post:* "Read my lips—I lied." The *Washington Post* headlined its front-page story of the statement (five columns wide above the fold) "Bush Abandons Campaign Pledge/Calls for New Taxes" and quoted Michael Dukakis as saying, "I told the truth and I paid the price. Mr. Bush did not and we're all going to have to pay the price now for that." In a *Post* editorial, Dale Rusakoff quoted Walter Mondale, the 1984 Democratic candidate, who said, "Let's hope we learn our lesson and start to talk honestly and openly in these campaigns" (*WP* June 28, 1990:A23).

In spite of White House attempts to shape the public perception of Bush in a positive direction, the "firestorm," originally predicted by the White House to last "twenty-four hours" (*WP* June 29, 1990:A4), never really died down. Patrick Buchanan surprised the Republican establishment by entering the primary lists against his sitting president and featured the "broken promise" in his campaign. Germond and Witcover (1993:135) quote part of Buchanan's stump speech: "We Republicans can no longer say it was all the liberals' fault...It was not some liberal Democrat who declared, 'Read my lips: No new taxes,' then broke his word to cut a seedy back-room deal with the big spenders on Capitol Hill."

Voter reaction to the idea that Bush had broken a promise became newsworthy in its own right. On June 14, 1992, the *New York Times* ran a major front-page piece by Jeffrey Schmalz under the head, "Words on Bush's Lips in '88 Now Stick in Voter's Craw," which heavily exploited the discourse of "lies." Schmalz, claiming to have interviewed hundreds of voters, found that they were "angered not so much that their taxes had been raised as by their belief that Mr. Bush had lied to them, breaking not a routine promise but a sacred compact." Schmalz argued that the "read my lips" factor was important in growing support for third-party candidate Ross Perot; voters, he said, preferred Perot's "vagueness" to "lies." Schmalz also reported an interview with William J. Bennett, Reagan's secretary of education and a self-appointed conservative ethicist, quoting him as saying, "You can't take the definition of yourself and flip it. I've found the American people don't have to agree with you. What they want is a straight line, being true to your word."

Attacks framed in the discourse of truth plagued Bush up to the very last days of his second campaign for the presidency. On October 11, 1992, the *Los Angeles Times* reported at length an attack on Bush by Democratic vice presidential candidate Albert Gore after Bush had ad-libbed that he would never, "ever, *ever*" raise taxes again. (Recall that Marlin Fitzwater had moved quickly into damage control mode, stating that Bush's remark was "not a pledge"—a remark that Mary Matalin, cited above, said referred to Bush's "taking the pledge" in New Hampshire in 1987, and not to the acceptance speech.) Gore, according to Sam Fulwood III (*LAT* October 11, 1992:A18), unleashed a torrent of sarcasm:

> Well, it sounds to me as if Marlin Fitzwater has learned to be a lip reader...We are now greatly in debt to Mr. Fitzwater for interpreting the President's comments...Bush has repeatedly said that the principal issue is whether or not he can be trusted...We now know that even when he bangs his fist on the table and says with a very determined look that he will never, ever, ever do something, he doesn't really mean it...We will have to wait for the interpretation from his official spokesman after he's checked with his handlers to get the truth of what he's really trying to say.

Note that Gore takes the characteristic discourse-of-truth position articulated by Kathleen Jamieson, that a highly socialized performance of message involving "handlers" and "spokesmen" necessarily indexes a failure of reference because truth, in this perspective, can emanate authentically only from the thoughts of a singular speaker.

An especially interesting attack on Bush in this vein appeared in a four-part series of articles by ace *Washington Post* reporter Bob Woodward. In "Making Choices: Bush's Economic Record," which ran for four days in the *Post* between October 4 and October 8, only a month before the 1992 election, Woodward turned the more socialized discourse of campaign specialists against Bush. By reporting the debate inside Bush's staff over whether the "Read my lips: No new taxes" line should stay in the 1988 acceptance speech, Woodward suggested that the line was put there by speech writers and media people, not by policy people—that is, it was an appeal to "emotion," not a reflection of Bush's "thought"—and implied that Bush "irresponsibly" accepted it (the word "irresponsible" appeared in a head in huge type on the inside page of the first article). Woodward stated that Bush practiced the line and found it hard to deliver convincingly until a staff member wrote it out for him with the pauses marked after each word. He thus denigrated Bush's performance accomplishment by implying that it showed that the words were wholly inauthentic. Bush's staff, Woodward claimed, was riven by "bitter infighting" and "turf wars," suggesting not the intricate social organization of the White House as a relational field but Bush's personal inability to control his staff.

On March 3, 1992, Bush admitted that he had "made a mistake." Andrew Rosenthal reported in the *New York Times* (March 4, 1992:A1, A17) that Bush was trying to "blunt the conservative attack of Patrick J. Buchanan" (then campaigning in the Georgia primary). Rosenthal quoted an interview Bush had given to the *Atlanta Journal:* "If I had to do it over, I wouldn't do what I did then, for a lot of reasons, including political reasons...I did it, and I regret it and I regret it [sic]" (*NYT* March 4, 1992:A17). Feeling that the Atlanta statement hadn't made enough impact, Bush's campaign managers had him apologize again during an interview with Barbara Walters that ABC aired on June 26, 1992, when he stated that the 1990 budget compromise "was a mistake, because it undermined to some degree my credibility with the American people" (*NYT* June 26, 1992:A13). According to Mary Matalin (Matalin and Carville 1994:223),the campaign was delighted with the interview: "The President's mea culpa restored credibility to a man with a deep sense of honor, it showed that he was big enough to admit a mistake, and it reasserted the universal Republican philosophy that any tax increase is bad policy."

Bush's use of the term "mistake" was exemplary "spin"—the lack of consistency between the acceptance speech and the budget compromise was that the latter was merely a political misstep, not a failure of reference. His statement was intended to neutralize Buchanan, who had been calling for Bush to apologize. Finally, as Matalin pointed out, the apology gave the campaign an opportunity to repeat the Republican message. This strategy, conceived in theatrical perspective, failed to overcome the widely held popular view that what was at issue was Bush's character, as indexed by referential continuity. James Gerstenzang and Art Pine, writing in the *Los Angeles Times* (March 4,

1992:A8) from within the discourse of truth, observed:

> While his confession may placate some conservatives, Bush's lat-
> est twist on the tax issue risks drawing attention not only to the
> fact that he abandoned the pledge—"Read my lips: No new
> taxes"—of his 1988 presidential campaign, but to his readiness
> to shift his position when he is under political fire.

CONCLUSION

Duranti (1993) concludes an article on Samoan political language
with the observation that the speech of a Samoan orator is "dangerous." So too, obviously, is the speech of American politicians. Local linguistic ideology may require precisely the most dangerous kind of
political speech, talk encoded in a form that can be taken as a
promise.[20] The performance of promising is heavily overdetermined.
The discourse of truth in American English language ideology pressures politicians to signal a commitment to referential continuity, a
principal manifestation of character, by speaking in the future tense.
These future-tense propositions cannot, however, be vague. The theatrical perspective requires regimentation of these propositions as definite, "the word" that a man will keep. This masculine word is "straight
talk," blunt, tough, colloquial, intense in its indications of orientation
to audience desire, because only this will produce the glass of audience
effervescence in which leadership is reflected. By promising in vivid
and specific language, presidential candidates become hyperpersons,
supermen invested to the highest degree with motives and qualities
that have come to be seen as necessary for the person who will be the
living symbol and center, the singular locus, of the American state.

Yet precisely this successful construction sets the trap that we saw
sprung in the case of George Bush. "Read my lips: No new taxes" can
easily be analyzed as one moment in a complex discursive field comprised of the intertextual series through which Republican fiscal policy
emerged in the 1970s and 1980s, and distributed across the intricate
institutional structure of the campaign organization itself as well as
across the social field of rivalries in the party. Journalists in the United
States are fully able to understand this contextual complexity of any
campaign utterance. Nonetheless, such an apprehension was seldom

evident in the mainstream journalistic discourse that evaluated Bush's "broken promise"; Bush was represented instead as a singular antihero.

Such a simplified construction is often attributed to the press's profit motive, to "sensationalism." But it seems worth considering that it is, rather, simply evidence of the fact that the metapragmatic discourse of truth is as ready to hand for journalists as for any other citizen and is the discourse considered to be most appropriate for evaluating political language (as opposed to discussing the craft of campaigning). The demolition of Bush from within this perspective can be seen not only as a manifestation of the moral stance made available by the discourse of truth, however. It was also an important moment of reproduction of personalist ideology and the project of engendering masculinity that is central to it. This ideology drives the theatrical regimentation of political utterances like "Read my lips: No new taxes" that permits them to be heard as "ironclad pledges," and at the same time filters the full range of journalistic understandings into the simplistic personalist discourses of individual motives that make our political world into a schoolyard inhabited by "wimps" and "tough guys."

Notes

1. Although the immediate cause of Hart's fall from grace was evidence of an extramarital affair, there was intense public concern about Hart's character even earlier, focused around a key piece of evidence for a failure of referential consistency in his career: Hart had changed his name (from Hartpence). A name change interrupts a central element of referentialist language ideology, the notion of an essential relationship between names and things. Furthermore, a change of name is gendered: It is something that American women do, but not American men. Hart was almost certainly trying to align his name with the monosyllabic norms of "straight talk" and toughness, but by working within the discourse of theater he ran afoul of the discourse of truth.

2. One of the important qualities for male politicians is a handshake so firm that hand injuries are an occupational hazard.

3. Thus, six years after Bush's famous acceptance speech, Senator Dennis DeConcini of Arizona attacked Republican congressman John Kyl, who eventually won DeConcini's seat, by saying, "You can't read John Kyl's lips any better than you could George Bush's, because they both talk out of both sides of their mouth" (*Arizona Daily Star*, March 19, 1994). Seven years out, in June 1995, at the

Wal-Mart greeting card rack—one of my favorite sites for research on popular usage— I found a birthday card that bore a caricature of George Bush saying, "Read my lips—no more birthdays." Inside, the card reads, "OK, I lied" (American Greetings).

4. Arnovick (1994) provides a different account, arguing that since the English modals "shall" and "will" no longer include "volitional implication," the "deontic intent" in promising must be covered by expanded discourse ("I absolutely promise…"). She contrasts this with an era, exemplified by *Beowulf*, when a single sentence could bind the speaker. However, I would argue that this expansion of promising is due instead to the ineluctable link between "truth" and "theater" implicit in Searle's account. One can imagine that vows in Beowulf's time were regimented by material props, gestures, gaze, witnesses, and the like. Indeed, the case cited by Arnovick (1994:176), where Hrothgar says, "Now, Beowulf, best of men, in my heart I will love you as a son," is in fact "expanded" in the elaborated address, the reference to the heart, and by the sentences that follow. Furthermore, Hrothgar is accompanied by his queen and her women, and by "much company," as he makes these vows. This is reminiscent of Duranti's account of the Samoan speech act *folafola*, a kind of commitment guaranteed by witnesses.

5. Ourousoff (1993) discusses a case of the evaluation of managers of a multinational firm in which the personalist discourse of "leadership" seemed to absolutely overwhelm any attention to actual results, even where a good deal of effort was put in to quantify and compare these. A manager evaluated as "tough" was praised and advanced, even though a factory under his leadership collapsed after he manifested his "toughness" by firing key personnel. Another manager, thought of as "weak," was replaced in spite of the fact that his factory was the most productive in the company.

6. "Promises, Promises: An RNC Republican Accountability Project" was the title of a series of publications put out by the Republican National Committee during the Carter administration (Fishel 1985:54). I am indebted to Paul Kroskrity for the observation that the intonation contours vary slightly among "red red" and "dinner dinner" versus "lies, lies," which is "emphatic repetition" (Kroskrity's term) and "promises, promises," usually uttered with an "ironic" intonation. However, while the intonational issue is definitely worth further research, I think the point still holds about the difference between "promise" and "lie."

7. The exceptions are the texts of the 1988 acceptance speech and the

statement issued on June 26, 1992, which are in the words of printed texts released by the Bush campaign and the White House staff respectively.

8. A spondee is a poetic meter in which every syllable is stressed (e.g., "What rough beast…"). One intertextual manifestation of the poetics of the famous utterance that later emerged was rhyme. As the controversy over the budget compromise escalated into the fall of 1990, Bush got off one of his most famous wisecracks. On October 10, a reporter accosted him as he was jogging, and said (referring to Bush's pet project of lowering the rate of the capital gains tax), "Are you ready to throw in the towel on capital gains?" Bush continued jogging, and, pointing to his "posterior" (in the language of the *Washington Post,* October 11, 1990), replied, "Read my hips."

9. Eastwood, a tall, wiry, rugged-looking actor famous for his steely blue squint, first gained fame as a gun-toting cowboy in Western films. He then made a series of movies in which he played a San Francisco police detective known as Dirty Harry, essentially a homicidal maniac redeemed only by the fact that the people he kills are crooks and bad guys. When Dirty Harry threatens, the viewer knows somebody is going to die.

10. Noonan attributes Bush's reluctance to say "I" to the rigid standards for modesty imposed on him by his mother (she proposes a ludicrous vision of Bush "raising his hand on the Capitol steps—'Do solemnly swear, will preserve and protect…'" (Noonan 1990:302). But the proscription on saying "I" is, in fact, widespread in American middle-class formal usage and may be particularly required of men. Philips and Reynolds (1987) found that men replying to *voir dire* examinations (the examination of potential jurors conducted during jury selection) deleted subject pronouns at a high rate of 17 percent, twice the rate of deletion by women. This speech pattern needs more attention, but its frequency does suggests that any relationship between first-person pronouns and "individualism" must be at best highly indirect.

11. There do seem to be limits on this kind of intertextual practice. Senator Joseph Biden of Delaware, an early leader among Democratic candidates in the 1988 primary season, was driven from the field in disgrace when critics pointed out that his stump speech drew heavily on a famous address by the British Labor Party leader Neil Kinnock, even adopting details of Kinnock's up-from-poverty autobiography that had nothing to do with Biden's own life (Cramer 1993).

12. Bush constantly faced this dilemma, which led to some of the more unfortunate moments of his career. Most widely remembered is his tough-guy remark following his debate with Democratic vice presidential candidate

Geraldine Ferraro in 1984, that he had "kicked a little ass." Fortunately, Bush's mother did not survive to hear him say this.

13. I owe this point to Michael Silverstein, who made it in discussion of the paper at the School of American Research seminar.

14. Matalin (Matalin and Carville 1994:310) observes that by 1992 the "poetry" of the Noonan speech had become problematic. Discussing the composition of Bush's acceptance speech by a "speech-construction circus" of an "army of Bushies," Matalin remarks, "We didn't want too many rhetorical flourishes, too much poetry in it, because we didn't want a repeat of 1988 and everyone saying, 'This is not George Bush, this is Peggy Noonan.'"

15. In spite of this sociocentric discourse, Matalin's attitude toward Bush as documented in her book was one of gushing worship of a hero who deserved to be exalted by the most expert staff and campaign skills.

16. On the allusion to Lincoln's decision to issue the Emancipation Proclamation, the *Post* quoted Representative Dan Rostenkowski (Democrat–Illinois), first elected to Congress in 1952: "Tell him, I knew Abe Lincoln, I worked with Abe Lincoln, and you're no Abe Lincoln." This, of course, did double duty by reminding voters that Bush's vice president was the nonentity Dan Quayle, who had been attacked with this same language by Lloyd Benson in the 1988 vice presidential debates, after Quayle compared himself to John F. Kennedy.

17. Challenged on the Quayle statement (since Bush had in fact agreed initially to the budget compromise on June 26, before the Iraqi invasion), Quayle's chief of staff, William Kristol, "disagreed that the Republicans had reinterpreted events. 'We're not rewriting history,' he said. 'The June 26 statement,' he added, 'was not signing on to a tax increase, it was putting taxes on the table'" (Dan Balz, *WP* July 24, 1992:A16).

18. Dan Balz and Ann Devroy (*WP* July 7, 1990:A1) stated that Democrats insisted that the words "to me" be included in this statement in order to pick Bush out as responsible. The Democrats were very concerned that they were going to be "sucker punched" with the sole responsibility for the tax increase.

19. Jamieson and Campbell (1992:100) single out the contrast between the vivid and memorable language of the original speech and the weaseling governmentese of the announcement of the compromise as a good example of an attempt to manipulate the media.

20. Many commentators argued in 1990–92 that there was something special about the Bush "betrayal." However, the scenario is very old in American

politics. Famous cases of betrayal involve Abraham Lincoln (who freed the slaves in violation of a campaign promise), Franklin D. Roosevelt (who betrayed the Eastern elite by breaking his promise to balance the federal budget), Lyndon Johnson (who promised that American boys would never do the fighting for Asian boys, and then doubled troop strength in Vietnam), Richard Nixon (who broke with his anticommunist image to open diplomatic relations with the People's Republic of China), Jimmy Carter (who betrayed his supporters on the left by lifting price controls on oil and gas), and most recently Bill Clinton (who broke his promise to eliminate restrictions against military service by gays when he was unable to convince top military leaders to accept the change).

8

Introducing Kaluli Literacy
A Chronology of Influences

Bambi B. Schieffelin

How do speakers in societies with language ideologies based on oral traditions respond to the introduction of language ideologies based on literate ones? To address this question, one must view both oral and literate practices as historically contingent and ideologically grounded, a set of culturally organized practices linked to the political, social, and economic forces that shape them. How a community "takes up" literacy, how it develops, how it is understood and deployed depends very much on the ideology and context of who is doing the introduction as well as on the ideology and context of those to whom it is being introduced. We know that societies differ significantly in ways of taking up and organizing literacy practices (or resisting them), and this relates to cultural as well as historical factors (Ferguson 1987; Graff 1981; Guss 1986; McKenzie 1987; Meggitt 1968). In this chapter I will explore the relationship between what is conceptualized as literacy in such a situation and how orality gets deployed and reconfigured.

CHRISTIAN MISSIONIZATION OF KALULI
Kaluli experienced their first contact with white people in 1935.

During the next few decades contact, mostly by government patrols, was intermittent. In the early 1970s two Australians, members of the Asia Pacific Christian Mission (APCM), began intensive activities in the Bosavi area of the Southern Highlands Province of Papua New Guinea, home to twelve hundred Kaluli. The missionaries, Keith and Norma Briggs, simultaneously introduced Christianity, literacy, and schooling, all part of a plan to transform Kaluli society. The agents and activities associated with the mission introduced Kaluli to new forms and sources of knowledge about their own and the outside world. They challenged and changed Kaluli notions of truth, knowledge, and authority, thereby affecting Kaluli linguistic as well as social structures.

These missionaries, who had had previous experience in Papua New Guinea, rapidly established a mission station that included an elementary school, clinic, and trade store around an airstrip. The station was additionally staffed by Papua New Guineans, all members of the APCM, including teachers, pastors, clinic orderlies, and nursing sisters. Mission staff held daily church services and Bible study groups for Kaluli. (For an overview of contact and the establishment of the mission, see Schieffelin and Crittenden 1991:262–68.)

During this time Kaluli also experienced intermittent contact with other Papua New Guinean nationals, predominantly government officers who patrolled the area and agricultural officers who tried to convince Kaluli to grow coffee, chili peppers, and other crops for cash. In addition, starting in 1966, anthropologists E. L. Schieffelin, Steve Feld, and I made visits at various times and of different durations that have continued into the present, visits I would like to think were relatively benign but not inconsequential. These mission, government, and anthropological intrusions introduced Kaluli to new ideas, languages, and language practices, changing the ways Kaluli would interpret events, establish facts, convey opinions, and imagine themselves.

The Christian mission presence was constant and assertive and played a strong role in effecting these changes. Christianity in Papua New Guinea is about missionizing, and this mission wanted to see change effected sooner rather than later. It is worth emphasizing that those who introduced Christianity in Papua New Guinea regarded their own culture as superior and the local society as in need of civilizing, in all respects inferior. Furthermore, the local people, confronted with missionaries, their goods, their stories, and their clear connections to wealth beyond imagination, came to question their own society and, in many cases, came to regard it as morally and technologically inferior.

This is the context in which missionaries organized, preached, discussed, and prayed, using English, Kaluli, and Tok Pisin, the most widely used national lingua franca. The new communicative resources that were created reflected the interests and beliefs of both the missionaries and the local Kaluli being missionized. Here, as in other situations of contact, it is important to remember that the roles of missionized and missionizer are not necessarily mutually exclusive or oppositional, as the missionized eventually become the missionizers in many cases. In Bosavi, for example, for several years before the arrival of the Australian evangelical Christian missionaries, the pastor in charge of the mission airstrip was a man from the Gogodala people, one of the first groups missionized by the Unevangelised Fields Mission. After Keith and Norma Briggs arrived in 1970, they imported additional Papua New Guinean pastors to help with evangelical activities, part of the mission agenda of localization.[1] Kaluli converts soon became active missionizers themselves, taking the opportunity to localize proselytizing activities through the vernacular.

Thus, although there is no question that the Christian evangelical project was conceptualized and implemented from a European vantage point, it is clear that several Kaluli, in addition to other Papua New Guineans, came to occupy the dual position of missionized and missionizer. Kaluli, in the role of missionizers, injected their own ideas about language and literacy into the creation and interpretation of new genres and information, thereby complicating the social, ideological, and textual forms and functions of these new genres and language practices. In examining processes of missionization and social change, one must examine shifting social roles over time and across activities.

This essay draws on a larger project that focuses on the impact of rapid missionization and the introduction of literacy on the communicative resources and social organization of Kaluli. It is based on ethnographic and sociolinguistic fieldwork I conducted between 1967 and 1995 and complements the extensive ethnographic and ethnomusicological research into Kaluli social, cultural, and expressive life carried out since 1966 (Feld 1988, 1990; Feld and Schieffelin 1982;

B. B. Schieffelin 1986a, 1990, 1996; Schieffelin and Feld 1998; E. L. Schieffelin 1976, 1981; Schieffelin and Crittenden 1991). Because I had the opportunity to carry out research on Kaluli language and social life before the mission was established, and was able to collect data at different times during periods of intense mission activity, I am able report on some of the resultant linguistic and social changes.[2]

This chapter takes the form of a chronology exploring several related linguistic and social activities which, when examined together, detail the development of literacy practices over a particular time period, the mid-1960s through the mid-1980s. This time frame is relatively short and recent; nevertheless I take a historical and ethnographic perspective to account for the multiple language ideologies, practices, and interpretive procedures introduced by different actors with a variety of interests and understandings. Analyzing the literacy practices and ideologies of both missionizers and missionized, I hope to demonstrate how everyday language practices, local metalinguistics, and language ideologies that are embedded in complex cultural and historical moments intersect in ongoing processes of social reproduction and rapid cultural change, certain outcomes of which may have been intended or planned, while others were not.

The chronology is composed of two types of analyses based on different kinds of data; taken together they offer complementary perspectives. The first analysis focuses on a set of written texts: a grammatical sketch of Kaluli prepared in 1964 by a missionary linguist and a series of vernacular literacy primers developed by the missionaries in Bosavi in the early 1970s. The grammatical sketch introduced new concepts into the language, naturalizing them through the use of the vernacular. The literacy primers (re)presented and (re)constructed social identities. Simple narratives about familiar, traditional village-based activities were presented in contrast to new events and options, ways of life that were being organized around the mission station. This analysis highlights how the mission inserted constructs about new social identities and ways to look and act "modern." The mission promoted the idea that Kaluli could change their culture while still speaking the vernacular.

The second analysis is based on an audiotaped 1984 literacy event that allows an examination of Kaluli literacy practices organized through talk. Here different language ideologies, practices, and interpretive procedures that arose and were elaborated in the contact situation are reflected in the emergence, shape, and social organization of such new genres as lessons and sermons—genres that combine oral and written practices in ways that allow for variation and novelty. So, for example, although the mission privileged reading over writing, for Kaluli the experience of reading during this time period (1970–84) was not silent, private, or contemplative but was, instead, deeply connected to their notions of orality. Thus Kaluli took literacy as an oral activity[3] and understood the practice of reading as transforming something that is visual into something oral. This transformation is connected to Kaluli ideas about sound and about saying and hearing as ways of knowing and remembering. The connection is apparent in the fact that reading is almost always done aloud, so that written texts are read and heard texts, which are then orally contextualized. Material read in classes and in church sermons is always discussed in some manner, most often guided by a teacher, pastor, or other Christian in charge.

Furthermore, Kaluli developed a vocabulary for talking about the activity of reading that included ways of talking about how words sound in terms of how they are spelled, in addition to what words mean. Books were granted a speaking role—as agents they spoke new words and the truth, and Kaluli were instructed to listen carefully and understand the new words that books said. Thus Kaluli ideas about speaking, and language in general, are critical to understanding many of the linguistic innovations found in literacy practices and demonstrate the different ways Kaluli themselves were participating in the linguistic and social reorganization of their society. The analysis of literacy practices shows how Kaluli were able to transform the understanding of written texts, eliciting verbal collaboration in order to achieve consensus about a different moral order. All of these efforts went toward creating a different kind of Kaluli person, one who, in spite of these changes, still spoke the vernacular.

ETHNOGRAPHIC APPROACHES TO LITERACY

The past decade or so has seen critical changes in the ways in which anthropologists think about and study literacy (see Collins 1995 and Street and Besnier 1994 for insightful reviews). Previously, literacy was viewed as a monolithic phenomenon, an autonomous and neutral technology whose introduction transforms "traditional" societies in much the same way regardless of other differences (Goody 1968, 1977). In contrast, more recent ethnographic work has demonstrated the importance of examining the diversity of meanings, functions, and ideological dimensions of literacy practices in particular communities (Besnier 1995; Boyarin 1993; Duranti and Ochs 1986; Finnegan 1988; Heath 1983; Kulick and Stroud 1990, 1993; Schieffelin and Gilmore 1986; Street 1984, 1993). Such ethnographic descriptions, set within a sociohistorical perspective, are a prerequisite for broader theorizing about any set of communicative practices, including those associated with literacy or literacies.

Although many scholars have argued against the "autonomous" view of literacy in favor of the "ideological" (Street 1984), the extent to which the social and textual aspects of literacy play a role in a variety of transformative processes, both positive and negative, is still subject to debate. Anderson (1991:24), for example, argues that the novel, the newspaper, and print capitalism facilitated "the birth of the imagined community of the nation" because they "made it possible for rapidly growing numbers of people to think about themselves, and to relate themselves to others, in profoundly new ways" (1991:36). He also suggests (1991:13) that for many religious communities sacred texts create a community out of signs, not sounds.

On a more negative note, Mühlhäusler (1996) puts literacy and derived technology at the center of an ongoing restructuring of the linguistic ecology of the Pacific. In his analysis of the transformation of the Pacific language region under the impact of colonization, modernization, and Westernization, he argues that the increasing loss of structural and semantic diversity is due not to "natural" causes but to cultural ones, specifically linguistic imperialism. Literacy, more than any other phenomenon, illustrates the impact of an introduced mode of behavior on the linguistic ecology; "it has led over the years to an almost total transformation of most Pacific societies and most languages spoken in the area" (Mühlhäusler 1996:212).[4] Although both positions are compelling, they tend to obscure what Kulick and Stroud (1990, 1993) pointed out in their study of how literacy was used among Gapun villagers of Papua New Guinea: Literacy *itself* does not have agentive force to change societies. It is humans who are the active force in any transformational processes accompanying the introduction of literacy. One institution in which human agency has played a particularly salient role in the introduction of literacy is the fundamentalist Christian mission.

In situations where literacy is introduced as part of Christian missionization, literacy activities are often shaped by competing epistemological and cultural frameworks. These frameworks are encoded in the ways in which information is presented, knowledge is talked about, and analogies are drawn; they are also apparent in the connections that cannot be made. Forms of resistance to literacy practices reflect not only linguistic ideologies but also broader social and historical forces. Therefore it is useful to situate this work within current ethnohistorical accounts of competing language ideologies that have played a role in shaping colonial and missionary encounters (Cohn 1985; Comaroff and Comaroff 1991; Fabian 1986; Mignolo 1992; Rafael 1988). There is a persistent problem, however, in documenting social and linguistic changes accompanied by literacy introduced as part of missionization: Scholars must rely on historical materials, most of it written by missionaries themselves, in order to reconstruct what types of communicative events constituted missionizing activities and how linguistic practices and views of the world might have shifted as a result of that contact. Most ethnohistorical studies therefore have focused on the missionaries' views, since little documentation exists from the perspective of those missionized.

Mission linguists in Papua New Guinea have provided some insights into linguistic issues that arise during missionization, for example, by focusing on how to achieve culturally appropriate Bible translations (e.g., Mundhenk 1990). Renck's (1990) study of how Lutherans implanted the Christian message in Yagaria society from the 1940s to the 1980s by means of the local languages analyzes the linguistic consequences of missionization. Viewing culture change resulting from missionization as inevitable, Renck proposes that language change (lexical innovation, semantic extension, borrowing) is one way a society copes with new information, though he argues that proclaiming the gospel in the vernacular does preserve Papua New Guinea's linguistic diversity.[5]

Several excellent studies (Besnier 1995; Burridge 1995; Gewertz and Errington 1991; Kulick and Stroud 1990; Lindstrom 1990) detail how particular societies and individuals in Papua New Guinea and other parts of the Pacific use literacy for their own political and social ends, demonstrating that the intentions of those introducing literacy and those receiving it have often been at odds. These studies address literacy in terms of local social organization, power relations, and gender issues; however, there has yet to be an ethnographic study that examines *how* literacy is introduced and enters into a society through texts and language practices as part of Christian missionization. We have little direct knowledge of how literacy practices develop over time from a local perspective, in large part due to the historical depth of Christianity in most places. For example, Besnier (1995:172–76) discusses Nukulaelae literacy practices as an example of "incipient literacy," in that reading and writing are "recent innovations, having been brought in just a little over a century ago" (1995:172). In spite of the fact that Besnier was able to reconstruct from historical documents the mission attitudes and language inputs to literacy, we do not know the processes and practices that constituted its introduction and early impact.

Furthermore, little is known about how technologies and vocabularies of literacy and literacy practices are introduced, developed, changed, or contested in a particular setting. Who does it, for what purpose, and with what ideological and linguistic orientations? In writing a language that previously has had no script, numerous practical as well as political problems must be solved. For example, in an area with extensive dialect variation, which dialect will be chosen for the phonemic analysis that would form the basis of the orthography? Orthographies are never neutral in terms of their logic (etymological or phonemic), as evidenced in the case of creole language debates (Ludwig 1989; Schieffelin and Doucet 1994) and many others (e.g., Collins 1998b). Similarly, the question of which dialect is chosen (often associated with a group, an area, or a set of villages) may be informed by social, political, or linguistic reasons or may be the result of pure accident—a matter, for example, of where the missionary or linguist ended up.

LOCATING IDEAS ABOUT LITERACY AND CHRISTIANITY IN A GRAMMATICAL SKETCH

After 1970 a concern echoed throughout Papua New Guinea that

"Papua New Guineans had to be Christians and live according to the Word of God within their own culture and not as brown-skinned Europeans. And it was argued that to train people to fit into their own culture could best be done within the framework of their own languages" (Neuendorf and Taylor 1977:423).

The APCM, which carried out the majority of its Papua New Guinea work in the Western and Southern Highlands Provinces, had a long-standing policy of working in vernacular languages and developing vernacular literacy. This explicitly went against the German and Australian colonial governments which, for the most part, promoted the colonial languages and opposed education in vernacular languages.[6] From the outset, missionary policy "in addition to 'evangelisation and education of the national people' was the translation of the Holy Scriptures into their mother tongue, the analysis of the local language, and the promotion of vernacular literacy were early priorities in each area" (J. Rule 1977:387–88). The APCM worked with groups that had little or no government contact, and they described the difficulties of their task: "Men who by force of circumstances were continually at war and whose central interest in life was head-hunting were not the ideal subjects for a sedentary and seemingly tame pursuit like vernacular literacy" (J. Rule 1977:388). Vernacular literacy, however, was explicitly viewed as integral to other evangelical activities.

Murray Rule, an experienced field linguist, Bible translator, and linguistic consultant to the APCM, emphasized that vernacular literacy had several functions relevant to the cultural as well as linguistic lives of those being missionized. He describes "seeing children become fluent readers and writers in their own language...thus helping to counteract their prevalent tendency to regard their tribal languages as 'bush' languages, and of little value in education" and observes, "as they write up the legends and folklore of their tribes, so these are being preserved" (W. M. Rule 1977a:1342). His goal was for local people to read "educational books, story books and the full New Testament," and he saw the use of the vernacular as critical for the "development of strong local churches, and local pastors with excellent grounding in the Christian faith" (1977a:1342). Rule described the importance of the vernacular for the mission in terms of his own activities. He was committed to working on grammatical descriptions "via the mother tongue believing it to be 'the shrine of the people's soul'" (1977a:1341). For Rule and his wife and coworker, Joan, this attention to the vernacular enabled them to "proclaim the Good News of the Christian Gospel to the people in their own languages" (Rule 1977a:1341).[7]

Murray Rule went to Bosavi in 1964 as part of the first missionary expedition there. Accompanied by fellow missionary Dick Donaldson, a large numbers of carriers, and Papuan Evangelists including Foi and Fasu speakers, he spent approximately five months in the area. The goal was to build an airstrip, a prerequisite for establishing a new mission station. The construction of an airstrip, the enormous influx of money and goods, and the experience of hearing God's word through Papuan pastors had a powerful impact on the Kaluli and other groups in the area (Schieffelin and Crittenden 1991:265–66).

While Donaldson organized the building of the airstrip, Rule established "schooling" in the language as another type of compensated labor. He collected linguistic material by interpretation from Fasu speakers via Police Motu, a Papuan lingua franca, and also from Huli, which he had analyzed previously (Rule 1964:1). But he eventually worked with two young Kaluli men, recording conversations directly onto paper and, to a lesser extent, on audiotape. His 1964 phonological and grammatical sketch of Kaluli was prepared to help the Australian missionaries who would run the Bosavi mission station to learn the language and translate the Bible.[8]

The grammatical sketch contains many of Rule's own ideas concerning literacy, Christianity, and other Western practices not yet present in Bosavi. These were simply slipped into the linguistic materials and treated as if they had always been there, or at least belonged there. Totally naturalized through Kaluli orthography and example sentences illustrating Kaluli morphology and syntax, there is nothing to distinguish what Kaluli were saying or doing at that time from what an Australian missionary linguist thought were good sentences illustrating linguistic structures. Consequently, anyone reading Rule's sketch would be apt to form the false impression that certain concepts, words, ideas, and activities were part of the Kaluli cultural and linguistic vocabulary in the mid-1960s, even though they were not.

For example, in a list of verbs, Rule included *momademA*,[9] glossed as 'write'. Since Kaluli were not literate at the time, this word obviously does not describe an activity that Kaluli habitually did. Example sentences illustrating grammatical points, for example, _mo:fo:so mogai momada:lo:biki halo:l_ ('because I wrote badly, I'm rubbing it out'),[10] reiterate Rule's literacy activities while introducing other literacy-related vocabulary: _mo:fos_ ('paper', from _mo:_ ['base', 'reason'], + _fo:s_ ['leaf']), _bene_ ('pen'), presumably based on English (Tok Pisin _ingpen_). Some words directly imported into Bosavi the phonological shape of Tok Pisin, and their Kaluli spelling had the effect of repidginizing them.[11] Rule used _buka_ ('book', Tok Pisin _buk_) and _wa:ilisi_ ('wireless radio', Tok Pisin _wailis_), both of which added final vowels to the Tok Pisin and were used in sentences with Kaluli morphology. The mission's introduction of books and wireless radios into the area, and their words for them with Kaluli morphology, made both these words and their referents instantly available as new Kaluli cultural vocabulary.

Rule coined the verb _sugulula:ma_ ('do school', Tok Pisin _skul_ + _a:la:ma_ ['do/say like that']) to describe his activity of working with speakers on the language. Kaluli use _walama_ ('show, instruct') or _wala sama_ ('show, instruct + say'); Rule lists _walama_ in his verb lists (glossed as 'teach, show'), but _sugulula:ma_ introduced a different concept. Although some of Rule's innovations have endured, such as _sugulula:ma_ and _hama_, glossed as 'erase' from 'rub out', others were not adopted. _Momadema_ ('write'), for example, was not accepted by Kaluli speakers. Local usage for this verb was and continues to be 'paint up or decorate oneself or a drum'.[12] At least as early as 1972, Kaluli themselves used _sasalima_ for write, meaning 'decorate, etch, mark'.[13] This new usage is found in the phrase _mo:fo:s sa:sa:lo:_ meaning 'letter' or 'something with print' as a noun phrase or 'someone wrote a letter' as an object-plus-verb utterance. (In spoken Kaluli, stress would disambiguate these meanings.)

The connection between linguistic activities and a religious agenda was very explicit during Rule's visit, and this too is evident in the grammatical sketch. Another introduced verb, _guliguli lan_[14] (glossed as 'pray'), is used in numerous illustrative sentences that also introduce _Gode_ ('God') and _A:dam_ ('Adam') to the Kaluli vocabulary. Sentences with religious messages or paraphrases from the Bible abound. Question-and-answer sequences model exchanges that the mission was there to achieve, such as, _ho:len tabo ge Godemo:wo: guliguli_ *lano:?* ('Do you [singular] pray to God everyday?') *A:! ne ho:len tabo guligulilan* ('Yes I pray every day'). Religious instructions illustrate switch reference structures; the morphology of same-subject, sequential action is shown by Old Testament verses translated into Kaluli. These sentences written in Kaluli appear as part of the Kaluli language alongside common utterances also used as illustrative sentences such as *da: wema: ola:bi* ('shoot it with that bow') and *ne mayab* ('I am hungry').

Finally, there are sentences about buying goods, an activity promoted through the establishment of a mission store where desired items—at that time cloth, beads, and tinned fish—could be purchased in exchange for the money earned for labor, for example, *helebe so:go: Mista Danisiniya: igesa kelilia:ibele?* ('When will Mr. Donaldson sell calico?'). Thus, as early as 1964, new sentences, ones that had not been uttered by Kaluli in any pre-mission context, began to register concerns about new goods, new ideas, and new moral values. It would not be long before such sentences entered the oral, vernacular Kaluli cultural vocabulary as well.

Anthropologists and missionaries alike used Rule's linguistic work to learn the language, but the two groups had very different ideas about how the language would be used and its relationship to local culture and cultural practices. For the anthropologists, language and culture were integrally linked symbolic systems used to index local aesthetics, a sense of place, social memory, and cultural identity. For the missionaries, the vernacular could be separated from cultural practices and used quite independently. It could be expanded, contracted, and changed in myriad ways, and it could express ideas that were foreign, while still being considered "the same" language. It had one function: effective evangelization.

CREATING THE LITERACY PRIMERS

Before the Bosavi mission station was established in 1970, there was little in the way of text or pictorial representation circulating among Kaluli people.[15] With the opening of the primary school in 1971, the fundamentalist missionaries introduced literacy and a view of literacy that emphasized reading over writing—a pattern that continues for many today, with the Tok Pisin Bible one of the few texts available in the Bosavi area. Reading was taught both to elementary-age school children at the mission station and to adults, using the syllable method, through a series of literacy primers produced by Norma Briggs. The orthographic conventions used in the literacy materials were based on W. M. Rule's (1964) alphabet. There was little linguistic consistency in the adoption of Rule's orthography, however, and little attention was paid to the morphological or grammatical analyses that he had provided and that could have made word boundaries and morpheme meanings consistent. There are several reasons for this. Those responsible for the local production of the primers had no linguistic training, and at the time these materials were produced Norma Briggs spoke a somewhat limited version of the vernacular. Especially in the first years of their mission work, the Briggses relied on Tok Pisin to communicate with their young male assistants, many of whom were the first to be trained as pastors and aid-post orderlies and for other mission-related positions. Additionally, education was not the mission's only focus; a clinic, a store, and numerous other projects competed for Norma Briggs's attention.

The mission produced a total of five primers, approximately one per year, with increasingly complex linguistic structures. The first appeared in 1972 and introduced the Kaluli alphabet of twenty phonemes.[16] Each page contained one letter and usually two pictures, simple line drawings of common animals, objects, and actions, with single-word labels. Rule's Kaluli alphabet was introduced in no particular order, and the objects pictured contained the selected sound/letter in initial, medial, or final position, without logical sequence.

The titles themselves indicate a linguistic mix. The first two in the series were titled in English, Kaluli Primer Book 1 and 2, while the third through fifth books had code-mixed titles, *Kaluli To* Book 3/Book 4/Book 5, composed of a Kaluli phrase *(Kaluli To* ['Kaluli language']), an English word (Book), and an Arabic numeral. The words "primer" and "book" are perhaps the first English words to be used in written materials for local consumption. Kaluli orthography does not employ /p/ or /r/, and the double vowel (oo) would be difficult to decode if reading the title. Clearly, the details of how the language was phonologically represented were not a priority.

The texts in Kaluli Primer Book 2 and *Kaluli To* Book 3 consist of simple stories with locally named characters and were illustrated with line drawings by Norma Briggs. According to J. Rule (1977:390), the literacy materials draw on "key words of basic interest in the culture and, from these foci build up into culturally relevant stories... [C]hoice of words which contain both the phonemes of most frequent occurrence and also basic interest and usability in story material has been crucial and...the criterion for choosing material has been that what is of interest to the adult male is also of interest to young people and to women, and for this reason, the hunting of pigs, and cassowaries, the building of houses and canoes, adventurous, eventful trading trips, pig feasts and singings, visits by plane to large (comparatively!) centers, have featured largely in the story content, with gardening, fishing, treatment of sickness, and other relevant everyday activities also having a place." The first five Kaluli primers featured gardening, hunting, and house building but lacked any mention of trading trips, pig feasts, and ceremonial singsings that were viewed by the mission as counter to Christian life (see E. L. Schieffelin 1978).

From a linguistic perspective, the orthography is inconsistent, resulting in decoding problems as well as semantic ambiguities in interpreting the meanings of sentences for Kaluli readers. Word and morpheme boundaries are also variably marked, making decoding difficult. Furthermore, the syntax is highly simplified, and except for imperatives, uses only subject-object-verb word order in simple declarative present-tense sentences without switch reference, clause chaining, or other features of adult syntax.[17] These primers are the Kaluli equivalent (or translation) of the "See Spot run!" readers, with pseudosentences such as *Ayo: bo:ba. Ayo: alan* ('Look at the house. The house is big'). In addition, the extensive use of third-person pronouns and subject-object-verb constituent sentences gives the syntax a foreign, definitely anglicized, pidginized, or "baby talk" feel. It is not until Book 4 that occasional past-tense and serial verb constructions are added. Sentences that introduce basic vocabulary, including personal names, kin terms, and pronouns, are repetitious in their syntactic form. Much of the reported speech would never have been spoken as it is represented, even by very young children. Although possibly useful for teaching literacy, the sentences still strike Kaluli speakers as *ko:li* ('odd and different').

The transformation of spoken Kaluli to a written version raises

Ami kaluwo: modo. yab.

Ko:suwo: a:la: yab.

Ka:na:ka kaisaleyo: tagilab

Aya nai ha:nab.

18

Ka na:ka kaluwo: Ami kaluwo:

ba:da:sege motagilab.

Ami kaluwo: ma:no: kililiyab.

Siabuluwo:, silemo:, aleko:,

yuno: o:liya: kililiyab.

19

FIGURE 8.1

English gloss: *Many army men come. Two planes come. Kanaka women are afraid. They run away to the longhouse. When the Kanaka men see the army men they are not afraid. Army men buy sweet potato, breadfruit, cabbage, and pitpit. (From* Kaluli To *Book 4 [© Asian Pacific Christian Mission 1980].)*

many interesting linguistic issues in terms of morphology, lexicon, syntax, and genre. My focus here, however, is on how particular ideas and labels become attached to persons and their cultural practices through these literacy primers in spite of the fact that they are composed of simple story lines and use unsophisticated or pidginized linguistic structures. The words do not make sense alone; they are supported by graphic and, in later literacy materials, photographic images. Although the language as written was not standardized, the labels and ideas pervasive in these texts are part of another type of standardization process—a codification or regimentation of identities that is based on cultural stereotyping and necessary for the narrative of religious transformation and conversion.

For example, the narratives in Primer 2 and Books 3 to 5 depict everyday subsistence activities that a Kaluli family would carry out in the mid-1970s. Father and son go hunting; women engage in subsistence activities. In Books 4 and 5, however, an element of change is introduced, with the dramatic moment marked by a break in the narrative: suddenly men hear airplanes, which land at the mission station.

This dramatic moment in fact marks a major activity for men at this time (1974–77), hanging around the mission station, while women carried out their usual domestic and subsistence activities. The inclusion of new activities provides an opportunity to introduce new ideas into the discursive space of literacy instruction, ideas that were being talked about as mission planes landed and things were changing.

One of the most striking features in the primers is how Kaluli people are named. In previous literacy materials, Kaluli are referred to by personal names or kin terms. Although several local terms were available to designate a group (for example, Bosavi, Kaluli, or *amisen* ['village'] people), the literacy texts do not use them. Instead, in Book 4 (which appeared in 1975), Kaluli people were referred to as *ka:na:ka,* a term from the Tok Pisin *kanaka* that means 'native, nonindentured person' but has long had a derogatory connotation of 'uncivilized, backward'. The labeling occurs in the context of Kaluli encounters with outsiders, the Papua New Guinean nationals who are part of the army and who visited for survey work and other activities (see fig. 8.1). It was not used by Kaluli in the 1970s to refer to themselves or anyone else, but those who knew any Tok Pisin at all knew the pejorative load of this word.[18]

In the use of this pejorative term in Book 4, Kaluli would have seen a reclassification of themselves from their status as individual Kaluli persons to undifferentiated members of a stigmatized group, one that was backward and in need of civilizing. In reading aloud, as was the local practice, they would be repeatedly referring to themselves in this derogatory manner. This label, which encodes a negative relationship to modernity and progress and situates Kaluli as backward, was introduced as part of the new ideas that literacy conveyed.

Under conditions of rapid social change, every language choice is a social choice that has critical links to the active construction of culture. The missionaries were familiar with the term *kanaka* from their experience in Papua New Guinea, where it was used in a derogatory manner both as address and reference on plantations and in urban settings. Whether or not it was a conscious move on the part of the mission cannot be determined; the point is that this term entered into a discursive space that had a particular directionality and focus. Kaluli people today remember that the word *kanaka* was introduced into their vocabulary at this time and in this way.

The vernacular literacy materials display many cultural, linguistic, and ideological continuities with Rule's 1964 grammatical sketch. They are all part and parcel of the same missionizing effort to transform persons. Although the first five primers make no explicit mention of Christianity, they include clear social change themes—for example, doing school, getting new goods such as soap and clothing, and returning to the village to get married after doing outside work—that are identical to Christian ones, particularly before there was the kind of government presence that linked these activities to becoming Papua New Guinean. Until the late 1970s, becoming a "new" Kaluli was presented as becoming a Christian man much more than becoming a Papua New Guinean.[19] Starting with the first primers, Kaluli social identities were (re)formulated, (re)presented, and (re)constructed in distinctive cultural and gendered ways, and the reading process elicited collaboration in a changing cultural and moral order.

These vernacular literacy primers are not neutral, nor do they have one function. They are used to introduce Kaluli to particular Western ways as well as to instruct them in basic literacy skills. Produced collaboratively by missionaries and missionized Kaluli who became active participants in the evangelical project, they portray conflicts between traditional Kaluli and "modern" practices (health, household arrangements, and so forth) as moral dilemmas with economic overtones.

By the mid-1970s it had become clear that mission activities were having a strong impact in Kaluli society. Despite the relatively small size of the average Kaluli village (approximately eighty people) and the low population of the area, there were differences in the ways people positioned themselves socially in terms of their participation in Christian activities (B. B. Schieffelin 1990). Missionization not only changed the social organization and material possessions of some families; it also changed the ways individuals talked about and imagined themselves. By 1975 Kaluli men had started leading church services. Reading aloud, syllable by syllable, from the Tok Pisin Bible, they translated passages orally into Kaluli during sermons. Vernacular literacy primers were sold for adult literacy instruction at the mission as well as in villages, and most families bought them. Local villages were divided into Christian and non-Christian living space.

Throughout the 1970s children attending the mission school

received literacy instruction, but very few became functionally literate in Kaluli. By 1973 the school was staffed exclusively by Papua New Guinean nationals, all Christians who were trained by the mission; none of them spoke the local language, and so they used Tok Pisin and English in accordance with the government policy. In addition, except for the primers, there was nothing to read in Kaluli. A handful of young men with various levels of elementary education spent time around the mission, spoke some Tok Pisin, and had received training in vernacular literacy classes held at the mission and sometimes in the villages; all were Christians.[20] Classes in vernacular literacy were taught by Christian Kaluli men and were occasions where a great deal of talk was generated; often the talk was more about religion than reading. For these teachers, the classes were social opportunities to have an audience, convey ideas, and be authoritative. Although many village people purchased the literacy booklets for a nominal fee, few developed more than rudimentary vernacular reading skills because adult literacy was not taught on a regular basis. In a way, it did not really matter if people learned to read; in the classes, they participated in guided discussions about who they had been and who they were going to become.

I see these as formative moments in representation and look to the sites of production in talk and texts. In contact situations, the constitution of situations, new types of audiences, classrooms, and congregations are telling. They are the contexts in which people are named, referred to, or represented in new ways.

Thus far the discussion has focused on the ways in which texts—a grammatical sketch and vernacular literacy materials—bring new cultural and linguistic vocabularies to a society. But these materials were not used as private texts to be read silently or alone. In family settings, primers or Bible passages were always read aloud, syllable by syllable, in unison with others.[21] Most of the time they were part of lessons or Bible classes that were oral and interactive, a context for correction and interpretation as well as innovation. The next sections examine an important set of linguistic innovations and practices in the mid-1980s that are deeply tied to Kaluli ideas about language. These practices highlight the active role Kaluli played in the development and shaping of literacy events, practices which gave significance to the texts.

A VOCABULARY FOR THE PRACTICES OF LITERACY

Language ideologies pertaining to literacy practices are often implicit, unarticulated, or out of awareness. Thus, to understand Kaluli ideas about literacy, one needs to examine what Kaluli do and say when they read and discuss texts.[22]

Critical to institutionalizing a new genre or activity, such as literacy, is the creation of a vocabulary for talking about doing it. For Kaluli, the development of metalinguistic terminology for literacy practices draws from three languages: English, Tok Pisin, and Kaluli. A few examples illustrate how Kaluli language ideologies permeate the vocabulary used in the mid-1980s and how local ideas about orality get entangled with Kaluli and Western ideas about print, spelling and reading, and understanding.

Kaluli have drawn on many linguistic processes in the construction of these new ways of talking. The words for reading and writing are the result of semantic expansions of Kaluli verbs. For example, the verb *agelema* ('count') was extended to 'reading' because when Kaluli first saw people looking at books, they thought they were counting the pages. The term is used today for both activities. *Sama agelema* ('read aloud', *sama* ['speak'] + *agalema* ['read']) is used in lessons to emphasize the oral, speaking nature of reading. The verb *bo:ba* ('look, see') is used to orient the reader to the book or page itself. And, as discussed above, the verb *sa:sa:lima* was adopted to refer to writing, an extension of its original meaning, 'to mark or etch' (with fine lines).

Both English and Tok Pisin contributed new vocabulary used in the lessons. Although English words such as "page," "spelling," "word," and "heading" were never used with Kaluli morphology, they were frequently borrowed within a Kaluli utterance or phrase, as in the following quote in which Kulu Fuale tells the fifth-grade class he is teaching his assessment of what Steve Feld and I know about Kaluli spelling:[23]

> 89) *nililo:* word we spelling *alano: eyo: mada dinafa ka asulab*
> our words here they really know a lot about the spelling

Tok Pisin words, for example, *buk* ('book'), *piksa* ('picture'), *lidisi* ('literacy'), *leson* ('lesson'), *namba* ('number'), and the numerals themselves—*wan, tu, tri, foa,* and so on—are used within the same utterance

with English and Kaluli. Kulu as well as the students often used a combination of these words, but only the Tok Pisin words received Kaluli
morphology, as in line 20. In lines 19 and 20, Kulu is trying to coordi-
nate the class to read on page three:

19)   page <u>tri</u> *a:na agelema:niki*
        on page three we will read

20)   page <u>tri</u>*yo: ba:ba:yo:?*
        do you see page three?

In this sequence, and throughout Kulu Fuale's lessons, Kaluli
numbers are not used in classroom contexts. As early as 1975 they
tended not to be used by younger people in situations of counting,
especially when counting introduced objects or items up to ten.[24] Tok
Pisin numerals are used exclusively to refer to page numbers and Bible
chapters and verses, or in counting to achieve a coordinated start for
singing hymns or reading, as in the example below:[25]

27)   *taminamilo: o:deyo: agela:bi* <u>wan tu</u>
        read the first part, one two
        (class reads in "unison," syllable by syllable)

Kaluli also compounded words from two languages to create new
words. The word *spellingmo:* ('syllable') is one example, composed of
the English 'spelling' and the Kaluli *mo:* ('base, reason'). *Spellingmo:* is
an important term, since reading was taught by the syllable method
(consonant-vowel or vowel), and sounds are referred to by their syllabic
rendering. Thus the syllable is the sound unit, the basis or reason for
spelling, and the sound was salient, as reading was always done aloud,
syllable by syllable.

In his lessons, Kulu talked about spelling in two ways. The first
referred to the general process and problems of spelling and to the text
itself, how the syllables were written, using the verbs 'do' as in *ha:lu ko:li
dimido:* ('done a little differently'), 'put down' as in *hala difa:* ('incorrectly put'), and 'written', as in *hala sa:sa:ido:lo:b* ('incorrectly written').
He is referring to the way the words were inscribed, their graphic representations, and how they looked, using the evidential *-lo:b* to mark the
visual nature of these graphic forms, their incorrectness being visually
obvious.

The second way referred to the specific readings or sayings of words, how the *spellingmo:* sounded when said. For example, after the class read a phrase aloud, Kulu frequently asked *to a:no: o:li salaba?* ('are these words said right?'), with the sense 'do these words sound all right?', and waited for the class to respond:

114) *a:no: o:sa:ma:niliki* **to a:no: o:li salaba?**
      and before talking about what it says, **are the words
      said all right?**

115) [Class] *o:li*
      all right

Kulu used the verb *sama* ('say, speak' in the sense of 'sound'). On numerous occasions when the class could sound out a word that made no sense, Kulu attributed it to incorrect spelling, referring to the missionary's incomplete knowledge of the language. He instructed the class on how to proceed:

106) *hala na ko:lo: taminamiyo: giyo: gimo:wo: aba siyo: ko:lo:
      a:ma: dimada ko:lo: a:la: agela:bi sa:lab aum*
      it's incorrect, I already told you about what he did, so
      you read it with the spelling like that

107) *"amisa:n" sama* (in the text)
      say 'village'

The class reads the text,

    amisa:n sawagalen o:liye. Ko:sega awagele
    with village children. But on Monday

but all struggle with the word *awagele* and cannot get beyond it. It is not the word for Monday, which is *agela:*, and the class is confused because Kulu himself had read it as *awagele,* which makes no sense. This is Kulu's solution:

    *a:no: o:bo:lo:bo:? "awagel nulu a:no:" to a:no: ha:lu o:li
    salaba?*

108) what is it [evidential]? 'on Monday night' are
      those words said a little all right?

109) [Class] *o:li salab*

it's said all right

110)   [Student] *mo: o:li*

not all right

111)   [KF] *mo: o:li salab a:la: asulo: mo:wo:*

not said all right he knew why

112)   *ha:lu dinafalo: mo:sa:sa:ido: ko:lo: tamina sa:sa:ido: ko:lo:*

it's a little not well written because it was written before

113)   *sama "a:no:"*

say 'it'

Telling the class to "read it with the spelling like that" (line 106), Kulu says the word, instructing the class to "say it," thus making it unnecessary for them to decode it. He uses a Kaluli language socialization strategy (lines 107 and 113) identical to one that caregivers use with young children (Schieffelin 1990:75–111). This literacy lesson, a language socialization context, conveys the idea that words can be read and understood even if the spelling, or the word, is incorrect. Once uttered, the printed syllables become transformed, heard and evaluated in a different way. Kulu never asks if the words are written properly, only if they sound all right, and students rarely say that something is not right with the text. They have been taught that if it is written, it is always right, that it speaks the truth with authority. This is especially the case when the source is mission related.

In addition to developing expressions for talking about reading, syllables, and books, Kaluli developed ways to refer to the spatial dimensions of the text and the page. A vocabulary was required that could orient readers to specific parts of the page, for example, *tamina* ('first in a list, line') to refer to the first part, so all the students could start at the same place and read in a coordinated manner. Kulu consistently used Kaluli spatial terms such as *wa:l* ('top') to refer to the top of the page and *ha:g* ('underneath, below') to refer to parts below.

27)   ***wa:la*** *a:no: o:bo:lo:bo:?* ***taminamilo:*** *o:deyo: agela:bi* <u>wan tu</u>

what is it (evid) **on the top** (of the page)? read the **first part,** one two

28)   *ha:ga a:no: agela:bi*
       what's **underneath,** read

Wa:l, whose customary spatial usage referred to surfaces and tops of horizontal objects, was extended to mean 'front' or 'cover', where Kulu was directing the class to look, as in the example below:

39)   *wa:la buko: a:no: bo:ba **wa:la wa:lamilo:** a:no: bo:ba*
       look **on the front** of the book, **on the front,** look **on the front** [drawing of mosquito on cover]

In addition to its spatial meaning, *ha:g* was also used in its metalinguistic sense of the underlying meaning of the message of the text, referring to *bale to* ('turned over words'). *Ha:g* was deployed as a way to guide interpretive work as well as to guide the reader to a place on the page:

210)   *o: **ha:gamilo:wo:** no wilo: salabo: Hamuleya:lo: salabo:*
       ***wa:l wenamilo:wo:** o: ho:bo:kilo:wo:mo:lo:bo:?*
       and the **meaning** and what does this say, what Hamule says, **on top,** to what is it directed (evid)?

Locative and spatial verbs and other constructions were also drafted for this purpose; for example, *tiya: fok* ('came down space') referred to the paragraph indentations. A great deal of attention was paid to orienting students to the page. Kulu frequently reminded the class to "hold the book carefully," "look at it," using Kaluli imperatives. Using Kaluli words and expressions in new ways, he verbally coordinated the reading of the text with selective borrowings from English and Tok Pisin. It is not surprising that Kaluli spatial terms were used rather than those in Tok Pisin, as the spatial lexicon of Kaluli is rich and important across genres.

The social organization of talk and the methods for displaying and acknowledging ideas drew from classroom pedagogy introduced by the mission (Schieffelin 1996:445), but the ways of thinking and speaking about language and talk were clearly marked by a Kaluli sensibility. Saying the words right was a prerequisite for understanding them, although they did not have to be spelled correctly. In the next section, we shift the focus from the sound-graphic relationship to the referential content of the text. Syllables do or do not sound all right, but it is the books that do the speaking; what they say is always correct, and what they are said to say comes to matter a great deal.

WHAT BOOKS SAY AND WHAT KALULI DO WITH BOOKS

Kaluli people have always been concerned with the source and truth of what they know. They have well-elaborated ideas of how truth is constituted, proved, and linguistically marked.[26] Through direct experience, the spoken word, and face-to-face interaction, cultural knowledge was orally represented; authority and responsibility could be argued, and often were. At a particular point in Kaluli history, however, written texts were granted authority as Kaluli constructed linguistic means for entitling texts and making them authentic and authoritative sources of factual knowledge. These linguistic changes were a notable response to missionization and underscore Kaluli concern with the sources and nature of knowledge and truth (B. B. Schieffelin 1996). Through the mid-1970s and into the 1980s, missionaries and those Kaluli who had accepted their views introduced into Kaluli society new ideas about the world through literacy lessons and sermons—contexts in which new moral discourses could be based on what books said and that were integral to transforming Kaluli society into a Christian one.

Literacy booklets become speaking texts through a number of morphological and lexical means. The lesson based on the booklet on malaria prevention, *Hamule e walaf bo:lo:* ('Hamule got sick'), contains multiple examples of how this was accomplished. The booklet tells the story of a young Kaluli boy who comes down with malaria. His father takes him to the mission doctor when his mother refuses to do so. The father receives information about the cause of malaria and its treatment; the child is treated and recovers. The story provides a context for moral evaluation of traditional Kaluli views of malaria and its treatment, in contrast to those of Western medicine; it also focuses on gender roles in terms of tradition and modernity. In talking about the information in this booklet, Kulu contrasts the source and manner of how things were known in the past—"what our fathers (knew) before"—with how things will be known now. He says to his class:

13)   *mo:lu nili doima:yo: ko:sega o:go: dinafa asulab **buko:***
        wema: walasalab
        before our fathers (ergative) but now we really know
        this book (ergative) shows/instructs

14)   *a:la:fo: ko:lo: **niliyo: buko: wena ba:da:sa:ga:***
        therefore **when we look at this book**

15)   *tif s/c taminamiyo: niyo: mo:asulo: ko:sega no niyo: nulu*
        alifo: alifo:labamiyo: kiso:wa:lo: nanog diabo: we
        aungabo:lo:do: a:la:bo:
        later [self-correction] before we did not know but
        when we are sleeping at night the work mosquitoes
        do is like this we now know

16)   ***buko: wenamilo: to salab we da:da:sa:ga: asuluma:niki***
        listening to what the words in this book say makes us
        know/understand

Kulu explains *buko: wema: walasalab* ('this book shows/instructs'). Note that "this book" is marked with an ergative/instrumental case marker, *buko: wema:,* it is the agent (or instrument) that instructs and shows (*wala sama,* 'show and speak'), and it is by looking at the book and listening to what the words in the book say that understanding or knowledge is obtained. The book is represented as speaking, as transmitting knowledge orally. When instructed to read, students are told to take the information by listening (*dabuma,* 'listen, hear'), which is the only way understanding can occur.

When Kulu refers to, elicits, or wants the class to focus on the content of what is written, he shifts to verbs and evidentials that mark speaking or sounding. For example, he uses a range of forms for the verbs *a:la:ma* ('say like that') and *sama* ('speak/say') to substantiate what he claims is in the text, as well as to give authority to the text, a verbal, spoken authority, an authority that can be listened to. He extends this authority to himself at the same time:

52)   *mada a:la:sa:ga: kalu nowo: walaf bo:lo:wamiyo: kalu*
        nowo: walaf ba:labamiyo: o: walafdo: a:na diya:sa:ga:
        *a:la:sa:ga: no ami dimianka: **a:la: salabka: wema:***
        really after one man gets sick, another man gets sick,
        (the mosquito) takes from the sick one and then

> gives it (malaria) to another man **it really says like
> that, this one does** (book, ergative)

53)   *walafdo: a:na diya:sa:ga: nowa dimianka:* **a:la: salab**
       walafdo: a:no: ho:bo:wo: wasuliya:sa:ga: nowa iliga:felai
       so:lo:lka: e mulumulo: a hononamilo: walaf ege owami
       a:na wa:ta:sa:ga: kalu amiyo: o:lanka:
       having taken from a sick one, it really gives to
       another **it says**, after mixing the blood of the sick
       one it sends (the sickness) to many **I'm really saying**,
       in the sickhouse over there, after drawing the sick-
       ness in the needle (stinger), (mosquito) really
       shoots (injects) a man

Kulu repeatedly emphasizes how the book (always marked with an ergative case marker) "speaks," "instructs," and "really says it well" to locate the source of his assertions about mosquitoes and disease. In addition he frequently adds *so:lo:ka:* ('I'm really saying'), combining a range of emphatic markers and other lexical items including *mada* ('really'), *hede* ('truly') with their own emphatics to intensify and emphasize his own authoritativeness. In a style almost identical to the style of sermons, Kulu's assertions are repeated throughout the lesson and are not to be discussed or challenged.

62)   *a:la:fo: ko:lo: o: walaf mo: a:no: o:go:* **buko: wema:** *iliki*
       nimo: **walasalab** *a:no:*
       therefore the sickness's beginning/cause now hav-
       ing **this book (erg) instructs** us about that
63)   *mo:wo: mada dinafa do:do:l*
       I really hear/understand the cause well
64)   *a:la:fo: ko:lo: ege buko:* **lidisi buko:** *wenami* **wema:yo:**
       mada nafa salab
       therefore uh [hesitation word] book, **in this literacy
       book this it (erg) really says it well**

Books become the source of understanding because they can be heard, and it is through hearing that understanding occurs. A printed word can be sounded, spoken; and to sound it, speak it, is to remember it. Memory is not graphic. Only through voicing does a text become a

circulable sign, discourse in the sense of repeatable, replicable, trans-
mutable material. For Kaluli, the materiality is oral.[27] This is Kaluli language ideology. When Kulu asserts, "I hear/understand the reason
from the book" and "We are really hearing new words spoken," and
reminds the class to think about and remember that what they are hearing is new, he is simply extending the paradigm to a new source of
information, retaining the verbal mode of knowing and remembering.

At the same time that Kaluli modes of knowing through speaking
are reflected through one set of practices, a contradictory, introduced
way of knowing through speaking is expressed through the social organization of talk. Thus throughout the lesson, and in all such activities
involving texts, we see the agency of both missionized and missionizers,
expressed at different levels of the language, coexisting:

68) *a:sa:ga: Papua Nugini us wenamiyo: taminamiyo:*
     asula:leno:? gimo: **a:dabu bo:do:lka: giliyo: sama**
     asula:leno:? *kiso:wa:yo: a:la: nanog diabami walafo:lo:*
     kalu amiyo: a:la: kaluka:isale amiyo: a:la: balabo:lo:b
     a:la:bo:
     in the Papua New Guinea interior here did we know
     this before? **I'm asking you all again, you all say it** did
     we know this before? that it was the mosquitoes, work
     that made men sick, men and women too we now
     know

69) [Class] *mo:asula:len*
     we didn't know

70) [KF] *mo:asula:len hede salab*
     we didn't know, that's truthfully said

71) *mo:asula:lenka: a:la: salab ko:lo: o: niliyo: hedele ho:gi to*
     salabo:lo:do: a:la: asula:sa:ga: dinafa asuluma:niki
     we didn't really know it says like that, we are really
     hearing new words spoken we now know after think-
     ing about them we will understand

This mode of achieving understanding is different from the ways
Kaluli usually learn: by listening to what many others say, arguing with
them, watching them, and being instructed while participating. What is
striking throughout the lesson is the importance of everyone partici-

pating in the same coordinated way, registering consensus by saying the words, and answering questions as a group with the one right answer. The social organization of talk in these lessons is not traditional Kaluli in several respects. For one, unison, which is the goal in this context, is not heard in traditional sound/song/music making activities (Feld 1988:82). Rather, the preferred sound aesthetic for Kaluli is *dulugu ganalan* ('lift-up-over-sounding'), a "non-hierarchical yet synchronous, layered, fluid group action" (Feld 1988:84), "a local gloss for social identity" (1988:76). The lessons are just the opposite: regimented and coordinated, indexing and trying to sound like and be a different social identity. Predictable, routinized answers are what is called for, not potentially unpredictable ones, which are dependent on the individual's ability to be clever (B. B. Schieffelin 1986b:180). Feld further suggests that this sound aesthetic is linked to a model of egalitarian interactional style that "simultaneously maximizes social participation and maximizes autonomy of self" (1988:83–84). This is not the way books speak or teachers instruct, nor is it the way lessons (or sermons) are structured. In these new genres, there are leaders and there are followers.

Combining reading with speaking by a knowledgeable leader, the literacy lesson closely resembles sermons in its essentially monologic style. The speaking takes place without the usual feedback that organizes traditional and other secular speech events and creates cohesion. Throughout this event, Kulu proposes that the class trust the language to mean what he says it does, to take it as literal truth; he assures the readers that the content is right although the spelling may be incorrect. The genre marks the activity as being one in which only truthfulness is asserted, as in sermons. It is monologic, without the presence of an interlocutory author, and without an author there is no one to argue with, no experiential knowledge to scrutinize. How one knows something is part of the negotiation and contestation that underlie all verbal claims for Kaluli people. With books the rules are different; Kaluli must assume that there is an experience immutably true on other grounds that is the source. They have yet to have a dialogue, or an argument, with a printed text.

CONCLUSION

This chronology of texts and the ideas and practices associated with them highlights the dynamics of particular cultures and language ideologies in contact over time and across contexts. Starting with the first prolonged linguistic encounter, the writing of the grammatical sketch, the language and cultural practices of Australian fundamentalist Christian missionaries and Kaluli became embedded in each other. As the contacts between members of these two cultures increased and others were added, new genres and regimes of language emerged.

To be sure, certain aspects of Kaluli language ideology can be found in the ways in which speaking is privileged in literacy events. It is also possible to detect the agency of Kaluli speakers in the development of a vocabulary for literacy. But what must be underscored is that colonial and missionary intrusions are premised on the principle of asymmetry: domination, control, and conversion to a particular point of view are shared goals of both enterprises. These forms of social control seem particularly salient in the larger discourse structures and in the social organization of talk. Particular communicative technologies, such as literacy, while not transformative in the simple, deterministic sense, do take on power by virtue of those who control those resources and set the participant structure. Such technologies often are not singular or isolated but exist as part of a constellation of activities and other technologies that are mobilized in one direction.

Kaluli who spent time around the mission station had ample opportunity to observe new communicative technologies that gave the missionaries the appearance of enormous wealth and power. The wireless radio made possible voice contact and information exchange with other mission stations. Tape recorders played religious tapes and music. Sacks of mail were delivered by airplanes on a regular basis, along with boxes of frozen meats, fish, and all manner of goods. The missionaries knew how to make things, how to fix things, and they organized Kaluli people and others to create a totally different type of social space, the mission station, where the missionaries were in control. Kaluli saw written materials used in conjunction with many of the tasks the missionaries performed. Manuals were consulted for repairing machines, and they worked. Lists and orders were written up for purchases. Letters were sent asking for goods, and they arrived. Translating the Tok Pisin Bible into Kaluli and writing it down took time and attention, as did the preparation of literacy materials. Kaluli imagined that by participating in the activities of bookmaking and book reading they could "get" the system. They were interested in acquiring not so much the specific knowledge but the larger logic of know-how and the practical mastery that would bring them closer to what the missionaries had hinted could be theirs.

The literacy booklets fit into this larger scheme of things. Written with the authority of the mission, they introduced new ways of knowing into Bosavi life. Although initially they were illustrated with simple line drawings, the later booklets on malaria prevention, tinned meat processing, and peanut growing used black-and-white photographs of local people engaged in the activity described in the narrative. While reading the texts, Kaluli could literally see themselves participating in new activities and taking on new identities.

One can only go so far, however, in examining the literacy primers as texts in order to understand how they function; one must also see how they are used in oral discourse, in activities such as lessons. It is through their use by Kaluli who have been granted authority as teachers and as Christians that their potential is realized. Sentences that are simple and lacking in detail are transformed from understated to elaborated messages whose meanings and moral values are discursively mediated and validated. For the Kaluli, without this critical step, the primers would be material artifacts, kept in net bags with other items. The same holds for the anthropologist; without examining how these materials are used and locally interpreted, analysis would be limited to what could be gleaned from the printed page. It is through literacy *activities* and the practices associated with them that the printed words are activated and expanded. The text is merely a starting point.

Moreover, it is not enough simply to add the talk in which literacy texts are embedded. These texts and the discursive frameworks that constitute them are interpreted against the meanings attributed to other genres. Literacy materials interact with other printed texts, with the ideas they present and the talk that surrounds them. For Kaluli, this is most evident with Bible materials, the other major source of text in the vernacular. Just as a single genre in the verbal repertoire of a people cannot be understood as an isolated entity, these materials and the talk in which they are embedded are the contexts in which other oppositional patterns emerge. Literacy materials prepared by missionaries in collaboration with Kaluli speakers are used in conjunction with

Bible texts in health lessons. Kaluli play these texts off against each other.

The use of booklets in literacy activities produced new participant structures and interpretive frames. The social organization of learning changed profoundly, largely due to the new kinds of knowledge that divide those who have it from those who do not. Texts themselves now demarcate authority. These new linguistic resources provide people with privileged access to authoritative information. Through creation of "local experts" such as teachers and pastors who speak with the authority of the mission and have access to books, Kaluli society is undergoing stratification. The use of books ratifies and participates in creating the same stratification that their content naturalizes.

For Kaluli, the activity of reading is saying, hearing, and understanding, and books impose a new type of authority on what is said. There was an imposition of the idea of passive consensus—silence giving consensus, as it were—rather than consensus achieved through verbal exchange. Particular kinds of speakers are created, and forms of stratification are created by having contexts in which there is only one right answer.

I offer this as a cultural view of Kaluli language that considers pragmatics, metalinguistics, and language ideology as well as the social organization of speech events. This linguistic view of Kaluli culture stresses the ways culture is constituted and social intentions are enacted through language, in this case through introduced forms of knowledge and cultural practices, specifically Christianity and literacy. More generally, the Kaluli case demonstrates that meaning in social action is emergent, co-constructed by participants. By taking an integrative historical perspective, I emphasize that under conditions of rapid social change, every language choice is a social choice that has critical links to the active construction of culture.

Notes

Research support for fieldwork with the Kaluli was generously provided by the National Science Foundation, the American Philosophical Society, and the Wenner-Gren Foundation for Anthropological Research and is gratefully acknowledged, as is a National Endowment for the Humanities Summer Fellowship that supported the writing of this chapter. Steven Feld, Don Kulick,

Stacey Lutz, Michael Silverstein, and Judy Irvine kindly provided invaluable comments reflecting their expertise at several critical stages.

1. For an account of the speed of missionization in Bosavi, in particular the role played by Papuan pastors, see E. L. Schieffelin (1981). The use of Papua New Guinean nationals was part of the policy of indigenization or localization of the churches. The Asia Pacific Christian Mission in Papua New Guinea, formerly the Unevangelised Fields Missions, gave rise to the Evangelical Church of Papua.

2. I carried out ethnographic and sociolinguistic fieldwork in 1967-68, 1975–79, 1984, 1990, and 1995. Tape-recorded speech was transcribed in collaboration with Kaluli speakers. Transcripts contain cultural translations and interpretations based on both social and linguistic knowledge. Linguistic analyses are based on naturalistic speech, a method that expands grammatical and pragmatic analyses rather than narrowing data through formal elicitation. These interpretive methods, drawn on ethnographic, linguistic, discourse and interactional analysis, are important because they reflect issues important to Kaluli themselves.

3. From the mid-1980s onwards, there were some changes in literacy practices, most notably around letter writing. Individuals silently read letters they received, though many read aloud letters from Kaluli living outside of the area. Although literacy was taking on a wider range of functions, in lessons and sermons the same patterns of use held true as of January 1995.

4. Mühlhäusler (1996:212) points out the absence of in-depth longitudinal studies illustrating the linguistic and conceptual restructuring and attrition of traditional modes of communication. He notes that Kulick and Stroud's work (1990, 1993) is an exception.

5. See Mühlhäusler (1996), Neuendorf and Taylor (1977), and chapters on missionary lingua franca (Wurm 1977:833-999) for overviews of mission language policies and practices in the Pacific; see Gilliam (1984) for a critique.

6. Historically the Australian colonial government insisted on English as the medium of instruction in schools and as a prerequisite for economic development. It viewed Tok Pisin as "a corruption of English, undemocratic and colonialistic" (Johnson 1977:444). The diversity and number of the vernaculars were deemed unsuitable to support politically, economically, or logistically, although the educational and social benefits of vernacular education were fully researched and acknowledged in the early 1950s. English was viewed as the national unifying language, and its use was tied to economic subsidies offered to schools, including mission schools that depended on government assistance. By

the late 1950s many missions, under protest, followed the policy of English as the sole medium of instruction in schools. This was maintained through the 1970s. Students speaking anything other than English could be punished, although language policing in rural areas was more difficult to enforce. In 1988 it became the official policy of Papua New Guinea to promote literacy in Tok Ples, that is, in the vernaculars or lingua francas.

7. Joan and Murray Rule, both of whom received master's degrees in linguistics at the University of Sydney, were linguistic consultants to the APCM. They had extensive experience preparing phonological and grammatical sketches on Western and Southern Highlands Provinces languages and collaborated on translating the New Testament into the Foi language (which they spelled "Foe"). Joan Rule, whose specialty was phonology, did not accompany her husband in 1964 to Bosavi as the area was thought to be too rough for women (taped interview with Murray Rule 1984). Rule makes no mention of the Bosavi dialects in his work.

8. Before starting fieldwork in 1966, E. L. Schieffelin wrote to Murray Rule asking about linguistic materials on Kaluli. Rule kindly sent him the fifty-page typescript.

9. Rule used underlining in his grammatical sketch to indicate nasalization. Some verbs were listed in the present imperative form; others were shown in four forms—present imperative, future imperative, first person future, and first person past. Words and sentences cited from Rule's grammar retain his original spellings and glosses.

10. This sentence has the evidential -lo:b infixed in the verb *momada:lo:biki* ('because I wrote') and must have been based on a spoken utterance. This evidential -lo:b ('obvious from visual information') would not be used in a written sentence except to quote an utterance. The oral has contacted the written.

11. I thank Steven Feld for pointing this out to me.

12. Kaluli no longer decorate themselves or their drums for ceremonial occasions.

13. In his discussion of the development of new terms in Yagaria (Eastern Highlands Province), Renck (1990:70) notes, "[T]he process of writing was denoted by an indigenous expression since it was obviously likened to the old technique of carving or burning decorative patterns into wood, bamboo and other materials."

14. *Guliguli lan* ('pray') is from the Motu *guriguri* ('pray'); *lan* is a contraction of the Kaluli verb *a:lan* from *a:la:ma* ('say like that'). This word was introduced by

Gogodala pastors. The APCM had been very active among Gogodala, and Briggs had worked there prior to coming to Bosavi.

15. A great deal of evangelical action took place while the airstrip was being built, and graphic posters were used to illustrate the positive consequences of listening to the Word (heaven) as well as the negative ones (hell). Papuan pastors also used these posters and other graphics, but print was not in local circulation.

16. The fricative /s/ is missing as a phoneme in Rule's phonemic inventory, but a word with that phoneme is used to illustrate another sound /u/ *us* ('egg').

17. Kaluli syntax can be SOV (subject-object-verb) or OSV. In most cases, after an initial three constituent utterance in a narrative, OV or SV syntax prevails. See B. B. Schieffelin (1986a).

18. Ironically, it is not only Kaluli who are depicted as unsophisticated. APCM missionary culture tended to view anyone who was not part of the church as being potentially suspect. Even the army men, PNG nationals who wear Western clothing and are set up in opposition to Kaluli as possible models for the future, are shown sitting on the ground and eating with their hands.

19. The APCM was not the only voice that promoted Christianity as a substitute for culture. The first vice chancellor of the University of Papua New Guinea, J. T. Gunther, argued that Christianity and English were the solution for both cultural and linguistic diversity (Johnson 1977:444).

20. For the first ten years or so, the mission school students were mostly boys; girls might spend a year or two before dropping out. Thus boys would learn more about life at the mission, in addition to picking up some Tok Pisin.

21. In terms of language socialization practices, families interested in becoming Christians made literacy activities part of everyday family life. Children heard not only Kaluli but a limited amount of Tok Pisin, and their conversations reflected new cultural knowledge and linguistic awareness.

Participation in these literacy activities resulted in several changes in terms of children's language practices (Schieffelin and Cochran-Smith 1984). First, children who were regularly involved in looking at the alphabet primers with their parents used referential language, especially labeling, in conversation, in ways significantly different from children not exposed to literacy activities. Second, very young children modeled their parents' behaviors with these primers. They quickly grasped the difference between "reading" the word and "saying" the name of the picture. They understood that reading was the pronunciation of printed words, aloud, syllable by syllable, and when pointing to the word-labels under the drawing, they would slowly and clearly enunciate each consonant-vowel syllable; in some utterances, vowel-initial case endings would be pronounced separately from their lexical forms. This was in contrast to saying the name of the pictures. Thus, from the age of two children exposed to these practices developed a heightened metalinguistic sensitivity to different ways to segment words. At this time Kaluli called reading (literacy) *mo:fo:s agelan* ('count/read printed pages') or *bugo: ba:dan* ('looking at books').

22. The transcript examples that follow are from a vernacular literacy lesson filmed and tape-recorded in 1984 at the Bosavi mission school by Steven Feld and myself. Kulu Fuale led this fifth grade class composed of twenty-four teenaged males; unless otherwise indicated, he is the speaker. He is teaching a health lesson based on a vernacular language booklet called *"Hamule e walaf bo:lo:"* ('Hamule got sick'), which is about malaria prevention and cure.

23. In examples where more than one language is used, Tok Pisin is underlined, English is in plain case, and Kaluli is italicized.

24. Wurm (1987) reports that traditional counting systems in Papua New Guinea that rely on body parts (as Kaluli did) quickly break down and shift to Tok Pisin and/or English abstract decimal systems.

25. Feld (1988:82) discusses the absence of unison in the Kaluli aesthetic and verbal repertoire. Counting to start hymns and reading was an effort to lead and unify, to have one voice, a style that was not consonant with the *dulugu ganalan* ('lift-up-over-speaking') style of verbal and musical expression.

26. Foley (1986:165-66) describes evidentials as an areal feature of the languages of the Southern Highlands, particularly Kewa and Fasu, and Rule (1977b, 1993) details the evidential system for the Foi. Ernst (1991) describes the empirical attitudes among the Onabasulu, a group neighboring Bosavi. See B. B. Schieffelin (1996) for an analysis of Kaluli evidentials and innovations in that system for marking authority, truth, and knowledge claimed to be in written texts.

27. I thank Steven Feld for helping me to articulate this.

9

Language Ideologies in the Expression and Representation of Arizona Tewa Identity

Paul V. Kroskrity

The concept of language ideologies has proved useful in this volume as a mode of analysis that permits a new appreciation of the role of language in the formation of both national and ethnic identities. In chapter 2, for example, Judith T. Irvine and Susan Gal demonstrate how language ideological processes like iconization, recursivity, and erasure produce patterns of differentiation that can be used by members of language communities and by nation-states to provide "the discursive or cultural resources to claim and thus attempt to create shifting 'communities,' identities, selves, and roles, at different levels of contrast within a cultural field." The attempts by states and their representatives to forge national identities using the anvil of standardized national languages, discussed in this volume as both a case study by Joseph Errington and a more general language development model by Michael Silverstein, suggest the ubiquity and importance of the connections between languages and identities.

In 1949, when Edward P. Dozier ascended the then narrow path up to First Mesa of the Hopi Reservation in northeastern Arizona, he began a remarkable but unappreciated episode in the history of

anthropological confrontations with various forms of identity. Dozier, a
Tewa Indian from Santa Clara Pueblo in New Mexico, was one of the
earliest "native" anthropologists. He studied the Arizona Tewa descendants of transplanted Southern Tewas who had abandoned colonial
New Mexico in the wake of the Second Pueblo Revolt of 1696.[1] His earliest published descriptions of this group presented them as paragons
of ethnic "persistence" (Dozier 1951:56). But he soon reversed this representation and emphasized their assimilation into the Hopi majority
(Dozier 1954, 1966:97).

Enjoying the great benefit of retrospection, I want to use the concept of language ideology to better understand its linked roles in the
Arizona Tewas' project of maintaining their ethnic identity and
Dozier's anthropological misrecognition of their multiethnic adaptation. Dozier was an especially gifted ethnographer, but his failure to
more fully attend to local Arizona Tewa language ideologies and
speech practices and his predisposition to emphasize assimilation can
be viewed as products of the marginalized treatment of language and
the influence of acculturation theory associated with his professional
language ideology as a cultural anthropologist working in the mid-
twentieth century. By professional language ideology, I mean the
assumptions about language in general and indigenous languages in
particular that shaped professional discourse within cultural and social
anthropology, especially in the treatment of language and identity.

This emphasis on professional language ideology complements
Charles Goodwin's (1994:606) concept of "professional vision," or
"socially organized ways of seeing and understanding events that are
answerable to the distinctive interests of a particular group"—by
extending focal concern beyond "seeing" to "hearing" and the sometimes invisible assumptions about language and communication that
influence ethnographic practices. It also extends professional vision by
emphasizing the role of macrolevel political economic factors (here
the influence of U.S. national policies regarding Native Americans) in
shaping actual anthropological research.[2]

In examining the influence of this professional regime on Dozier,
this chapter joins several others in this volume in demonstrating the
role of these discourses in constraining interpretation. Jane H. Hill's
work, for example, treats the competing discourses of truth and theater

in the perception of George Bush's promise of no new taxes, and Susan U. Philips's chapter examines the role of Tongan magistrates in imposing and enforcing traditionalizing models of speech behavior by extending the avoidance behavior of brother and sister to all Tongans. By attempting to get at the language ideological assumptions underlying Dozier's ethnography, my chapter also resembles Michael Silverstein's essay on the presuppositions of Benedict Anderson's language ideological assumptions and their putative role in the formation of national identity. And since the professional ideological emphasis on acculturation theory is closely related to national policies and programs emphasizing Indian assimilation, my analysis attempts to expose linkages between national Indian policy and conventional theories and practices of cultural anthropology, which, in turn, significantly influenced Dozier's ethnographic observation and analysis.

In an age when the image of diaspora is routinely applied to the increasingly common dislocation and transnational relocation of cultural groups, it is sobering to remember that this process is not new to indigenous peoples like the Arizona Tewas. Almost three hundred years ago, their Southern Tewa ancestors left the oppression of the Spanish colonial regime based in Santa Fe, New Mexico, to accept repeated invitations from Hopi clan chiefs to move west and help rid Hopi lands of marauding enemies. In exchange for their mercenary activity, the Southern Tewas were to be given land adjacent to that of the First Mesa Hopis. Today, despite significant change and accommodation to both Hopis and Euro-Americans, the Arizona Tewas continue to live as a distinct cultural group—the only post–Pueblo Revolt diaspora group to maintain its ancestral language and associated ethnic identity.

This chapter is about the association of language and ethnicity. In particular, I am concerned with the role a dominant language ideology plays in providing cultural resources for language and ethnic boundary maintenance and in shaping the multilingual and multiethnic adaptation of the Arizona Tewas to their Hopi neighbors. I will also confront the professional misrecognition of the multiethnic adaptation of the Arizona Tewas. Since professional ideologies of language tended to marginalize communication and language use in favor of a reflectionist vision of language that recognized only its referential functions, even a native anthropologist like Dozier did not—and perhaps could not—

view either language use or language ideology as contributing factors in the creation of an Arizona Tewa repertoire of identity (Kroskrity 1993:178–210), a form of multiethnic adaptation.

Dozier was limited both by neglect of language use and by uncritical use of then dominant professional language ideologies. He imported many of the assumptions about language and identity that characterized Linton's (1940) acculturation paradigm. Without access to some of the most telling forms of the discursive construction of local identities (use of their linguistic repertoire, codeswitching, language ideologies) and without conceptual resources from his field that would allow for appreciation of the Arizona Tewas' multiethnic adaptation, even a highly gifted native ethnographer could become confused. In his first writings, Dozier wavered dramatically in his representation of the Arizona Tewas. Initially he presented them as paragons of ethnic persistence (Dozier 1951), but soon he reversed this interpretation and characterized them as moving toward "complete assimilation" to the Hopi Indian majority (Dozier 1954).

My focus on Dozier's professional language ideology is actually directed at a cluster of influences on his ethnographic treatment of language in his Arizona Tewa research. These influences include the conventional practices and assumptions of the cultural anthropology of the day toward "field" languages and the special status of native ethnographers who knew them, and the "expert" language of the researcher. These influences in turn are informed by such macrolevel forces as the political-economic influence of U.S. policy in administering to Native American tribal groups as domestic colonies and by such microcultural phenomena as uncritically accepted beliefs about language and identity.

This chapter then is a parable (Clifford 1986), or perhaps a cautionary tale taken from the pre-"experimental" (Marcus and Fischer 1986) period of sociocultural anthropology in which British social anthropology and American cultural anthropology were combined in an attempt to achieve an integrated and especially authoritative professional voice. At that time, prior to the current "linguistic turn," linguistic anthropology existed primarily to teach students of sociocultural anthropology how to learn field languages. Linguistic anthropologists in this period wrote of "the divorce of linguistic work from cultural investigation" (Voegelin and Harris 1945:356–57) and the failure of ethnologists to study patterns in the use of languages (Greenberg 1948; Hymes 1970). Dell Hymes had yet to name or even invoke the enterprise later known as the "ethnography of speaking" (Hymes 1962).

But this chapter is not so much a historical account of some dark age of linguistic anthropology as an opportunity to appreciate more fully the role and utility of languages, including the ideologies of their speakers, in the formation of ethnic groups and boundaries and to recognize more fully the power of professional language ideologies in the ongoing anthropological construction of identity (Barth 1969; Kroskrity 1993) and community (Anderson 1983; Silverstein 1996b). This parable, then, consists of two stories: (1) how a local language ideology contributed to the maintenance of Arizona Tewa as both a language and an ethnic identity, and (2) how a professional ideology of language produced a very different representation of that identity.

LOCAL IDEOLOGIES OF LANGUAGE

Language ideologies have served the Arizona Tewas as resources for the discursive construction of ethnic, village, and other social identities (Kroskrity 1992, 1993, 1998) in two major ways. First, as a group of microcultural preferences that extend the ideals of 'ceremonial speech' *(te'e hiili)* well beyond the strictly sacred domain of the kiva, they promote a unifying model for speech behavior that crosscuts clan and class divisions. Second, individual or component ideological preferences such as indigenous purism and strict compartmentalization provide specific cultural resources for maintaining maximally distinctive languages that can serve as the symbolic and communicative vehicles for their indexically associated social identities. In this section I briefly summarize some of the previous discussion on Tewa language ideologies that is particularly pertinent to the theme of erasure (Irvine and Gal, this volume) of social difference as a means of creating group identity and to the emergence of Arizona Tewa in a repertoire of languages and identities.

For the first of these themes it is useful to begin with recent research on the Western Pueblos that has greatly undermined earlier images of groups such as the Hopi as "an apolitical, egalitarian society" (Whiteley 1988:64). In both Peter Whiteley's (1988) *Deliberate Acts* and Jerold Levy's (1992) *Orayvi Revisited,* we find a welcome examination of political-economic concerns and a confrontation with Hopi social inequality. Far from representing the Hopi as a kind of Redfieldian "folk society," these works examine intracultural diversity and suggest the stark disparities within and across Hopi classes and clans. Though neither book specifically treats the Arizona Tewas, the pattern of social stratification described is generalizable to the traditional social organization of all Pueblos and is especially germane to understanding Arizona Tewa social variation, since their Southern Tewa ancestors adopted many features of kinship and social organization from their Hopi neighbors (Dozier 1954:305; Ortiz 1969).

In Whiteley (1988), for example, we see a clear distinction between *pavansinom* ('ruling people') and *sukavuungsinom* ('common people'). Levy's (1992) reanalysis of earlier research by the anthropologist Mischa Titiev reveals how inequality of land distribution made some large clans into virtual tenant farmers for other clans. Levy demonstrates a patterned relationship between ceremonial standing and the control of land, indicating that clans that "owned" the most important ceremonies also controlled the best land. Levy goes still further, stating that the ceremonial system not only rationalized a hierarchy but also masked it by offering an alternative ideology of equality and mutual dependence. For both the Hopis and the Arizona Tewas, a village's ritual success depends critically upon the participation of almost all villagers and not just the members of the sponsoring clan or clans. The cumulative effect of these practices, and of related practices such as clan exogamy and the extension of kinship relations along ceremonial lines, promotes a sense of ceremonial mobility and produces what Levy (1992:76) calls a "ceremonial ideology":

> Although an ideology emphasizing the importance of all Hopis and all ceremonial activities was probably an essential counterbalance to the divisiveness of social stratification, it is important to recognize that the integrative structural mechanisms [e.g., clan exogamy, ceremonial "parents", and so on] were also an important ingredient. Opportunity for participation in the ceremonial life was sufficient to prevent the alienation of the common people under the normal conditions of life.

Here Levy builds on earlier ethnographic work by demonstrating how the ceremonial system works to provide what the Pueblo ethnologist Fred Eggan (1964) had earlier identified as "major horizontal strands holding Hopi society together" and by preventing what Titiev (1944:69) saw as clan divisiveness and "the constant potential danger of [Hopi towns] dividing into their component parts." Ceremonial activity, then, like the kiva speech performed in religious chambers when sacred altars are erected, has the net effect of erasing clan and class distinctions by indexing these activities to the ethnic group as a whole. Levy's "ceremonial ideological" analysis thus provides a complementary view to that of a language ideological analysis as mutually dependent processes in a "duality of structure" (Giddens 1984).

Levy's analysis invokes the role of political economy and the macroculture of social and ceremonial organization, whereas the language ideological perspective emphasizes how these macrocultural features are produced and reproduced in the cooperative and communicative displays of members. This linkage of social forms associated with the ceremonial ideology and the discursive practices of kiva speech also helps to explain the emergence and appeal of kiva speech as a dominant language ideology (Kroskrity 1998), a contestable but ultimately "naturalized" belief (Bourdieu 1977:164). For ceremonial activity does not only validate the authority of a ceremonial elite (the 'Made People', or *paa t'owa*); it also motivates the participation of the relatively powerless (the 'Weed People', or *wae t'owa*), both through the promise of ceremonial mobility and the microcultural production of group identity, thus providing a critical complicity (Bourdieu 1991:113). Today even those Tewas who challenge the specific dictates of the political or ritual order, through personal disaffection or conversion to a Euro-American religion, still view the ceremonial system as an appropriate medium for constructing their local identities as Arizona Tewas. Given the importance and power of ritual performance as a rite of unification, it is no wonder that the kiva serves as the paramount "site" of the Arizona Tewa dominant language ideology (Silverstein 1998).

The specific discursive preferences traceable to kiva speech as a model have also provided useful resources in the historical project of ethnic boundary maintenance. In the diaspora of the Pueblo Revolts of 1680 and 1696, the Arizona Tewas were the only outmigrating group to retain their language into the present. Maintenance of the Tewa language served not only to perpetuate an ethnic boundary but also to mask a pattern of dramatic cultural change in adapting to Hopi dry-farming techniques and patterns of kinship and social organization that emphasize wide distribution of limited resources and that evolved in response to the harsh Western Pueblo environment (Dozier 1951). The Arizona Tewa saying *Naa-bí hiili naa-bí woowaci na-mu* 'My language is my life (history)' reveals the intimate relationship between language, history, and identity that this migration promoted and the cultural salience of the connection. The unique history of the Arizona Tewas magnifies a pan-Pueblo emphasis on language.

Though the role of native language maintenance in response to their Hopi hosts is somewhat peculiar to the Arizona Tewas, the cultural prominence of 'kiva talk' *(te'e hiili)* is common to all Pueblo societies. As a key site of Tewa language ideology, kiva talk embodies four closely related cultural preferences: regulation by convention, indigenous purism, strict compartmentalization, and linguistic indexing of identity. I have described these preferences elsewhere (Kroskrity 1992, 1993:36–39, 1998) and will provide only an abbreviated summary here.

Regulation by convention. In the kiva, ritual performers rely on fixed prayer and song texts, and innovation is neither desired nor tolerated. Ritual performance should replicate past conventions; if such repetition is impossible, the ritual should not be performed at all. Culturally valued genres involving either histories or traditional stories must conform to the formal precedents associated with those genres.

This ideological preference for traditional form, perhaps better understood as a preference for "traditionalizing" discursive practices (see, for instance, Bauman 1992), has its most visible model in the unchanging discourse of kiva speech. As a resource in ethnic identity maintenance, it serves as an instruction to not only "speak the past" by including traditionalizing discourse conventions like the particle *ba* 'so, it is said' (Kroskrity 1985, 1993:143–61) but, more generally, to use the past as a model for the present. As in other communities where a dominant theocratic ideology prompts members to carefully reproduce the future on the model of the past, this ideological preference for convention and precedent clearly supports the maintenance of traditional speech practices such as kinship terms for address forms, conventional greetings, public announcements, and, of course, the Tewa language in which they are encoded. Public announcements for secular activities, for example, show remarkable intonational and content similarities to the chants of crier chiefs and are uniformly encoded in Tewa (Kroskrity 1992, 1997). By speaking their traditional ethnic language, Arizona Tewa people retain it as a vehicle for expressing their oldest ethnic or social identity.

Indigenous purism and *strict compartmentalization* are two dimensions of Arizona Tewa language ideology that, though analytically distinguishable, are intimately joined in most linguistic practices, especially those of the kiva. During ritual performance, ceremonial leaders require and enforce an explicit proscription against the use of foreign words and/or native vocabulary clearly identified with an equally alien social dialect (such as slang, defined as recently manufactured words lacking any association with prestigious individuals or activities [Newman 1955:345–46]). As for enforcement, consider the experience of Frank Hamilton Cushing, anthropology's "original participant-observer" (Eggan 1979), who was struck forcefully across the arms by a whipper kachina for uttering a Spanish word in a Zuni kiva. After being so purified, he was instructed to say the Zuni equivalent of "Thank you." The fact that such "verbal crimes" receive such swift and public sanction in ritual contexts makes them especially salient to all villagers.

In everyday speech, speakers regulate language mixing from languages that they highly value and use proficiently. Certainly many Arizona Tewa social identities are performed in the nonethnic languages of Hopi and English (Kroskrity 1993:177–210). Hopi is an essential medium of intervillage communication and the appropriate language for relating to Hopi kinsmen. Command of English has permitted the Arizona Tewas to gain significant economic and political advantages over the Hopis in their role as cultural brokers, mediating between Euro-Americans and the more conservative Hopis (Dozier 1966). Fluency in these languages is necessary for full participation in Arizona Tewa society. Such fluency is never criticized by the Tewas, but language mixing between languages is routinely and consistently devalued. The absence of loanwords from other languages indicates, in part, both a promotion of the indigenous language and a preference for extending native vocabulary. When the Arizona Tewas needed to develop a word for 'clan', for example, they chose to extend their word for 'people' *(t'owa)* rather than to borrow the Hopi term. Thus, even though Arizona Tewa kinship was remodeled along Hopi lines, Tewa terms were consistently retained.[4] This treatment is not unique but rather part of a well-established pattern that has also limited the number of incorporated Spanish loanwords to seventeen despite about 130 years of Southern Tewa contact prior to the Pueblo Revolts.

The third value, *strict compartmentalization,* is also of great importance to the understanding of Arizona Tewa language ideology. Essential to kiva talk is the maintenance of a distinctive linguistic variety dedicated to a well-demarcated arena of use. Kiva talk would lose its integrity if it admitted expressions from other languages or linguistic levels. Likewise, the use of kiva talk outside of ceremonial contexts would constitute a flagrant violation. This strict compartmentalization of language forms and uses has often been recognized as a conspicuous aspect of the language attitudes of Pueblo cultures (Dozier 1956; Sherzer 1976:244). What is novel here is the recognition that this value, like regulation by convention and indigenous purism, is traceable to the kiva as the ideological site that confers its "naturalizing" linguistic prestige. Just as ceremonial practitioners may not mix linguistic codes or use them outside of their circumscribed contexts of use, so Tewa people, ideally, observe comparable compartmentalization of their various languages and linguistic levels in their everyday speech.

As an ideological preference, strict compartmentalization is tangible not only in the "practical consciousness" of Arizona Tewa speech behavior but also in the "discursive consciousness" (Giddens 1984) of some members. One older man who was very experienced in ceremonial matters offered the following agricultural imagery in describing kiva talk:

> This way we keep kiva speech separate from our everyday speech reminds me of the way we plant corn. You know those different colors of corn just don't happen. If you want blue corn, if you want red corn, you must plant your whole field only in that color. If you plant two colors together you get mixed corn. But we need to keep our colors different for the different ceremonies and social dances which require that color. That's why we have so many fields far from one another. Same way our languages. If you mix them they are no longer as good and use-

ful. The corn is a lot like our languages—we work to keep them separate.[5]

This discussion suggests that Tewa strict compartmentalization is not always unconscious but on occasion can surface as a discursively conscious strategy. Despite the natural imagery of the corn simile, botanical or linguistic distinctiveness is not seen as being "in the nature of things" but rather emphasizes the contributing role of humans in maintaining an existing "natural" order.

It is important to note the selectivity of most members' awareness since some compartmentalizing practices, like codeswitching, are routinely outside of the awareness of Tewa conversationalists. Trilingual Tewa individuals, when asked to describe their use of different languages, usually report an idealized spatial determinism in which Tewa is said to be the language of the home and the village and Hopi the language of Hopi villages and the Hopi Tribal Council. Although such folk correlations with cultural spaces do partially capture a statistical pattern, members' models rarely acknowledge the interactional dynamics of codeswitching and instead conform to putative universal patterns of member awareness that locate folk consciousness at the level of the word rather than of the grammar (Silverstein 1981). Thus, despite the complex nature of codeswitching, which involves the alternation of three very different languages, members show little awareness of its practice and may even deny its occurrence because they view it as a form of inappropriate linguistic borrowing (Kroskrity 1993:194).

By permitting linguistic diversification without apparent convergence between languages, the preferences of indigenous purism and compartmentalization have a clear impact not only on the Arizona Tewa linguistic repertoire but also on its associated repertoire of identity. In practice, this preference fosters both native language maintenance and the development of a linguistic repertoire of maximally distinct codes such as languages, dialects, and registers. These distinct codes thus become symbolically available for signaling discrete indexical identities (for instance, ethnic, social, and gender identities) as members iconically (Irvine and Gal, this volume) construct and naturalize connections between linguistic differences and social categories.

Linguistic indexing of identity. The final dimension of Tewa linguistic

ideology is the preference for locating the speaking self in a linguistically well-defined, possibly positional, sociocultural identity and the
belief that speech behavior in general expresses important information
about the speaker's identity. The model of ritual speech foregrounds
the importance of explicit positional rather than personal identities
and the use of appropriate role-specific speech. Outside of kiva talk, we
find similar emphases in the more mundane genres of traditional stories and public announcements, where Tewa speakers mark relevant
social identities through the use of self-reference and evidential parti-
cles (Kroskrity 1993:143–63).

This use of linguistic resources that enable Tewa speakers to socio-
linguistically claim opposed but nested identities, the intraindividual
aspect of the language ideological process of "recursiveness" (Irvine
and Gal, this volume), provides evidence of the inadequacy of the reification of the individual that seems to be foundational to a Barthian
(1969) notion of ethnic boundary maintenance. For the Tewa have
symbolic rights to many different identities and will use their linguistic
resources to signal relevant interactional identity. Barthian imagery
seems excessively brittle and inappropriate in its emphasis on a single,
continuously ascribed ethnic identity. A model based on a repertoire of
identities better fits the pattern of intraindividual variation and the
preference for explicitly signaling relevant identity through selection
of an associated language form.

In the following brief example of codeswitching, note how speaker
G uses languages iconically and recursively to construct an interactional identity as a Tewa. Three older men are talking in a home over-
looking the plaza in Tewa Village atop the Hopi First Mesa in the
summer of 1985. Their conversation is immediately contexted by news
that, after years of contention, the Hopi Tribal Council has selected a
site for a high school on the eastern reservation. Significantly, the site,
as for other public buildings including a jail built about five years earlier, is on Arizona Tewa land. Although Tewa is the expected language
in Tewa homes, these trilingual (Tewa, Hopi, and English) men are following a conversational norm of talking about the Hopi Reservation as
a whole by using Hopi.

F: [Hopi] *Tutuqayki-t qa-naanawakna.*

Schools were not wanted.

G: [Tewa] *Wé-dí-t'ókán-k'ege-na'a-di im-bí akhon-i-di.*

They didn't want a school on their land.

H: [Tewa] *Naembí eeyae nqelqe-mo díbí-t'ó-'ám-mí kqayį 'į wé-di-mu:-di.*

It's better our children go to school right here rather than far away.

Embedded in almost two hours of conversation on a wide range of topics, this brief passage clearly demonstrates how the Arizona Tewas identify both as Hopi and as Tewa and use these distinct languages to interactionally construct discrete identities from their repertoire of identities. For the Arizona Tewas can rightfully claim identities as members of the Hopi Tribe (in accord with official, federal recognition) as well as members of the Arizona Tewa ethnic group. As the Arizona Tewa elder Albert Yava (1979:129–30) wrote,

> We are interrelated with Hopi families in all the villages. Many of us have become members of the various Hopi Kiva Societies. We share dances and festival days with the Hopis. We belong to the same clans. We are usually represented on the Hopi Tribal Council…In many ways we are indistinguishable from them, and often you hear us say in conversations, "We Hopis," not because we have forgotten that we are Tewas but because we identify with the Hopi in facing the outside world.[6]

Just as Yava helps us to understand how Arizona Tewas can invoke Hopi identities, the previous interactional segment illustrates how quickly Hopi identity can be cast aside in favor of constructing the speaking self as a Tewa. Speaker G's abrupt shift to Tewa, and the reference to the Hopis as "they," clearly show how a new we-they dichotomy is invoked. The Tewas may identify with the Hopis in facing the outside world, but in political confrontations with the Hopis, Tewa ethnic identity readily emerges. Here the codeswitch to Tewa underscores the speaker's disapproval of the Hopi conservatism, indecision, and intra-group discord that led to the failure to locate a new high school on the reservation for several decades beginning in the mid-twentieth century. Since many Tewas advocated for a local school long ago and a large majority of both Hopis and Tewas regard the off-reservation boarding schools as failed experiments, many Tewas take special satisfaction in their role in finally bringing a high school to the reservation in the mid-1980s. A discussion of schools therefore often produces a switch to Tewa in order to disassociate speakers from the "incorrect" Hopis and align themselves with the "correct" stance endorsed by the majority of their own ethnic group.

In the comparative study of codeswitching in multilingual social groups, researchers such as Myers-Scotton (1993:478–81) often recognize cases in which "unmarked" codeswitching is used to signal a "mixed" or bicultural identity, as in Monica Heller's (1988) study of strategic ambiguity in the use of English and French in Montreal, where a speaker's seemingly unmotivated switches from one language to another are designed to show a third identity not available through the exclusive use of either of the other languages. But in the Arizona Tewa case, a local ideology works to eliminate ambiguity by encouraging speakers first to speak multiple languages without reducing their distinctiveness and, second, to iconically index each of these languages to particular identities. In sum, the dominant language ideology of the Arizona Tewas has promoted the production and reproduction of a repertoire of languages and identities that offer critical resources for providing multiplicity while maintaining maximal distinctiveness. As in the growing of distinct colors of corn, this was for many Arizona Tewa people at least partially a deliberate cultivation of difference.

DOZIER'S PROFESSIONAL LANGUAGE IDEOLOGY

In examining Arizona Tewa language ideology, I have attempted to locate its source in the model of kiva speech and identify it as a contributing resource for the expression and maintenance of an Arizona Tewa ethnic identity in a multiethnic society. In this section I demonstrate that these are patterns that Dozier did not recognize, in part because of his own professional socialization and the selective attention to language and communication that it entailed. Though this may seem to be an especially ironic instance of professional socialization desensitizing a native to an indigenous cultural pattern, closer examination reveals something quite different. If, as Clifford (1986a) contends, cultural description can be viewed as consisting of partial truths, then perhaps all cultural members can be usefully construed as partial members.

As the son of a Santa Clara Tewa mother and a Franco-American father, Edward P. Dozier inherited the resources of two quite distinct cultures. From his mother and her family he heard the Santa Clara dialect of Tewa and became a native speaker of it. His father's influence is more difficult to characterize and is customarily ignored by most anthropologists. Despite the bilateral pattern of descent in Euro-American kinship and the patrilineal emphasis among the Santa Clara Tewas, most anthropological writers emphasized the matrilineal connection as better suited to constructing Dozier as an unambiguously indigenous anthropologist. Marilyn Norcini (1995) provides the first biographically based treatment of Dozier that permits us to see a paternal influence. Dozier's father seemed very interested in the Tewa heritage into which he had married; he wrote about Tewa history, kinship, and culture and involved his son in such efforts (Norcini 1995:42–47). The younger Dozier was not ceremonially initiated at Santa Clara and was thus ineligible for full participation in the traditional religion of his native pueblo (Norcini 1995).[7] My goal here, however, is not to further examine Dozier's biography but rather to use his published work as evidence of his professional stance on language, communication, and identity.

It is useful to begin by examining Dozier's status as a native anthropologist. Today this notion has been significantly problematized and exemplified so as to call attention to the need for such anthropologists to position themselves within local communities, to ask, as did Kirin Narayan (1993), how "native" a native anthropologist is (Abu-Lughod 1988; Kondo 1990; Limón 1991). But as one of the earliest native anthropologists, Edward Dozier did not enjoy the benefits of more recent critical discussion. Whereas today the literature critically treats such issues as the internal diversity of cultural groups, the dual accountability of "member" anthropologists, and the need for ethnographers to use culturally appropriate styles of discourse to legitimate their status as members (Morgan 1997), in Dozier's day the appeal of native anthropology lay in its promise of validation of anthropological authority. Native anthropologists knew the cultures they studied as insiders and also acquired the approved methodological sophistication and the endorsed technologies of scientific representation (Clifford 1983).

My goal here is not to inventory all of the social science tropes that had acquired some conventionality in American anthropology at the time of Dozier's ethnographic research but rather to focus specifically on those involving language and communication. One of the validating appeals of native anthropologists to an anthropological paradigm that emphasized objective description and analysis was their special linguistic qualifications, which preadapt them both to establish rapport with members and to interpret the insider's point of view. In their foreword to Dozier's *Hano, A Tewa Indian Community in Arizona,* George and Louise Spindler (1966:v–vi) write,

> This case study is unusual. It was written by a man who knows Hano, the Tewa Indian community of which he writes, in a somewhat different way than most anthropologists know pueblo communities. He is accepted as a friend, as an insider, and speaks the language fluently. He never violates this friendship and acceptance in what he writes about the Tewa and yet the reader achieves a feeling of directness and intimacy that is often lacking in descriptions of pueblo life.

Dozier's special linguistic qualifications are also a central theme in professional reviews of his monograph "The Hopi-Tewa of Arizona" (Dozier 1954):

> Not the least of its virtues lies in the simplicity and lucidity of Dozier's English. He is capable of expressing himself without resort to the esoteric jargon…One may infer that his facility with his native Tewa is equally fluent, a fact that adds measurably to the reader's confidence in his understanding and interpretation of his informants.[8] (Smith 1956:325)

Smith, like the Spindlers, presupposes that Dozier had an insider's level of fluency and further assumes Dozier to be a "balanced bilingual" whose fluency in English must indicate comparable skill in Tewa. But in order to construct Dozier as an authoritative native anthropologist, both Smith and the Spindlers avoid seriously examining his actual level of fluency.

What *does* it mean to say that someone "speaks the language"? As a linguist, I am first struck by the effect of the definite determiner "the," which contributes to the uniformist assumption of a singular, undifferentiated language. As a linguistic anthropologist who has conducted approximately three years of cumulative research in the Arizona Tewa community over a twenty-five-year period (Kroskrity 1993), I am further struck by the erasure of relevant regional, class, clan, gender, and other voices in order to create an idealized, shared, and uniform code spoken by all Tewa Others. To what extent could Dozier be said to be fluent in "the language"? Certainly he was highly fluent in his maternal language, Santa Clara Tewa. His pronunciation of words, use of morphologically complex verbs, and ability to use the language in spontaneous conversation can be readily established from published work, recorded materials, and the reports of the Arizona Tewas[9] (although there is no evidence that he possessed any esoteric knowledge of the language, since he received no specialized training in his home pueblo).

But Dozier was not a native speaker of Arizona Tewa, a form of the language even more dissimilar than a regional dialect. Although the basic vocabulary in both Arizona and Santa Clara Tewa is about 90 percent cognate, significant phonological and grammatical differences make it difficult for many Arizona Tewas to follow Santa Clara speech. Santa Clara is the most divergent of the Rio Grande Tewa dialects, and even cognate terms can sound quite exotic when pronounced with r, j, and f—sounds that do not occur in Arizona Tewa. Dozier's treatment of Arizona Tewa in the orthography section of his 1954 monograph (Dozier 1954:261–62) makes any extension of his fluency in Santa Clara to Arizona Tewa quite problematic. The system he detailed is his native Santa Clara system, not that of the Arizona Tewas, as evidenced by his inclusion of the distinctive sounds mentioned above and his exclusion of Arizona Tewa's aspirated stop series (ph, th, kh, kyh, kwh) as well as hy and hw. I do not think that Dozier merely lacked the linguistic sophistication to represent Arizona Tewa properly; this orthographic treatment suggests, rather, that he did not speak the local form of Tewa. Although many older speakers I talked to reported that they were able to use Arizona Tewa with him and to understand his Santa Clara speech after a period of adjustment to its sound system, they also mentioned that Dozier's speech marked him as someone from outside the village. Those current elders, who were in their twenties at the time of Dozier's fieldwork, also described difficulties in understanding Dozier's speech and continue to regard Santa Clara as less than completely intelligible.

Dozier thus may not have enjoyed quite the linguistic advantages that his colleagues were willing to confer on him. He himself seems to have been aware of social boundaries erected by the Arizona Tewas that excluded him from the complete participation ascribed to native anthropologists, but he nonetheless attempted to claim a special insider status. Thus, for example, he writes,

> In June 1949, I visited First Mesa for a preliminary survey of the Hopi-Tewa. As a native Tewa-speaking member of Santa Clara Pueblo, a village of the Rio Grande Tewa in New Mexico, I was received with considerable warmth—as any visitor from my village would have been. Only after several weeks did I make known my desire to study, and even then, I mentioned only the language. (Dozier 1954:260)

Here Dozier not only makes a special claim to insider status but also reveals his attempt to conform to expected standards of scientific objectivity—a requirement of both the Boasian and functionalist theories that so influenced him (Norcini 1995) and one from which Dozier, even as a native anthropologist, was hardly exempt (Smith 1956). Dozier himself acknowledges that his access to insider knowledge had its limits, particularly with regard to gendered knowledge and ceremonial knowledge. In the first case, Dozier (1954:325) notes his inability to attend birth rites, which are normally performed only by women and religious specialists. In the second, Dozier hits the wall of "internal secrecy" (Brandt 1980) and admits his inability to even "learn the names for the second and fourth katcina [sic] ceremonies" (Dozier 1954:347).

In unpublished field notes Dozier concedes, "I was able to secure only very sketchy and inadequate information about societies. There are societies among them but I was unable to learn how they fit into the clan system" (Norcini (1995:187). He questions the information he did receive about initiation, because society members refused to provide independent data and only seemed to agree with him that the system worked as it did at his home pueblo. Dozier interpreted this as a polite refusal to disagree with his leading questions but, in retrospect, it seems more likely a result of his status as an outsider subject to strict rules of information control. Thus Dozier's linguistic skills and the special access to community knowledge they supposedly ensured must be problematized in light of a close analysis of his own writings, inferences regarding his apparent skills, and the perceptions of them reported by the Arizona Tewas.

In addition to unpacking assumptions about native anthropologists, this attempt to disclose Dozier's professional ideology of language includes two additional key points, one regarding his reflectionist ideology of language, the other an ideological stance on language and identity. Dozier's ideological position on language is an academic variant of the reflectionist stance so common in Western Europe and the United States.[10] In this view language is epiphenomenal, removed from the social structures and processes as well as the cultural artifacts and activities produced by members; it thus merely reflects the "real" world.

In Dozier's version of this position, language structure is privileged over language use, resulting in a view of language as simply referring to a preexisting sociocultural world. An alternative view, one preferred by most linguistic anthropologists today, might see language use as a form of social action that plays a creative role in the social reproduction of cultural forms (Blom and Gumperz 1972; Gumperz 1982). But this was neither Dozier's view nor one that was available in the academic marketplace during the time when he wrote.

As mentioned above, Dozier's writings on the ethnic identity of the Arizona Tewas display important inconsistencies that suggest the influence of both additional field research and further professional socialization. His 1951 article, which he described as "a preliminary report on one aspect of a research project on culture change now in progress at Tewa Village...based on four months of field work; the study will continue for another eight months" (Dozier 1951:56), focused on the Arizona Tewas' "resistance" as their most remarkable attribute:

> The most pronounced feature of the Tewa of First Mesa, Hopi, Arizona, is their persistence in maintaining cultural, linguistic, and personality distinction from a numerically larger group, the Hopi. In a contact situation which seems favorable for complete acculturation and assimilation, this insistence on uniqueness is

> provocative. Moreover the Tewa have succeeded, while main-
> taining cultural distinctiveness, in elevating themselves from a
> subordinate, minority status, to a respected and favored posi-
> tion on First Mesa. Investigation of this phenomenon promises
> to reveal significant information on the dynamics of culture
> change. (Dozier 1951:56)

Framed in this manner, Dozier's article examines "cultural manifestations which seem to have been accommodating devices fostering
or maintaining the distinctive minority group" (Dozier 1951:57).
Foremost among these devices was the presence of the "linguistic
curse" placed on the Hopi by the Tewa and entextualized in Arizona
Tewa clan migration legends:

> This curse has probably been the most important cultural
> mechanism for maintaining Tewa self-esteem. It is a constantly
> recurring theme in the traditional myths as well as in topics of
> conversation among themselves and with visiting Indian and
> white confidants and sympathizers. Invocation of the curse in
> ceremonials, reference to it in their informal talks, teaching
> children about it—all these have given the Tewa confidence as
> individuals and reassured them as a group of their respected,
> dominant position on First Mesa. (Dozier 1951:60)

In addition to the linguistic curse, which I further treat below,
Dozier notes three other devices. Two of these involve kinship: the proscription of intermarriage in the early period of intergroup relations,
and Tewa kinship change toward a Hopi model in the more recent
period. Regarding the former, Dozier (1951:60) explains,

> In the early contact period, restriction of marriage was probably
> an essential mechanism to provide an atmosphere in which cul-
> tural distinctiveness could be maintained and ideas of group
> pride could be implanted. In time the restriction was lifted, and
> today the Tewa are thoroughly mixed with the Hopi; in fact an
> examination of present-day marriages makes Tewa village
> appear to be an exogamous pueblo. So strong was the feeling
> for cultural independence, however, that the autonomous Tewa
> pueblo endured despite biological assimilation.

Regarding the second kinship device, Dozier observes that the Arizona Tewa kinship system has shifted from its former patrilineal descent pattern to produce a matrilineal system involving clans, like that of the Hopi. He concludes,

> It is interesting that when elements could be incorporated within the Tewa pattern without endangering aloofness, borrowing was in order...The kinship system, although similar to the Rio Grande in terminology, is structurally like the Hopi...so much so that intermarriage causes no disruption in residence or kinship behavior. (Dozier 1951:61)

Here Dozier fails to note the role of Tewa language ideology's emphasis on indigenous purism in effacing local awareness of kinship change by maintaining Tewa vocabulary, thus naturalizing the application of traditional kinship terms to kinsmen who embodied changed kinship roles and practices.

The fourth device Dozier lists is the Tewa maintenance of a discrete set of ceremonial practices from which Hopis are excluded. The essay concludes with an extended discussion of Merton's (1948) "self-fulfilling prophecy" and the importance of local definitions of the situation as an important factor in "the successful execution of the accommodating mechanisms" (Dozier 1951:62). This is interesting for at least two reasons. First, the notion of a self-fulfilling prophecy was one of the few available models to focus on microcultural production of cultural patterns rather than the more usual materialist emphasis on macrolevel economic determinism. By emphasizing local definitions of the situation, such an approach opened the possibility of appreciating the role of linguistic and discursive practices in making a "false" definition evoke a new behavioral response, which, in turn, makes the originally false conception come true. As an analytical tool, this notion seems quite attuned to an emphasis on the role of both Tewa discourse and Tewa language ideology. Given Dozier's emphasis on the linguistic curse and his somewhat neglected opportunity to interpret the role of language in promoting kinship while masking apparent cultural change through the proscription of borrowed kinship terms, his early data clearly suggested the wisdom of an approach that emphasized the roles of Tewa discourse practices, native perceptions, and local ideologies.

Although Dozier seemed inclined to emphasize Tewa resistance on the basis of his early fieldwork, another eight months of research offered evidence to suggest that in both kinship behavior and ceremonial activity the Arizona Tewas were not maintaining the level of distinctiveness he had valorized. The additional field research revealed them to be so like their Hopi neighbors that Dozier found them to be "assimilating" and "merging." This reversal apparently was caused not solely by additional field experience but also by a theoretical change that emphasized social structure, functionalism, and acculturation theory (Norcini 1995:153).

In Dozier's most extensive monograph on the Arizona Tewas (Dozier 1954), language enters in a more highly circumscribed fashion than in his earlier article. The opening chapter identifies the Arizona Tewas as "the Tewa-speaking community in Northern Arizona"—a professionally acceptable way of identifying bounded sociocultural units in accordance with what Barth (1969:11) has called "the ideal type" anthropological definition of an ethnic group in which race = culture = language = society. This survival of a Herderian view dominated anthropological thinking throughout more than half of the twentieth century and, as Blommaert and Verschueren (1998) have reminded us, is still highly visible in European nationalist ideologies.

Dozier next mentions the Tewa language as a methodological resource, emphasizing its dual role in the establishment of rapport and the collection of data. The remainder of the monograph incorporates few details about language and discourse other than a reflectionist treatment of kin terms (to be discussed later), but Dozier does treat one culturally salient feature of language ideology and use: the linguistic curse that the Arizona Tewas placed on the Hopi as a form of cultural revenge. The text of this narrative is represented solely through Dozier's translation (Dozier 1954:292):

> When our ancestors had defeated the Utes and made life safe for the Hopi, they petitioned for the land, women and food which had been promised to them. But the Hopi refused to give them these things. Then it was that our poor ancestors had to live like beasts, foraging on the wild plants and barely subsisting on the meager supply of food. Our ancestors lived miserably,

beset by disease and starvation. The Hopi, well-fed and healthy, laughed and made fun of our ancestors. Finally our clan chiefs dug a pit between Tewa Village and the Hopi towns and told the Hopi clan chiefs to spit into it. When they had all spat, our clan chiefs spat above the spittle of the Hopi, the pit was refilled, and then our clan chiefs declared: "Because you have behaved in a manner unbecoming to human beings, we have sealed knowledge of our language and our way of life from you. You and your descendants will never learn our language and our ceremonies, but we will learn yours. We will ridicule you in both your language and our own."

Here Dozier reveals more narrative detail than in his earlier article. But he reveals less than an insider's knowledge when he says, "Like all Pueblo Traditions, those of the Tewa are couched in a mystical, fanciful language. It is impossible to tell what is fact or fancy in the migration legend" (Dozier 1966:18). Rather than appreciating or explicating such legends as discourse genres of another culture, he instead implicitly imposes the evaluation metric of truth. Although he never explains what he finds so "fanciful" about these narratives, Dozier does reserve for the "linguistic curse" the only effort he extends to understand a local language ideology and related language use. He notes, for example, that Hopis may acquire the Tewa language through marriage yet comply with the curse by not speaking it except, perhaps, when social restraints are relaxed due to inebriation (Dozier 1954:292).

Dozier observes the role of the curse in maintaining self-esteem at a time when the Arizona Tewas were stigmatized by the Hopi majority at First Mesa, but this point is not highlighted. More elaborate treatment, including chapter-length development, is devoted to such topics as ceremonial organization and social structure, with linguistic topics and native discourse receiving only brief mention. In a short section titled "Linguistic Ability," Dozier (1954:302) states that the Arizona Tewas are "completely bilingual in Hopi and Tewa. They change from one language to the other with great facility.". He goes on to remark that many Arizona Tewas also know English and Navajo, but he never explores multilingualism as a key element in Tewa adaptation to the Hopis. Instead of treating the linguistic curse as an indicator of the tremendous importance of language practices and beliefs in this contact situation, he dismissively exoticizes it as an aspect of native discourse, reducing it to a functionalist account in which it instills ethnic pride.

Dozier's functionalist views of language are also apparent in a brief section of his chapter on social organization (Dozier 1954:339–42), in which he describes gossip as "the most common form of social control" and notes the Arizona Tewas' fear of witchcraft accusations even though "there are apparently no open accusations of witchcraft, no trials, and no executions" (1954:340). An extended quotation from "a highly acculturated Hopi-Tewa man" (1954:340) provides an especially valuable local perspective:

> People are never told they are witches to their face…No one wants bad things said about him or his family, and this family will then try to help the village in work and with the ceremonies. If this family does not do this, then people will continue to think that they are witches and the family will have a hard time because "people will talk about them and act strangely toward them."

Dozier observes that both sacred clowns and volunteer or appointed clowns "often ridicule individuals during plaza dances" and quotes an anonymous Arizona Tewa consultant (1954:339):

> According to informants, the antics of the clowns today are mild, and it is said "they are afraid to make fun of town members." Instead, Navaho and whites become the subjects for ridicule.

Dozier describes his own experience at a plaza dance, when clowns ridiculed his heavy smoking by yelling "Fire! Fire!" and dousing him with a bucket of water.

Dozier limits any further mention of Tewa in this monograph to the role of language as reference, or "names for things." In this he follows then-current cultural anthropological linguistic practice, Western scientific discourse in its quest, since Locke, to limit language to reference (Bauman and Briggs, this volume), and folk models that locate language in lexical reference (Silverstein 1981). Dozier's linguistic representations of the Arizona Tewas suggest that even "native" anthropologists must display appropriate attention to the "validating" (Hymes 1970) function of the native language and must send lexical "postcards from the field" to show "you were there" (Tedlock 1979). Rather than focusing on native discourse, Dozier treats only terms or terminological sets. In the chapter on social organization, for example, he employs Tewa terminology to invoke various sets of dyadic relationships and organize information about norms of kinship behavior and actual practices that he observed in Tewa households. The following discussion is representative (Dozier 1954:320):

Older Sister <————————————> Younger Sister

kaakáh <————— ——————————> *tíyee*

> The relation of sisters to one another is very intimate and life-long. Sisters rear and care for their children in the same household and cooperate in all household tasks. An older sister may often assume an importance equal to that of the mother in the household, particularly if she is the oldest daughter in the household and the other children are considerably younger than she. There is in Hopi-Tewa a special term, *kaakáh*, to distinguish older sister from *tíyee*, younger sibling.

This treatment goes beyond strict reference by including information about typified role relationships and their behavioral routines. Rather than appealing to genealogical positions alone in unpacking these kin categories, Dozier also equates the kin terms with typical kinship roles and behaviors.

Absent from this discussion, although briefly noted earlier in the monograph (1954:305), is any treatment of how *kaakáh* is an unusual Arizona Tewa word. It is, in fact, the only kinship term borrowed from Hopi and one of very few Hopi loanwords into Arizona Tewa, despite at least three centuries of Arizona Tewa multilingualism and a century of intermarriage between the groups (Kroskrity 1993:73). Dozier does not explore members' awareness of the source of this term or the ideological preferences for compartmentalization and indigenous purism that make it so anomalous in Arizona Tewa. Since, in his view, language only labels kinship and social organization, its manifold roles in Arizona Tewa multiethnic adaptation are ignored. He includes many other dyadic relations to give a more complete sense of the kinship system. But here, and in the naming of ceremonies, Dozier defers to linguistic standards of anthropological authentication, which seem to fetishize the denotational function of language.

Dozier's reflectionist stance is even more clear in "Two Examples of Linguistic Acculturation: The Yaqui of Sonora and the Tewa of New Mexico" (Dozier 1956), a contrastive study of Spanish loanwords in Yaqui and Rio Grande Tewa. Here Dozier explains why the former language shows a pattern of syncretism while the latter displays compartmentalization. Rather than considering the possibility that differing linguistic ideologies may affect contact outcomes, Dozier attempts to demonstrate that the facts of the contact situation (for example, whether it is forced or permissive) alone determine the pattern of linguistic diffusion. This is a critical dismissal of language ideologies or even language attitudes, excluding the role of local knowledge and local interests as well as the limits of members' linguistic awareness (Silverstein 1981). For Dozier (1956:147), "linguistic acculturation… reflects acculturation in other aspects of culture," and the results of language contact are a residue of historical forces that language merely reflects. This dismissal of a "culture of language" has interpretive consequences. Compartmentalization and indigenous purism are traced to resistance to the Spanish colonial regime rather than located as indigenous products of local theocracies. Regarding the Tewas' preference for neologisms rather than Spanish loans, Dozier (1956:157) states,

> The reticence of the Tewa in this regard is paralleled by their reluctance to give out information about their way of life. This is a typical Pueblo linguistic trait, apparently deeply rooted. It is undoubtedly associated with the suppression of native customs by missionaries and Spanish authorities experienced by their forefathers and handed down by word of mouth to the present generation.

Here again Dozier's reflectionist stance reduces language to a mirror of historical factors. Were the Pueblos missionized by more tolerant Jesuits rather than the militant Franciscans, he suggests, the Tewas, like the Yaquis, would have produced a linguistic syncretism. I think this is especially doubtful, even outright wrong. Dozier's attempt to view purism and compartmentalization as a version of secrecy traceable to Spanish hegemonic rule critically ignores the fact that the most tenacious control of sacred knowledge is directed from within, in what Brandt (1980:125) has called "internal secrecy." The power of a priestly elite rests in part on its detailed, strictly controlled knowledge of ceremonial performance. Dozier also fails to account for Southern Tewa indigenous purism, which preexisted contact with the Spanish, as well as that of the Arizona Tewas in response to the Hopi (Kroskrity 1993:60–77).

Dozier's ideological position on language and identity is also noteworthy. His early images of the "ethnically persistent" Arizona Tewas were based on his early welcome, including the introductions and establishing of clan relationships—encounters in which the Arizona Tewas spoke their native language and emphasized their Tewa ancestry. Dozier (1954:261) brought several Santa Clara Tewas to Tewa Village for a visit and a social dance and also transported Tewa Villagers to Santa Clara. This exposure to the Tewa side of the Arizona Tewa multicultural adaptation confirmed the persistence of a Tewa culture and the language metonymically associated with it. It was only later, when Dozier's long-term fieldwork exposed him to Hopi aspects of this adaptation, that he realized how Hopi this same group could be. But rather than looking to their multilingual practices as a key to their multicultural identity, Dozier was guided by ideal-type understandings of language and identity (such as that mentioned above) and the theory of "acculturation." In principle, acculturation theory admitted the possibility of a spectrum of culture contact (see, for example, Linton 1940), but in practice it seemed to presuppose assimilation as an ideal (Nagata 1974) and to rationalize hegemonic rule over native populations which, through (Euro-)Americanizing in any way, would lose their right to a distinctive cultural voice (Jorgenson 1971). These "narratives of assimilation," which Edward Bruner (1986) describes as typical of the period, were the academic rationalization for an assimilationist federal Indian policy that treated reservation communities as domestic colonies.

Dozier was no stranger to acculturation theory. Ralph L. Beals, a prominent member of his UCLA dissertation committee, was a Latin

Americanist whose work at the time strongly emphasized this theme
(Beals 1953) and whose 1950 presidential address to the American
Anthropological Association was entitled "Urbanism, Urbanization,
and Acculturation" (Beals 1951). Like functionalist theory, acculturation theory depicted cultures and cultural groups as organic and integrated wholes. Since even minimal changes caused by culture contact
would impact all parts of the system, cultural contact was represented as
an especially stressful state. In a textbook formulation on applied
anthropology and acculturation, Beals and Hoijer (1953:735) wrote,

> Cultures, because they are integrated wholes, do not merely
> add or subtract traits in the process of change. Each new ele-
> ment accepted is, rather, fitted into a functioning whole, often
> undergoing considerable modification in the process; if it can
> not be fitted it may not be accepted.

This emphasis on integration and the possibility of rejection provides a very democratic vision in which systems in contact mutually regulate according to cultural compatibility. But Beals (1953:626–27), in
distinguishing "acculturation" from "diffusion," noted an association of
the former with "force": "In such discussions, force is broadly treated to
include not only overt or naked force but pressures resulting from
deprivations, introduction of compelling new goals, or psychological
pressures arising from sentiments of inferiority and superiority."
Americanists were well aware that Native American societies were the
objects of acculturative forces arising from subordination within
nation-states and that any culture change, with the exception of the
appropriation and commodification of native cultures, would be unidi-
rectional and shaped to the interests of the nation-state (see, for example, Urban and Sherzer 1991).

Although Hopi Indians would never have the hegemonic powers
available to nation-states, their superior numbers and control of local
resources, in comparison to the Arizona Tewas, permitted an extension
of the acculturation model that would predict assimilation. In addition,
the professional ideology that prescribed an iconic linkage of language
and identity promoted only confusion when confronted with a stable,
multilingual adaptation. The Arizona Tewas were either Tewa or Hopi;
they could not be both. By not attending to either their multilingual

practices (such as compartmentalization and codeswitching) or their ideology of language, Dozier could not hear the Arizona Tewa people using their languages as resources in the creation of multicultural identities. Instead of being guided by Tewa discourse, Dozier was influenced by English language academic discourse modeled on the same assumptions that shaped federal policy.

As U.S. nationalism's postwar emphasis on the melting pot metaphor became hegemonic, federal programs of "termination" and "relocation" (Fixico 1986; Jorgenson 1978:22; Officer 1971:45–47) were offered by legislators to promote what they termed "assimilation and freedom" to Indians. This ironic label did little more than signal a new form of state oppression to Indian people as a sequel to "underdevelopment" (Jorgenson 1971). Although they were presented in a discourse of liberation and national integration, "the policies adopted were based not only on the needs of an expanding economy for land and other natural resources, but also on the need for ready supplies of cheap labor" (Littlefield 1991).

CODA

Having concluded my two stories, I am reminded that Euro-Americans, unlike the Arizona Tewas, may expect a moral as part of this blurred genre. Despite Edward Dozier's preadaptation as a native anthropologist and his extraordinary skill as an ethnographer, his lack of attention to Tewa language ideology and use and his uncritical use of then current ideologies of language and culture contact inherent in "narratives of assimilation" (Bruner 1986:124–25) deafened his ability to hear the discursive production of Tewa identity by the Arizona Tewa themselves.

Notes

1. For a more complete discussion of the Pueblo diaspora, interested readers should consult Knaut (1995), Sando (1992:63–78), Schroeder (1979), and Simmons (1979). This extended use of "diaspora" follows the descriptive model suggested by Clifford (1994) rather than the prescriptive one endorsed by Safran (1991) and others. For additional discussion, see Kroskrity (1998:118–19).

2. This influence is quite profound when one considers that the Indian

Claims Commission employed anthropologists as expert witnesses to testify about such topics as traditional land usage. National policy, in attempting to provide some tribes with resources that would make them self-sufficient and possible candidates for termination of reservation status, clearly encouraged a past-oriented study with heavy emphasis on the oral testimony of elders rather than a more participant-observation-based study of contemporary patterns (Fixico 1986; Jorgenson 1978).

3. I am using a slightly different orthography here than the one I used in an earlier treatment (Kroskrity 1993:xv–xvii). As in the earlier treatment, all secondary articulations conventionally represented in Americanist practice with superscripts (like aspiration, labialization, etc.) appear as digraphs. Vowel length is represented here by doubling the vowel (e.g., *aa*) as opposed to using a colon (e.g., *a:*). The apparent vowel cluster, *ae,* is simply a low, midfront vowel, an accent mark indicates high tone, and subscripted hooks indicate nasal, as opposed to oral, vowels.

4. One of only two words from Hopi that appear to be loanwords is *kaakáh* 'older sister' (Kroskrity 1993:73). It should be emphasized that though the Arizona Tewas have managed lexical convergence by proscribing mixing, grammatical and discourse convergence has occurred between the two languages, in part, because these other linguistic levels escape the same awareness, scrutiny, and evaluation that speakers more routinely impose on the lexicon (Kroskrity 1993:71–77; Silverstein 1981).

5. This quotation is translated from a senior Corn Clan man's response to my informal questions about growing corn. We were relaxing one morning in July 1983 after cultivating a field near Keams Canyon. I used the social credit my assistance provided to inquire about why this individual, like many older and relatively "traditional" men, seemed to have many fields that were not at all contiguous. Although the connection between corn and language was not coaxed by any leading questions on my part, my professional interest in the Tewa language was recognized by all of my senior consultants, who occasionally helped me see connections between language and cultural practices that they believed to be important and not obvious to me. I never heard this metaphor used in discussions among Tewa people themselves, but it emerged on several occasions in intercultural encounters like this as a rationalization from the perspective of "Others."

6. Albert Yava, an Arizona Tewa man, was the official interpreter for the Hopi Tribe. He was also ceremonially active in Hopi and Tewa ceremonial soci-

eties. For more on Yava, consult his life history (Yava 1979) and my brief comments (Kroskrity 1993:208).

7. According to the late Alfonso Ortiz (personal communication), the fact that Dozier was not initiated into the ceremonial life of his native pueblo should not necessarily be viewed as an indication of his individual or family stance on participation in native religion. Initiation was not available during his youth because of the breakdown of Santa Clara's moiety system and the requirement that both moieties be cooperatively involved in such ceremonies.

8. I am indebted to Marilyn Norcini for locating and interpreting this useful review.

9. I was able to obtain information from a number of Tewa people who interacted with Dozier during his fieldwork on First Mesa. This group includes Albert Yava, Dewey and Juanita Healing, and Edith Nash

10. This reference-dominated view of language is a robust part of non-academic folk models (Silverstein 1979, 1981, 1985, 1996a).

References

Aarsleff, Hans

1982   *From Locke to Saussure: Essays on the Study of Language and Intellectual History.* Minneapolis: University of Minnesota Press.

1994   Locke's Influence. In *The Cambridge Companion to Locke.* Vere Chappell, ed. Pp. 252–89. Cambridge: Cambridge University Press.

Abbott, Andrew

1990   Self-Similar Social Structures. Manuscript. Dept. of Sociology, University of Chicago.

Abiven, O.

n.d.   *Annales réligieuses de St.-Joseph de Ngasobil, 1849–1929.* Archevêché de Dakar.

Abrahams, Roger D.

1974   Black Talking on the Streets. In *Explorations in the Ethnography of Speaking.* Richard Bauman and Joel Sherzer, eds. Pp. 240–62, 461. Cambridge: Cambridge University Press.

Abrams, Philip

1988   Notes on the Difficulty of Studying the State. *Journal of Historical Sociology* 1(1):58–89.

Abu-Lughod, Lila

1988   Fieldwork of a Dutiful Daughter. In *Arab Women in the Field.* S. Altorki and

C. Fawzi El-Solh, eds. Pp. 139–61. Syracuse: Syracuse University Press.

Alisjahbana, S. Takdir

1961   *Indonesia in the Modern World.* B. R. O'G. Anderson, trans. New Delhi: Office for Asian Affairs Congress for Cultural Freedom.

1976   Politik bahasa nasional dan pembinaan bahasa Indonesia. [National language politics and the development of Indonesian.] In *Politik bahasa nasional,* vol. 1. Amran Halim, ed. Pp. 37–53. Jakarta: Pusat Pembinaan dan Pengembangan Bahasa, Departemen Pendidikan dan Kebudayaan.

Alonso, Ana Maria

1994   The Politics of Space, Time, and Substance: State Formation, Nationalism, and Ethnicity. *Annual Review of Anthropology* 23:379–405.

1995   *Thread of Blood: Colonialism, Revolution, and Gender on Mexico's Northern Frontier.* Tucson: University of Arizona Press.

Anderson, Benedict R. O'Gorman

1966   The Languages of Indonesian Politics. *Indonesia* 1:89–116. (Reprinted in Anderson 1990.)

1972   The Idea of Power in Javanese Culture. In *Culture and Politics in Indonesia.* C. Holt, ed. Pp. 1–69. Ithaca: Cornell University Press. (Reprinted in Anderson 1990.)

1990   *Language and Power: Exploring Political Cultures in Indonesia.* Ithaca: Cornell University Press.

1991   *Imagined Communities: Reflections on the Origin and Spread of Nationalism.*
[1983]   2d ed. London: Verso.

Andriotes, Nic. P.

1957   *The Confederate State of Skopje and Its Language.* Athens, n.p.

Appadurai, Arjun

1990   Disjuncture and Difference in the Global Cultural Economy. *Public Culture* 2:1–24.

Arnovick, Leslie Katherine

1994   The Expanding Discourse of Promises in Present-Day English: A Case Study in Historical Pragmatics. *Folia Linguistica Historica* 15:175–92.

Bacon, Francis

1863   *Novum Organum.* James Spedding, Robert Leslie Ellis, and
[1620]   Douglas Denon Heath, eds. Boston: Taggard and Thompson.

Bakhtin, Mikhail M.

1981   *The Dialogic Imagination: Four Essays.* Caryl Emerson and Michael Holquist, trans., Michael Holquist, ed. Austin: University of Texas Press.

Bakić-Hayden, Milica, and Robert Hayden

1992   Orientalist Variations on the Theme "Balkans." *Slavic Review* 51:1–15.

Balibar, Etienne

1991   The Nation Form: History and Ideology. In *Race, Nation, Class: Ambiguous Identities.* Etienne Balibar and Immanuel Wallerstein, eds. Pp. 86–106. London: Verso.

Barilli, Renato
1989   *Rhetoric.* Giuliana Menozzi, trans. Minneapolis: University of Minnesota Press.

Barnard, F. M.
1965   *Herder's Social and Political Thought.* Oxford: Clarendon Press.
1969   *Herder on Social and Political Culture.* Cambridge: Cambridge University Press.
1993   The Nationalization and Internationalization of Folklore: The Case of Schoolcraft's "Gitshee Gauzinee." *Western Folklore* 52:247–69.

Barth, Fredrik
1969   *Ethnic Groups and Boundaries.* Boston: Little, Brown, and Company.

Barthes, Roland
1967   *Elements of Semiology.* Annette Lavers and Colin Smith, trans. New York: Hill and Wang. ✓

Basso, Keith H.
1979   *Portraits of "the Whiteman": Linguistic Play and Cultural Symbols among the Western Apache.* New York: Cambridge University Press.

Bateson, Gregory
1936   *Naven.* Cambridge: Cambridge University Press.

Bauman, Richard
1992   Contextualization, Tradition, and the Dialogue of Genres: Icelandic Legends of the *Kraftaskald.* In *Rethinking Context.* A. Duranti and C. Goodwin, eds. Pp. 125–45. New York: Cambridge University Press.

Bauman, Richard, and Charles L. Briggs
1990   Poetics and Performance as Critical Perspectives on Language and Social Life. *Annual Review of Anthropology* 19:59–88.

Beals, Ralph L.
1951   Urbanism, Urbanization, and Acculturation. *American Anthropologist* 53:1–10.
1953   Acculturation. In *Anthropology Today.* A. L. Kroeber, ed. Pp. 621–41. Chicago: University of Chicago Press.

Beals, Ralph L., and Harry Hoijer
1953   *Introduction to Anthropology.* New York: Macmillan.

Belić, Alexandr
1919   *La Macédoine: Études ethnographiques et politiques.* Paris and Barcelona: Bloud & Gay.

Bendix, Regina
1997   *In Search of Authenticity: The Formation of Folklore Studies.* Madison: University of Wisconsin Press.

Berlin, Isaiah
1976   *Vico and Herder.* New York: Vintage.

Berman, Morris
1978   *Social Change and Scientific Organization: The Royal Institution, 1799–1844.* Ithaca: Cornell University Press.

REFERENCES

Bernstein, Basil
√ 1971 *Class, Codes, and Control.* London: Routledge & Kegan Paul.
1975 *Class, Codes, and Control: Theoretical Studies Towards a Sociology of Language.* New York: Shocken.

Besnier, Niko
1989 Information Withholding as a Manipulative and Collusive Strategy in Nukulaelae Gossip. *Language in Society* 18:315–41.
1995 *Literacy, Emotion, and Authority: Reading and Writing on a Polynesian Atoll.* New York: Cambridge University Press.

Bhaba, Homi, ed.
√ 1990 *Nation and Narration.* New York: Routledge.

Blackall, Eric
1978 *The Emergence of German as a Literary Language, 1700–1775.* Ithaca: Cornell University Press.

Blom, Jan-Petter, and John J. Gumperz
1972 Social Meaning in Linguistic Structure: Codeswitching in Norway. In *Directions in Sociolinguistics.* J. J. Gumperz and D. H. Hymes, eds. Pp. 407–34. New York: Holt.

√ **Blommaert, Jan, and Jef Verschueren**
1992 The Role of Language in European Nationalist Ideologies. *Pragmatics* 2(3):355–76.
1998 The Role of Language in European Nationalist Ideologies. In *Language Ideologies: Practice and Theory.* Bambi B. Schieffelin. Kathryn A. Woolard, and Paul V. Kroskrity, eds. Pp.189–210. New York: Oxford University Press.

Bloomfield, Leonard
1933 *Language.* New York: Henry Holt.
1944 Secondary and Tertiary Responses to Language. *Language* 20:44–55.
1987a A Set of Postulates for the Science of Language. In *A Leonard Bloomfield*
[1926] *Anthology,* abridged ed. Charles F. Hockett, ed. Pp. 70–80. Chicago: University of Chicago Press.
1987b Literate and Illiterate Speech. In *A Leonard Bloomfield Anthology,*
[1927] abridged ed. Charles F. Hockett, ed. Pp. 84–93. Chicago: University of Chicago Press.
1987c Language or Ideas? In *A Leonard Bloomfield Anthology,* abridged ed.
[1936] Charles F. Hockett, ed. Pp. 220–26. Chicago: University of Chicago Press.
1987d Review of *La Nueva Filologia,* by Morris Swadesh. In *A Leonard Bloomfield*
[1943] *Anthology,* abridged ed. Charles F. Hockett, ed. Pp. 277–78. Chicago: University of Chicago Press.

Boas, Franz
1911 Introduction. In *Handbook of North American Indian Languages.* Franz Boas, ed. Part 1, pp.1–83. *Bulletin of the Bureau of American Ethnology,* vol. 40. Washington, DC: U.S. Government Printing Office.

1928   *Anthropology and Modern Life*. New York: W. W. Norton & Co.

1940a   The Classification of American Languages. In *Race, Language, and*
[1920]   *Culture*. Pp. 211–18. New York: Macmillan.

1940b   Classification of American Indian Languages. In *Race, Language, and*
[1929]   *Culture*. Pp. 219–25. New York: Macmillan.

1966   Introduction to *Handbook of American Indian Languages by Franz Boas and*
[1911]   *Indian Linguistic Families of America North of Mexico by J. W. Powell*. Preston
            Holder, ed. Pp. 1–79. Lincoln: University of Nebraska Press.

Bourdieu, Pierre

1977   *Outline of a Theory of Practice*. Richard Nice, trans. Cambridge:
            Cambridge University Press.

1984   *Distinction: A Social Critique of the Judgment of Taste*. R. Nice, trans.
            Cambridge: Harvard University Press.

1991   *Language and Symbolic Power*. Cambridge: Harvard University Press.

Boyarin, Jonathan, ed.

1993   *The Ethnography of Reading*. Berkeley: University of California Press.

Brailsford, Henry

1906   *Macedonia: Its Races and Its Future*. London: Methuen.

Brancoff, Dimitur M.

1905   *La Macédoine et sa population chrétienne*. Paris: Plon.

Brandt, Elizabeth A.

1980   On Secrecy and Control of Knowledge. In *Secrecy: A Cross-Cultural
            Perspective*. Stanton Teft, ed. Pp. 123–46. New York: Human Sciences
            Press.

Braunschwig, Henri

1974   *Enlightenment and Romanticism in Eighteenth-Century Prussia*. Chicago:
            University of Chicago Press.

Brenneis, Donald

1984   Grog and Gossip in Bhatgaon: Style and Substance in Fiji Indian
            Conversation. *American Ethnologist* 11:487–506.

Briggs, Charles L.

1992   Linguistic Ideologies and the Naturalization of Power in Warao
            Discourse. *Pragmatics* 2:387–404.

1993   Metadiscursive Practices and Scholarly Authority in Folkloristics. *Journal
            of American Folklore* 106:387–434.

1998   "You're a Liar—You're Just Like a Woman!": Constructing Dominant
            Ideologies of Language in Warao Men's Gossip. In *Language Ideologies:
            Practice and Theory*. Bambi B. Schieffelin, Kathryn A. Woolard, and Paul
            V. Kroskrity, eds. Pp. 229–55. New York: Oxford University Press.

Broce, Gerald

1981   Discontent and Cultural Relativism: Herder and Boasian Anthropology.
            Annals of Scholarship 2:1–3.

Brown, Keith

1995   Of Meanings and Memories: The National Imagination in Macedonia.
            Ph.D. diss., Department of Anthropology, University of Chicago.

REFERENCES

Bruner, Edward M.
1986   Experience and Its Expressions. In *The Anthropology of Experience*. V. W.
          Turner and E. M. Bruner, eds. Pp. 124–58. Urbana: University of Illinois
          Press.

Bryant, Alfred T.
1949   *The Zulu People*. Pietermaritzburg: Shuter and Shooter.

Buci-Glucksmann, Christine
1982   Hegemony and Consent. In *Approaches to Gramsci*. Anne Showstack
          Sassoon, ed. Pp.116–26. London: Writers and Readers Publishing
          Cooperative Society.

Budiman, Arief, ed.
1990   *State and Civil Society in Indonesia*. Clayton, Australia: Center of Southeast
          Asian Studies, Monash University.

Bull, William E.
1960   *Time, Tense, and the Verb: A Study in Theoretical and Applied Linguistics with
          Particular Attention to Spanish*. University of California Publications in
          Linguistics, vol. 19. Berkeley and Los Angeles: University of California
          Press.

Bundy, McGeorge
1980   Shadow and Substance in 1980. In McGeorge Bundy and Edmund S.
          Muskie, *Presidential Promises and Performance*. Pp. 23–54. New York: The
          Free Press.

Burhan, Jazir
1989   Politik bahasa nasional dan pengajaran bahasa. [National language poli-
          tics and language instruction.] In *Politik bahasa nasional*. Amran Halim,
          ed. Pp. 65–83. Jakarta: Balai Pustaka.

Burridge, Kenelm
1995   *Mambu: A Melanesian Millennium*. Princeton: Princeton University Press.
[1960]

Calhoun, Craig, ed.
1992   *Habermas and the Public Sphere*. Cambridge: MIT Press.
1993   Nationalism and Ethnicity. *Annual Review of Sociology* 19:211–39.

Cameron, Deborah
1990   Demythologizing Sociolinguistics: Why Language Does Not Reflect
          Society. In *Ideologies of Language*. John Joseph and Talbot J. Taylor, eds.
          London: Routledge.

Chafe, Wallace L.
1980   The Deployment of Consciousness in the Production of a Narrative. In
          The Pear Stories. Wallace L. Chafe, ed. Pp. 9–50. Norwood, NJ: Ablex.

Chomsky, Noam
1957   Syntactic Structures. *Janua Linguarum*, no. 4. 's Gravenhage: Mouton.
1965   *Aspects of the Theory of Syntax*. Cambridge: MIT Press.

Churchill, R. S.

1966   *Winston S. Churchill.* Boston: Houghton Mifflin.

Clark, Robert J., Jr.

1969   *Herder: His Life and Thought.* Berkeley and Los Angeles: University of
         California Press.

Clifford, James

1983   On Ethnographic Authority. *Representations* 1:118–45.

1986   On Ethnographic Allegory. In *Writing Culture.* J. Clifford and G. E.
         Marcus, eds. Pp. 98–121. Berkeley: University of California Press

1988   *The Predicament of Culture: Twentieth-Century Ethnography, Literature, and
         Art.* Cambridge: Harvard University Press.

1994   Diasporas. *Cultural Anthropology* 9:302–38.

Cocchiara, Giuseppe

1981   *The History of Folklore in Europe.* Philadelphia: ISHI.
[1952]

Cohn, Bernard

1985   The Command of Language and the Language of Command. *Subaltern
         Studies* 4:276–329.

Cohn, Bernard, and Nicholas Dirks

1988   Beyond the Fringe: The Nation State, Colonialism, and the
         Technologies of Power. *Journal of Historical Sociology* 1(2):224–29.

Collins, James T.

1995   Literacy and Literacies. In *Annual Review of Anthropology 24.* W. Durham,
         E. V. Daniel, and Bambi B. Schieffelin, eds. Pp. 75–93. Palo Alto: Annual
         Reviews Inc.

1998   *Malay, World Language: A Short History.* Kuala Lumpur: Dewan Bahasa
         dan Pustaka.

1998   Our Ideologies and Theirs. In *Language Ideologies: Practice and Theory.*
         Bambi B. Schieffelin, Kathryn A. Woolard, and Paul V. Kroskrity, eds.
         Pp. 256–70. New York: Oxford University Press.

Comaroff, Jean, and John Comaroff

1991   *Of Revelation and Revolution.* Chicago: University of Chicago Press.

Cramer, Richard Ben

1993   *What It Takes.* New York: Vintage Books.

Crétois, Père Léonce

1972   *Dictionnaire Sereer-Français.* Dakar: Centre de Linguistique Appliquée de
         Dakar.

Crosby, Alfred W.

1997   *The Measure of Reality: Quantification and Western Society, 1250–1600.*
         Cambridge: Cambridge University Press.

Cust, Robert Needham

1883   *A Sketch of the Modern Languages of Africa.* London: Trübner.

Cvijić, J.
1907   *Remarques sur l'ethnographie de la Macédoine.* Paris: Georges Roustan.

Derrida, Jacques
1967   *Writing and Difference.* Alan Bass, trans. Chicago: University of Chicago
        Press.
√ 1974 *Of Grammatology.* Gayatri Chakravorty Spivak, trans. Baltimore: Johns
[1967] Hopkins University Press.

Denoon, D.
1992   Dependence and Interdependence: Southern Africa from 1500 to 1800.
        In *General History of Africa V: Africa from the Sixteenth to the Eighteenth
        Century.* B. A. Ogot, ed. Pp. 683–702. Berkeley: University of California
        Press, for UNESCO.

de Tressan, M. de L.
1953   *Inventaire linguistique de l'Afrique Occidentale Française et du Togo.* Mémoires
        #30. Dakar: Institut Français d'Afrique Noire.

Deutsch, Karl W.
1953   *Nationalism and Social Communication.* Redding, MA: MIT Press/John
        Wiley & Co.

Diagne, Pathé
1967   *Pouvoir politique traditionnel en Afrique Occidentale.* Paris: Présence
        Africaine.

Dimitrovski, Todor, Blaze Koneski, and Trajko Stamatoski, eds.
1978   *About the Macedonian Language.* Skopje: Macedonian Language Institute.

Dohrn-van Rossum, Gerhard
1996   *History of the Hour: Clocks and Modern Temporal Orders.* Thomas Dunlap,
        trans. Chicago: University of Chicago Press.

Doke, Clement
1961   *Textbook of Zulu Grammar.* 6th ed. Johannesburg: Longmans.

Doke, Clement, and B. W. Vilakazi
1958   *Zulu-English Dictionary.* 2nd ed. Johannesburg: Witwatersrand University
        Press.

Dozier, Edward P.
1951   Resistance to Acculturation and Assimilation in an Indian Pueblo.
        American Anthropologist 53:56–66.
1954   The Hopi-Tewa of Arizona. *University of California Publications in American
        Archaeology and Ethnology* 44[3]:257–376. Berkeley: University of
        California Press.
1956   Two Examples of Linguistic Acculturation: The Yaqui of Sonora and the
        Tewa of New Mexico. *Language* 32:146–57.

1966   *Hano, A Tewa Indian Community in Arizona.* New York: Holt, Rinehart and Winston.

Duranti, Alessandro

1990   Politics and Grammar: Agency in Samoan Political Discourse. *American Ethnologist* 17:646–66.

1993   Intentions, Self, and Responsibility: An Essay in Samoan Ethnopragmatics. In *Responsibility and Evidence in Oral Discourse.* Jane H. Hill and Judith T. Irvine, eds. Pp. 24–47. Cambridge: Cambridge University Press.

1994   *From Grammar to Politics: Linguistic Anthropology in a Western Samoan Village.* Berkeley: University of California Press.

Duranti, Alessandro, and Elinor Ochs

1985   Literacy Instruction in a Samoan Village. In *The Acquisition of Literacy: Ethnographic Perspectives.* Bambi B. Schieffelin and Perry Gilmore, eds. Pp. 213–32. Norwood, NJ: Ablex.

Eggan, Fred

1964   Alliance and Descent in a Western Pueblo Society. In *Process and Patterns in Culture.* Robert A. Manners, ed. Pp. 175–84. Chicago: Aldine.

1979   Foreword. In *Zuni: Selected Writings of Frank Hamilton Cushing.* Jesse Green, ed. Pp. xi–xiv. Lincoln: University of Nebraska Press.

Ehrenpreis, Marcus

1928   *The Soul of the East: Experiences and Reflections.* New York: Viking.

Ellem, Elizabeth W.

1981   Queen Salote Tupou III and Tungi Mailefihi: A Study of Leadership in Twentieth-Century Tonga (1918–41). Ph.D. diss., University of Melbourne.

Ergang, Robert

1966   *Herder and the Foundations of German Nationalism.* New York:
[1931]   Octagon Books.

Ernst, Thomas M.

1991   Empirical Attitudes among the Onabasulu. In *Man and A Half: Essays in Pacific Anthropology and Ethnobiology in Honor of Ralph Bulmer.* A. Pawley, ed. Pp. 199–207. Memoir 48, The Polynesian Society, Auckland.

Errington, Joseph

1986   Continuity and Discontinuity in Indonesian Language Development. *Journal of Asian Studies* 45(2):329–53.

1988   *Structure and Style in Javanese: A Semiotic View of Linguistic Etiquette.* Philadelphia: University of Pennsylvania Press.

1989   Exemplary Centers, Urban Centers, and Language Change in Java. *Working Papers and Proceedings of the Center for Psychosocial Studies,* no. 30. Chicago: Center for Psychosocial Studies.

1998a   *Shifting Languages: Javanese Indonesian Interaction and Identity.* Cambridge: Cambridge University Press.

1998b   Indonesian('s) Development: On the State of a Language State. In *Language Ideologies: Practice and Theory.* Bambi B. Schieffelin, Kathryn A. Woolard, and Paul V. Kroskrity, eds. Pp. 271–84. New York: Oxford University Press.

Escobar, Arturo

1992   Imagining a Post-Development Era? Critical Thought, Development, and Social Movements. *Social Text* 31/32:20–56.

Evans-Pritchard, Edward E.

1940   *The Nuer.* Oxford: Clarendon Press.

Fabian, Johannes

1986   *Language and Colonial Power.* Cambridge: Cambridge University Press.

Faidherbe, Louis Léon César

1865   Etude sur la langue Kuégem ou Sérère-Sine. In *Annuaire du Sénégal pour l'année 1865.* Pp. 175–245. Saint-Louis: Imprimerie du Gouvernement.

1882   *Grammaire et vocabulaire de la langue poul.* Paris: Maisonneuve.

Fasold, Ralph W.

1984   Introduction to Sociolinguistics. Vol. 1, *The Sociolinguistics of Society.* Oxford: Blackwell.

Feld, Steven

1985   Aesthetics as Iconicity of Style, or, 'Lift-up-over-Sounding': Getting into the Kaluli Groove. *Yearbook for Traditional Music* 20:74–113.

1990   *Sound and Sentiment: Birds, Weeping, Poetics, and Song in Kaluli Expression.* 2d ed. Philadelphia: University of Pennsylvania Press.

Feld, Steven, and Bambi B. Schieffelin

1982   Hard Words: A Functional Basis for Kaluli Discourse. In *Georgetown University Roundtable on Languages and Linguistics 1981.* D. Tannen, ed. Pp. 351–71. Washington, DC: Georgetown University Press.

Ferguson, Charles

1987   Literacy in a Hunting-Gathering Society: The Case of the Diyari. *Journal of Anthropological Research* 4(3):223–37.

1994   Dialect, Register, and Genre: Working Assumptions about Conventionalization. In *Sociolinguistic Perspectives on Register.* D. Biber and E. Finegan, eds. Pp. 15–30. New York: Oxford University Press.

Fichte, Johann Gottlieb

1845–46 Reden an die deutsche Nation. In *Sämmtliche Werke,* vol. 7. I. H. Fichte, ed. Pp. 264–499. Berlin: Veit.

Finlayson, Rosalie

1978 A Preliminary Survey of Hlonipha among the Xhosa. *Taalfasette* 24:48–63.

1982 Hlonipha—the Women's Language of Avoidance among the Xhosa. *South African Journal of African Languages* 1(1).

1984 The Changing Nature of Isihlonipho Sabafazi. *African Studies* 43:137–46.

Finnegan, Ruth

1985 *Literacy and Orality: Studies in the Technology of Communication.* Oxford: Blackwell.

Fischer, John L.

1958 Social Influences on the Choice of a Linguistic Variant. *Word* 14:47–56.

Fishel, Jeff

1985 *Presidents and Promises.* Washington, DC: Congressional Quarterly Press.

Fixico, Donald.

1986 *Termination and Relocation: Federal Indian Policy, 1945–1960.* Albuquerque: University of New Mexico.

Florida, Nancy

1987 Reading the Unread in Traditional Javanese Literature. *Indonesia* 44:1–15.

Foley, William A.

1986 *The Papuan Languages of New Guinea.* Cambridge: Cambridge University Press.

Formigari, Lia

1985 Théories du langage et théories du pouvoir en France, 1800–1848. *Historiographia Linguistica* 12:63–83.

1988 *Language and Experience in Seventeenth-Century British Philosophy.* Amsterdam: John Benjamins.

1993 *Signs, Science and Politics: Philosophies of Language in Europe 1700–1830.* William Dodd, trans. Amsterdam: John Benjamins.

Foster, Robert J., ed.

1995 *Nation Making: Emergent Identities in Postcolonial Melanesia.* Ann Arbor: University of Michigan Press.

Foucault, Michel

1970 *The Order of Things: An Archaeology of the Human Sciences.* New York: Random House.

1972 *The Archaeology of Knowledge.* A. M. Sheridan Smith, trans. New York: Harper and Row.

1980 *Power/Knowledge: Selected Interviews and Other Writings, 1972–1977.* Colin Gordon et al., trans. New York: Pantheon.

REFERENCES

Fraser, Nancy

✓ 1993   Rethinking the Public Sphere: A Contribution to the Critique of Actually Existing Democracy. In *The Phantom Public Sphere*. Bruce Robbins, ed. Pp. 1–32. Minneapolis: University of Minnesota Press.

Friedman, Victor

1975   Macedonian Language and Nationalism during the Nineteenth and Early Twentieth Centuries. *Balkanistica* 2:83–98.

1985   The Sociolinguistics of Literary Macedonian. *International Journal of the Sociology of Language* 52:31–57.

1989   Macedonian: Codification and Lexicon. In *Language Reform: History and Future*, vol. IV. I. Fodor and C. Hagège, eds. Pp. 329–334. Hamburg: Helmut Buske.

1995   Persistence and Change in Ottoman Patterns of Code-Switching in the Republic of Macedonia: Nostalgia, Duress and Language Shift in Contemporary Southeastern Europe. In *Summer School: Code-Switching and Language Contact*. Durk Gorter et al., eds. Pp. 58–67. Ljouwert/Leeuwarden, Netherlands: Fryske Academy.

1996   The Turkish Lexical Element in the Languages of the Republic of Macedonia from the Ottoman Period to Independence. *Zeitschrift für Balkanologie* 32(2):133–50.

Fugate, Joe K.

1966   *The Psychological Basis of Herder's Aesthetics*. The Hague: Mouton.

Gaier, Ulrich

1990   "Volk" und "Völker." In *Volkslieder, Übertragungen, Dichtungen*. Johann Gottfried Herder, *Werke*, vol. 3. Pp. 865–78. Frankfurt-am-Main: Deutscher Klassiker Verlag.

Gal, Susan

1979   *Language Shift: Social Determinants of Language Change in Bilingual Austria*. New York: Academic Press.

1987   Codeswitching and Consciousness in the European Periphery. *American Ethnologist* 14:4:637–53.

1989   Language and Political Economy. *Annual Review of Anthropology* 18:345–67.

1991   Bartók's Funeral: Representations of Europe in Hungarian Political Rhetoric. *American Ethnologist* 18:440–58.

1992   Multiplicity and Contention among Ideologies. *Pragmatics* 2:445–50.

1993   Diversity and Contestation in Linguistic Ideologies: German Speakers in Hungary. *Language in Society* 22:337–59.

1998   Multiplicity and Contention among Language Ideologies: A Commentary. In *Language Ideologies: Practice and Theory*. Bambi B. Schieffelin, Kathryn A. Woolard, and Paul V. Kroskrity, eds. Pp. 317–31. New York: Oxford University Press.

Gal, Susan, and Judith T. Irvine

1995   The Boundaries of Languages and Disciplines: How Ideologies
        Construct Difference. *Social Research* 62(4):967–1001.

Gal, Susan, and Kathryn A. Woolard

1995   Constructing Languages and Publics. Special issue. *Pragmatics* 5(2).

Garnett, Lucy

1904   *Turkish Life in Town and Country.* New York: Putnam.

Garvin, Paul L.

1964   The Standard Language Problem: Concepts and Methods. In *Language*
[1959] *in Culture and Society: A Reader in Linguistics and Anthropology.* Dell Hymes,
        ed. Pp. 521–23. New York: Harper & Row.

1993   A Conceptual Framework for the Study of Language Standardization.
        International Journal of the Sociology of Language 100/101:37–54.

Garvin, Paul L., and Madeleine Mathiot

1968   The Urbanization of the Guaraní Language: A Problem in Language
[1956] and Culture. In *Readings in the Sociology of Language.* Joshua A. Fishman,
        ed. Pp. 365–74. The Hague: Mouton.

Geertz, Clifford

1973   The Politics of Meaning. In *The Interpretation of Cultures.* Pp. 311–26. New
        York: Basic Books.

1980   *Negara.* Princeton: Princeton University Press.

1983   *Local Knowledge.* New York: Basic Books.

Gellner, Ernest

1964   *Thought and Change.* London: Weidenfeld and Nicholson.

1983   *On Nations and Nationalism.* Ithaca: Cornell University Press.

1994   *Encounters with Nationalism.* Oxford: Blackwell.

Germond, Jack W., and Jules Witcover

1993   *Mad as Hell: Revolt at the Ballot Box, 1992.* New York: Warner Books.

Gewertz, Deborah, and Fredrick Errington

1991   *Twisted Histories, Altered Contexts.* Cambridge: Cambridge University Press.

Geyer, Michael

1989   Historical Fictions of Autonomy and the Europeanization of National
        History. *Central European History* 22:316–42.

Giddens, Anthony

1984   *The Constitution of Society.* Berkeley: University of California Press.

Giliomee, Hermann

1989   The Eastern Frontier, 1770–1812. In *The Shaping of South African Society,
        1652–1840.* Richard Elphick and Hermann Giliomee, eds. Pp. 421–71.
        Middletown, CT: Wesleyan University Press.

REFERENCES

Gilliam, Angela

1984   Language and "Development" in Papua New Guinea. *Dialectical Anthropology* 8:303–18.

Goff, A., and Hugh A. Fawcett

1921   *Macedonia: A Plea for the Primitive.* London: John Lane.

Goffman, Erving

1979   Footing. *Semiotica* 25:1–29.

Goodwin, Charles

1994   Professional Vision. *American Anthropologist* 96:606–33.

Goody, Jack

1968   Introduction. In *Literacy in Traditional Societies.* J. Goody, ed. Pp. 1–26. Cambridge: Cambridge University Press.

1977   *The Domestication of the Savage Mind.* Cambridge: Cambridge University Press.

Goody, Jack, ed.

1968   *Literacy in Traditional Societies.* Cambridge: Cambridge University Press.

Goody, Jack, and Ian Watt

1968   The Consequences of Literacy. In *Literacy in Traditional Societies.* Jack
[1963]   Goody, ed. Pp. 27–68. Cambridge: Cambridge University Press.

Gordon, Tamar

1990   Inventing the Mormon Tongan Family. In *Christianity in Oceania: Ethnographic Perspectives.* John Barker, ed. Pp. 197–219. Lanham, MD: University Press of America.

Gossen, Gary H.

1974   To Speak with a Heated Heart: Chamula Canons of Style and Good Performance. In *Explorations in the Ethnography of Speaking.* Richard Bauman and Joel Sherzer, eds. Pp. 389–413. Cambridge: Cambridge University Press.

Graff, Harvey, ed.

1981   *Literacy and Social Development in the West.* Cambridge: Cambridge University Press.

✓ **Gramsci, Antonio**

1971   *Selections from the Prison Notebooks.* New York: International Press.

Greenberg, Joseph H.

1948   Linguistics and Ethnology. *Southwestern Journal of Anthropology* 4:140–47.

1963   The Languages of Africa. *International Journal of American Linguistics* 29(1), Part II.

Grice, H. Paul

1975   Logic and Conversation. In *Syntax and Semantics 3: Speech Acts.* Peter

Cole and Jerry Morgan, eds. Pp. 41–58. New York: Academic Press.

Grimm, Jacob

1984   *On the Origin of Language.* Raymond A. Wiley, trans. Leiden: E. Brill.
[1851]

Grimm, Jacob, and Wilhelm Grimm

1987   Preface to the Second Edition of *Die Kinder- und Hausmärchen.* In *The*
[1819]   *Hard Facts of the Grimms' Fairy Tales.* Maria Tatar, ed. Pp. 215–22.
        Princeton: Princeton University Press.

Gruner, Rolf

1977   *Theory and Power: On the Character of Modern Sciences.* Amsterdam: B. R.
        Gruner.

Guiraudon, T. G. de

1894   *Bolle Fulbe: Manuel de la langue foule, parlée dans la sénégambie et le soudan.*
        Grammaire, textes, vocabulaire. Paris and Leipzig: H. Welter.

Gumperz, John

1958   Dialect Differences and Social Stratification in a North Indian Village.
        American Anthropologist 60:668–82.

1962   Types of Linguistic Communities. *Anthropological Linguistics* 4:28–40.

1982   *Discourse Strategies.* New York: Cambridge University Press.

Gumperz, John, and Dell Hymes, eds.

1964   The Ethnography of Communication. *American Anthropologist* 66(6), Part
        2 (special publication).

1972   *Directions in Sociolinguistics: The Ethnography of Communication.* New York:
        Holt, Rinehart, & Winston.

Guss, David

1986   Keeping It Oral: A Yekuana Ethnology. *American Ethnologist*
        13(3):413–29.

Guyer, Paul

1994   Locke's Philosophy of Language. In *Cambridge Companion to Locke.* Vere
        Chappell, ed. Pp. 115–45. Cambridge: Cambridge University Press.

Habermas, Jürgen

1989   *The Structural Transformation of the Public Sphere: An Inquiry into a Category*
[1962]   *of Bourgeois Society.* Thomas Burger and Frederick Lawrence, trans.
        Cambridge: MIT Press.

Hall, A. Rupert

1963   *From Galileo to Newton, 1630–1720.* New York: Harper and Row.

Hall, Robert A., Jr., ed.

1987   *Leonard Bloomfield: Appraisals of His Life and Work.* Amsterdam: John
        Benjamins. Also published in *Historiographia Linguistica* 14(1–2).

Hall, Stuart

1981   Cultural Studies: Two Paradigms. In *Culture, Ideology and Social Process.*
         Tony Bennett, Graham Martin, Colin Mercer, and Janet Woollacott, eds.
         Pp. 19–37. London: The Open University and BT Batsford Ltd.

1986   Gramsci's Relevance for the Study of Race and Ethnicity. *Journal of
         Communication Inquiry* 10(2):5–27.

1992   Cultural Studies and Its Theoretical Legacies. In *Cultural Studies.*
         Lawrence Grossberg, Cary Nelson, and Paula A. Treichler, eds. Pp.
         277–86. New York: Routledge.

Hanks, William

1987   Discourse Genres in a Theory of Practice. *American Ethnologist*
         14:668–92.

Hansen, Miriam

1993   Foreword. In *Public Sphere and Experience: Toward an Analysis of the
         Bourgeois and Proletarian Public Sphere,* by Oskar Negt and Alexander
         Kluge. Pp. ix–xli. Minneapolis: University of Minnesota Press.

Harinck, Gerrit

1969   Interaction Between Xhosa and Khoi: Emphasis on the Period
         1620–1750. In *African Societies in Southern Africa.* Leonard Thompson, ed.
         Pp. 145–70. London: Heinemann.

Havránek, Bohuslav

1964   The Functional Differentiation of the Standard Language. In *A Prague
[1932]   School Reader on Esthetics, Literary Structure, and Style.* Paul L. Garvin, trans.
         & ed. Pp. 3–16. Washington, DC: Georgetown University Press.

Heath, Shirley Brice

1977   Social History. In *Bilingual Education: Current Perspectives.* Vol. I: *Social
         Science.* Pp. 53–72. Arlington, VA: Center for Applied Linguistics.

1980   Standard English: Biography of a Symbol. In *Standards and Dialects in
         English.* Timothy Shopen and Joseph M. Williams, eds. Pp. 3–32.
         Cambridge, MA: Winthrop Publishers, Inc.

1983   *Ways with Words.* Cambridge: Cambridge University Press.

Heller, Monica

1988   Strategic Ambiguity: Codeswitching in the Management of Conflict. In
         Codeswitching: Anthropological and Sociolinguistic Perspectives. M. Heller, ed.
         Pp. 77–96. Berlin: Mouton de Gruyter.

Herbert, Robert K.

1990   The Sociohistory of Clicks in Southern Bantu. *Anthropological Linguistics*
         32:295–315.

Herder, Johann Gottfried

1833   *The Spirit of Hebrew Poetry.* James Marsh, trans. 2 vols. Burlington, VT:
[1782]   Edward Smith.

1966   Essay on the Origin of Language. In *On the Origin of Language.* John H.
[1787]   Moran and Alexander Gode, trans. Pp. 85–166. Chicago: University of
            Chicago Press.

1967   *Sämtliche Werke.* Bernhard Suphan, ed. 33 vols. Hildesheim: Georg Olms
[1877–   Verlagsbuchhandlung.
1913]

1968   *Reflections on the Philosophy of the History of Mankind.* Chicago: University
[1784–91]of Chicago Press.

1969   *Herder on Social and Political Culture.* F. M. Barnard, ed. Cambridge:
            Cambridge University Press.

1992   *Selected Early Works, 1764–1767.* Ernest A. Menze and Karl Menges, eds.,
            Ernest A. Menze with Michael Palma, trans. University Park:
            Pennsylvania State University Press.

1993   *Against Pure Reason: Writings on Religion, Language, and History.* Marcia
            Bunge, trans. and ed. Minneapolis: Fortress Press.

Heryanto, Ariel
1988   Language of Development and Development of Language: The Case of
            Indonesia. N. Lutz, trans. *Indonesia* 46:1–24.

Hervas y Panduro, Lorenzo
1800–   *Catalogo de las lenguas de las naciones conocidas, y numeración, división, y*
1805   *clases de estas segun la diversidad de sus idiomas y dialectos.* Madrid: Renz.

Herzfeld, Michael
1987   *Anthropology Through the Looking Glass.* Cambridge: Cambridge University
            Press.

Hibbard, Stephen
1989   Whorf and Scientific Relativity: The Influence of the Theory of Physical
            Relativity on Benjamin Lee Whorf's Linguistics. M.A. paper, Master of
            Arts Program in the Social Sciences, University of Chicago.

Hill, Jane H.
1992   "Today There Is No Respect": Nostalgia, "Respect," and Oppositional
            Discourse in Mexicano (Nahuatl) Language Ideology. *Pragmatics*
            2(3):263–80.

1998   "Today There Is No Respect": Nostalgia, "Respect," and Oppositional
            Discourse in Mexicano (Nahuatl) Language Ideology. In *Language
            Ideologies: Practice and Theory.* Bambi B. Schieffelin, Kathryn A. Woolard,
            and Paul V. Kroskrity, eds. Pp. 103–22. New York: Oxford University
            Press.

Hill, Jane H., and Kenneth C. Hill
1978   Honorific Usage in Modern Nahuatl: The Expression of Social Distance
            and Respect in the Nahuatl of the Malinche Volcano Area. *Language*
            54:123–55.

1980   Mixed Grammar, Purist Grammar, and Language Attitudes in Modern
          Nahuatl. *Language in Society* 9:321–48.

Hill, Jane H., and Judith T. Irvine
1993   Introduction. In *Responsibility and Evidence in Oral Discourse*. Jane H. Hill
          and Judith T. Irvine, eds. Pp. 1–23. Cambridge: Cambridge University
          Press.

Hill, Jane H., and Ofelia Zepeda
1993   Mrs. Patricio's Trouble: The Distribution of Responsibility in an Account
          of Personal Experience. In *Responsibility and Evidence in Oral Discourse*.
          Jane H. Hill and Judith T. Irvine, eds. Pp. 197–226. Cambridge:
          Cambridge University Press.

Hobbes, Thomas
1968   *The Leviathan*. C. B. MacPherson, ed. Harmondsworth, Middlesex:
[1651]   Penguin.

Hobsbawm, Eric, and Terence Ranger, eds.
1983   *The Invention of Tradition*. Cambridge: Cambridge University Press.

Hoenigswald, Henry M.
1966   A Proposal for the Study of Folk Linguistics. In *Sociolinguistics*. William
          Bright, ed. Pp. 16–20. The Hague: Mouton.

Hubatsch, Walther
1975   *Frederick the Great of Prussia: Absolutism and Administration*. London:
          Thames and Hudson.

Humboldt, Wilhelm von
1988   *On Language: The Diversity of Human Language-Structure and Its Influence*
[1836]   *on the Mental Development of Mankind*. Peter Heath, trans. Cambridge:
          Cambridge University Press.

Huntsman, Judith, and Antony Hooper
1975   Male and Female in Tokelau Culture. *Journal of the Polynesian Society*
          84:415–30.

Hutchins, Edwin
1995   *Cognition in the Wild*. Cambridge: MIT Press.

Hymes, Dell H.
1962   The Ethnography of Speaking. In *Anthropology and Human Behavior*. T.
          Gladwin and W. Sturtevant, eds. Pp. 13–53. Washington, DC:
          Anthropological Society of Washington.
1964   Introduction: Toward Ethnographies of Communication. In *The
          Ethnography of Communication*. John J. Gumperz and Dell Hymes, eds.
          Pp.1–34. Special publication. *American Anthropologist* 66(6), part 2.

Hymes, Dell

1968   Linguistic Problems in Defining the Concept of "Tribe." In *Essays on the Problem of Tribe: Proceedings of the 1967 Annual Spring Meeting of the American Ethnological Society.* June Helm, ed. Pp. 23–48. Seattle: University of Washington Press (for the A.E.S.).

1970   Linguistic Method in Ethnography. In *Method and Theory in Linguistics.* Paul L. Garvin, ed. Pp. 249–311. The Hague: Mouton.

1974   *Foundations in Sociolinguistics: An Ethnographic Approach.* Philadelphia: University of Pennsylvania Press.

1980   Speech and Language: On the Origins of Inequality among Speakers. In *Language in Education: Ethnolinguistic Essays.* Dell Hymes, ed. Pp.119–61. Washington, DC: Center for Applied Linguistics.

1981   *In Vain I Tried to Tell You.* Philadelphia: University of Pennsylvania Press.

Irvine, Judith T.

1985   Status and Style in Language. *Annual Review of Anthropology* 14:557–81.

1987   Domains of Description in the Ethnography of Speaking: A Retrospective on the "Speech Community." In *Performance, Speech Community and Genre: Working Papers and Proceedings of the Center for Psychosocial Studies,* no. 11. Pp. 13–24. Chicago: Center for Psychosocial Studies.

1989   When Talk Isn't Cheap: Language and Political Economy. *American Ethnologist* 16:248–67.

1990   Registering Affect: Heteroglossia in the Linguistic Expression of Emotion. In *Language and the Politics of Emotion.* Catherine Lutz and Lila Abu-Lughod, eds. Pp. 126–61. New York: Cambridge University Press.

1992   Ideologies of Honorific Language. In special issue on Language Ideologies. Paul Kroskrity, Bambi Schieffelin, and Kathryn Woolard, eds. *Pragmatics* 2:251–62.

1993   Mastering African Languages: The Politics of Linguistics in Nineteenth-Century Senegal. In special issue on Nations, Colonies and Metropoles. D. Segal and R. Handler, eds. *Social Analysis* 33:27–46.

Jakobson, Roman

1957   *The Framework of Language.* Ann Arbor: University of Michigan Press.

1960   Concluding Statement: Linguistics and Poetics. In *Style in Language.* Thomas Sebeok, ed. Pp. 350–73. Cambridge: MIT Press.

Jamieson, Kathleen

1988   *Eloquence in an Electronic Age.* Oxford: Oxford University Press.

Jamieson, Kathleen, and Karlyn Kohrs Campbell

1992   *The Interplay of Influence.* Belmont, CA: Wadsworth Publishing Company.

Johnson, R. K.

1977   Administration and Language Policy in Papua New Guinea. In *Language, Culture, Society, and the Modern World.* Fascicle 1, New Guinea

Area Languages and Language Study, vol. 3, Pacific Linguistics Series C, no. 40. S. A. Wurm, ed. Pp. 429–59. Canberra: Australian National University.

Jorgenson, Joseph

1971   Indians and the Metropolis. In *The American Indian in Urban Society*. Jack Waddell and O. Michael Watson, eds. Pp. 66–113. Boston: Little, Brown, and Company

1978   A Century of Political Economic Effects on American Indian Societies, 1880–1980. *Journal of Ethnic Studies* 6(3):1–82.

Joseph, Gilbert, and Daniel Nugent, eds.

1994   *Everyday Forms of State Formation: Revolution and the Negotiation of Rule in Modern Mexico*. Durham: Duke University Press.

Joseph, John E.

1989   Bloomfield's Saussureanism. *Cahiers Ferdinand de Saussure* 43:43–53.

Kamenetsky, Christa

1973   The German Folklore Revival in the Eighteenth Century: Herder's Theory of *Naturpoesie*. *Journal of Popular Culture* 6:836–48.

Karakasidou, Anastasia

1993   Policing Culture: Negating Ethnic Identity in Greek Macedonia. *Journal of Modern Greek Studies* 11:1–28.

Keeler, Ward

1987   *Javanese Shadow Plays, Javanese Selves*. Princeton: Princeton University Press.

Kelly, John D.

1997   The Privileges of Citizenship: Nations, States, Markets, and Narratives. In *Nation Making*. Robert J. Foster, ed. Pp. 253–73. Ann Arbor: University of Michigan Press.

Klein, Martin

1968   *Islam and Imperialism in Senegal: Sine-Saloum 1847–1914*. Stanford: Stanford University Press.

Knaut, Andrew. L.

1995   *The Pueblo Revolt of 1680: Conquest and Resistance in Seventeenth Century New Mexico*. Norman: University of Oklahoma Press.

Kobès, Alois

1869   *Grammaire de la langue volofe*. Saint-Joseph de Ngasobil (Sénégambie): Imprimerie de la mission.

Koerner, E. F. Konrad

1992   The Sapir-Whorf Hypothesis: A Preliminary History and a Bibliographical Essay. *Journal of Linguistic Anthropology* 2:173–98.

Kolben, Peter

1731   *The Present State of the Cape of Good Hope; or, a Particular Account of the Several Nations of the Hottentots, their Religion, Government, Laws, Customs, Ceremonies, and Opinions; their Art of War, Professions, Language, Genius, etc.; Together with a Short Account of the Dutch Settlement at the Cape.* London: W. Innys.

Kondo, D.

1990   *Crafting Selves: Power, Gender, and Discourses of Identity in a Japanese Workplace.* Chicago: University of Chicago Press.

Koneski, Blaze

1980   Macedonian. In *The Slavic Literary Languages: Formation and Development.* Alexander Schenker and Edward Stankiewicz, eds. Pp. 53–64. New Haven: Yale Concilium on International and Area Studies.

Krige, Eileen

1950   *The Social System of the Zulus.* Pietermaritzburg: Shuter and Shooter.
[1936]

Kripke, Saul A.

1972   Naming and Necessity. In *Semantics of Natural Language.* 2nd ed. Donald Davidson and Gilbert Harman, eds. Pp. 253–355, 763–69. Dordrecht: D. Reidel Publishing Co.

Kristeva, Julia

1980   *Desire in Language.* Leon S. Roudiez, ed. New York: Columbia University
[1977]   Press.

1989   *Language, the Unknown: An Initiation into Linguistics.* Anne M. Menke,
[1981]   trans. New York: Columbia University Press.

Krohn, Kaarle

1971   *Folklore Methodology: Formulated by Julius Krohn and Expanded by Nordic*
[1926]   *Researchers.* Roger Welsch, trans. Austin: University of Texas Press.

Kroskrity, Paul V.

1985   "Growing With Stories": Line, Verse, and Genre in an Arizona Tewa Text. *Journal of Anthropological Research* 41:183–200.

1992   Arizona Tewa Public Announcements: Form, Function, and Language Ideology. *Anthropological Linguistics* 34:104–16.

1993   *Language, History, and Identity: Ethnolinguistic Studies of the Arizona Tewa.* Tucson: University of Arizona Press.

1998   Arizona Tewa Kiva Speech as a Manifestation of a Dominant Language Ideology. In *Language Ideologies: Practice and Theory.* Bambi B. Schieffelin, Kathryn A. Woolard, and Paul V. Kroskrity, eds. Pp.103–22. New York: Oxford University Press.

Kroskrity, Paul, Bambi Schieffelin, and Kathryn Woolard, eds.

1992   Special issue on Language Ideologies. *Pragmatics* 2(3).

REFERENCES

Kula, Witold

1984 *Measures and Men.* Richard Szreter, trans. Princeton: Princeton
University Press.

Kulick, Don, and Christopher Stroud

1990 Christianity, Cargo and Ideas of Self. *Man,* n.s., 25:70–88.

1991 Conceptions and Uses of Literacy in a Papua New Guinean Village. In
Cross-Cultural Approaches to Literacy. B. Street, ed. Pp. 30–61. Cambridge:
Cambridge University Press.

Kunene, Daniel P.

1958 Notes on Hlonepha among the Southern Sotho. *African Studies*
17:159–82.

Labov, William

1963 The Social Motivation of a Sound Change. *Word* 19:273–309.

✓ 1966 *The Social Stratification of English in New York City.* Washington, DC:
Center for Applied Linguistics.

✓ 1972a *Language in the Inner City: Studies in the Black English Vernacular.*
Philadelphia: University of Pennsylvania Press.

1972b *Sociolinguistic Patterns.* Philadelphia: University of Pennsylvania Press.

1972c The Transformation of Experience in Narrative Syntax. In *Language in
the Inner City.* Pp. 354–96. Philadelphia: University of Pennsylvania Press.

1979 Locating the Frontier Between Social and Psychological Factors in
Linguistic Variation. In *Individual Difference in Language Abilities and
Behavior.* Charles J. Fillmore, Daniel Kempler, and William S.-Y. Wang,
eds. Pp. 327–39. New York: Academic Press.

Laffan, R. D. G.

1918 *The Guardians of the Gate: Historical Lectures on the Serbs.* Oxford:
Clarendon Press.

Lamoise, Père.

1873 *Grammaire de la langue sérère avec des exemples et des exercices renfermant des
documents très-utiles.* Saint-Joseph de Ngasobil (Sénégambie): Imprimerie
de la mission.

Lamouche, Léon

1899 *La Péninsule balkanique: Esquisse historique, ethnographique, philologique et lit-
téraire.* Paris: Paul Ollendorff.

Landes, David S.

1983 *Revolution in Time: Clocks and the Making of the Modern World.* Cambridge:
Harvard University Press/Belknap Press.

Landes, Joan

1988 *Women and the Public Sphere in the Age of the French Revolution.* Ithaca:
Cornell University Press.

Latukefu, Sione

1974   *Church and State in Tonga.* Canberra: Australian National University Press.

Le Goff, Jacques

1980   *Time, Work, and Culture in the Middle Ages.* Arthur Goldhammer, trans. Chicago: University of Chicago Press.

Lenneberg, Eric H.

1953   Cognition in Ethnolinguistics. *Language* 29:463–71.

Lepsius, Karl Richard

1863   *Standard Alphabet for Reducing Unwritten Languages and Foreign Graphic Systems to a Uniform Orthography in European Letters.* 2nd ed. London: Williams and Norgate; Berlin: W. Hertz.

Levy, Jerold E.

1990   *Orayvi Revisited.* Santa Fe: School of American Research Press.

Liddle, William

1988   *Politics and Culture in Indonesia.* Ann Arbor: University of Michigan Press.

Limón, José

1991   Representation, Ethnicity, and Precursory Ethnography: Notes of a Native Anthropologist. In *Recapturing Anthropology.* Richard Fox, ed. Pp. 115–35. Santa Fe: School of American Research Press.

Lindstrom, Lamont

1985   *Knowledge and Power in a South Pacific Society.* Smithsonian Series in Ethnographic Inquiry. Washington, DC: Smithsonian Institution Press.

Linton, Ralph

1940   *Acculturation in Seven American Indian Tribes.* New York: D. Appleton-Century Company.

Littlefield, Alice

1991   Native American Labor and Public Policy in the United States. In *Marxist Approaches in Economic Anthropology.* Monographs in Economic Anthropology, no. 9. Alice Littlefield and Hill Gates, eds. Pp. 219–32. Lanham, MD: Society for Economic Anthropology/University Press of America.

Locke, John

1959   *An Essay Concerning Human Understanding.* Alexander Campbell Fraser,
[1690]   ed. 2 vols. New York: Dover.

1960   *Two Treatises on Government.* New York: New American Library.
[1690]

1968   *Epistola de Tolerantia/A Letter on Toleration.* Raymond Klibansky, ed., Latin text; J. W. Gough, trans. and ed., English text. Oxford: Clarendon Press.

1971   *Of the Conduct of the Understanding.* New York: Burt Franklin.
[1881]
1989   *Some Thoughts Concerning Education.* Oxford: Clarendon Press.
[1693]

Louw, J. A.
1977   The Adaptation of Non-Click Khoi Consonants in Xhosa. *Khoisan Linguistic Studies* 3:74–92.

Lowenburg, Peter
1983   Lexical Modernization in Bahasa Indonesia: Functional Allocation and Variation in Borrowing. *Studies in Linguistic Sciences* 13(2):73–86.

Lowth, Robert
1969   *Lectures on the Sacred Poetry of the Hebrews.* 2 vols. Hildesheim: Georg Olms
[1787]   Verlag.

Lucy, John A.
1985   Whorf's View of the Linguistic Mediation of Thought. In *Semiotic Mediation: Sociocultural and Psychological Perspectives.* Elizabeth Mertz and Richard J. Parmentier, eds. Pp. 73–97. Orlando: Academic Press.
1992a   *Grammatical Categories and Cognition: A Case Study of the Linguistic Relativity Hypothesis.* Cambridge: Cambridge University Press.
1992b   *Language Diversity and Thought: A Reformulation of the Linguistic Relativity Hypothesis.* Cambridge: Cambridge University Press.

Lucy, John A., ed.
1993   *Reflexive Language: Reported Speech and Metapragmatics.* Cambridge: Cambridge University Press.

Lucy, John A., and James V. Wertsch
1987   Vygotsky and Whorf: A Comparative Analysis. In *Social and Functional Approaches to Language and Thought.* Maya Hickmann, ed. Pp. 67–86. Orlando: Academic Press.

Ludwig, Ralph, ed.
1989   *Les Créoles Français entre l'Oral et l'Ecrit.* Tübingen: Gunter Narr Verlag.

Lunt, Horace
1959   The Creation of Standard Macedonian: Some Facts and Attitudes. *Anthropological Linguistics* 16:19–26.
1984   Some Sociolinguistic Aspects of Macedonian and Bulgarian. In *Language and Literary Theory.* Ben Stoltz, I. R. T. Hunik, and Lubomire Dolezel, eds. Pp. 83–132. Ann Arbor: University of Michigan Press.

McKenzie, D. F.
1991   The Sociology of a Text: Oral Culture, Literacy and Print in Early New Zealand. In *The Social History of Language.* P. Burke and R. Porter, eds. Pp. 161–97. Cambridge: Cambridge University Press.

MacLaury, Robert E.

1993   Vantage Theory: An Introduction. In *Language and the Cognitive Construal of the World*. John R. Taylor and Robert E. MacLaury, eds. Pp. 231–76. Berlin: Mouton de Gruyter.

McNeill, William

1964   *Europe's Steppe Frontier, 1500–1800*. Chicago: University of Chicago Press.

MacPherson, C. B.

1962   *The Political Theory of Possessive Individualism: Hobbes to Locke*. Oxford: Oxford University Press.

Mahina, 'Okusitino

1986   Religion, Politics and the Tu'i Tonga Empire. Master's thesis, University of Auckland.

Maier, Hendrik M. J.

1993   From Heteroglossia to Polyglossia: The Creation of Malay and Dutch in the Indies. *Indonesia* 56:37–65.

Marcus, George E., and Michael M. J. Fischer

1986   *Anthropology as Cultural Critique*. Chicago: University of Chicago Press.

Marshall, John

1994   *John Locke: Resistance, Religion and Responsibility*. Cambridge: Cambridge University Press.

Matalin, Mary, and James Carville, with Peter Knobler

1993   *All's Fair: Love, War, and Running for President*. New York: Random House.

Mather, Lynn, and Barbara Yngvesson

1981   Language, Audience, and the Transformation of Disputes. *Law and Society Review* 15:775–821.

Matsuki, Keiko

1995   Creating Showa Memories in Contemporary Japan: Discourse, Society, History, and Subjectivity. Ph.D. diss., Department of Anthropology, University of Arizona.

Meggitt, Mervin

1968   Uses of Literacy in New Guinea and Melanesia. In *Literacy in Traditional Societies*. J. Goody, ed. Pp. 300–309. Cambridge: Cambridge University Press.

Menze, Ernest, and Karl Menges

1992   Commentary to the Translations. In Johann Gottfried Herder, *Selected Early Works, 1764–1767*. Ernest A. Menze and Karl Menges, eds., Ernest A. Menze with Michael Palma, trans. Pp. 235–333. University Park: Pennsylvania State University Press.

Merton, Robert K.

1948   The Self-Fulfilling Prophecy. *Antioch Review* 8:193–210.

Mignolo, W. D.
1992   On the Colonization of Amerindian Languages and Memories: Renaissance Theories of Writing and the Discontinuity of the Classical Tradition. *Comparative Studies in Society and History* 32:310–30.

Mills, Mary Beth
1997   Contesting the Margins of Modernity: Women, Migration, and Consumption in Thailand. *American Ethnologist* 21(1):37–61.

Milroy, Lesley
1980   *Language and Social Networks.* Oxford: Blackwell.

Moeliono, Anton M.
1993   The First Efforts to Promote and Develop Indonesian. In *The Earliest Stage of Language Planning: The "First Congress" Phenomenon.* J. Fishman, ed. Pp. 129–142. Berlin: Mouton de Gruyter.

Moore, Frederick
1906   *The Balkan Trail.* London: Smith, Elder and Co.

Morgan, Marcyliena
1997   Conversational Signifying: Grammar and Indirectness among African American Women. In *Interaction and Grammar.* E. Ochs, E. Schegloff, and S. Thompson, eds. Pp. 405–34. New York: Cambridge University Press.

Morton, Michael
1989   *Herder and the Poetics of Thought.* University Park: Pennsylvania State University Press.

Mudimbe, V. Y.
1988   *The Invention of Africa.* Bloomington: Indiana University Press.

Mühlhäusler, Peter
1996   *Linguistic Ecology: Language Change and Linguistic Imperialism in the Pacific Region.* New York: Routledge.

Müller, F. Max
1855   *The Languages of the Seat of War in the East.* 2nd ed. London: Williams and Norgate.
1861   *Lectures on the Science of Language.* London.

Mundhenk, Norm
1985   Linguistic Decisions in the Tok Pisin Bible. In *Melanesian Pidgin and Tok Pisin.* John W. M. Verhaar, ed. Pp. 345–73. Amsterdam: John Benjamins.

Murray, Stephen O.
1985   A Pre-Boasian Sapir? *Historiographia Linguistica* 12:267–69.

Myers-Scotton, Carol.
1993   Common and Uncommon Ground: Social and Structural Factors in Codeswitching. *Language in Society* 22:475–503.

Nagata, Judith

1974   What is a Malay? Situational Selection of Ethnic Identity in a Plural
         Society. *American Ethnologist* 1:331–50.

Narayan, Kirin

1993   How Native is a "Native" Anthropologist? *American Anthropologist*
         95:671–85.

Negt, Oskar, and Alexander Kluge

1993   *The Public Sphere and Experience.* Peter Labanyi, Jamie Daniel, and
         Assenka Oksiloff, trans. Minneapolis: University of Minnesota Press.

Nelson, Cary, Paula A. Treichler, and Lawrence Grossberg

1990   Cultural Studies: An Introduction. In *Cultural Studies.* Cary Nelson,
         Paula A. Treichler, and Lawrence Grossberg, eds. Pp. 1–16. New York:
         Routledge.

Neuendorf, A. K., and A. J. Taylor

1977   The Churches and Language Policy. In *Language, Culture, Society and the
         Modern World.* Fascicle 1. New Guinea Area Languages and Language
         Study, vol. 3, Pacific Linguistics Series C, no. 40. S. A. Wurm, ed. Pp.
         413–28. Canberra: Australian National University.

Neustepny, J.

1974   Basic Types of Treatment of Language Problems. In *Advances in
         Language Planning.* J. Fishman, ed. Pp. 37–48. The Hague: Mouton.

Newman, Stanley

1953   Vocabulary Levels: Zuni Sacred and Slang Usage. *Southwestern Journal of
         Anthropology* 11:345–54.

Nicolaïdes, Cleanthes

1899   *Macedonien: Die geschichtliche Entwicklung der macedonischen Frage im
         Altertum, in Mittelalter und in der neueren Zeit.* Berlin: Verlag von Johannes
         Räder.

Noonan, Peggy

1990   *What I Saw at the Revolution.* New York: Random House.

Norcini, Marilyn

1995   Edward P. Dozier: A History of Native American Discourse in
         Anthropology (Ethnohistory). Ph.D. diss., University of Arizona.

Officer, James

1971   The American Indian and Federal Policy. In *The American Indian in
         Urban Society.* Jack Waddell and O. Michael Watson, eds. Pp. 8–65.
         Boston: Little, Brown, and Company.

Okey, Robin

1982   *Eastern Europe 1740–1985: Feudalism to Communism.* Minneapolis:

University of Minnesota Press.

Olender, Maurice

1992   *The Languages of Paradise.* Cambridge: Harvard University Press.

Olson, Ernest

1997   Leaving Anger Outside of the Kava Circle: An Important Context in
Conflict Management in Tonga. In *Cultural Variations in Conflict
Resolutions: Alternatives for Reducing Violence.* Douglas Fry and Kaj
Bjorkqvist, eds. Nashwah, NJ: Lawrence Erlbaum.

Ophuysen, Ch. A. van

1901   *Kitab logat Melajoe: Woordenlijst voor de spelling der Maleishe taal met
Latijnsch karakter.* Batavia: Landsrukkerij.

Ortiz, Alfonso

1969   *The Tewa World.* Chicago: University of Chicago Press.

Östreich, Karl von

1905   Die Bevölkerung von Makedonien. *Geographische Zeitschrift* XI:268–92.

Ourousoff, Alexandra

1992   Illusions of Rationality: False Premises of the Liberal Tradition. *Man*
28:281–98.

Peirce, Charles S.

1931–58 *Collected Papers of Charles Sanders Peirce.* Charles Hartshorne and Paul
Weiss, eds., vols. 1–6; Arthur W. Burks, ed., vols. 7–8. Cambridge:
Harvard University Press/Belknap Press.

1955   Logic as Semiotic: The Theory of Signs. In *Philosophical Writings of Peirce.*
Justus Buchler, ed. Pp. 98–119. New York: Dover.

Pemberton, John

1993   *On the Subject of "Java."* Ithaca: Cornell University Press.

Philips, Susan U.

1991   Tongan Speech Levels: Practice and Talk about Practice in the Cultural
Construction of Social Hierarchy. In *Currents in Pacific Linguistics: Papers
on Austronesian Languages and Ethnolinguistics in Honour of George Grace.*
Robert Blust, ed. Pp. 369–82. Canberra: Australian National University.

1998   *Ideological Diversity in Judges' Courtroom Discourses: Due Process Rights in
Practice.* Oxford: Oxford University Press.

Philips, Susan U., and Anne Reynolds

1987   The Interaction of Variable Syntax and Discourse Structure in Men's
and Women's Speech. In *Language, Gender and Sex in Comparative
Perspective.* Susan U. Philips, Susan Steele, and Christine Tanz, eds. Pp.
71–94. Cambridge: Cambridge University Press.

Pichl, W. J.

1966   *The Cangin Group: A Language Group in Northern Senegal.* Pittsburgh:

Duquesne University Press, for the Duquesne University Institute of African Affairs.

Pinet-Laprade, E.
1865   Notice sur les Sérères. *Annuaire du Sénégal pour l'année 1865.* Pp. 131–71. Saint-Louis: Imprimerie du Gouvernement.

Pinker, Steven
1994   *The Language Instinct: How the Mind Creates Language.* New York: William Morrow & Co.

Pinto, Vivian
1980   Bulgarian. In *The Slavic Literary Languages: Formation and Development.* Alexander Schenker and Edward Stankiewicz, eds. Pp. 37–52. New Haven: Yale Concilium on International and Area Studies.

Poulton, Hugh
1995   *Who Are the Macedonians?* Bloomington: Indiana University Press.

Prins, Frans E., and Hester Lewis
1992   Bushmen as Mediators in Nguni Cosmology. *Ethnology* 31:133–48.

Purver, Margery
1967   *The Royal Society: Concept and Creation.* Cambridge: MIT Press.

Putnam, Hilary
1975   The Meaning of 'Meaning.' In *Philosophical Papers, vol. 2: Mind, Language, and Reality.* Pp. 215–71. Cambridge: Cambridge University Press.
1987   *The Many Faces of Realism.* La Salle, IL: Open Court Publishing Co.

Quine, Willard V.
1960   *Word and Object.* Cambridge: MIT Press.
1968   Ontological Relativity. *Journal of Philosophy* 65:185–212.

Rafael, Vincente
1988   *Contracting Colonialism: Translation and Christian Conversion in Tagalog Society under Early Spanish Rule.* Ithaca: Cornell University Press.

Renck, Günther
1985   *Contextualization of Christianity and Christianization of Language: A Case Study from the Highlands of Papua New Guinea.* Erlangen: Verlag der Evang.-Luth. Mission.

Riantiarno, N.
1990   *Suksesi.* Jakarta: Teater Coma.

Ricoeur, Paul
1986   *Lectures on Ideology and Utopia.* G. Taylor, ed. New York: Columbia University Press.

Robins, R. H.

1990   *A Short History of Linguistics.* 3d ed. London: Longman.

Robison, Richard

1983   Culture, Politics, and Economy in the Political History of the New Order. *Indonesia* 1–29.

Rogers, Garth

1977   The Father's Sister Is Black: A Consideration of Female Rank and Power in Tonga. *Journal of the Polynesian Society* 86:157–82.

Rollins, Peter C.

1972   Benjamin Lee Whorf: Transcendental Linguist. Ph.D. diss., Program in American Studies, Harvard University.

1980   *Benjamin Lee Whorf: Lost Generation Theories of Mind, Language, and Religion.* Ann Arbor: University Microfilms International for Popular Culture Association.

Rosaldo, Michelle

1981   The Things We Do with Words: Ilongot Speech Acts and Speech Act Theory in Philosophy. *Language in Society* 11:203–37.

Ruby, Jay, ed.

1982   *Crack in the Mirror: Reflexive Perspectives in Anthropology.* Philadelphia: University of Pennsylvania Press.

Rule, Joan

1977   Vernacular Literacy, Western and Lower Southern Highlands. In *Language, Culture, Society and the Modern World.* Fascicle 1, New Guinea Area Languages and Language Study, vol. 3, Pacific Linguistics Series C, no. 40. S. A. Wurm, ed. Pp. 387–401. Canberra: Australian National University.

Rule, W. Murray

1964   Customs, Alphabet and Grammar of the Kaluli People of Bosavi, Papua. Mimeo, Unevangelised Fields Missions.

1977a   Institutional Framework of Language Study: The Asia Pacific Christian Mission. In *Language, Culture, Society and the Modern World.* Fascicle 2, New Guinea Area Languages and Language Study, vol. 3, Pacific Linguistics Series C, no. 40. S. A. Wurm, ed. Pp. 1341–44. Canberra: Australian National University.

1977b   *A Comparative Study of the Foe, Huli and Pole Languages of Papua New Guinea.* Oceania Linguistic Monographs, no. 20. Sydney: University of Sydney, Australia.

1985   *The Culture and Language of the Foe: The People of Lake Kutubu, Southern Highlands Province, Papua New Guinea.* Merewether, New South Wales: W. Murray Rule.

Rumsey, Alan

1990   Wording, Meaning, and Linguistic Ideology. *American Anthropologist*
         92:346–61.

Safran, William

1991   Diasporas in Modern Societies: Myth of Homeland and Return. *Diaspora*
         1:83–99.

Said, Edward

1978   *Orientalism.* New York: Pantheon.   ✓

Salim, Ziad

1977   The Growth of the Indonesian Language: The Trend Towards Indo-
         Saxonization. *Indonesian Quarterly* 5(2):75–93.

Sandfeld, Karl

1930   *Linguistique balkanique: Problèmes et résultats.* Paris: C. Klincksieck.

Sando, Joe S.

1991   *Pueblo Nations: Eight Centuries of Pueblo Indian History.* Santa Fe: Clear
         Light Press.

Santino, Jack

1988   The Tendency to Ritualize: The Living Celebration Series as a Model for
         Cultural Presentation and Validation. In *The Conservation of Culture:
         Folkloristics in the Public Sector.* Burt Feintuch, ed. Pp. 118–31. Lexington:
         University Press of Kentucky.

Sapir, Edward

1908   Herder's "Ursprung der Sprache." *Modern Philology* 5:109–42.

1913   Review of Carl Meinhof, *Die Sprachen der Hamiten. Current Anthropological
         Literature* 2:21–27.

1949a   Culture, Genuine and Spurious. In *Selected Writings of Edward Sapir in*

[1924]   *Language, Culture, and Personality.* David G. Mandelbaum, ed. Pp. 308–31.
         Berkeley: University of California Press.

1949b   *Language: An Introduction to the Study of Speech.* New York: Harcourt,

[1921]   Brace & World.

1949c   The Status of Linguistics as a Science. In *Selected Writings of Edward Sapir*

[1929]   *in Language, Culture, and Personality.* David G. Mandelbaum, ed. Pp.
         160–67. Berkeley: University of California Press.

Saussure, Ferdinand de

1916   *Cours de linguistique générale.* Charles Bally and Albert Sechehaye, eds.   ✓
         Lausanne–Paris: Payot.

Schieffelin, Bambi B.

1986a   The Acquisition of Kaluli. In *The Cross-Linguistic Study of Language
         Acquisition*, Vol. 1. Dan I. Slobin, ed. Pp. 525–93. Hillsdale, NJ: Lawrence
         Erlbaum Associates.

1986b   Teasing and Shaming in Kaluli Children's Interactions. In *Language Socialization across Cultures*. E. Ochs and Bambi B. Schieffelin, eds. Pp. 165–81. New York: Cambridge University Press.

1990   *The Give and Take of Everyday Life: Language Socialization of Kaluli Children.* New York: Cambridge University Press.

1996   Creating Evidence: Making Sense of Written Words in Bosavi. In *Interaction and Grammar*. E. Ochs, E. Schegloff, and S. Thompson, eds. Pp. 435–60. Cambridge: Cambridge University Press.

Schieffelin, Bambi B., and Marilyn Cochran–Smith

1984   Learning to Read Culturally: Literacy before Schooling. In *Awakening to Literacy*. H. Goelman, A. Oberg, and Frank Smith, eds. Pp. 3–23. Exeter, NH: Heineman.

Schieffelin, Bambi B., and Rachelle Doucet

1994   The "Real" Haitian Creole: Ideology, Metalinguistics, and Orthographic Choice. *American Ethnologist* 21(1):176–200.

Schieffelin, Bambi B., and Steven Feld

1998   *Bosavi-English-Tok Pisin Dictionary*. Pacific Linguistics Series C-153. Canberra: Australian National University.

Schieffelin, Bambi B., and Perry Gilmore

1984   *The Acquisition of Literacy: Ethnographic Perspectives*. Norwood, NJ: Ablex.

Schieffelin, Bambi B., Kathryn A. Woolard, and Paul V. Kroskrity, eds.

1998   *Language Ideologies: Practice and Theory*. New York: Oxford University Press.

Schieffelin, Edward L.

1976   *The Sorrow of the Lonely and the Burning of the Dancers*. New York: St. Martin's Press.

1977   The End of Traditional Music, Dance and Body Decoration in Bosavi, Papua New Guinea. Discussion Papers nos. 30, 31, and 32. Port Moresby: Institute of Papua New Guinea Studies. Reprinted in *The Plight of Peripheral Peoples*, vol.1, Occasional Paper no.7, *Cultural Survival*. R. Gordon, ed. Peterborough, NH: Transcript Printing Co., 1981.

1981   Evangelical Rhetoric and the Transformation of Traditional Culture in Papua New Guinea. *Comparative Studies in Society and History* 23(1):150–56.

Schieffelin, Edward L., and Robert Crittenden

1991   *Like People You See in a Dream: First Contact in Six Papuan Societies*. Stanford: Stanford University Press.

Schleicher, August

1869   *Darwinism Tested by the Science of Language*. Alexander Bikkers, trans. London: John Camden Hotten. First published 1863 as *Die Darwinsche Theorie und die Sprachwissenschaft*.

Schoeffel, Penelope
1977   Gender, Status and Power in Western Samoa. *Canberra Anthropology* 1(2):69–81.

Schroeder, Albert H.
1978   Pueblos Abandoned in Historic Times. In *Handbook of North American Indians,* vol. 9, *The Southwest.* Alfonso Ortiz, ed. Pp. 236–54. Washington, DC: Smithsonian Institution.

Schütze, Martin
1921   The Fundamental Ideas in Herder's Thought III. *Modern Philology* 19:113–30.

Scollon, Ronald, and Suzanne Scollon
1981   *Narrative, Literacy, and Face.* New York: Ablex.

Searle, John
1969   *Speech Acts.* Cambridge: Cambridge University Press.
1983   *Intentionality: An Essay in the Philosophy of Mind.* New York: Cambridge University Press.

Shaklee, Margaret
1980   The Rise of Standard English. In *Standards and Dialects in English.* Timothy Shopen and Joseph M. Williams, eds. Pp. 33–62. Cambridge, MA: Winthrop Publishers.

Shapin, Steven
1994   *A Social History of Truth: Civility and Science in Seventeenth-Century England.* Chicago: University of Chicago Press.

Shapin, Steven, and Simon Schaffer
1985   *Leviathan and the Air-Pump: Hobbes, Boyle, and the Experimental Life.* Princeton: Princeton University Press.

Sheldon, William
1970   *The Intellectual Development of Justus Möser: The Growth of a German Patriot.* Osnabruck: Kommissionsverlag H. Th. Wenner.

Sherzer, Joel
1976   *An Areal-Typological Study of American Indian Languages, North of Mexico.* Amsterdam: North Holland.

Silverstein, Michael
1976   Shifters, Linguistic Categories, and Cultural Description. In *Meaning in Anthropology.* Keith Basso and Henry Selby, eds. Pp. 11–55. Albuquerque: University of New Mexico Press.
1978   Review of *The View from Language: Selected Essays, 1948–1974,* by Charles F. Hockett. *International Journal of American Linguistics* 44:235–53.
1979   Language Structure and Linguistic Ideology. In *The Elements: A Parasession on Linguistic Units and Levels.* Paul R. Clyne, William F. Hanks,

REFERENCES

and Carol L. Hofbauer, eds. Pp.193–247. Chicago: Chicago Linguistic
Society.

1981   *The Limits of Awareness*. Working Papers in Sociolinguistics, no. 84.
Austin: Southwest Educational Development Library.

1985   Language and the Culture of Gender: At the Intersection of Structure,
Usage and Ideology. In *Semiotic Mediation: Sociocultural and Psychological
Perspectives*. Elizabeth Mertz and Richard J. Parmentier, eds. Pp. 219–59.
Orlando: Academic Press.

1986   The Diachrony of Sapir's Synchronic Linguistic Description; or, Sapir's
"Cosmographical" Linguistics. In *New Perspectives in Language, Culture,
and Personality: Proceedings of the Edward Sapir Centenary Conference*.
William Cowan, Michael K. Foster, and Konrad Koerner, eds. Pp.
67–110. Amsterdam: John Benjamins.

1987   The Three Faces of "Function": Preliminaries to a Psychology of
Language. In *Social and Functional Approaches to Language and Thought*.
Maya Hickmann, ed. Pp. 17–38. Orlando: Academic Press.

1992   The Uses and Utility of Ideology: Some Reflections. *Pragmatics*
2(3):311–24.

1993   Metapragmatic Discourse and Metapragmatic Function. In *Reflexive
Language: Reported Speech and Metapragmatics*. John A. Lucy, ed. Pp.
33–58. Cambridge: Cambridge University Press.

1996a   Monoglot "Standard" in America: Standardization and Metaphors of
Linguistic Hegemony. In *The Matrix of Language: Contemporary Linguistic
Anthropology*. D. Brenneis and R. Macaulay, eds. Pp. 284–306. Boulder:
Westview Press.

1996b   Encountering Languages and the Languages of Encounter in North
American Ethnohistory. *Journal of Linguistic Anthropology* 6:126–44.

1996c   Indexical Order and the Dialectics of Sociolinguistic Life. In *Proceedings
of the Third Annual Symposium About Language and Society—Austin*. Risako
Ide, Rebecca Parker, and Yukako Sunaoshi, eds. Pp. 266–95. *Texas
Linguistic Forum*, vol. 36. Austin: University of Texas Department of
Linguistics.

1996d   Monoglot "Standard" in America: Standardization and Metaphors of
[1987] Linguistic Hegemony. In *The Matrix of Language: Contemporary Linguistic
Anthropology*. Donald Brenneis and Ronald K. S. Macaulay, eds. Pp.
284–306. Boulder: Westview Press.

1998   The Uses and Utility of Ideology: A Commentary. In *Language Ideologies:
Practice and Theory*. Bambi B. Schieffelin, Kathryn A. Woolard, and Paul
V. Kroskrity, eds. Pp.123–45. New York: Oxford University Press.

Simmons, Marc
1979   History of Pueblo-Spanish Relations to 1821. In *Handbook of North
American Indians*, vol. 9, *The Southwest*. Alfonso Ortiz, ed. Pp.178–93.
Washington, DC: Smithsonian Institution.

Sís, Vladimír

1918   *Mazedonien: Eine Studie über Geographie, Geschichte, Volkskunde und die*
         wirtschaftlichen und kulturellen Zustände des Landes mit statistischen
         Ergängzungen. Zürich: Art. Institut Orell Füssli.

Smith, Anthony D.

1983   *Theories of Nationalism.* 2nd ed. New York: Holmes and Meier, Publishers.

Smith, Marion V.

1996   Linguistic Relativity: On Hypotheses and Confusions. *Communication and*
         Cognition 29:65–90.

Smith, Watson

1956   Review of Dozier's *The Hopi-Tewa of Arizona. American Antiquity* 21:324–25.

Smithies, Michael

1982   The Vocabulary of the Elite: An Examination of Contemporary Loan
         Words in Indonesian. *Indonesian Quarterly* 10(2):105–13.

Spier, Leslie, A. Irving Hallowell, and Stanley S. Newman, eds.

1941   *Language, Culture, and Personality: Essays in Memory of Edward Sapir.*
         Menasha, WI: Sapir Memorial Publication Fund.

Spindler, George, and Louise Spindler.

1966   Foreword. In *Hano, A Tewa Indian Community in Arizona,* by Edward
         Dozier. Pp. v–vi. New York: Holt, Rinehart, and Winston.

Spitulnik, Debra

1992   Radio Time Sharing and the Negotiation of Linguistic Pluralism in
         Zambia. *Pragmatics* 2(3):335–54.

1998   Mediating Unity and Diversity: The Production of Language Ideologies
         in Zambian Broadcasting. In *Language Ideologies: Practice and Theory.*
         Bambi B. Schieffelin, Kathryn A. Woolard, and Paul V. Kroskrity, eds.
         Pp.163–88. New York: Oxford University Press.

Sprat, Thomas

1958   *History of the Royal Society.* Jackson I. Cope and Harold Whitmore Jones,
[1667]   eds. St. Louis: Washington University Studies.

Staub, Shalom

1988   Folklore and Authenticity: A Myopic Marriage in the Public Sector. In
         The Conservation of Culture. Burt Feintuch, ed. Pp. 166–79. Lexington:
         University Press of Kentucky.

Steinhauer, Hein

1994   The Indonesian Language Situation and Linguistics: Problems and
         Possibilities. *Bijdragen tot de taal-, land- en volkenkunde* 150(4):755–84.

Stewart, Susan

1991   Notes on Distressed Genres. *Journal of American Folklore* 104:5–31.

REFERENCES

Stewart, William A.
1968   A Sociolinguistic Typology for Describing National Multilingualism. In *Readings in the Sociology of Language.* Joshua A. Fishman, ed. Pp. 531–45. The Hague: Mouton.

Street, Brian V.
1984   *Literacy in Theory and Practice.* New York: Cambridge University Press.

Street, Brian V., ed.
1993   *Cross-Cultural Approaches to Literacy.* New York: Cambridge University Press.

Street, Brian, and Niko Besnier
1985   Aspects of Literacy. In *Companion Encyclopedia of Anthropology.* T. Ingold, ed. Pp. 527–62. London: Routledge.

Stoianovich, Traian
1958   The Conquering Balkan Orthodox Merchant. *Journal of Economic History* XX:234–313.

Suharto
1971   *Kumpulan Kata-Kata Presiden Soeharto 1967–1971.* [Words of President Suharto 1967–1971.] Djakarta: Sekretariat Kabinet R.I.

Sweetser, Eve
1987   The Definition of "Lie." In *Cultural Models in Language and Thought.* Dorothy Holland and Naomi Quinn, eds. Pp. 43–66. Cambridge: Cambridge University Press.

Tambiah, Stanley
1976   *World Conqueror and World Renouncer.* Cambridge: Cambridge University Press.

Tautain, L.
1885   Etudes critiques sur l'ethnologie et l'ethnographie des peoples du bassin du Sénégal. *Revue d'Ethnographie* 4:61–80, 137–47, 254–68.

Taylor, Charles
1985   Language and Human Nature. In *Philosophical Papers,* vol. 1. Cambridge: Cambridge University Press.

Taylor, Talbot J.
1990a   Liberalism in Lockean Linguistics. In *North American Contributions to the History of Linguistics.* Francis P. Dinneen and E. F. Konrad Koerner, eds. Pp. 99–109. Amsterdam: John Benjamins.
1990b   Which Is to Be Master? The Institutionalization of Authority in the Science of Language. In *Ideologies of Language.* John E. Joseph and Talbot J. Taylor, eds. Pp. 9–26. London: Routledge.

Tedlock, Dennis
1978   The Analogical Tradition and the Emergence of a Dialogical
         Anthropology. *Journal of Anthropological Research* 35:387–400.

Teeuw, A.
1973   *Pegawai bahasa dan ilmu bahasa,* trans. of *Taalambtenaren en Indonesische
         Taalwetenschap.* Paper given to a special course in Leiden in 1971.
         Jakarta: Bhratara.

Thomason, Sarah G., and T. Kaufman
1988   *Language Contact, Creolization, and Genetic Linguistics.* Berkeley and Los
         Angeles: University of California Press.

Thompson, Stith
1946   *The Folktale.* New York: Dryden.

Titiev, Mischa
1944   *Old Oraibi: A Study of the Hopi Indians of Third Mesa.* Papers of the
         Peabody Museum of American Archaeology and Ethnology, vol. 2, no. 1.
         Cambridge: Harvard University Press.

Todorova, Maria
1990   Language as a Cultural Unifier in a Multilingual Setting: The Bulgarian
         Case during the Nineteenth Century. *East European Politics and Societies*
         4(3):439–50.
1994   The Balkans: From Discovery to Invention. *Slavic Review* 53(2):453–82.

Tsing, Anna
1993   *In the Realm of the Diamond Queen: Ethnography in an Out-of-the-Way Place.*
         Princeton: Princeton University Press.

Urban, Greg, and Joel Sherzer, eds.
1991   *Nation-States and Indians in Latin America.* Austin: University of Texas
         Press.

van Dülmen, Richard
1992   *The Society of the Enlightenment: The Rise of the Middle Class and
         Enlightenment Culture in Germany.* New York: St. Martin's Press.

Vikors, Lars
1992   *Spelling Discussions and Reforms in Indonesian and Malaysian, 1900–1972.*
         No. 133, Verhandelingen de Koninklijk Instituut voor de Taal-, Land-,
         en Volkenkunde. Dordrecht, Holland: Foris.

Voegelin, C. F., and Z. S. Harris
1944   Linguistics in Ethnology. *Southwestern Journal of Anthropology* 1:455–65.

Wagner, Roy
1991   Fractal Persons. In *Big Men and Great Men: Personifications of Power in
         Melanesia.* Maurice Godelier and Marilyn Strathern, eds. Pp. 159–73.
         Cambridge: Cambridge University Press.

Weber, Eugen
1976   *Peasants into Frenchmen.* Stanford: Stanford University Press.

Weinreich, Uriel
1966   On the Semantic Structure of Language. In *Universals of Language.* 2nd
[1963] ed. Joseph H. Greenberg, ed. Pp. 142–216. Cambridge: MIT Press.

Weinreich, Uriel, William Labov, and Marvin Herzog
1968   Empirical Foundations of Linguistic Theory. In *Directions for Historical Linguistics.* W. Lehmann and Y. Malkiel, eds. Pp. 95–195. Austin: University of Texas Press.

Whiteley, Peter M.
1986   *Deliberate Acts.* Tucson: University of Arizona Press.

Whorf, Benjamin Lee
1946a   The Hopi Language, Toreva Dialect. In Harry Hoijer et al. *Linguistic Structures of Native America.* Pp. 158–83. Viking Fund Publications in Anthropology, vol. 6. New York: Viking Fund, Inc.
1946b   The Milpa Alta Dialect of Aztec. In Harry Hoijer et al. *Linguistic Structures of Native America.* Pp. 367–97. Viking Fund Publications in Anthropology, vol. 6. New York: Viking Fund, Inc.
1949   *Four Articles on Metalinguistics.* Washington, DC: Foreign Service Institute, Department of State.
✓ 1956a   A Linguistic Consideration of Thinking in Primitive Communities. In
[c. 1936] *Language, Thought, and Reality: Selected Writings of Benjamin Lee Whorf.* John B. Carroll, ed. Pp. 65–86. Cambridge: MIT Press.
1956b   Some Verbal Categories of Hopi. In *Language, Thought, and Reality.*
[1938] John B. Carroll, ed. Pp. 112–24. Cambridge: MIT Press.
1956c   Gestalt Technique of Stem Composition in Shawnee. In *Language,*
[1940] *Thought, and Reality.* John B. Carroll, ed. Pp. 160–72. Cambridge: MIT Press.
1956d   Science and Linguistics. In *Language, Thought, and Reality.*
[1940] John B. Carroll, ed. Pp. 207–19. Cambridge: MIT Press.
1956e   Linguistics as an Exact Science. In *Language, Thought, and Reality.*
[1940] John B. Carroll, ed. Pp. 220–32. Cambridge: MIT Press.
1956f   Languages and Logic. In *Language, Thought, and Reality.* John B. Carroll,
[1941] ed. Pp.233–45. Cambridge: MIT Press.
1956g   The Relation of Habitual Thought and Behavior to Language. In
✓ ⟶ [1941] *Language, Thought, and Reality.* John B. Carroll, ed. Pp. 134–59. Cambridge: MIT Press.
1956h   Grammatical Categories. In *Language, Thought, and Reality.* John B.
[1945] Carroll, ed. Pp. 87–101. Cambridge: MIT Press.

Whorf, Benjamin Lee, and George L. Trager
1937   The Relationship of Uto-Aztecan and Tanoan. *American Anthropologist* 39:609–24.

Wilkinson, Henry R.

1951   *Maps and Politics: A Review of the Ethnographic Cartography of Macedonia.* Manchester: Manchester University Press.

Williams, Brackette F.

1991   *Stains on My Name, War in My Veins: Guyana and the Politics of Cultural Struggle.* Durham, NC: Duke University Press.

Williams, Raymond

1983   Notes on English Prose, 1780–1950. In *Writing in Society.* Pp. 67–118. London: Verso.

Willner, Ann

1966   *The Neotraditional Accommodation to Political Independence: The Case of Indonesia.* Center for International Studies Research, monograph no. 26. Princeton: Woodrow Wilson School for Public and International Studies.

Wilson, John

1990   *Politically Speaking. The Pragmatic Analysis of Political Language.* Oxford: Blackwell.

Wilson, W. A. A.

1988   Atlantic. In *The Niger-Congo Languages.* J. Bendor-Samuel, ed. Pp. 81–104. Lanham, MD: University Press of America.

Wilson, William A.

1973   Herder, Folklore, and Romantic Nationalism. *Journal of Popular Culture* 6:819–35.

Wolff, Larry

1994   *Inventing Eastern Europe: The Map of Civilization in the Mind of the Enlightenment.* Stanford: Stanford University Press.

Woolard, Kathryn A.

1985   Language Variation and Cultural Hegemony: Towards an Integration of Sociolinguistic and Social Theory. *American Ethnologist* 12:738–48.

1989   Sentences in the Language Prison: The Rhetorical Structuring of an American Language Policy Debate. *American Ethnologist* 16:268–78.

1998   Introduction: Language Ideology as a Field of Inquiry. In *Language Ideologies: Practice and Theory.* Bambi B. Schieffelin, Kathryn A. Woolard, and Paul V. Kroskrity, eds. Pp. 3–47. New York: Oxford University Press.

Woolard, Kathryn A., and Bambi B. Schieffelin

1994   Language Ideology. *Annual Review of Anthropology* 23:55–82.

Woolhouse, Roger

1997   Introduction. In John Locke, *An Essay Concerning Human Understanding.* Pp. ix–xxiv. New York: Penguin Books.

REFERENCES

Wurm, Steven A.
1987   Language Death and Disappearance. *Diogène* 153:1–18.

Wurm, Steven A., ed.
1977   *Language, Culture, Society and the Modern World.* Fascicles 1 and 2, New
            Guinea Area Languages and Language Study, vol. 3, Pacific Linguistics
            Series C, no. 40. Canberra: Australian National University.

Yava, Albert
1979   *Big Falling Snow.* New York: Crown.

Yolton, John W.
1970   *Locke and the Compass of Human Understanding: A Selective Commentary on
            the "Essay."* Cambridge: Cambridge University Press.
1993   *A Locke Dictionary.* Oxford: Blackwell.

Index

School of American Research Advanced Seminar Series

PUBLISHED BY SAR PRESS

PUBLISHED BY UNIVERSITY OF CALIFORNIA PRESS

WRITING CULTURE: THE POETICS
AND POLITICS OF ETHNOGRAPHY
James Clifford &
George E. Marcus, eds.

PUBLISHED BY UNIVERSITY OF ARIZONA PRESS

THE COLLAPSE OF ANCIENT STATES AND
CIVILIZATIONS
Norman Yoffee &
George L. Cowgill, eds.

PUBLISHED BY UNIVERSITY OF NEW MEXICO PRESS

NEW PERSPECTIVES ON THE PUEBLOS
Alfonso Ortiz, ed.

STRUCTURE AND PROCESS IN LATIN AMERICA
Arnold Strickon &
Sidney M. Greenfield, eds.

THE CLASSIC MAYA COLLAPSE
T. Patrick Culbert, ed.

METHODS AND THEORIES OF
ANTHROPOLOGICAL GENETICS
M. H. Crawford & P. L. Workman, eds.

SIXTEENTH-CENTURY MEXICO:
THE WORK OF SAHAGUN
Munro S. Edmonson, ed.

ANCIENT CIVILIZATION AND TRADE
Jeremy A. Sabloff &
C. C. Lamberg-Karlovsky, eds.

PHOTOGRAPHY IN ARCHAEOLOGICAL
RESEARCH
Elmer Harp, Jr., ed.

MEANING IN ANTHROPOLOGY
Keith H. Basso & Henry A. Selby, eds.

THE VALLEY OF MEXICO: STUDIES IN
PRE-HISPANIC ECOLOGY AND SOCIETY
Eric R. Wolf, ed.

DEMOGRAPHIC ANTHROPOLOGY:
QUANTITATIVE APPROACHES
Ezra B. W. Zubrow, ed.

THE ORIGINS OF MAYA CIVILIZATION
Richard E. W. Adams, ed.

EXPLANATION OF PREHISTORIC CHANGE
James N. Hill, ed.

EXPLORATIONS IN ETHNOARCHAEOLOGY
Richard A. Gould, ed.

ENTREPRENEURS IN CULTURAL CONTEXT
Sidney M. Greenfield, Arnold Strickon,
& Robert T. Aubey, eds.

THE DYING COMMUNITY
Art Gallaher, Jr. & Harlan Padfield, eds.

SOUTHWESTERN INDIAN RITUAL DRAMA
Charlotte J. Frisbie, ed.

LOWLAND MAYA SETTLEMENT PATTERNS
Wendy Ashmore, ed.

SIMULATIONS IN ARCHAEOLOGY
Jeremy A. Sabloff, ed.

CHAN CHAN: ANDEAN DESERT CITY
Michael E. Moseley & Kent C. Day, eds.

SHIPWRECK ANTHROPOLOGY
Richard A. Gould, ed.

ELITES: ETHNOGRAPHIC ISSUES
George E. Marcus, ed.

THE ARCHAEOLOGY OF LOWER CENTRAL
AMERICA
Frederick W. Lange &
Doris Z. Stone, eds.

LATE LOWLAND MAYA CIVILIZATION:
CLASSIC TO POSTCLASSIC
Jeremy A. Sabloff &
E. Wyllys Andrews V, eds.

Photo by Katrina Lasko

Participants in the School of American Research advanced seminar "Language Ideologies," Santa Fe, New Mexico, April 1994. Front row, seated, from left: Jane H. Hill, Susan Gal, Judith T. Irvine. Second row, from left: Susan U. Philips, Richard Bauman, Bambi B. Schieffelin. Back row and standing: Charles Briggs, Michael Silverstein, Paul V. Kroskrity, Joseph Errington.

Made in the USA